VOLUME 568

MARCH 2000

THE ANNALS

of The American Academy *of* Political
and Social Science

ALAN W. HESTON, *Editor*
NEIL A. WEINER, *Assistant Editor*

THE STUDY OF AFRICAN AMERICAN PROBLEMS: W.E.B. DU BOIS'S AGENDA, THEN AND NOW

Special Editors of this Volume

ELIJAH ANDERSON
TUKUFU ZUBERI
University of Pennsylvania
Philadelphia

 Sage Publications, Inc. *THOUSAND OAKS   LONDON   NEW DELHI*

Origin and Purpose. The Academy was organized December 14, 1889, to promote the progress of political and social science, especially through publications and meetings. The Academy does not take sides in controverted questions, but seeks to gather and present reliable information to assist the public in forming an intelligent and accurate judgment.

Meetings. The Academy occasionally holds a meeting in the spring extending over two days.

Publications. THE ANNALS of the American Academy of Political and Social Science is the bimonthly publication of The Academy. Each issue contains articles on some prominent social or political problem, written at the invitation of the editors. Also, monographs are published from time to time, numbers of which are distributed to pertinent professional organizations. These volumes constitute important reference works on the topics with which they deal, and they are extensively cited by authorities throughout the United States and abroad. The papers presented at the meetings of The Academy are included in THE ANNALS.

Membership. Each member of The Academy receives THE ANNALS and may attend the meetings of The Academy. Membership is open only to individuals. Annual dues: $61.00 for the regular paperbound edition (clothbound, $90.00). Add $12.00 per year for membership outside the U.S.A. Members may also purchase single issues of THE ANNALS for $14.00 each (clothbound, $19.00). Add $2.00 for shipping and handling on all prepaid orders.

Subscriptions. THE ANNALS of the American Academy of Political and Social Science (ISSN 0002-7162) is published six times annually—in January, March, May, July, September, and November. Institutions may subscribe to THE ANNALS at the annual rate: $327.00 (clothbound, $372.00). Add $12.00 per year for subscriptions outside the U.S.A. Institutional rates for single issues: $59.00 each (clothbound, $66.00).

Periodicals postage paid at Thousand Oaks, California, and additional mailing offices.

Single issues of THE ANNALS may be obtained by individuals who are not members of The Academy for $20.00 each (clothbound, $31.00). Add $2.00 for shipping and handling on all prepaid orders. Single issues of THE ANNALS have proven to be excellent supplementary texts for classroom use. Direct inquiries regarding adoptions to THE ANNALS c/o Sage Publications (address below).

All correspondence concerning membership in The Academy, dues renewals, inquiries about membership status, and/or purchase of single issues of THE ANNALS should be sent to THE ANNALS c/o Sage Publications, Inc., 2455 Teller Road, Thousand Oaks, CA 91320. Telephone: (805) 499-0721; FAX/Order line: (805) 499-0871. *Please note that orders under $30 must be prepaid.* Sage affiliates in London and India will assist institutional subscribers abroad with regard to orders, claims, and inquiries for both subscriptions and single issues.

Printed on recycled, acid-free paper

THE ANNALS

© 2000 by The American Academy *of* Political *and* Social Science

Editorial Office: 3937 Chestnut Street, Philadelphia, PA 19104.

For information about membership* (individuals only) and subscriptions (institutions), address:

SAGE PUBLICATIONS, INC.
2455 Teller Road
Thousand Oaks, CA 91320

Sage Production Staff: MARIA NOTARANGELO, LISA CUEVAS, DORIS HUS, and ROSE TYLAK

From India and South Asia, write to:	From Europe, the Middle East, and Africa, write to:
SAGE PUBLICATIONS INDIA Pvt. Ltd	SAGE PUBLICATIONS LTD
P.O. Box 4215	6 Bonhill Street
New Delhi 110 048	London EC2A 4PU
INDIA	UNITED KINGDOM

*Please note that members of The Academy receive THE ANNALS with their membership.
International Standard Serial Number ISSN 0002-7162
International Standard Book Number ISBN 0-7619-2227-X (Vol. 568, 2000 paper)
International Standard Book Number ISBN 0-7619-2226-1 (Vol. 568, 2000 cloth)
Manufactured in the United States of America. First printing, March 2000.

The articles appearing in the ANNALS are abstracted or indexed in *Academic Abstracts, Academic Search, America: History and Life, Asia Pacific Database, Book Review Index, CAB Abstracts Database, Central Asia: Abstracts & Index, Communication Abstracts, Corporate ResourceNET, Criminal Justice Abstracts, Current Citations Express, Current Contents: Social & Behavioral Sciences, e-JEL, EconLit, Expanded Academic Index, Guide to Social Science & Religion in Periodical Literature, Health Business FullTEXT, HealthSTAR FullTEXT, Historical Abstracts, International Bibliography of the Social Sciences, International Political Science Abstracts, ISI Basic Social Sciences Index, Journal of Economic Literature on CD, LEXIS-NEXIS, MasterFILE FullTEXT, Middle East: Abstracts & Index, North Africa: Abstracts & Index, PAIS International, Periodical Abstracts, Political Science Abstracts, Sage Public Administration Abstracts, Social Science Source, Social Sciences Citation Index, Social Sciences Index Full Text, Social Services Abstracts, Social Work Abstracts, Sociological Abstracts, Southeast Asia: Abstracts & Index, Standard Periodical Directory (SPD), TOPICsearch, Wilson OmniFile V,* and *Wilson Social Sciences Index/Abstracts,* and are available on microfilm from University Microfilms, Ann Arbor, Michigan.

Information about membership rates, institutional subscriptions, and back issue prices may be found on the facing page.

Advertising. Current rates and specifications may be obtained by writing to THE ANNALS Advertising and Promotion Manager at the Thousand Oaks office (address above).

Claims. Claims for undelivered copies must be made no later than six months following month of publication. The publisher will supply missing copies when losses have been sustained in transit and when the reserve stock will permit.

Change of Address. Six weeks advance notice must be given when notifying of change of address to ensure proper identification. Please specify name of journal. **POSTMASTER:** Send address changes to: THE ANNALS of the American Academy of Political and Social Science, c/o Sage Publications, Inc., 2455 Teller Road, Thousand Oaks, CA 91320.

THE ANNALS

of The American Academy *of* Political *and* Social Science

ALAN W. HESTON, *Editor*
NEIL A. WEINER, *Assistant Editor*

--------------------- FORTHCOMING ---------------------

THE AFRICAN AMERICAN MALE IN
AMERICAN LIFE AND THOUGHT
Special Editor: Jacob U. Gordan

Volume 569   May 2000

DIMENSIONS OF GLOBALIZATION
Special Editors: Louis Ferleger and Jay R. Mandle
Volume 570   July 2000

FEMINIST VIEWS OF THE SOCIAL SCIENCES
Special Editor: Christine L. Williams
Volume 571   September 2000

See page 2 for information on Academy membership and
purchase of single volumes of **The Annals.**

CONTENTS

PREFACE

The articles were prepared for a conference titled "The Study of African American Problems," held at the University of Pennsylvania on February 23 and 24, 1999. These words are a manifestation of the rich scholarly legacy created by W.E.B. Du Bois at the end of the nineteenth century, a legacy that continues to bear fruit at the turn of the twentieth. While the works in this volume of *The Annals* are based on Du Bois's prospectus, "The Study of the Negro Problems," originally published in this journal 100 years ago and reprinted here, they follow strongly the spirit rather than the letter of that article. This is because times have changed, even as the problems persist. Du Bois's article was written as a prospectus for apprehending the problem of the Negro people as they confronted industrialism and increasing urbanization in the dual context of white supremacy and American democracy, for coming to terms with the problem of black immigration into the American economy and society. Du Bois acknowledged that blacks were disadvantaged compared to European immigrants both because of their lack of human capital with which to compete for place and position—the result of centuries of slavery—and because of their devalued skin color. For Du Bois the question was, How do you study this?

Born and raised in Great Barrington, Massachusetts, Du Bois received his first B.A. at Fisk University in Tennessee and a second B.A. and then his Ph.D. at Harvard. He subsequently taught for two years at Wilberforce University, a black college in Ohio, before being invited to Philadelphia by Susan Wharton under the auspices of the University of Pennsylvania in order to study the black population of the city. A great believer in science, in this case social science, Du Bois felt that if the situation of African Americans was systematically described and analyzed, the findings would be used by the leaders of society to change the situation for the better. Then living in the old Seventh Ward, which stretched along Pine and Lombard streets from Sixth to Twenty-third, this community indeed yielded a wealth of information on the topics Du Bois had identified—in particular, why employers were not using black labor as they were white immigrant labor. But, to Du Bois's dismay and eventual disillusionment, his study did not immediately change attitudes or conditions. Although he went on to conduct similar social research in Atlanta, after the publication of *The Philadelphia Negro* Du Bois began to lose faith in social science and became more of an activist. His writing turned increasingly to pamphleteering and literary portrayals of the black experience, such as *The Souls of Black Folk*.

Du Bois's methodology changed, but his purpose did not. His life's work was to focus the attention of society on the problems of African Americans, and these were centered on the need to develop leadership and social capital for blacks within a wider system that was unwilling to include them. Du Bois felt that this effort had to encompass the black race in its fullness by developing the most complete possible picture of the black community. To this end, he identified four broad areas of study: social interpretation, historical study, statistical investigation, and anthropological measurement. The articles in this issue of *The Annals* expand these practical divisions, adding issues of gender, for example, and broaden the definition of others, but all the topics fall within the purview of what Du Bois saw as affecting blacks in all sections of the land.

Du Bois felt scholars were missing an important opportunity by not studying blacks. In pushing the academic community to take blacks seriously from a scientific perspective, he manifested great faith in the power of knowledge to lead to positive change in the world. But he also thought such study would make an important contribution to world scholarship. Here were people caught up in the problems of slavery and post-slavery, the study of whom offered social scientists a wonderful opportunity to explore the human condition and the way members of such a population related among themselves and to the wider society. In a sense, the articles here continue to place this broad issue in front of the American public. A century after Du Bois, we are still dealing with this issue. How prescient he was in laying out a program that is still relevant today. The University of Pennsylvania also is to be credited with realizing the need for the work that became *The Philadelphia Negro* and setting the agenda—and the standard—for further study.

Our purpose here is not to critique Du Bois but to reflect on the issues that were first raised by him and to relate those themes to work that is being done today, to advance "The Study of the Negro Problems." To that end, scholars write both of their work and of the inspiration provided by Du Bois. In that sense, the conference celebrated the scholarly life of this seminal and highly influential thinker. The result, I hope, is a volume of which Du Bois would have been proud. The special editors, who have shared equally in the work and satisfaction of assembling the volume, hope the readers find this tribute to Du Bois to be as exciting an intellectual exercise as they did. We would like to express our gratitude to the following discussants for their valuable contributions to the conference and hence to this volume: Thomas D. Boston, Vivian Gadsden, Oscar Gandy, Paul Jefferson, Douglas Massey, William J. Moses, Robert Murray, Kenneth Shropshire, Robert Washington, and Howard Winant. The special editors would like to take this opportunity to express our gratitude to the following for their support and sponsorship of the conference: the Department of Sociology, the School of Arts and Sciences, the Population Studies Center, the Annenberg School for Communication, and the Du Bois Collective Research Institute, all of the University of Pennsylvania.

ELIJAH ANDERSON

Introduction: The Study
of African American Problems

We often have been blessed with individuals who, by their personality, intelligence, and efforts to better our world, leave an indelible mark on each and every one of us. The destruction of the color line has been distinguished by such persons: David Walker, Sojourner Truth, Harriet Tubman, Frederick Douglass, Martin Delany, John Brown, Alexander Crummell, Anna Julia Cooper, Marcus Garvey, Malcolm X, and Nelson Mandela.

In this distinguished company of activist scholars stands W. E. Burghardt Du Bois. As a scholar he transcended disciplinary boundaries and genre. Since the Enlightenment, conceptions of identity have defined the very core of questions about human difference in the Western world. Sociology, for example, was founded by intellectuals who believed that "the world" (that is, Europe or the West) was changing; social theorists such as Karl Marx, Max Weber, and Emile Durkheim examined the ways in which individual identity was shaped by the transformation of traditional societies into modern ones.[1] Traditional preindustrial societies were seen as the embodiment of a collective identity in which individuals were aware of who they are and why they exist. The clarity of traditional identities is blurred by the transition to the modern division of labor. As modern capitalism develops and rational behaviors dominate, the problems of identity are left behind. Yet the same social theorists who founded sociology had little to say about the role of race in modern society (Marx [1867] 1976; Weber [1920-21] 1958; Durkheim [1893] 1933; Greenberg 1980, chaps. 1 and 2, esp. 9-11; Liebersohn 1987, 123-31). Marx treated racial inequality as a problem secondary to the class struggle. Weber treated race as an unsubstantiated category with marginal significance for understanding national identity, which he defined in opposition to ethnicity and race.[2] Du Bois recognized the importance of identity for the modern worldview, and he developed a critique of the theories of modern society in his thesis of the color line. He emphasized the importance of racial stratification:[3] one could not understand the impact of the modern division of labor, he argued, unless one understood African enslavement in the Americas, "on which modern commerce and industry was founded" (Du Bois [1935] 1992,

30; Du Bois 1903). Du Bois's formulation of the problem presents race and class as significant, twin aspects of the modern division of labor.

Called to be an activist scholar—a seer to provide vision and leadership out of the house of racial domination and human suffering—Du Bois's contributions to our understanding of the question of racial colonialism, racial enslavement, the African question, the role of theory in social change, and the role of race in the dehumanization of the African and the African diaspora have been surpassed by few and serve as a model for those with intelligence and courage.

Du Bois is an essential intellectual in the broadest sense of the term. He stands with the greatest of minds of the nineteenth and twentieth centuries. On 23 and 24 February 1999, at a conference titled "The Study of African American Problems: Papers Presented in Honor of W.E.B. Du Bois" and convened at the University of Pennsylvania, we undertook the difficult task of evaluating Du Bois's contribution to understanding the African American problems and of building on these attempts as we extended his shortcomings into goals for future generations.

"The Study of African American Problems" brings an interdisciplinary eye to focus on Du Bois's sociology—a sociology that is historical, statistical, demographic, biological, and cultural. In "The Study of the Negro Problems," published in 1898 in *The Annals* of the American Academy of Political and Social Science and the basis on which this conference was organized, Professor Du Bois wrote:

It is not *one* problem, but rather a plexus of social problems, some new, some old, some simple, some complex; and these problems have their one bond of unity in the act that they group themselves about those Africans whom two centuries of slave-trading brought into the land. (Du Bois 1898, 3)

Du Bois challenges the world, the nation, universities, and scholars to set out on an academic and activist journey. At the turn of the twentieth century, Du Bois's blueprint is as vital, relevant, and inspirational as it was at the turn of the nineteenth. This volume of *The Annals* on the study of African American problems honors this effort by Du Bois. This volume brings together prominent scholars in the field of African American studies to look at the study of African American problems.

In "The Study of the Negro Problems," Du Bois outlines the elements necessary to conduct a scientific sociological investigation of the problems of African Americans: (1) the historical development of these problems; (2) the necessity for their careful systematic study; (3) the results of the scientific study up to this time; (4) the scope and method which future scientific inquiry should take; and (5) the agencies by which this work could best be carried out. We might ask what has happened over the last 100 years. To what extent has Du Bois's research plan been carried out? Have studies of the African American population been based on a thorough knowledge of details? Have they been systematic? Have they been critical? The articles in this issue of *The Annals* aim to answer these questions.

For Du Bois, "a social problem is ever a relation between conditions and action, and as conditions and actions vary and change from group to group from time to time and from place to place, so social problems change, develop and grow" (Du Bois 1898, 3). Thus, he placed the study of the African American population into two categories: the study of African Americans as a social group, and the study of African Americans' peculiar social environment. As Du Bois himself recognized, these two categories are difficult to separate in practice, and therefore we have not attempted to do so.

This volume focuses attention on a number of subjects that affect the African American population as a social group and its peculiar social environments. Du Bois did his work and he did it well. It is hoped that the authors of this volume have emulated him while extending his scope and vision. The following words by Du Bois both remind us of the importance of our task and inspire us to continue:

We are still prone in spite of all our culture to sneer at the heroism of the laboratory while we cheer the swagger of the street broil. At such a time true lovers of humanity can only hold higher the pure ideals of science, and continue to insist that if we would solve a problem we must study it, and that there is but one coward on earth, and that is the coward that dare not know. (Du Bois 1898, 23)

TUKUFU ZUBERI

Notes

1. "In its simplest sense the Enlightenment was the creation of a new framework of ideas about man, society, and nature, which challenged existing conceptions rooted in a traditional world-view, dominated by Christianity. The key domain in which Enlightenment intellectuals challenged the clergy, who were the main group involved in supporting existing conceptions of the world, concerned the traditional view of nature, man, and society which was sustained by the Church's authority and its monopoly over the information media of the time" (Hamilton 1996, 24). Three classic texts are helpful for grasping the significance of modernization to the founders of European social science (Marx [1867] 1976; Weber [1920-21] 1958; Durkheim [1893] 1933).

2. In *Economy and Society*, Weber asserts that "We shall call 'ethnic groups' those human groups that entertain a subjective belief in their common descent because of similarities of physical type or of customs or both, or because of memories of colonization and migration; this belief must be important for the propagation of group formation; conversely, it does not matter whether or not an objective blood relationship exists. Ethnic membership (*Gemeinsamkeit*) differs from the kinship group precisely by being a presumed identity, not a group with concrete social action, like the latter. In our sense, ethnic membership does not constitute a group; it only facilitates group formation of any kind, particularly in the political sphere. On the other hand, it is primarily the political community, no matter how artificially organized that inspires the belief in common ethnicity. This belief tends to persist even after the disintegration of the political community, unless drastic differences in the custom, physical type, or, above all, language exist among its members" (Weber [1956] 1978, 389). Weber expressed some of the most advanced thinking on the issue of race among nineteenth-century social scientists of European origin. For Weber, racial identity was a particular form of ethnic identity, and both "dissolved" in the context of the

nation. Also, Weber's article suggests a heavy debt to Du Bois. In fact, Weber was himself influenced by and predisposed to Du Bois's work (see Aptheker 1973, 106). Yet his notion of ethnic group identity differed significantly from Du Bois's idea of racial identity. Du Bois was careful to distinguish between ethnic and racial identity and social processes.

3. Racial stratification means the differentiation of a given population into hierarchically superposed racial groups. Its basis and very essence demand an unequal distribution of rights and privileges among the members of a society.

References

Aptheker, Herbert, ed. 1973. *The Correspondence of W.E.B. Du Bois*. Vol. 1. Amherst: University of Massachusetts Press.

Du Bois, W.E.B. 1898. The Study of the Negro Problems. *The Annals* of the American Academy of Political and Social Science, Jan.:1-23.

———. 1903. *The Souls of Black Folk*. Chicago: A. C. McClurg.

———. [1935] 1992. *Black Reconstruction*. New York: Atheneum.

Durkheim, Emile. [1893] 1933. *The Division of Labor in Society*. New York: Free Press.

Greenberg, Stanley B. 1980. *Race and State in Capitalist Development*. New Haven, CT: Yale University Press.

Hamilton, Peter. 1996. The Enlightenment and the Birth of Social Science. In *Modernity: An Introduction to Modern Societies*, ed. Stuart Hall, David Held, Don Hubert, and Kenneth Thompson. Cambridge, MA: Blackwell.

Liebersohn, Harry. 1987. Weber's Concept of National Identity. In *Weber's Protestant Ethic: Origins, Evidence, Contexts*, ed. Hartmut Lehmann and Guenther Roth. New York: Cambridge University Press.

Marx, Karl. [1867] 1976. *Capital: A Critique of Political Economy*. New York: International Publishers.

Weber, Max. [1920-21] 1958. *The Protestant Ethic and the Spirit of Capitalism*. New York: Scribner.

———. [1956] 1978. *Economy and Society*. Berkeley: University of California Press.

The Study of the
Negro Problems

W. E. BURGHARDT DU BOIS
University of Pennsylvania

T he present period in the development of sociological study is a trying one; it is the period of observation, research and comparison—work always wearisome, often aimless, without well-settled principles and guiding lines, and subject ever to the pertinent criticism: What, after all, has been accomplished? To this the one positive answer which years of research and speculation have been able to return is that the phenomena of society are worth the most careful and systematic study, and whether or not this study may eventually lead to a systematic body of knowledge deserving the name of science, it cannot in any case fail to give the world a mass of truth worth knowing.

Being then in a period of observation and comparison, we must confess to ourselves that the sociologists of few nations have so good an opportunity for observing the growth and evolution of society as those of the United States. The rapid rise of a young country, the vast social changes, the wonderful economic development, the bold political experiments, and the contact of varying moral standards—all these make for American students crucial tests of social action, microcosmic reproductions of long centuries of world history, and rapid—even violent—repetitions of great social problems. Here is a field for the sociologist—a field rich, but little worked, and full of great possibilities. European scholars envy our opportunities and it must be said to our credit that great interest in the observation of social phenomena has been aroused in the last decade—an interest of which much is ephemeral and superficial, but which opens the way for broad scholarship and scientific effort.

NOTE: *This article was originally published in the January 1898 issue of* The Annals *of the American Academy of Political and Social Science. —Ed.*

In one field, however,—and a field perhaps larger than any other single domain of social phenomena, there does not seem to have been awakened as yet a fitting realization of the opportunities for scientific inquiry. This is the group of social phenomena arising from the presence in this land of eight million persons of African descent.

It is my purpose in this paper to discuss certain considerations concerning the study of the social problems affecting American Negroes; first, as to the historical development of these problems; then as to the necessity for their careful systematic study at the present time; thirdly, as to the results of scientific study of the Negro up to this time; fourthly, as to the scope and method which future scientific inquiry should take, and, lastly, regarding the agencies by which this work can best be carried out.

1. DEVELOPMENT OF
THE NEGRO PROBLEMS.

A social problem is the failure of an organized social group to realize its group ideals, through the inability to adapt a certain desired line of action to given conditions of life. If, for instance, a government founded on universal manhood suffrage has a portion of its population so ignorant as to be unable to vote intelligently, such ignorance becomes a menacing social problem. The impossibility of economic and social development in a community where a large per cent of the population refuse to abide by the social rules of order, makes a problem of crime and lawlessness. Prostitution becomes a social problem when the demands of luxurious home life conflict with marriage customs.

Thus a social problem is ever a relation between conditions and action, and as conditions and actions vary and change from group to group from time to time and from place to place, so social problems change, develop and grow. Consequently, though we ordinarily speak of the Negro problem as though it were one unchanged question, students must recognize the obvious facts that this problem, like others, has had a long historical development, has changed with the growth and evolution of the nation; moreover, that it is not *one* problem, but rather a plexus of social problems, some new, some old, some simple, some complex; and these problems have their one bond of unity in the act that they group themselves about those Africans whom two centuries of slave-trading brought into the land.

In the latter part of the seventeenth and early in the eighteenth centuries, the central and all-absorbing economic need of America was the creation of a proper labor supply to develop American wealth. This question had been answered in the West Indies by enslaving Indians and Negroes. In the colonies of the mainland it was answered by the importation of Negroes and indentured servants. Immediately then there arose the question of the legal status of these slaves and servants; and dozens of enactments, from Massachusetts to Georgia, were made "for the proper regulation of slaves and servants." Such statutes sought to solve problems of labor and not of race or color. Two circumstances, however, soon began to differentiate in the problem of labor, problems which concerned slaves for life from those which concerned servants for limited periods; and these circumstances were the economic superiority of the slave system, and the fact that the slaves were neither of the same race, language nor religion as the servants and their masters. In laboring classes thus widely separated there naturally arose a difference in legal and social standing. Colonial statutes soon ceased to embrace the regulations applying to slaves and servants in one chapter, and laws were passed for servants on the one hand and for Negro slaves on the other.

As slave labor, under the peculiar conditions of colonial life, increased in value and efficiency, the importations of Africans increased, while those of indented servants decreased; this gave rise to new social problems, namely, those of protecting a feeble civilization against an influx of barbarism and heathenism. Between 1750 and 1800 an increasing number of laws began to form a peculiar and systematic slave code based on a distinct idea of social caste. Even, as this slave code was developing, new social conditions changed the aspect of the problems. The laws hitherto had been made to fit a class distinguished by its condition more than by its race or color. There arose now, however, a class of English-speaking Negroes born on American soil, and members of Christian churches; there sprang from illicit intercourse and considerable intermarriage with indentured servants, a number of persons of mixed blood; there was also created by emancipation and the birth of black sons of white women a new class of free Negroes: all these developments led to a distinct beginning of group life among Negroes. Repeated attempts at organized insurrection were made; wholesale running away, like that which established the exiles in Florida, was resorted to; and a class of black landholders and voters arose. Such social movements brought the colonists face to face with new and serious problems; which they sought at first to settle in curious ways, denying the rite of baptism, establishing the legal presumption that all Negroes and mulattoes were slaves, and finally changing the Slave Code into a Black Code, replacing a caste of condition by a caste of race, harshly stopping legal sexual intercourse, and seeking to prevent further complications by restricting and even suppressing the slave-trade.

This concerted and determined action again changed the character of the Negro problems, but they did not cease to be grave. The inability of the Negro to escape from a servile caste into political freedom turned the problems of the group into problems of family life. On the separated plantations and in households the Negro became a constituent member of the family, speaking its language, worshiping in its churches, sharing its traditions, bearing its name, and sometimes sharing its blood; the talented slaves found large freedom in the intimate intercourse with the family which they enjoyed; they lost many traditions of their fatherland, and their ideals blended with the ideals of their new country. Some men began to see in this development a physical, economic and moral danger to the land, and they busied themselves with questions as to how they might provide for the development of white and black without demoralizing the one or amalgamating with the other. The solution of these difficulties was sought in a widespread attempt to eliminate the Negro from the family as he had formerly been eliminated from the state, by a process of emancipation that made him and his sons not even half-free, with the indefinite notion of colonizing the anomalous serfs thus created. This policy was carried out until one-half the land and one-sixth of the Negroes were quasi-freemen.

Just as the nation was on the point of realizing the futility of colonization, one of those strange incalculable world movements began to be felt throughout civilized states—a movement so vast that we call it the economic revolution of the nineteenth century. A world demand for crops peculiarly suited to the South, substituted in Europe the factory system for the house industry, and in America the large plantation slave system for the family patriarchy; slavery became an industrial system and not a training school for serfdom; the Black Codes underwent a sudden transformation which hardened the lot of the slave, facilitated the slave trade, hindered further emancipation and rendered the condition of the free Negro unbearable. The question of race and color in America assumed a new and peculiar importance when it thus lay at the basis of some of the world's greatest industries.

The change in industrial conditions, however, not only affected the demands of a world market, but so increased the efficiency of labor, that a labor system, which in 1750 was eminently successful, soon became under the altered conditions of 1850 not only an economic monstrosity, but a political menace, and so rapidly did the crisis develop that the whole evolution of the nation came to a standstill, and the settlement of our social problems had to be left to the clumsy method of brute force.

So far as the Negro race is concerned, the Civil War simply left us face to face with the same sort of problems of social condition and caste which were beginning to face the nation a century ago. It is these problems that we are to-day somewhat helplessly—not to say carelessly—facing, forgetful that they are living, growing social questions whose progeny will survive to curse the nation, unless we grapple with them manfully and intelligently.

2. THE PRESENT
NEGRO PROBLEMS.

Such are some of the changes of condition and social movement which have, since 1619, altered and broadened the social problems grouped about the American Negro. In this development of successive questions about one centre, there is nothing peculiar to American history. Given any fixed condition or fact—a river Nile, a range of Alps, an alien race, or a national idea— and problems of society will at every stage of advance group themselves about it. All social growth means a succession of social problems—they constitute growth, they denote that laborious and often baffling adjustment of action and condition which is the essence of progress, and while a particular fact or circumstance may serve in one country as a rallying point of many intricate questions of adjustment, the absence of that particular fact would not mean the absence of all social problems. Questions of labor, caste, ignorance and race were bound to arise in America; they were simply complicated here and intensified there by the presence of the Negro.

Turning now from this brief summary of the varied phases of these questions, let us inquire somewhat more carefully into the form under which the Negro problems present themselves to-day after 275 years of evolution. Their existence is plainly manifested by the fact that a definitely segregated mass of eight millions of Americans do not wholly share the national life of the people; are not an integral part of the social body. The points at which they fail to be incorporated into this group life constitute the particular Negro problems, which can be divided into two distinct but correlated parts, depending on two facts:

First—Negroes do not share the full national life because as a mass they have not reached a sufficiently high grade of culture.

Secondly—They do not share the full national life because there has always existed in America a conviction—varying in intensity, but always widespread—that people of Negro blood should not be admitted into the group life of the nation no matter what their condition might be.

Considering the problems arising from the backward development of Negroes, we may say that the mass of this race does not reach the social standards of the nation with respect to

(a) Economic condition.
(b) Mental training.
(c) Social efficiency.

Even if special legislation and organized relief intervene, freedmen always start life under an economic disadvantage which generations, perhaps centuries, cannot overcome. Again, of all the important constituent parts of our nation, the Negro is by far the most ignorant; nearly half of the race are absolutely illiterate, only a minority of the other half have thorough common school training, and but a remnant are liberally educated. The great deficiency of the Negro, however, is his small knowledge of the art of organized social life—that last expression of human culture. His development in group life was abruptly broken off by the slave ship, directed into abnormal channels and dwarfed by the Black Codes, and suddenly wrenched anew by the Emancipation Proclamation. He finds himself, therefore, peculiarly weak in that nice adaptation of individual life to the life of the group which is the essence of civilization. This is shown in the grosser forms of sexual immorality, disease and crime, and also in the difficulty of race organization for common ends in economic or in intellectual lines.

For these reasons the Negro would fall behind any average modern nation, and he is unusually handicapped in the midst of a nation which excels in its extraordinary economic development, its average of popular intelligence and in the boldness of its experiments in organized social life.

These problems of poverty, ignorance and social degradation differ from similar problems the world over in one important particular, and that is the fact that they are complicated by a peculiar environment. This constitutes the second class of Negro problems, and they rest, as has been said, on the widespread conviction among Americans that no persons of Negro descent should become constituent members of the social body. This feeling gives rise to economic problems, to educational problems, and nice questions of social morality; it makes it more difficult for black men to earn a living or spend their earnings as they will; it gives them poorer school facilities and restricted contact with cultured classes; and it becomes, throughout the land, a cause and excuse for discontent, lawlessness, laziness and injustice.

3. THE NECESSITY OF CAREFULLY STUDYING THESE PROBLEMS.

Such, barely stated, are the elements of the present Negro problems. It is to little purpose however to name the elements of a problem unless we can also say accurately to what extent each element enters into the final result: whether, for instance, the present difficulties arise more largely from ignorance than from prejudice, or *vice versa*. This we do not know, and here it is that every intelligent discussion of the American Negro comes to a standstill. Nearly a hundred years ago Thomas Jefferson complained that the nation had never studied the real condition of the slaves and that, therefore, all general conclusions about them were extremely hazardous. We of another age can scarcely say that we have made material progress in this study. Yet these problems, so vast and intricate, demanding trained research and expert analysis, touching questions that affect the very foundation of the republic and of human progress, increasing and multiplying year by year, would seem to urge the nation with increasing force to measure and trace and understand thoroughly the underlying elements of this example of human evolution.

Now first we should study the Negro problems in order to distinguish between the different and distinct problems affecting this race. Nothing makes intelligent discussion of the Negro's position so fruitless as the repeated failure to discriminate between the different questions that concern him. If a Negro discusses the question, he is apt to discuss simply the problem of race prejudice; if a Southern white man writes on the subject he is apt to discuss problems of ignorance, crime and social degradation; and yet each calls the problem he discusses *the* Negro problem, leaving in the dark background the really crucial question as to the relative importance of the many problems involved. Before we can begin to study the Negro intelligently, we must realize definitely that not only is he affected by all the varying social forces that act on any nation at his stage of advancement, but that in addition to these there is reacting upon him the mighty power of a peculiar and unusual social environment which affects to some extent every other social force.

In the second place we should seek to know and measure carefully all the forces and conditions that go to make up these different problems, to trace the historical development of these conditions, and discover as far as possible the probable trend of further development. Without doubt this would be difficult work, and it can with much truth be objected that we cannot ascertain, by the methods of sociological research known to us, all such facts thoroughly and accurately. To this objection it is only necessary to answer that however difficult it may be to know all about the Negro, it is certain that we can know vastly more than we do, and that we can have our knowledge in more systematic and intelligible form. As things are, our opinions upon the Negro are more matters of faith than of knowledge. Every schoolboy is ready to discuss the matter, and there are few men that have not settled convictions. Such a situation is dangerous. Whenever any nation allows impulse, whim or hasty conjecture to usurp the place of conscious, normative, intelligent action, it is in grave danger. The sole aim of any society is to settle its problems in accordance with its highest ideals, and the only rational method of accomplishing this is to study those problems in the light of the best scientific research.

Finally, the American Negro deserves study for the great end of advancing the cause of science in general. No such opportunity to watch and measure the history and development of a great race of men ever presented itself to the scholars of a modern nation. If they miss this opportunity— if they do the work in a slip-shod, unsystematic manner—if they dally with the truth to humor the whims of the day, they do far more than hurt the good name of the American people; they hurt the cause of scientific truth the world over, they voluntarily decrease human knowledge of a universe of which we are ignorant enough, and they degrade the high end of truth-seeking in a day when they need more and more to dwell upon its sanctity.

4. THE WORK
ALREADY ACCOMPLISHED.

It may be said that it is not altogether correct to assert that few attempts have been made to study these problems or to put the nation in possession of a body of truth in accordance with which it might act intelligently. It is far from my purpose to disparage in any way the work already done by students of these questions; much valuable effort has without doubt been put upon the field, and yet a careful survey of the field seems but to emphasize the fact that the work done bears but small proportion to the work still to be done.*

Moreover the studies made hitherto can as a whole be justly criticized in three particulars: (1) They have not been based on a thorough knowledge of details; (2) they have been unsystematical; (3) they have been uncritical.

In few subjects have historians been more content to go on indefinitely repeating current traditions and uninvestigated facts. We are still gravely told that the slave trade ceased in 1808, that the docility of Africans made slave insurrections almost unknown, and that the Negro never developed in this country a self-conscious group life before 1860. In the hasty endeavor to cover a broad subject when the details were unknown, much superficial work has been current, like that, for instance, of a newspaper reporter who spent "the odd intervals of leisure in active newspaper work" for "nearly eighteen months," in the District of Columbia, and forthwith published a study of 80,000 Negroes, with observations on their institutions and development.

Again, the work done has been lamentably unsystematic and fragmentary. Scientific work must be subdivided, but conclusions which affect the whole subject must be based on a study of the whole. One cannot study the Negro in freedom and come to general conclusions about his destiny without knowing his history in slavery. A vast set of problems having a common centre must, too, be studied according to some general plan, if the work of different students is to be compared or to go toward building a unified body of knowledge. A plan once begun must be carried out, and not like that of our erratic census reports, after allowing us to follow the size of farms in the South for three decades, suddenly leave us wondering as to the relation of farms and farm families. Students of black codes should not stop suddenly with 1863, and travelers and observers whose testimony would be of great value if arranged with

---

*A bibliography of the American Negro is a much needed undertaking. The existing literature may be summarized briefly as follows: In the line of historical research there are such general studies of the Negro as Williams' "History of the Negro Race in America," Wilson's, Goodell's, Blake's, Copley's, Greeley's and Cobb's studies of slavery, and the treatment of the subject in the general histories of Bancroft, Von Holst and others. We have, too, brief special histories of the institution of slavery in Massachusetts, Connecticut, New York, New Jersey, Pennsylvania, the District of Columbia, Maryland and North Carolina. The slave trade has been studied by Clarkson, Buxton, Benezet, Carey and others; Miss McDougall has written a monograph on fugitive slaves; the Slave Codes have been digested by Hurd, Stroud, Wheeler, Goodell and Cobb; the economic aspects of the slave system were brilliantly outlined by Cairnes, and a great amount of material is available, showing the development of anti-slavery opinion. Of statistical and sociological material the United States Government has collected much in its census and bureau reports; and congressional investigations, and state governments and societies have added something to this. Moreover, we have the statistical studies of DeBow, Helper, Gannett and Hoffman, the observations of Olmsted and Kemble, and the studies and interpretations by Chambers, Otken, Bruce, Cable, Fortune, Brackett, Ingle and Tourgée; foreign students, from De Tocqueville and Martineau to Halle and Bryce, have studied the subject; something has been done in collecting folklore and music, and in studying dialect, and some anthropological material has been collected. Beside this, there is a mass of periodical literature, of all degrees of value, teeming with opinions, observations, personal experiences and discussions.

some system and reasonably limited in time and space, must not ramble on without definite plan or purpose and render their whole work of doubtful value.

Most unfortunate of all, however, is the fact that so much of the work done on the Negro question is notoriously uncritical; uncritical from lack of discrimination in the selection and weighing of evidence; uncritical in choosing the proper point of view from which to study these problems, and, finally, uncritical from the distinct bias in the minds of so many writers. To illustrate, the layman who does not pretend to first hand knowledge of the subject and who would learn of students is to-day woefully puzzled by absolutely contradictory evidence. One student declares that Negroes are advancing in knowledge and ability; that they are working, establishing homes, and going into business, and that the problem will soon be one of the past. Another student of equal learning declares that the Negro is degenerating—sinking into crime and social immorality, receiving little help from education, still in the main a menial servant, and destined in a short time to settle the problem by dying entirely out. Such and many other contradictory conclusions arise from the uncritical use of material. A visitor to a great Negro school in the South catches the inspiration of youth, studies the work of graduates, and imbibes the hopes of teachers and immediately infers from the situation of a few hundred the general condition of a population numbering twice that of Holland. A college graduate sees the slums of a Southern city, looks at the plantation field hands, and has some experience with Negro servants, and from the laziness, crime and disease which he finds, draws conclusions as to eight millions of people, stretched from Maine to Texas and from Florida to Washington. We continually judge the whole from the part we are familiar with; we continually assume the material we have at hand to be typical; we reverently receive a column of figures without asking who collected them, how they were arranged, how far they are valid and what chances of error they contain; we receive the testimony of men without asking whether they were trained or ignorant, careful or careless, truthful or given to exaggeration, and, above all, whether they are giving facts or opinions. It is so easy for a man who has already formed his conclusions to receive any and all testimony in their favor without carefully weighing and testing it, that we sometimes find in serious scientific studies very curious proof of broad conclusions. To cite an extreme case, in a recently published study of the Negro, a part of the argument as to the physical condition of all these millions, is made to rest on the measurement of fifteen black boys in a New York reformatory.

The widespread habit of studying the Negro from one point of view only, that of his influence on the white inhabitants, is also responsible for much uncritical work. The slaves are generally treated as one inert changeless mass, and most studies of slavery apparently have no conception of a social evolution and development among them. The slave code of a state is given, the progress of anti-slavery sentiment, the economic results of the system and the general influence of man on master are studied, but of the slave himself, of his group life and social institutions, of remaining traces of his African tribal life, of his amusements, his conversion to Christianity, his acquiring of the English tongue—in fine, of his whole reaction against his environment, of all this we hear little or nothing, and would apparently be expected to believe that the Negro arose from the dead in 1863. Yet all the testimony of law and custom, of tradition and present social condition, shows us that the Negro at the time of emancipation had passed through a social evolution which far separated him from his savage ancestors.

The most baneful cause of uncritical study of the Negro is the manifest and far-reaching bias of writers. Americans are born in many cases with deep, fierce convictions on the Negro question, and in other cases imbibe them from their environment. When such men come to write on the subject, without technical training, without breadth of view, and in some cases without a deep sense of the sanctity of scientific truth, their testimony, however interesting as opinion, must of necessity be worthless as science. Thus too often the testimony of Negroes and their friends has to be thrown out of court on account of the manifest prejudice of the writers; on the other hand, the testimony of many other writers in the North and especially in the South has to be received with reserve on account of too evident bias.

Such facts make the path of students and foreign observers peculiarly thorny. The foreigner's views, if he be not exceptionally astute, will depend largely on his letters of introduction; the home student's views, on his birthplace and parentage. All students are apt to fail to recognize the magnitude and importance of these problems, and to succumb to the vulgar temptation of basing on any little contribution they make to the study of these problems, general conclusions as to the origin and destiny of the Negro people in time and eternity. Thus we possess endless final judgments as to the American Negro emanating from men of influence and learning, in the very face of the fact known to every accurate student, that there exists to-day no sufficient material of proven reliability, upon which any scientist can base definite and final conclusions as to the present condition and tendencies of the eight million American Negroes; and that any person or publication purporting to give such conclusions simply makes statements which go beyond the reasonably proven evidence.

5. A PROGRAM
OF FUTURE STUDY.

If we admit the deep importance of the Negro problems, the necessity of studying them, and certain shortcomings in work done up to this time, it would seem to be the clear duty of the American people, in the interests of scientific knowledge and social reform, to begin a broad and systematic study of the history and condition of the American Negroes. The scope and method of this study, however, needs to be generally agreed upon beforehand in its main outlines, not to hinder the freedom of individual students, but to systematize and unify effort so as to cover the wide field of investigation.

The scope of any social study is first of all limited by the general attitude of public opinion toward truth and truth-seeking. If in regard to any social problem there is for any reason a persistent refusal on the part of the people to allow the truth to be known, then manifestly that problem cannot be studied. Undoubtedly much of the unsatisfactory work already done with regard to the Negro is due to this cause; the intense feeling that preceded and followed the war made a calm balanced research next to impossible. Even to-day there are certain phases of this question which we cannot hope to be allowed to study dispassionately and thoroughly, and these phases, too, are naturally those uppermost in the public mind. For instance, it is extremely doubtful if any satisfactory study of Negro crime and lynching can be made for a generation or more, in the present condition of the public mind, which renders it almost impossible to get at the facts and real conditions. On the other hand, public opinion has in the last decade become sufficiently liberal to open a broad field of investigation to students, and here lies the chance for effective work.

The right to enter this field undisturbed and untrammeled will depend largely on the attitude of science itself. Students must be careful to insist that science as such—be it physics, chemistry, psychology, or sociology—has but one simple aim: the discovery of truth. Its results lie open for the use of all men—merchants, physicians, men of letters, and philanthropists, but the aim of science itself is simple truth. Any attempt to give it a double aim, to make social reform the immediate instead of the mediate object of a search for truth, will inevitably tend to defeat both objects. The frequent alliance of sociological research with various panaceas and particular schemes of reform, has resulted in closely connecting social investigation with a good deal of groundless assumption and humbug in the popular mind. There will be at first some difficulty in bringing the Southern people, both black and white, to conceive of an earnest, careful study of the Negro problem which has not back of it some scheme of race amalgamation, political jobbery, or deportation to Africa. The new study of the American Negro must avoid such misapprehensions from the outset, by insisting that historical and statistical research has but one object, the ascertainment of the facts as to the social forces and conditions of one-eighth of the inhabitants of the land. Only by such rigid adherence to the true object of the scholar, can statesmen and philanthropists of all shades of belief be put into possession of a reliable body of truth which may guide their efforts to the best and largest success.

In the next place, a study of the Negro, like the study of any subject, must start out with certain generally admitted postulates. We must admit, for instance, that the field of study is large and varying, and that what is true of the Negro in Massachusetts is not necessarily true of the Negro in Louisiana; that what was true of the Negro in 1850 was not necessarily true in 1750; and that there are many distinct social problems affecting the Negro. Finally, if we would rally to this common ground of scientific inquiry all partisans and advocates, we must explicitly admit what all implicitly postulate—namely, that the Negro is a member of the human race, and as one who, in the light of history and experience, is capable to a degree of improvement and culture, is entitled to have his interests considered according to his numbers in all conclusions as to the common weal.

With these preliminary considerations we may say that the study of the Negro falls naturally into two categories, which though difficult to separate in practice, must for the sake of logical clearness, be kept distinct. They are (a) the study of the Negro as a social group, (b) the study of his peculiar social environment.

The study of the Negro as a social group may be, for convenience, divided into four not exactly logical but seemingly most practicable divisions, viz:

1. Historical study.
2. Statistical investigation.
3. Anthropological measurement.
4. Sociological interpretation.

The material at hand for historical research is rich and abundant; there are the colonial statutes and records, the partially accessible archives of Great Britain, France and Spain, the collections of historical societies, the vast number of executive and congressional reports and documents, the state statutes, reports and publications, the reports of institutions and societies, the personal narratives and opinions of various observers and the periodical press covering nearly three centuries. From these sources can be gathered much new information upon the economic and social development of the Negro, upon the rise and decline of the slave-trade, the character, distribution and state of culture of the Africans, the evolution of the slave codes as expressing the life of the South, the rise of such peculiar expressions of Negro social history, as the Negro church, the economics of plantation life, the possession of private property by slaves, and the history of the oft-forgotten class of free Negroes. Such historical research must be subdivided in space and limited in time by the nature of the subject, the history of the different colonies and groups being followed and compared, the different periods of development receiving special study, and the whole subject being reviewed from different aspects.

The collection of statistics should be carried on with increased care and thoroughness. It is no credit to a great modern nation that so much well-grounded doubt can be thrown on our present knowledge of the simple matters of number, age, sex and conjugal condition in regard to our Negro population. General statistical investigations should avoid seeking to tabulate more intricate social conditions than the ones indicated. The concrete social status of the Negro can only be ascertained by intensive studies carried on in definitely limited localities, by competent investigators, in accordance with one general plan. Statistical study by groups is apt to be more accurately done and more easily accomplished, and able to secure more competent and responsible agents than any general census. General averages in so complicated a subject are apt to be dangerously misleading. This study should seek to ascertain by the most approved methods of social measurement the size and condition of families, the occupations and wages, the illiteracy of adults and education of children, the standard of living, the character of the dwellings, the property owned and rents paid, and the character of the organized group life. Such investigations should be extended until they cover the typical group life of Negroes in all sections of the land and should be so repeated from time to time in the same localities and with the same methods, as to be a measure of social development.

The third division of study is anthropological measurement, and it includes a scientific study of the Negro body. The most obvious peculiarity of the Negro—a peculiarity which is a large element in many of the problems affecting him—is his physical unlikeness to the people with whom he has been brought into contact. This difference is so striking that it has become the basis of a mass of theory, assumption and suggestion which is deep-rooted and yet rests on the flimsiest basis of scientific fact. That there are differences between the white and black races is certain, but just what those differences are is known to none with an approach to accuracy. Yet here in America is the most remarkable opportunity ever offered of studying these differences, of noting influences of climate and physical environment, and particularly of studying the effect of amalgamating two of the most diverse races in the world—another subject which rests under a cloud of ignorance.

The fourth division of this investigation is sociological interpretation; it should include the arrangement and interpretation of historical and statistical matter in the light of the experience of other nations and other ages; it should aim to study those finer manifestations of social life which history can but mention and which statistics can not count, such as the expression of Negro life as found in their hundred newspapers, their considerable literature, their music and folklore and their germ of esthetic life—in fine, in all the movements and customs among them that manifest the existence of a distinct social mind.

The second category of studies of the Negro has to do with his peculiar social environment. It will be difficult, as has been intimated, to separate a study of the group from a study of the environment, and yet the group action and the reaction of the surroundings must be kept clearly distinct if we expect to comprehend the Negro problems. The study of the environment may be carried on at the same time with a study of the group, only the two sets of forces must receive distinct measurement.

In such a field of inquiry it will be found difficult to do more than subdivide inquiry in time and space. The attempt should be made to isolate and study the tangible phenomena of Negro prejudice in all possible cases; its effect on the Negro's physical development, on his mental acquisitiveness, on his moral and social condition, as manifested in economic life, in legal sanctions and in crime and lawlessness. So, too, the influence of that same prejudice on American life and character would explain the otherwise inexplicable changes through which Negro prejudice has passed.

The plan of study thus sketched is, without doubt, long, difficult and costly, and yet is not more than commensurable with the size and importance of the subject with which it is to deal. It will take years and decades to carry out such a plan, with the barest measure of success, and yet there can be no doubt but that this plan or something similar to it, points to the quickest path toward the ultimate solution of the present difficulties.

6. THE PROPER
AGENTS FOR THIS WORK.

In conclusion it will not be out of place to suggest the agencies which seem best fitted to carry out a work of this magnitude. There will, without doubt, always be room for the individual working alone as he wills; if, however, we wish to cover the field systematically, and in reasonable time, only organized and concerted efforts will avail; and the requisite means, skill and preparation for such work can be furnished by two agencies alone: the government and the university.

For simple, definite inquiries carried out periodically on a broad scale we should depend on the national and state governments. The decennial census properly organized under civil service rules should be the greatest single agency for collecting general information as to the Negro. If, however, the present Congress cannot be induced to organize a census bureau under proper Civil Service rules, and in accordance with the best expert advice, we must continue for many years more to depend on clumsy and ignorant methods of measurement in matters demanding accuracy and trained technique. It is possible also for the different national bureaus and for the state governments to study certain aspects of the Negro question over wide areas. A conspicuous example of this is the valuable educational statistics collected by Commissioner Harris, and the series of economic studies just instituted by the Bureau of Labor.

On the whole it may be laid down as axiomatic that government activity in the study of this problem should confine itself mainly to the ascertainment of simple facts covering a broad field. For the study of these social problems in their more complicated aspects, where the desideratum is intensive study, by trained minds, according to the best methods, the only competent agency is the university. Indeed, in no better way could the American university repay the unusual munificence of its benefactors than by placing before the nation a body of scientific truth in the light of which they could solve some of their most vexing social problems.

It is to the credit of the University of Pennsylvania that she has been the first to recognize her duty in this respect, and in so far as restricted means and opportunity allowed, has attempted to study the Negro problems in a single definite locality. This work needs to be extended to other groups, and carried out with larger system; and here it would seem is the opportunity of the Southern Negro college. We hear much of higher Negro education, and yet all candid people know there does not exist today in the centre of Negro population a single first-class fully equipped institution devoted to the higher education of Negroes; not more than three Negro institutions in the South deserve the name of *college* at all; and yet what is a Negro college but a vast college settlement for the study of a particular set of peculiarly baffling problems? What more effective or suitable agency could be found in which to focus the scientific efforts of the great universities of the North and East, than an institution situated in the very heart of these social problems, and made the centre of careful historical and statistical research? Without doubt the first effective step toward the solving of the Negro question will be the endowment of a Negro college which is not merely a teaching body, but a centre of sociological research, in close connection and co-operation with Harvard, Columbia, Johns Hopkins and the University of Pennsylvania.

In this direction the Negro conferences of Tuskeegee and Hampton are tending; and there is already inaugurated an actual beginning of work at Atlanta University. In 1896 this university brought into correspondence about one hundred Southern college-bred men and laid before them a plan of systematic investigation into certain problems of Negro city life, as, for instance, family conditions, dwellings, rents, ownership of homes, occupations, earnings, disease and death-rates. Each investigator took one or more small groups to study, and in this way fifty-nine groups, aggregating 5000 people in various parts of the country, were studied, and the results have been published by the United States Bureau of Labor. Such purely scientific work, done with an eye single to ascertaining true conditions, marks an era in our conception of the place of the Negro college, and it is certainly to be desired that Atlanta University may be enabled to continue this work as she proposes to do.

Finally, the necessity must again be emphasized of keeping clearly before students the object of all science, amid the turmoil and intense feeling that clouds the discussion of a burning social question. We live in a day when in spite of the brilliant accomplishments of a remarkable century, there is current much flippant criticism of scientific work; when the truth-seeker is too often pictured as devoid of human sympathy, and careless of human ideals. We are still prone in spite of all our culture to sneer at the heroism of the laboratory while we cheer the swagger of the street broil. At such a time true lovers of humanity can only hold higher the pure ideals of science, and continue to insist that if we would solve a problem we must study it, and that there is but one coward on earth, and that is the coward that dare not know.

ANNALS, *AAPSS*, **568**, March 2000

Black Feminists and Du Bois: Respectability, Protection, and Beyond

By FARAH JASMINE GRIFFIN

ABSTRACT: Throughout his life, W.E.B. Du Bois was an advocate for black women. However, in his article of 1898, "The Study of the Negro Problems," he posits a model of the intellectuals, the investigators who analyze Negro problems, as male. In other writings, the most important being "The Damnation of Women," Du Bois focuses his attention on black women as mothers, workers, and activists but not as intellectuals. This is why contemporary black feminist intellectuals continue to claim him as an important ancestor even as they critique some of his failures around gender. The author's research attempts to enhance and extend the intellectual agendas Du Bois set in motion by being attentive to both gender and race.

Farah Jasmine Griffin, associate professor of English at the University of Pennsylvania, is the author of Who Set You Flowin'? The African American Migration Narrative *(1985), editor of* Beloved Sisters and Loving Friends: The Addie Brown–Rebecca Primus Correspondence *(1999), and the co-editor of* Stranger in the Village: Two Centuries of African American Travel Writing *(1998). She has also published several essays on literature, history, music, and politics.*

MORE than any other African American thinker of his time or before, W.E.B. Du Bois devoted a great deal of his attention to the condition of black women specifically and distinct from black men. That attention is not apparent in his article "The Study of the Negro Problems." One assumes he includes black women under the rubric of Negro, though his analysis of "Negro problems" is articulated in masculinist language: "these problems that we are . . . facing . . . will survive to curse the nation, unless we grapple with them manfully and intelligently" (Du Bois 1898, 6). The intellectuals, the investigators, the people who analyze Negro problems are male. This, of course, simply means that Du Bois is speaking the language of his time. Gender as a category of analysis did not exist until the latter part of the last century.[1]

In this article, I outline the way some contemporary black feminist intellectuals write about Du Bois and then offer a brief discursive analysis of his most important writings on black women. In the last section of the article, I use my own research as a means of demonstrating one way black feminist scholarship might enhance and extend the intellectual agendas Du Bois set in motion.

BLACK FEMINIST PERSPECTIVES ON DU BOIS

For the most part, black feminist intellectuals acknowledge Du Bois's sexism in his personal life (specifically his treatment of his daughter), but many of them also applaud his efforts on behalf of black women and claim him as an intellectual ancestor. Beverly Guy-Sheftall has named him as one of the founding parents of the discipline of black women's studies.

Guy-Sheftall takes the title of her study, *Daughters of Sorrow*, from Du Bois's essay "The Damnation of Women." To situate him in the context of his time, Guy-Sheftall cites Du Bois's fight with Monroe Trotter over admitting women into the Niagara Movement and notes that Du Bois later helped to organize the women's auxiliary. Guy-Sheftall does recognize Du Bois's "idealized image of black women, much in the same way that southern white men paid homage to the shrine of womanhood." This idealized image "reveals the extent to which black men subscribed to the notion that since women are the weaker sex they must be protected by their men from the evils of the world" (Guy-Sheftall 1990, 161).

More recently, Claudia Tate, in *Psychoanalysis and Black Novels*, also notes that Du Bois was an exception among black intellectuals. As with Guy-Sheftall, Tate notes Du Bois's "chivalric idealization of female sexuality" (Tate, 1998, 49).

In *Transcending the Talented Tenth: Black Leaders and American Intellectuals*, Joy James provides a framework for understanding Du Bois's "profeminism" as well as his "masculinism." Hers is one of the most complex analyses of Du Bois's gender politics: "Since masculinism does not explicitly advocate male superiority or rigid gender roles, it is not identical to patriarchal ideology. Masculinism can share patriarchy's presupposition of the male as norma- tive without anti-female politics and rhetoric." James explains that, "without misogynist dogma," Du Bois naturalized black male intellec- tual dominance (James 1997, 35). At the same time that Du Bois advo- cated women's rights, he "veiled the individual achievements of women such as [Anna Julia] Cooper and [Ida Wells] Barnett from the political landscape" (37). Furthermore, Du Bois had troublesome relationships with independent black women activists.

The most critical voice among con- temporary black feminists to wrestle with Du Bois, black British critic Ha- zel Carby, extends James's critique. In *Race Men*, Carby initiates an ex- tended critical discussion of the work of black male artists and intellectu- als, and she posits the ways that the black intellectual tradition has been constructed as masculine. In a chap- ter that is as much a critique of Cor- nel West as it is of Du Bois, Carby ar- gues that Du Bois's

complete failure to imagine black women as intellectuals and race leaders . . . [his] failure to incorporate black women into the sphere of intellectual equality . . . is not merely the result of the sexism of Du Bois's historical moment . . . it is a concep- tual and political failure of imagination that remains a characteristic of the work of contemporary African American male intellectuals. (Carby 1998, 10)

In contrast to Guy-Sheftall and Tate, for Carby "there is, unfortunately, no simple correspondence between anyone's support for female equality and the ideological effect of the gen- dered structures of thought and feel-

ing at work in any text one might write and publish" (Carby 1998, 12). Carby's focus on ideology and on Ray- mond Williams's concept of "struc- tures of feeling" move her critique be- yond the "intent" of an individual author. Structures of feeling are de- scribed by Tony Bennett as "a shared set of ways of thinking and feeling which, displaying a patterned regu- larity, form and are formed by the 'whole way of life' which comprises the 'lived culture' of a particular ep- och, class or group" (quoted in Turner 1990, 57). Interestingly, in turning to Williams, Carby utilizes paradigms of a male intellectual who was cer- tainly far less attentive to black women as thinkers or subjects of his- tory than was Du Bois.

Carby goes on to assert that her critique of Du Bois is necessary in order to "struggle to be critically aware of the ways in which ideologies of gender have undermined . . . the past and continue to do so in the pres- ent" (Carby 1998, 33).[2]

DU BOIS ON THE DISTINCT PROBLEMS FACING BLACK WOMEN

I imagine Du Bois might have been taken aback at the vehemence of Carby's critique of his sexism, for he most certainly would have believed himself to be a champion of black women and progressive on issues of importance to their advancement. Certainly, Du Bois was sexist, just as he was elitist and "color-struck." Were he not, he would have been even more unique among his contemporaries. For instance, although critics such as Carby have argued that early black authors chose to privilege biracial characters in their fiction because such characters served as mediators and as persons embodying the absurdity of race purity, I have never lost sight of the fact that most of the authors of these texts believed fairer-skinned black people to possess more beauty, intelligence, and worth than those of a darker hue. This is in no way to diminish their commitment to racial uplift and justice, but instead to demonstrate their contradictions and their own internalization of the very ideologies against which they fought.[3] Under these circumstances, we might consider how Du Bois advanced our understanding of the oppression of black women even as we are critically aware of his limitations.

W.E.B. Du Bois's arguments on behalf of black women are most apparent in four works: the poem "The Burden of Black Womanhood" (1907) and the essays "The Black Mother" (1912), "Hail Columbia" (1913), and "The Damnation of Women" (1920). Of these, I focus briefly on "The Damnation of Women." Du Bois opens the essay with a description of four women of his boyhood: his widowed mother; his beautiful cousin Inez; Emma, the victim of a sexual double standard; and Ide Fuller, the outcast. These four women represent the limitations American society places on women when denying them social, political, and economic freedom. Of them Du Bois writes, "They existed not for themselves, but for men; they were named after the men to whom they were related and not after the fashion of their own souls."

Du Bois launches a critique of inhibitions to the development of women's intellect and leadership:

Only at the sacrifice of intelligence and the chance to do their best work can the majority of modern women bear children. This is the damnation of women. . . . All womanhood is hampered today because the world on which it is emerging is a world that tries to worship both virgins and mothers and in the end despises motherhood and despoils virgins. (Du Bois 1995, 300)

He does not critique the false divisions between the Madonnas and virgins (and I would add whores) but instead focuses on the contradictory impulses of despising one icon while despoiling the other, and consequently leaving no space for real, human women.

In the final analysis, Du Bois argues, "The future woman must have a life work and economic independence. She must have knowledge. She must have the right of motherhood at her own discretion" (1995, 300). This paragraph holds within it the seeds of what emerges decades later as a feminist politics: women must have access to educational and economic opportunity free of their relationships to husbands, fathers, and brothers.

Interestingly, where others have found the seeds of an emasculating black matriarchy, Du Bois applauds the emergence of economically independent black women. Furthermore, he asserts the necessity of women's control over their reproduction. Finally, there is an emerging critique of the "promise of protection," which I will discuss in detail later. He writes,

"Not by guarding the weak in weakness do we gain strength, but by making weakness free and strong" (1995, 300). This is as progressive a stance on black women to emerge from the pen of a black man since Frederick Douglass. It echoes the demands of feminists such as Anna Julia Cooper and Margaret Sanger. In fact, it is doubtful that even black women thinkers were as explicit in their demands. For the most part, it is only in the context of veiled allusions in their fiction that black women writers and thinkers of the time approach any discussion of sexuality and birth control.

Du Bois situates the contemporary condition of black women in the historical context of slavery, where they had no protection from the abuses and exploitation of their masters. However, he not only focuses on the victimization of black women during slavery, but he also notes their agency as well by citing women such as Harriet Tubman and Sojourner Truth. Although the turn to black women's agency is an early contribution to black feminist revisions of African American history, Du Bois's delineation of black female types is somewhat disturbing because of its implied class and color politics. While hailing the courage and contributions of Tubman and Truth, he writes of them:

Such strong, primitive types of Negro womanhood in America seem to exhaust its capabilities. They know less of a not more worth, but a finer type of black woman wherein trembles all of that delicate sense of beauty and striving for self realization which is as characteristic of the Negro soul as its quaint strength and sweet laughter. (Du Bois 1995, 307)

In other words, America thinks that these "primitive" types are the best the race has to offer, but they know nothing of those delicate ladies of beauty and refinement. The perfect examples of this type of womanhood of beauty and intelligence he gives in the following: "Mary Shadd . . . was tall and slim . . . of that ravishing dream born beauty, that twilight of the races which we call mulatto. Well educated, vivacious, with determination shining from her sharp eyes, she threw herself single-handed into the great Canadian pilgrimage" (Du Bois 1995, 307). For a full three sentences prior to stating her contribution to the black freedom struggle, he writes of Shadd's appearance, her beauty, her color. He describes Louise De Mortie as "a free born Virginia girl . . . her high forehead, swelling lips and dark eyes marked her for a woman of feeling and intellect" (307-8). Her looks are what mark her intellect. In contrast, he describes Sojourner Truth as "a tall, gaunt black unsmiling sibyl, weighted with the woe of the world" (306).

Now, oddly enough, Du Bois moves from this focus on the physical attributes of the representative women of the race to launch into a critique of the white world for caring only about the way a woman looks:

When in this world a man comes forward with a thought, a deed, a vision we ask not, how does he look, but what is his message? . . . This which is axiomatic among men, has been in past ages but partially true if the messenger was a woman. The world still wants to ask that a woman primarily be pretty and if she is not, the mob . . . asks querulously what are women for. (Du Bois 1995, 310)

In contrast, Du Bois claims black people have respect for women's attributes beyond their physical appearance:

Their sturdier minds have concluded that if a woman be clean, healthy and educated, she is as pleasing as God wills and far more useful than most of her sisters. If in addition to this she is pink and white and straight haired and some of her fellow men prefer this, well and good; but if she is black or brown and crowned in curled mist (and this to us is the most beautiful thing on earth), this is surely the flimsiest excuse for spiritual incarceration or banishment. (Du Bois 1995, 310)

Du Bois acknowledges that some black men judge black women by a white standard of beauty, but he is quick to claim he is not one of them. Nonetheless, he asserts that even those women not considered pleasing to the eye are not condemned. He writes, "for black women . . . 'Handsome is as handsome does' and they are asked to be no more beautiful than God made them, but they are asked to be efficient, to be strong, fertile, muscled, and able to work" (Du Bois 1995, 310).

Significantly, he closes the essay with a chivalric tribute to and assertion of the beauty and femininity of black women:

Their beauty,—their dark and mysterious beauty of midnight eyes, crumpled hair, and soft, full-feature faces—is perhaps more to me than it is to you, because

I was born to its warm and subtle spell; but their worth is yours as well as mine. No other woman on earth could have emerged from the hell of force and temptation which once engulfed and still surrounds black women in America with half the modesty and womanliness that they retain. I have known the women of many lands and nations, I have known and seen and lived beside them, but none have I known more sweetly feminine, more unswervingly loyal, more desperately earnest, and more instinctively pure in body and in soul than the daughters of my black mothers. (Du Bois 1995, 311-12)

The irony of this passage, and for the essay as a whole, is that, while he argues for women's freedom, he occupies many of the stances of which he is critical. He is caught in a bind that many feminists, black and white, later find themselves in. Do we argue for the rights of women based on their equality with or their difference from men? How do we argue for their equality while at the same time acknowledging their need for protection? This is an especially dangerous trap for black women who certainly have needed more protection than their white counterparts. Also, given white supremacists' assaults on black beauty, even black feminists have had to come to terms with the contradictory impulses of needing to counter these assaults by focusing on physical attributes at the expense of dismissing all hierarchies of beauty as oppressive. Of course, this focus on black beauty is one means of healing the psychic wounds of white supremacy. Another more significant attempt has resulted in a politics of respectability.

THE POLITICS OF RESPECTABILITY

For African American leaders and intellectuals, the politics of respectability first emerged as a way to counter the images of black Americans as lazy, shiftless, stupid, and immoral in popular culture and the racist pseudosciences of the nineteenth century. Paradoxically, as black leaders attempted to counter racist discourses and their consequences, the politics of respectability also reflected an acceptance and internalization of these representations. The politics of respectability seeks to reform the behavior of individuals and as such takes the emphasis away from structural forms of oppression such as racism, sexism, and poverty.

Evelyn Brooks Higginbotham notes the scathing critiques against nonconformity that accompany the politics of respectability. She writes:

The politics of respectability equated non-conformity with the cause of racial inequality and injustice. The conservative and moralistic dimension tended to privatize racial discrimination thus rendering it outside the authority of government regulation. (Higginbotham 1993, 203)

The politics of respectability emerged in a sincere attempt to address the conditions of black people both internally and externally. It marked an attempt to instill dignity and self-respect while also challenging negative, stereotypical images of African Americans. However, it fails to recognize the power of racism to enforce itself upon even the most respectable and well-behaved black people. Such a politics leaves little room for those who choose not to conform.

If this was a guiding principle in the political work of black leaders, it also informed the paradigms of the early days of Afro-American studies as well. Afro-American studies was born outside of the academy in the late nineteenth century with the goal of counteracting negative images and claims of genetic inferiority. Today, after a century of practicing a politics of respectability, a century of being concerned with presenting "positive images" of black life, we have so policed our own intellectual efforts that often we find ourselves caught up with narrow representations that in no way allow for the full complexity and humanity of black people, particularly black women. Black popular culture has always been a site that resists the confines of the politics of respectability.

One manifestation of the politics of respectability is something I call the "promise of protection." Discussions of protection are not original to me. Both Nancy Cott (1987) and Deborah Gray White (1999) offer analyses of the protection dilemma. Elsewhere, I have written at length about the politics of protection (Griffin forthcoming). Here, I provide a more succinct working definition.

THE PROMISE OF PROTECTION

Because black women were denied the privileges of femininity and protection from physical and discursive violence, black intellectuals and activists developed a discourse of protection. My term "promise of protection" is influenced by Jacqueline Dowd Hall's term, "rhetoric of protection." Hall uses the phrase to describe the discourses of a pure and protected white womanhood in the American South: "the rhetoric of protection [was] reflective of a power struggle between men . . . the right of the southern lady to protection presupposed her obligation to obey" (Hall 1983, 335). I have chosen not to use the word "rhetoric" because I want to avoid the implications of the word that suggest a discourse lacking in conviction or earnest feeling. Black male desire to "protect" black women grows out of a sincere concern for their emotional, psychic, and physical safety; it is also reflective of the power struggle between black and white men and black men and black women.

Nonetheless, many black women understandably have been willing to accept the terms of this contract. The promise of patriarchal protection was certainly much better than the methodical abuse suffered by black women throughout much of their history in the New World. The promise of protection has a long history in black thought and politics. The National Association of Colored Women was formed in 1896 in part to protect the name and image of black women. Leaders like Du Bois and Alexander Crummell simultaneously called for the protection of black women from rape, physical abuse, and economic poverty.

Malcolm X, the Nation of Islam, and Louis Farrakhan are contemporary proponents of a promise of protection. A promise of protection addresses two important concerns of black nationalism: it restores a sense of masculinity to black men while granting black women at least one of the privileges of femininity.

This is not without its cost. The promise of protection assumes a stance of victimization on the part of those who need to be protected, without allowing much room for their agency in other spheres. It places the woman in the hands of her protector—who may protect her, but who also may decide to further victimize her. In either case, her well-being is entirely dependent on his will and authority.

Protection is not in and of itself a bad thing. Patriarchal societies such as ours foster misogyny from which all women need protection. A racist patriarchal society is particularly dangerous for black women. Of course, until the day arrives when we no longer live in a patriarchal society, women need to be protected from misogyny; however, protection need not be equated with possession. We must be careful to recognize offers of protection that are made in a context that places limitations on women's freedom. Our intellectual and social movements ought to be guided by a vision that not only seeks to protect women from misogyny but also helps to eradicate patriarchy as well as racism. As we have seen, Du Bois himself recognized this: "Not by guarding the weak in weakness do we gain strength, but by making weakness free and strong" (Du Bois 1995, 300). The promise of protection is one dimension or outcome of the practice of a politics of uplift and respectability.

BEYOND THE POLITICS OF RESPECTABILITY AND THE PROMISE OF PROTECTION

Despite Du Bois's contradictions, we ought to be grateful to him for keeping black women at the forefront of his vision, and we ought to learn from his limitations and mistakes and move on. Contemporary black male intellectuals and activists ought to be criticized for not moving beyond these limitations in matters of gender, sexuality, and class. Unlike Du Bois, they have access to the history and analytical frames and paradigms made available by the work of politically engaged black feminist intellectuals such as Patricia Hill Collins, Joy James, Wahneemah Lubiano, and Kimberly Crenshaw, to name a few. In "The Damnation of Women," Du Bois names all of the intellectuals he cites except Anna Julia Cooper. Today, many black male intellectuals name black women, but all too often they do not seriously engage their intellectual work. There are exceptions to this. A bevy of younger scholars such as Robin D. G. Kelly, Lewis Gordon, Kevin Gaines, and Brent Edwards have work that proves to be promising in this regard.

At this point, I think a more productive black feminist research agenda might be one that makes sure contemporary debates are informed by black women's insights, reconceptualizing African American intellectual, social, political, and cultural history in a way that accounts for black women's experiences. What does Reconstruction look like when we add black women? How do analyses of racism change if we include gender along with race as an analytical category? Such questions make us reexamine dominant understandings of Reconstruction and force an analysis of the construction of black masculinity. Black feminist intellectuals must continue the work of recovering, analyzing, and theorizing those aspects of black life that have been subsumed because of past adherence to sexist, elitist, and heterosexist norms.

Du Bois identifies four divisions for the study of Negro problems: (1) historical study, (2) statistical investigation, (3) anthropological measurement, and (4) sociological interpretation. I would add to them cultural analysis as well. In earlier work, I have used cultural analysis as a means of researching that which Du Bois includes under anthropological measurement:

a scientific study of the Negro body. The most obvious peculiarity of the Negro—a peculiarity which is a large element in many of the problems affecting him—is his physical unlikeness to the people with whom he has been brought into contact. This difference is so striking that it has become the basis of a mass of theory, assumption and suggestion which is deep-rooted. (Du Bois 1898, 19)

Of historical study he writes, "The material at hand for historical research is rich and abundant, there are ... the collections of historical societies . . . the personal narratives" (Du Bois 1898, 18). These hold information about "the history of the oft-forgotten class of free Negroes" among other aspects of black life. One of the objects of historical study is to show the dynamic nature of black life and the changing nature of the problems confronting black people. Furthermore, historical study reveals the diversity of the population of people who fall under the racial category "Negro."

In articles on the response of black women artists and intellectuals to racist categorizations of black bodies, I have attempted to address the issues he raises here. However, for now I want to focus on two projects that fall under the rubric of historical study and my added category of cultural analysis. Two areas of research identified by Du Bois in "The Study of the Negro Problems" resonate with my own intellectual agenda, especially two forthcoming projects: a collection of letters between two nineteenth-century black women and a cultural analysis of the construction of various Billie Holiday icons and the cultural work they perform.

In the more historical of these projects, *Beloved Sisters and Loving Friends* (Griffin 1999), I have attempted to fill in gaps left by Du Bois in his seminal work, *Black Reconstruction* ([1935] 1969). While he praises the Yankee schoolteachers, particularly white women, who went south to teach the freedmen following the Civil War, he cites no black women. Once again, he ignores the work of black women as intellectuals. Rebecca Primus, one of the

"oft-forgotten class of free-blacks" was one such dedicated teacher. Her letters found their way to the Connecticut Historical Society in 1932, three years before the publication of *Black Reconstruction*.

This project also focuses on a member of the black working poor not as a problem but as a vibrant, intelligent woman—Addie Brown. Brown was a member of the black poor and working class that Du Bois did not imagine: she is not only burdened by the problems of poverty and exploitation; she is also a vibrant, intellectual, funny, sensual woman. Furthermore, the letters reveal as much about the private lives of these two women as they do about their public lives. The correspondence makes clear the two shared a romantic/erotic relationship as well. Despite these differences, the letters project does share Du Bois's concern that historical research demonstrate the complexity and heterogeneity of antebellum and postbellum black life.

Given his early disdain of the black subcultures that produced jazz, Du Bois probably would not have encouraged a study that centers on Billie Holiday—a foul-mouthed, promiscuous drug-addicted musical genius. The Billie Holiday project is a means of challenging and confronting silences demanded by the politics of respectability and uplift without ignoring the need for such a politics at the time of their emergence. Billie Holiday has often been cast as a victim in need of protection. Black male intellectuals want to protect her from white men. Feminist intellectuals want to protect her from men, particularly black men. Of course, anyone familiar with Holiday's life would not disagree with her need for protection. However, there were instances when she neither desired nor needed protection.

The Holiday project also provides me the opportunity to explore the class origins and context out of which she emerged and to demonstrate, contrary to Du Bois's suggestion, that these conditions can also create and nurture black genius. Such an analysis turns a critical eye on those powers that deny the expression of such genius on a broader stage, while recognizing that the black elite have no monopoly on talent or brilliance. Finally, the Holiday book, as with the letters, adds a much needed analysis of gender to Du Bois's research agenda.

Because I make no pretense of an objective analysis in this project, I make my agenda explicit. In addition to demonstrating the way that various representations of Holiday serve the interests of those who create them, I try to posit an alternative representation as well. In an attempt to offer an alternative subjectivity for contemporary and future black women to occupy, perform, and live, I try to reconstruct an understanding of Holiday as a woman who at times needed protection but who also happened to be a highly gifted jazz artist, who preferred the fast life, who indulged in her appetite for pleasure, and who practiced and refined her artistry not simply as entertainment but as a form of creative expression and self-realization. As such, I do

hope that the scholarship entailed in the project will serve to inform contemporary conceptions of black women's lives and potential.

In closing, as a black feminist scholar I am most indebted to Du Bois not so much for his identification of areas in need of analysis but for his model as an activist intellectual. To be a black feminist scholar in the truest sense, one must be both an intellectual and an activist: simultaneously broad in scope and deep in analysis and committed in theory and praxis to black freedom. I am also indebted to Du Bois for the very notion of demanding that the problems confronting black people, as well as their cultural contributions, are worthy of serious scholarly inquiry and that inquiry might in some way be related to relieving their problems. I do not share his article's optimism about knowledge as the means toward the end of racism and his identification of the university as the "only competent agency" to study the complexities of black life. I believe the university might be one such site, though it is profoundly limited. Because of this, we are in desperate need of the creation of others. Perhaps this kind of institution-building outside of the academy might be one of the projects of future generations of black intellectuals.

Finally, black people are confronted with enormous poverty—a maldistribution of cultural and economic capital—and continued state violence; they are also confronted with ideological structures that define them for the world and all too often for themselves. Consequently, in addition to research that leads directly to policy initiatives, we are also in need of cultural analysis that reveals the contours of these ideologies and that encourages critical rather than conspiratorial thinking. Our own historical context demands an analytic category not only of race but also of class (which Du Bois would later discover); not only gender but sexuality as well. Most important, our context demands an understanding of the ways that all of these categories intersect, each defining our experience of the other.

Notes

1. Joy James (1997) and Hazel Carby (1998) disagree with me here. James argues that black women intellectuals and activists who were Du Bois's contemporaries—Anna Julia Cooper and Ida B. Wells—did provide gender-based critiques. I thoroughly agree with this, but would suggest that, although they did critique sexism and the relationship to masculinity and power, gender as the kind of analytical category that we have come to know did not exist. Similarly, although Du Bois is clearly aware of class conflict and differences, he does not use class as an analytical category until he published *Black Reconstruction* (Du Bois [1935] 1969).

2. In addition to those discussed here, black feminists such as Tera Hunter have also offered critiques of Du Bois (see Hunter 1998).

3. For an excellent discussion of these contradictions between Du Bois's contemporaries, see Davis 1994.

References

Carby, Hazel. 1998. *Race Men*. Cambridge, MA: Harvard University Press.

Cott, Nancy. 1987. *The Grounding of Modern Feminism*. New Haven, CT: Yale University Press.

Davis, Thadious. 1994. *Nella Larsen, Novelist of the Harlem Renaissance: A Woman's Life Unveiled*. Baton Rouge: Louisiana State University Press.

Du Bois, W.E.B. 1898. The Study of the Negro Problems. *The Annals* of the American Academy of Political and Social Science Jan.:1-23.

———. [1935] 1969. *Black Reconstruction in America; An Essay Toward a History of the Part Which Black Folk Played in an Attempt to Reconstruct Democracy in America 1860-1880*. New York: Atheneum.

———. 1995. "The Damnation of Women." In *W.E.B. Du Bois: A Reader*, ed. David Levering Lewis. New York: Henry Holt.

Griffin, Farah Jasmine. Forthcoming. Ironies of the Saint: Malcolm X and the Politics of Protection. In *Black Women in the Civil Rights and Black Power Movements*, ed. Bettye Collier Thomas and V. P. Franklin. Philadelphia: Temple University Press.

———, ed. 1999. *Beloved Sisters and Loving Friends: Letters from Rebecca Primus of Royal Oak, Maryland, and Addie Brown of Hartford, Connecticut, 1854-1868*. New York: Knopf.

Guy-Sheftall, Beverly. 1990. *Daughters of Sorrow: Attitudes Toward Black Women, 1880-1920*. New York: Carlson.

Hall, Jacqueline Dowd. 1983. The Mind That Burns in Each Body: Women, Rape, and Racial Violence. In *Powers of Desire: The Politics of Sexuality*, ed. Ann Snitow, Christine Stansell, and Sharon Thompson. New York: Monthly Review Press.

Higginbotham, Evelyn Brooks. 1993. *Righteous Discontent: The Women's Movement in the Black Baptist*

Church, 1880-1920. Cambridge, MA: Harvard University Press.

Hunter, Tera. 1998. The "Brotherly Love" for Which This City Is Proverbial Should Extend to All: Working Class Women in Philadelphia and Atlanta in the 1890's. In *W.E.B. Du Bois, Race and the City: The Philadelphia Negro and Its Legacy*, ed. M. B. Katz and T. J. Sugrue. Philadelphia: University of Pennsylvania Press.

James, Joy. 1997. *Transcending the Talented Tenth: Black Leaders and American Intellectuals*. New York: Routledge.

Lewis, David Levering. 1993. *W.E.B. Du Bois: Biography of a Race, 1868-1919*. New York: Henry Holt.

Tate, Claudia. 1998. *Psychoanalysis and Black Novels: Desire and Protocols of Race*. New York: Oxford University Press.

Turner, Graeme. 1990. *British Cultural Studies: An Introduction*. New York: Routledge.

White, Deborah Gray. 1999. *Too Heavy a Load: Black Women in Defense of Themselves, 1894-1994*. New York: W. W. Norton.

ANNALS, *AAPSS*, **568**, March 2000

Gender, Black Feminism, and Black Political Economy

By PATRICIA HILL COLLINS

ABSTRACT: This article uses two dimensions of Black feminist standpoint epistemology to investigate Black political economy. It suggests that centering on Black women's experiences and analyzing those experiences via intersectional paradigms fosters rethinking the significance of family within gender, sexuality, race, class, and nation. The article concludes by identifying how these new views of family might inform gendered analyses of Black political economy.

Patricia Hill Collins is Charles Phelps Taft Professor of Sociology and chair of the Department of African-American Studies at the University of Cincinnati. She is the author of the award-winning Black Feminist Thought: Knowledge, Consciousness, and the Politics of Empowerment *(1990);* Race, Class, and Gender: An Anthology, *now in its third edition (1988); and* Fighting Words: Black Women and the Search for Justice *(1998).*

L IKE others of his era, William E. B. Du Bois believed that the tools of social science could be used to address racial segregation, poverty, urbanization, industrialization, and other important social issues affecting U.S. society. In this context, one important contribution of Du Bois's sociological work concerns his implicit use of intersectional paradigms of race, class, and nation in explaining Black political economy. Du Bois saw race, class, and nation not primarily as personal identity categories but as social hierarchies that shaped African American access to status, property, and power. Understanding and addressing the social problems plaguing U.S. Blacks required analyses that examined the basic ideologies and practices of American racism, that evaluated how capitalism used these ideologies and practices, and that investigated how U.S. nation-state policies reinforced social inequalities. Moreover, rather than viewing these systems of power as either parallel—race, class, and nation as free-standing, distinct systems that resemble one another on some dimensions and differ from one another on others—or as derivative of one another—the case when racism becomes treated as a subset of capitalism or vice versa—Du Bois placed Black political economy within a context of mutually constructing systems of race, class, and nation. Thus, Du Bois advanced arguments concerning Black political economy that saw U.S. social structures and African American cultural patterns not only as interconnected but as shaped by intersecting systems of race, class, and nation.

Despite this important contribution, one might ask, What about gender? On the one hand, it can be argued that Du Bois's work contains an incipient gender analysis (Gilkes 1996). Du Bois actually talked of African American women during a time when Black women were treated as objects of knowledge (Collins 1998a, 95-123). Some of his work does center on African American women and indicates his awareness of the distinctive experiences that characterized Black women's lives. For Du Bois, Black women carried a special burden—not only were they Black, poor, and second-class citizens, but they were female as well. Du Bois identified Black women's suffering as a "social fact that provided an important and distinct angle of vision," and for Du Bois, three great revolutions were at work: those involving "women, labor, and black folk. In various writings, he observed that black women embodied all three of these revolutions in their historical roles in the family, the community, and the labor force" (Gilkes 1996, 112).

Du Bois may have acknowledged African American women's centrality within these three revolutions, but this does not mean that he afforded gender the same analytical importance as race and class in explaining them. For Du Bois, race and class constituted important systems of power that explained Black political economy, yet gender far too often remained a personal identity category that described Black women's special circumstances in dealing with the more fundamental (and thereby more important) oppressions of race, class, and nation. As a result, Du Bois could be simultaneously progressive yet paternalistic—his intersectional analyses of race, class, and nation coupled with his recognition of Black women's special situation distanced him from avowedly sexist approaches yet did little to challenge masculine authority. His stance on gender was better than most but not as good as it could have been. This raises the question of whether interpretations of gender were available to Du Bois that afforded gender theoretical significance comparable to that afforded to race, class, and nation. Joy James (1996) argues that not only did such perspectives exist but that Du Bois ignored them. Thus, one can argue that Du Bois did have access to what we now call Black feminist analyses that view Black women's experiences as honed at the intersection of race, class, nation, and gender but that he rejected them.

James suggests, for example, that Du Bois was familiar with the ideas of both Anna Julia Cooper and Ida B. Wells-Barnett, two prominent turn-of-the-century Black feminist thinkers. Both women used gendered analyses to explain important social issues. For example, Cooper's *A Voice from the South* contends that only when Black women got their rights would African Americans as a collectivity be empowered (Cooper 1892). Similarly, Ida B. Wells-Barnett's analysis of lynching and institutionalized rape points to the significance of gender in explaining patterns of sexual violence confronting U.S. Black men and women (Wells-

Barnett 1995). Neither Cooper nor Wells-Barnett elevated gender above other factors, but both clearly identified its importance both for Black women and as a fundamental principle of African American social organization.

Why Du Bois failed to make use of these paradigms is a matter of speculation, but that he did not grant gender the same theoretical weight as that placed on race, class, and nation seems fairly straightforward. This has been a loss, because Du Bois did not incorporate into the corpus of his work two distinctive and important elements of U.S. Black feminism drawn upon by Gilkes and James, respectively, in their analyses of Du Bois. When read together, Gilkes and James identify two dimensions of Black feminist standpoint epistemology that might inform a gendered analysis of Black political economy.[1]

From Gilkes, we learn the potential utility of centering on Black women's experiences. Stressing the interconnectedness of group experiences and collective knowledge, this methodological approach stresses the significance of Black women's experiences for generating new questions, issues, and interpretations. Centering work on the experiences of U.S. Black women can provide new angles of vision not just on the African American experience but on the basic concepts used to describe that experience. For example, research on U.S. Black women community leaders argues that such women hold and use different views of what constitutes the "political" from those used by Black men in similar situations.

This approach not only reveals new knowledge just about Black women's lives but enriches our theoretical understanding of the meaning of the political (Collins 2000). Within this logic, had Du Bois centered his theories of work on Black women's labor as well as that of Black men, more complex analyses of the effects of industrial capitalism on African Americans might have emerged. This centering approach is not designed to be static—one does not simply replace one normative group with another. Instead, by pivoting the center and theorizing from multiple angles of vision—in this case, those provided by both African American men and women—new themes, approaches, and questions become visible.

From James, we encounter another dimension of Black feminist standpoint epistemology: the significance of using paradigms of intersectionality in interpreting social phenomena (Anthias and Yuval-Davis 1992; Collins 1998a, 201-28; Collins 2000). Centering on Black women's experiences produces not only new knowledge but new ways of thinking about such knowledge. Thus, intersectionality constitutes an interpretive framework that can be seen as one outcome of such centering. Cooper and Wells-Barnett foreshadow one important element in contemporary U.S. Black feminism: the significance of intersectional paradigms in explaining not just Black women's experiences but the overall organization of social structure and culture itself. Unlike Du Bois, they were more likely to see the complexities of

intersections of race, class, nation, and gender. Again, their analyses may differ from contemporary sensibilities, yet their approach remains highly important. The works of these and other turn-of-the-century Black women intellectuals do not just illustrate a recounting of the experiences that accompany the special circumstances of living life as a Black woman but also suggest how this placement in U.S. society can foster a distinctive analysis. Stated differently, these club women provided an intersectional analysis that accompanied the distinctive angle of vision available to them. Centering on the experiences of African American women as well as listening to what they said about what they saw—the hallmarks of U.S. Black feminism then and now—could foster paradigmatic shifts that would come more slowly to those not so situated.

Invoking these two dimensions of Black feminist standpoint epistemology—placing Black women's experiences at the center of analysis as well as interpretive frameworks that rely on intersectional paradigms—promises to shed light on one important question: how might a gendered analysis shift our understanding of Black political economy? This is different from adding the "special burden" born by African American women into preexisting paradigms of race, class, and/or nation. Rather, this question asks what new insights concerning Black political economy emerge both when Black women's experiences become central to analysis and when intersectionality is used as a theoretical frame.

THE WORK/FAMILY NEXUS
AND BLACK WOMEN'S POVERTY

Placing U.S. Black women's experiences at the center of analysis reveals the significance of work and family in analyses of Black political economy. Because African American women have long worked outside the home, their paid labor in the labor market as well as their unpaid labor in their family households do not fit within prevailing understandings of work and family as separate spheres of social organization (Collins 1998a, 11-32). Black women's experiences do not simply challenge views of work as a public, male domain, and family as a private, female haven; they also suggest how the framework of a work/family nexus provides new directions for understanding Black women's poverty.

Because gender hierarchies affect African American women's work and family experiences in ways that differ from those of Black men, centering on Black women's experiences highlights two important contributions of a work/family nexus framework. One concerns how gender hierarchies affect Black women's income in ways that go beyond simple gender-based wage discrimination. This income-based approach not only addresses the types of jobs U.S. Black women get but also examines their unpaid family labor, how child care strains the income that they do garner, and patterns of consumer racism that affect the purchasing power of their income.

In some ways, U.S. Black women are poor for many of the same reasons that U.S. Black men are poor—both lack access to steady, well-paying jobs that ensure an adequate income. Yet African American women's confinement to a small segment of low-paying jobs reveals how race and gender converge. Black women's disadvantaged labor market status in turn has important implications for patterns of Black family organization and income, and subsequently higher rates of Black poverty (Collins 2000).

Income-based approaches also highlight the importance of Black women's unpaid labor for their higher poverty rates.[2] Cooking, cleaning, home repair, and other domestic labor that African American women do for free could also be done for pay. Moreover, despite the fact that caring for children is often seen as something that women "naturally" do better than men, child care also constitutes unpaid labor. A considerable portion of Black women's time goes into caring for children—their own and those of others. Moreover, patterns of consumer racism that fall more heavily on Black women affect the purchasing power of their income. Because African American women usually are responsible for families, they do much of the shopping for housing, food, clothing, health care, transportation, recreation, and other consumer goods. Consumer racism in all of these areas means that Black women's depressed incomes simply do not have the same purchasing power as those of White men or women.

The situation of African American single mothers highlights the convergence of these components of how gender affects income. Such women are likely to be disadvantaged in the labor market, and without partners, they lack access to both men's unpaid household labor as well as adequate child support from their children's fathers. The combination of these factors often means that Black women's time goes into unpaid labor, thus hindering their ability to work for pay. Racial segregation means that their consumer dollars do not stretch as far.

Centering on Black women's experiences also highlights a second way that the work/family nexus framework provides new directions for understanding Black women's poverty. In general, Black women lack assets, property, or wealth. Income-based approaches emphasize a well-paying job as an important source of Black women's income. In contrast, wealth-based approaches stress access to income-generating property—that is, property that enables women to generate their own income as well as financial and nonfinancial support from family members (Austin 1997).

This emphasis on property highlights the significance of marriage as an important social institution that regulates the disposition of wealth. When it comes to marriage, love matters, but property matters even more. Black diasporic feminisms in particular identify the lack of access to income-generating property by women of African descent as crucial and point to important connections between wealth, marriage, and family.[3] In such feminisms, the links between property and marriage rival those between love and marriage.

Applying this focus on income-producing property to U.S. Black women generates new angles of vision on gendered structures of wealth in the United States as well as the marital relations required to regulate them. In particular, they suggest that African American women's status as single mothers, especially never-married single mothers, operates as an important conduit for a racialized social class system.

Centering on U.S. Black women points out how two sets of laws—those concerning interracial marriage and inheritance of property—foster a distinctive work/family nexus that in turn influences the overall patterns of Black political economy. Laws against interracial marriage were only abolished in the 1960s. One objective of these laws was to deter African American men from marrying White women. The increasing number of U.S. Black men who now date and marry White women reinforces notions that these two groups did in fact have a long-standing sexual attraction. However, another interpretation of anti-miscegenation laws examines their effect on African American women. Such laws regulated property relations and thus regulated the inter-generational accumulation of wealth. Historically, White women's property was intertwined with that of their fathers and spouses, and Black men remained poor. Thus, neither White women nor Black men could bring substantial property to marriages. For Black men, such laws regulated sexuality. In contrast, if African American women were allowed to marry White men—propertied White men who ran things or working-class White men who claimed the family wage as their birthright—African American women theoretically gained access to White male property. More important, their mixed-race but legally Black children did too. Within prevailing gender hierarchies, for Black women, such laws regulated wealth.

The second set of laws concerns the intergenerational inheritance of property. As opposed to examining how U.S. Black and White families facilitate the intergenerational transfer of cultural capital, such families can also be seen as sites where property or material capital is accumulated, invested, and transferred from one generation to the next. In a similar fashion, debt and poverty can also be inherited. Rules that rendered the biologically White children of legal marriages legitimate and thus entitled to the property of their White fathers also worked to deny Black and/or mixed-race children access to the property of their White fathers. In a context of antimiscegenation laws that rendered mixed-race children with White fathers born to nonmarried Black mothers illegitimate, claims on their fathers' property had little meaning. Instead, African American social institutions—primarily African American extended families—were forced to bear the cost of raising not just the children fathered by Black men but those fathered by White men as well.

Overall, wealth differences between races as well as gender distinctions within races that originated under slavery have meshed with an intergenerational class disadvantage organized through and passed on via Black women's placement in a distinctive work/family nexus. Until the 1970s, the combination of legal restrictions against interracial marriage and Black men's lower income meant that the majority of Black women could not marry wealth nor could their mixed-race children inherit it. Moreover, in a context where the presence or absence of state-sanctioned marriage conferred differential political rights on women and men based on their marital status, racial classification, and assets, Black women remained severely disadvantaged.

THE WORK/FAMILY NEXUS AS
A SITE OF INTERSECTIONALITY

Centering scholarship on U.S. Black women's experiences reveals how rethinking the work/family nexus might influence Black political economy. But this new focus on links between work and family also stimulates new interpretive frameworks. In this regard, Black feminist standpoint epistemology not only provides new angles of vision on the African American work/family nexus, but it also fosters the use of intersectional paradigms.

As opposed to examining gender, sexuality, race, class, and nation as separate systems of oppression, the construct of intersectionality references how these systems mutually construct one another. Intersectional paradigms suggest that certain ideas and/or practices surface repeatedly across multiple systems of oppression. Serving as focal points for intersecting systems of oppression, these ideas and practices may be central to how gender, sexuality, race, class, and nation mutually construct one another. Family broadly defined may serve as one such privileged exemplar of intersectionality (Collins 1998b). In particular, the traditional family ideal whereby men work and women stay at home constitutes one particular work/family nexus—one that reappears across many systems of oppression.

Ideas about family certainly contribute to the continued stigmatization of U.S. families headed by Black single mothers. But the significance of family goes beyond this. Ideas about family also operate as a cognitive scaffold used to construct intersecting systems of oppression. In the United States, the power of the traditional family ideal lies in its dual function as both an ideological construction and a fundamental principle of social organization. As ideology, family rhetoric provides a flexible, interpretive framework that accommodates a range of meanings. Just as reworking the rhetoric of family for their own political agendas is a common strategy for conservative movements of all types, family rhetoric is often invoked to symbolize the aspirations of oppressed groups. The conservative right and African American nationalists alike both invoke the language of family in advancing their political agendas. However, because it operates as a fundamental principle of social organization, the traditional family ideal is much more than an ideological

construction. U.S. social institutions and social policies often reflect family rhetoric. Families constitute multiple sites of belonging—to families understood as kinship groups linked by a common biology; to communities conceptualized as imagined families occupying geographically identifiable, racially segregated neighborhoods; to so-called racial families historically codified in science and law; and to the American nation-state conceptualized as an imagined national family marked by citizenship and alien status (Collins 1998b).

Ideas and practices organized through the rhetoric of family thus permeate intersecting oppressions of gender, sexuality, race, class, and nation. Each social hierarchy relies on the work/family nexus that in turn frames particular understandings of property. Specifically, gender hierarchies depend on family rhetoric and practices to shape differential male and female access to property. Historically, whether property was inherited from their fathers, given to them by their husbands, or acquired via the working-class male "property" of the family wage, women typically gained access to property via their relationships with men. Families that are organized around married heterosexual couples form a site for intergenerational control over and transfer of racialized wealth. These same social locations also constitute an important site for intergenerational male control of property. Because they lack access to current male income as well as past and present male property, families maintained by Black single mothers are especially penalized within this system.

Sexual hierarchies privilege heterosexism by requiring heterosexual marriage as the route for women's access to property. Not only is marriage designed to regulate heterosexual sexual activity—witness U.S. controversies in the 1990s regarding the efforts of gays, lesbians, and transgendered individuals to obtain legal marriage—but marital status differentially positions women to rights and entitlements associated with other categories of belonging, primarily citizenship. For example, taxation policies have long taken marital status into consideration as have social welfare policies. The unmarried, whether by choice or by necessity, remain disadvantaged in this legal context.

Racial hierarchies also rely on family rhetoric and practices to structure property relations. Marriage and family operate as important sites for reproducing both racial meanings and actual populations of "races." Regulating biological notions of race and racial purity required regulating who could marry whom. In the U.S. racial context, restricting interracial marriage not only worked to ensure that property controlled by Whites would remain within White families; it also bundled biological notions of race with ideas about property. When racially homogeneous family units serve as primary conduits for the intergenerational transmission of assets, concerns about declining property values in racially desegregated neighborhoods gain credence.

By their nature, social class hierarchies are most directly associated with property, and here, too, family matters. The traditional family ideal includes home ownership. For most American families, their house constitutes one of their more important assets. In their actions as both income-generating units as well as sites of inherited property relations, families constitute important sites for organizing and managing property. Since family operates as a site of intergenerational transfer of wealth (and the opportunities it generates), marriage and family become key in reproducing social class relations across time. In particular, asset-rich families inherit advantages across generations. Conversely, debt-ridden families inherit debt and the lack of opportunities.

Gender, sexuality, race, and class hierarchies all require a favorable political climate. While U.S. nation-state policies regarding marriage and family reflect dominant moral codes, they also regulate property relations. Assumptions about marriage and, by implication, desired family forms remain supported by governmental policy, corporate policies, and the legal system. For example, denying slaves legal marriages, forbidding interracial marriages, using marital status to determine taxation policies and social welfare state entitlements, and refusing legal marriage to sexually stigmatized individuals all reflect nation-state interest in regulating an allegedly natural institution. Just as the sedimented disadvantages of institutionalized racism are passed on intergenerationally to African Americans as a collectivity, the benefits accruing to families fitting state-sanctioned marital patterns encounter comparable cumulative advantages.

TOWARD A GENDERED ANALYSIS OF BLACK POLITICAL ECONOMY

The contributions of Black feminist standpoint epistemology suggest several implications for developing a more complex understanding of Black political economy. One concerns the importance of asset-building strategies for Black women, regardless of their marital status and/or relationship to Black men (Austin 1997). Asset-building strategies seemingly challenge current initiatives that argue that strengthening African American men's capacity as marital partners will in effect address Black women's poverty. Within this logic, one helps Black women by helping Black men first. Certainly, providing good jobs for Black men is a much needed and worthwhile endeavor, but having good jobs does not automatically encourage Black men to marry Black women. The asset-building approach takes marriage out of the equation altogether and refocuses attention on the actual financial needs of African American women.

Most current policy outcomes stress getting income to poor Black women, primarily through job training and transfer payments. Ironically, qualifying for such support often requires depleting one's assets. Whereas these policies are important, they might be supplemented by public and private asset-development programs targeted toward Black women. For example, taxation policies whose goal is to foster investment by Black women, especially those who are single mothers, could provide substantial benefits without the stigma attached to so-called Black programs. Private initiatives might also make important contributions. As illustrated by their support of Black churches, often on very little income, African American women already demonstrate the capacity to budget, save, and invest. Economic development strategies designed to encourage what Regina Austin (1997) calls a "nest egg" for African American women would go a long way toward removing the need to "catch" a propertied male for financial security.

A second implication of the preceding analysis concerns the importance of family as an analytical tool in theorizing Black political economy. Certainly, family status serves as a mechanism for reproducing social class hierarchies. But the significance of the work/family nexus suggested by Black women's experiences also lies in how it shifts the very categories of class analysis. Existing class analyses rely on the individual as the primary unit of investigation and build social class categories by sorting individuals by preselected characteristics and aggregating them into classes. In contrast, viewing African American families as the unit of analysis allows for construction of social class categories around actual historical material relations. Individuals may come and go, but the racial families that have been constructed from biological families persist across time. Using the individual as the unit of analysis elevates the importance of male income for Black political economy. But moving from individuals to families as another unit of social class analysis shifts the gender equation and makes women more central to class analysis. It also reveals the importance of collectively held, historical family assets to contemporary patterns of affluence and poverty. In this view, differential distributions of occupations and income among individuals are less causes of disparities in wealth than outcomes of property ownership.

Conceptualizing social class via institutionalized patterns of group access to wealth not only gets at the stability of social class formations over time; it adds the important gendered analysis of U.S. Black women's access to property. Within these assumptions, the traditional family ideal and Black single mothers' seeming repudiation of it may be more heavily implicated in social class organization in the United States than imagined. Within this class-stratified family hierarchy, families headed by single mothers become especially vulnerable because, as intergenerational debtors, it may be impossible for them to get ahead. In the absence of asset-generating strategies targeted to Black women, there is little of material value that can be passed on and used to broker opportunities from one generation to the next. More ominously, U.S. Blacks threaten to become an intergenerational class of debtors, especially in the absence of

any unified political program that addresses the distribution not just of income but of intergenerational wealth.

A final implication concerns how centering on African American women challenges some basic assumptions that permeate analyses of Black political economy. As feminist scholarship quite rightly points out, the very categories of public and private, work and family, structure and culture rely heavily on specific gender configurations—public, work, and structure become coded as masculine endeavors, whereas private, family, and culture become the preserve of women. But what is less often noted is how race, class, and nation become examined as public sphere processes while gender and sexuality are treated as private sphere endeavors. Analyses of Black political economy that leave these basic dichotomies unchallenged merely replicate them.

Grounding analyses of Black political economy in issues of state power, industrial and labor market practices, and other public sphere social institutions affords African American family processes secondary status. Within this logic, gender becomes confined to Black women, and Black women become studied in the context of family. Similarly, associating African American culture with the activities of Black families and Black civil society, and juxtaposing that culture to seemingly more important public sphere activities, again renders gender of secondary importance. Culture becomes reproduced in the private sphere of family or in community spaces coded as domestic—women's space. In this fashion, gender and sexuality as systems of power become coded as private matters; they only emerge into public sphere activities when worn as identity categories by Black women. Just as seemingly masculine endeavors remain routinely elevated above feminine ones, because race, class, and nation seemingly constitute public sphere endeavors, they acquire greater importance than the seemingly private sphere practices of gender and sexuality. Reminiscent of Du Bois's treatment of social inequalities, race, class, gender, nation, and sexuality as systems of power may all be mentioned within discussions of Black political economy, yet their actual conceptualization affords them unequal theoretical weight. Overall, moving toward a gendered analysis of Black political economy requires much more diligence than simply reforming preexisting paradigms by adding Black women's experiences to them. Instead, as Black feminist standpoint epistemology suggests, the very categories of analysis require a more thorough transformation, one begun by Du Bois but one that contemporary social science can take even further.

Notes

1. Black feminist epistemology involves the rules used to guide knowledge-construction and knowledge-validation processes. In *Black Feminist Thought*, I identify four distinguishing features of a knowledge-validation process that have been functional for U.S. Black women as a collectivity (Collins 2000, chap. 11). In *Fighting Words*, I examine the significance of Black feminist epistemology for the larger question of developing an epistemology of empowerment for social justice projects (Collins 1998a, 229-52).

2. A related body of Black feminist scholarship places more credence on capitalism for explaining African American economic status, especially African American women's poverty (Brewer 1993; Omolade 1994; Mullings 1997). Such work also analyzes Black women's labor but expands the analysis beyond work for pay to include unpaid labor. Within this scholarship, Black women's paid and unpaid work (productive and reproductive labor) emerge as important features of Black political economy. Women heading households without adult male partners thus face a double dilemma—they lack access to male wages and must take on the duties of reproductive labor without male assistance.

3. Black diasporic feminisms constitute a large and growing literature (see Nnaemeka 1998), and I highlight only some suggestive contributions here.

References

Anthias, Floya and Nira Yuval-Davis. 1992. *Racialised Boundaries: Race, Nation, Gender, Colour and Class in the Anti-Racist Struggle*. New York: Routledge.

Austin, Regina. 1997. Nest Eggs and Stormy Weather: Law, Culture, and Black Women's Lack of Wealth. *University of Cincinnati Law Review* 65(3):765-86.

Brewer, Rose. 1993. Theorizing Race, Class and Gender: The New Scholarship of Black Feminist Intellectuals and Black Women's Labor. In *Theorizing Black Feminisms: The Visionary Pragmatism of Black Women*, ed. Stanlie M. James and Abena P. A. Busia. New York: Routledge.

Collins, Patricia Hill. 1998a. *Fighting Words: Black Women and the Search for Justice*. Minneapolis: University of Minnesota Press.

————. 1998b. It's All in the Family: Intersections of Gender, Race, and Nation. *Hypatia* 13(3):62-82.

————. 2000. *Black Feminist Thought: Knowledge, Consciousness, and the Politics of Empowerment*. 2d ed. New York: Routledge.

Cooper, Anna Julia. 1892. *A Voice from the South; by a Black Woman of the South*. Xenia, OH: Aldine Printing House.

Gilkes, Cheryl Townsend. 1996. The Margin as the Center of a Theory of History: African-American Women, Social Change, and the Sociology of W.E.B. Du Bois. In *W.E.B. Du Bois on Race and Culture*, ed. Bernard W. Bell, Emily R. Grosholz, and James B. Stewart. New York: Routledge.

James, Joy. 1996. The Profeminist Politics of W.E.B. Du Bois with Respects to Anna Julia Cooper and Ida B. Wells Barnett. In *W.E.B. Du Bois on Race and Culture*, ed. Bernard W. Bell, Emily R. Grosholz, and James B. Stewart. New York: Routledge.

Mullings, Leith. 1997. *On Our Own Terms: Race, Class, and Gender in the Lives of African American Women*. New York: Routledge.

Nnaemeka, Obioma. 1998. Introduction: Reading the Rainbow. In *Sisterhood, Feminisms, and Power: From Africa to the Diaspora*, ed. Obioma Nnaemeka. Trenton, NJ: Africa World Press.

Omolade, Barbara. 1994. *The Rising Song of African American Women*. New York: Routledge.

Wells-Barnett, Ida. 1995. Lynch Law in America. In *Words of Fire: An Anthology of African-American Feminist Thought*, ed. Beverly Guy-Sheftall. New York: New Press.

ANNALS, *AAPSS*, **568**, March 2000

The Emerging Philadelphia African American Class Structure

By ELIJAH ANDERSON

ABSTRACT: In *The Philadelphia Negro*, W.E.B. Du Bois presented a four-class typology of the black community. Today the situation has changed greatly. The enormous social changes of the twentieth century, culminating in the civil rights movement and followed by civil disorders occurring on a wide scale in urban America, resulted in attempts by the wider society to incorporate black Americans through federally mandated social programs such as affirmative action, fair housing legislation, set-asides, and major civil rights legislation. These initiatives helped to defuse much of the tension of the 1960s, but they also set the stage for much greater black participation in American society, leading to tremendous growth in the black middle class. At the same time, these measures of black incorporation, as realized over the past 30 years, have greatly changed the traditional castelike system of race relations. In conjunction with deindustrialization and the simultaneous growth of the global economy, these changes have contributed to a more complex class configuration among blacks.

Elijah Anderson is the Charles and William L. Day Professor of the Social Sciences and professor of sociology at the University of Pennsylvania. He is the author of A Place on the Corner: A Study of Black Street Corner Men *(1978);* Streetwise: Race, Class and Change in an Urban Community *(1990); and* Code of the Street: Decency, Violence, and the Moral Life of the Inner City *(1999).*

I N 1899, W.E.B. Du Bois made sense of the social organization of the Philadelphia black community by developing a typology of four classes: the well-to-do; the decent hard workers, who were doing quite well; the "worthy poor," who were working or trying to work but barely making ends meet; and the "submerged tenth," who were beneath the surface of socioeconomic viability. This stratification system was seen in the social and economic context of increasing industrialization of the time (Du Bois [1899] 1996).

Today, a century later, much has happened that requires modification of Du Bois's typology. The intervening historical period has seen two world wars, the emergence of industrialism on a huge scale, and a massive black migration from the rural South to Philadelphia, and other urban areas, North and South. Blacks competed with European immigrants and faced significant racial discrimination, and segregation and black ghettoization became institutionalized (see Massey and Denton 1993). Immigrants leapfrogged the blacks, pushing them out of job niches through group pressure and violence (Lieberson 1981; Davis and Haller 1998). The civil rights movement and the widespread 1960s' civil disorders followed, and in response the wider socioeconomic system opened up to blacks in major ways.

Affirmative action and other public policies of racial incorporation ameliorated immediate racial tensions. These policies resulted in a growing black middle class and have created among blacks a sense of inclusion, albeit guarded; but in time, these inclusion efforts provoked in a growing number of whites feelings of unfairness and a generalized sense of threat (Blumer 1958; Glazer 1989).

In addition, a social and economic split developed between the black working class and middle class as deindustrialization, the global economy, and other factors eliminated the manufacturing jobs that once provided working-class employment in the city (Wilson 1987). White people and, later, upper- and middle-class black people followed the jobs out of the city, leaving the inner-city working class and poor in neighborhoods that became generally perceived as dangerous, poor, and black and, therefore, undesirable. Ghettos grew and persisted, city services declined, and police, schools, and other institutions often abdicated their responsibilities to serve and to protect black residents (Spear 1967; Franklin 1979; Massey and Denton 1993).

Over the last 15 years, Philadelphia has lost upward of 100,000 jobs, and its manufacturing employment has declined 53 percent, dislocating massive numbers of black workers, who now encounter great difficulty finding family-sustaining employment in the emerging high-technology and service economy. Consequently, many of their communities have become noted for their high concentrations of ghetto poverty. In such areas, the drug trade and other elements of the underground economy have moved in and proliferated, providing economic opportunity for the most desperate elements, while the wider economy provides little (Wacquant and Wilson 1989; Anderson 1990, 1999a).

THE OLD CLASS STRUCTURE

Along with slavery, which was probably the most important single factor distinguishing the black community in the United States, came a white supremacist ideology that defined black people as less than human, as genetically inferior to the country's white majority. Even after emancipation, this ideology persisted, all but negating the prospect of equality between the races. Accordingly, as blacks migrated to cities of the industrial North and South, they were relegated mainly to the most menial positions. In Philadelphia, the talented or educated were at times allowed a somewhat better situation, serving as schoolteachers, doctors, lawyers, ministers, and small-business operators, but the situation for the largest portion of African Americans was social and economic subjugation. Generally, blacks could obtain only the least desirable, lowest-paying positions, and they were very often the last hired and first fired (see Du Bois [1899] 1996).

Moreover, blacks were also consistently treated as second-class citizens. For several decades before and after Du Bois wrote, recurring waves of European immigration consistently leapfrogged the black population, the immigrants' white skin easily parlayed into better social and economic positions than those available to blacks (Lieberson 1981; Davis and Haller 1998). The employers of the day effectively collaborated with the new labor from Europe, placing the black population at the back of the employment queue. This economic system effectively supported and elaborated the castelike system of racial exclusion that Du Bois described. In time, however, an expanding economy offered improved industrial opportunities to blacks over the first half of the twentieth century so that Du Bois's four-class typology required reexamination by the 1950s.

The colortocracy

In the context of racial apartheid, the well-to-do identified by Du Bois effectively constituted an upper-class colortocracy of the black community. Their relatively privileged ancestors were the offspring of slaves and slave masters. Even before the Civil War, many of them were educated in freedmen's schools and occasionally mingled with whites in northern (and sometimes southern) cities. Essentially, they made up the early African American professional class, serving within the segregated black community as doctors, lawyers, professors, undertakers, and other small-business operators. In some cases, their light complexion made them somewhat ambiguous in terms of race—they were marginal and felt it. But that same marginality gave members of this class a form of human capital by forcing them to think somewhat independently of any particular group, and a form of social capital that allowed them to negotiate with whites in positions of authority. Despite their marginality, however, as they gravitated to northern and southern urban centers, they were lumped with or identified with the black community. The darker-complexioned blacks who made up the bulk of that community usually accepted them as a higher class but as blacks nonetheless. Accordingly, these lighter-complexioned men and women often served the community as "race" men and women, or leaders of the race (Frazier 1939, chap. 20; Drake and Cayton 1945; Anderson 1997).

In these circumstances, they became a caste apart and also the ones most inclined—and able—to represent that community to the wider white society socially, politically, and economically. Moreover, in the social context of white supremacy, lighter skin color conferred on them greater rights, obligations, and duties, and both lighter- and darker-complexioned blacks accepted that fact. The result was a normative arrangement that gave the members of the colortocracy the ability to navigate the wider system and to distinguish themselves from darker-skinned blacks, while mimicking the behaviors and values of white society. With their superior status in the black community but inferior status in the white community, they were strongly encouraged to embrace the idea of leadership of the black community, to enact, as Du Bois put it, the role of the "talented tenth" of their race.

Strikingly, this black elite was at pains to cultivate and to maintain its position. And these privileged blacks did so in part by imbuing light skin color with ever more value and social significance, usually socializing and marrying among themselves to create and maintain a legacy. This selective intermarriage nonetheless often resulted in the retention of African facial features as well so that the offspring of the colortocracy evolved a somewhat distinctive appearance, different from the more Negroid phenotype common among the rest of the black population.

Individual members of the colortocracy at times developed a notorious but distinctive racial complex involving an ideology that set them apart from those they viewed as their inferiors. They would take excessive pride in their "white" features, including light skin, thin noses and lips, and "good" (not kinky) hair if they had it. Often "colorstruck," seeing themselves as superior to the average darker-complexioned blacks, they sometimes mimicked and voiced the anti-black prejudices of whites, whose fears, concerns, and values they understood and partly shared. In fact, the lighter-skinned blacks had a greater license than whites for putting blacks down because they could do so from the position of insiders and thus avoid being labeled racist. Ironically, darker-skinned blacks often looked up to them, seeing them as leaders of the race and claiming them as their own. So these leaders came to embody the aspirations of the whole black community, often because of their physical features but also because of their more polished behavior and accomplishments. Their successes inspired feelings of racial pride and were seen as reflecting positively on all blacks. As doctors, lawyers, preachers, undertakers, and other business-men, they were generally looked up to and accepted by the entire black community as the "best people of the race."

Light skin was so highly valued that the folk dictum "If you're light, you're right; if you're brown, stick around; but if you're black, get back" became widely voiced among blacks. At so-called brown-and-tan clubs frequented by the elite, people were required to pass the notorious brown-bag test to be admitted—their skin could not be darker than the bag. Such practices continued well into the 1950s and 1960s. A light complexion was strongly associated with high status, prosperity, and decency, a dark one with low status, badness, uncouthness, or the "street." The closer a person's skin tone and phenotype was to white, the more acceptable he or she was to the wider society as well, encouraging some to try to pass for white. Though somewhat deemphasized by the civil rights and cultural nationalist movements of the 1960s, these invidious distinctions persist in the black community to this day and continue to create tensions and differential opportunities for advancement and upward mobility for black people of different hues (Domhoff and Zweigenhaft 1998; Graham 1998).

The middle class

At the time Du Bois wrote *The Philadelphia Negro*, a new middle class was emerging. Its occupants were not so light-complexioned; they were more brown, sometimes even dark (Frazier 1939, chap. 20). By the 1950s, this class was becoming firmly established, if still relatively small in size. Their origins were humble, but they were beginning to obtain access to education. Often, they served the local community as ministers, schoolteachers, postal workers, and storekeepers. Although relatively less prominent than the elite group, many saw themselves and were often viewed as leaders of the race whose accomplishments reflected positively on the local black community.

The working class

Below the middle class was the solid working class, people who tended to be dark-complexioned and not long off the land even decades after emancipation. Generally, they migrated from the South, particularly South Carolina, North Carolina, Virginia, and Maryland, during the manufacturing era. The industrious among them formed the folk icon of the black family, colloquially known as Mr. and Mrs. Johnson (Anderson 1999a). Typically, men in this group were employed as laborers in factories, steel mills, municipal work, and construction; they were excluded from the skilled building trades, including carpentry, plumbing, and electrical work. Their wives tended to work as domestics in the homes of middle- and upper-middle-class whites. In the first half of the century, such people were constantly competing with or being displaced from their jobs by European immigrants, but with the increased opportunities brought on by the wartime industrial boom of the 1940s and sustained through the 1950s, many were able to achieve some semblance of the American dream. They often were able to purchase a nice home and a new automobile, and their children would sometimes attend the historically black colleges of the old South.

Such people emphasized strong family values, including decency, the work ethic, religion, and male authority. They also tended to have a strong, almost ritualistic sense of place. Cultural products of the powerful forces of the Jim Crow castelike segregation of the old South, they adapted to lives of second-class citizenship in Philadelphia. They generally accepted their place in the system, accommodating but not always fully. Their communities were socially organized around the idea that black people were discriminated against by the wider society and that this was to be resisted. But, like members of the colortocracy, many were not convinced that the wider society was completely wrong. Generally, the way to overcome these social and economic barriers, in their view, was to respect the wider society but also to strive to be better than the average white person—to be more decent, to work harder, and to always obey the law. Such an almost ritualistic inclination to accommodate the system and to overcompensate for one's supposed shortcomings was one of the enduring effects of class and race subordination (Frazier 1957).

The submerged tenth

Below the solid working class were the very poor who worked sporadically if at all: Du Bois's "submerged tenth." While they generally

struggled to make ends meet economically, some were also engaged in illegal or shady occupations, and some were criminals (Du Bois [1899] 1996; Lane 1986; Drake and Cayton 1945). Even in the 1950s, they were often relatively new arrivals from the South who had yet to make their way and become acculturated to life in the big cities like Philadelphia. And, as a residual social category, they were often put down by the more established members of the working-class black communities as "country" or "street."

Memorably chronicled by Du Bois ([1899] 1996), Drake and Cayton (1945), Frazier (1939, 1957), and Myrdal ([1944] 1964), these four categories—the elite, the middle class, the working class, and the very poor—endured, with variations, from slavery into the 1950s in urban America.

MAJOR CHANGES BEGIN:
THE CIVIL RIGHTS MOVEMENT

In 1978, William J. Wilson presented the first observations of the fundamental change that was occurring in the black class structure. In *The Declining Significance of Race* (1978), he argued that, for the first time in American history, class was becoming more important than race in determining the life chances of black Americans, that the castelike system of race relations around which the black community long had been organized was changing. This shift was related to the great successes of the civil rights movement of the 1950s and 1960s, the ground for which had been laid in the manufacturing centers during the first half of the century.

In addition, the two world wars and the full advent of industrialism created an advantageous situation for African Americans. Because of labor shortages, particularly of unskilled labor, blacks coming from the South readily found employment in the mills and factories of the North. At times, they worked side by side with immigrants from western Europe, southeastern Europe, and other areas of the world. But, as noted, with the passage of time, the white immigrants would outstrip them socially and economically, if not in their own lives, then in their children's (Ignatiev 1996).

These developments in themselves did little to dismantle or even unsettle the castelike system of race relations existing in the United States. But they signaled a new, more critical, perception of self by black Americans in relation to the wider system of social stratification (Pettigrew 1980). With continuing immigration, the fuller participation of black soldiers in the world wars, and full-blown industrialism, including an improved standard of living for large numbers of African Americans, they began to question their second-class status. And their leaders, race men all, turned their attention to challenging the wider system and petitioning for even fuller inclusion of black Americans.

These are the circumstances in which the modern civil rights movement was born (Pettigrew 1980; Morris 1984; Williams 1988). Sit-ins, demonstrations, and mass boycotts were the weapons of the civil rights activists. In the South, numerous cities were targeted, and segregation was increasingly challenged, questioned, and in places made to appear untenable and subsequently defeated. With moderate leaders like Whitney Young and the Reverend Martin Luther King, Jr., and militants like Stokely Car-michael, H. Rap Brown, and Malcolm X, progress was made toward full citizenship and greater inclusion of blacks.

The civil disorders that began with the Watts riots in Los Angeles in 1965 began a new era of the civil rights movement. These disorders became politically and socially contagious, occurring in city after city. After Watts burned, Seattle, Kansas City, Chicago, and Detroit, among many other major and minor cities, experienced major civil disorders. Many younger black people had all but given up on a system that called on them for sacrifice while withholding the fruits and privileges of citizenship.

In general, the black community was deeply disturbed. Those who were most agitated made their feelings known through even more demonstrations, civil disorders, and, ultimately, urban riots. Between 1965 and 1968, the year Martin Luther King was assassinated, many cities sustained heavy damage, physical as well as social. Each winter and spring, local and national officials fearfully looked forward to a long hot summer of urban riots and civil disorders (National Advisory Commission 1968).

At the same time, increasing numbers of black people were being educated and securing jobs that placed them in the growing black middle class, thereby serving as a counterweight to the civil disorder. There were increasing numbers of black college students, professors, schoolteachers, businessmen, postal workers, social workers, policemen, doctors, lawyers, and elected officials.

But this emerging middle class was still more akin to what had been described by E. Franklin Frazier in *Black Bourgeoisie* (1957): it was growing in the context of the traditional castelike system of race relations. It was widely assumed that many of these professionals would serve in largely circumscribed roles. In fact, as second-class citizens, black professionals often continued to labor under the so-called master status of race: whatever else they might claim to be, they often were treated as black first, and that status usually overrode any professional status (Hughes 1945).

As the riots persisted, powerful white allies of the civil rights movement raised their demands for greater incorporation of the black population into American society. President John F. Kennedy in 1963 issued an executive order prescribing affirmative action as a remedy to race discrimination in the American workplace. After Kennedy's assassination, President Lyndon Johnson was even more direct, supporting affirmative action in various areas of American life. But during the heat of the riots and civil disorders, affirmative action, particularly in white-owned ghetto shops and stores, could be described as informal, petty tokenism or as mere window

dressing. In the prevailing crisis environment, it was not clear whether such informal actions were simply cynical attempts to cool the anger of so many local ghetto black people or were serious signals of far-reaching change. In time, however, what began as an informal policy evolved into long-overdue formal government legislation mandating genuine incorporation of the black population into American society (Landry 1988; Collins 1997; Anderson 1999b).

When the civil rights movement began, many blacks could be described as accommodating, even docile. They may not have been happy about their place vis-à-vis white society, but many were resigned to it and often did not want to rock the boat. It was widely accepted that the social structure with which they were familiar was simply the established order of things, that black people somehow deserved the low positions they had, and that such an order maintained social stability.

The changes brought about by the movement were not substantial at first. In the forefront was the middle class, whose members observed most clearly the discrepancy between their place in society and that of whites. The leaders were concerned with helping the whole race achieve its rightful place in society. Although not always representing the majority of blacks, they were able to gain the attention and support of many of both races. They strongly emphasized the discrepancies between the status of blacks and that of whites in society and strongly embraced the idea of racial equality. Led mostly by middle-class ministers, such as the Reverend Dr. Martin Luther King, Jr., they focused on small but obvious manifestations of inequality, such as being required by law to sit at the back of buses. Their goal was racial equality: to achieve for blacks the same rights, obligations, and duties that whites enjoyed as American citizens (see Morris 1984; Sitkoff 1981).

Essentially, the civil rights movement called into question the country's racially oppressive social stratification system. The focus of the movement was the inequality between blacks and whites. In calling the wider system into account, black leaders were joined by many liberal whites who believed their grievances to be justified. But they were also joined by more militant blacks, who spun off into the cultural nationalist movement, and by others whose anger and frustration finally culminated in the riots of the mid- to late 1960s. Only a minority of blacks were demonstrating, but all the leaders were constantly invoking the profound racial inequality of American society (National Advisory Commission 1968). King in particular was expert at drawing attention to this point on both the national and international stage.

The response of the establishment was a conviction that something must be done to quell the turmoil and dissension. Increasing the pressure on the government to act was the fact that these events were occurring during the Cold War. The image sent around the world was that the United States as leader of the free world was not extending full rights to all of its own citizens, thus undermining U.S. influence in trying to extend democracy around the world. This situation was resolved by a concerted effort of the white academic, corporate, and governmental elite to work to incorporate blacks, the centerpiece of the strategy being the passing of civil rights legislation mandating voting rights, affirmative action, and fair housing policies. In effect, this amounted to a form of reparations for the injustices blacks had suffered, but this implication of the legislation was seldom acknowledged. Strikingly, support for these racially inclusive policies was by no means unanimous, and to this day, perhaps especially in this day, many conservatives disagree profoundly with them. But with the success of the policies, documented by the fact that more and more black people were holding major positions in the system, the riots began to die down, and peace and comity emerged among the races, at least for a while.

The social changes brought on by these policies were enormous. One of the most unappreciated but profound consequences was the destabilization of the former castelike system under which black society had long been set apart from white society and internally organized on the basis of human capital mediated through skin shade. Strikingly, affirmative action policies—largely indifferent to skin shade among blacks—effectively worked to blur these differences in the black community by providing qualified dark-complexioned black people from the old working class with the same opportunities as light-complexioned members of the old colortocracy.

Hence, affirmative action policies inserted a certain egalitarianism into the emerging black class configuration. The colortocracy's privileged position vis-à-vis other blacks was diminished. Blacks of all hues, for example, began attending formerly white universities and joining the faculties there, working in formerly white companies, working in formerly white hospitals, and teaching in formerly white elementary and high schools. These developments reverberated to formerly all-black institutions, which could no longer afford to so boldly discriminate in favor of the colortocracy. In general, the barriers of racial caste were slowly giving way to a more inclusive atmosphere.

As corporations, universities, and government agencies usurped control from the colortocracy, they became the major arbiters and shapers of black mobility. And status in the black community became less arbitrary. In time, class positions became increasingly dependent on achievement and less on ascription. Strikingly, the light-skinned descendants of the colortocracy and the dark-skinned descendants of the working class were encountering one another on equal terms in the affirmative action programs of the wider American institutions, including universities, corporations, and governmental agencies. A major consequence has been a certain political and social integration within the black community. As the civil rights movement gathered steam,

privileged light-skinned young people embraced black consciousness and very often joined with their darker-skinned peers in criticizing both the exclusionary white system and the elitist black old guard; at times, they became extremely militant. Thus, one of the significant effects of affirmative action was its role in beginning to challenge the old color caste arrangements that had existed within the black community since slavery.

THE EMERGING
CLASS CONFIGURATION

As indicated previously, the social forces of racial incorporation and deindustrialization had a strong impact upon the old black class structure, simultaneously undermining the castelike system of racial exclusion and creating a new social class configuration among black Philadelphians. Today, the social classes within the African American community are qualitatively different from those of Du Bois's time, but we can still discern four basic groups: the growing black elite, the middle class, the working class, and the underclass. Racism and market forces strongly influence all four segments. Overall, though blacks can now be found at all levels of mainstream society, the community continues to be socially organized around issues of racial oppression and calls for political and economic unity.

An important feature of the emerging class structure is the fact that black residence, while still largely segregated, has with mixed reception penetrated formerly white areas throughout the city and the region (see Massey and Denton 1993). Originally, most black people resided in the ghetto—the old Seventh Ward in Du Bois's day. Later, black migration patterns from the rural South, and black and white residential migration around the city, resulted in ever larger black enclaves while fair housing laws opened residence to those blacks who could afford it in all sections of Philadelphia. Typically, as blacks moved into various white neighborhoods, whites moved out. Today, the elite live in predominantly white and well-to-do areas like Chestnut Hill, Cheltenham, and Society Hill, while the middle class can be found in racially mixed Mount Airy, Germantown, Yeadon, West Philadelphia, and parts of North Philadelphia such as West Oak Lane. High concentrations of ghetto poverty may be found in South, Southwest, West, and North Philadelphia.

The elite

Unlike in the old system of racial caste, the new black elite emerges from a wide diversity of backgrounds. Today, some are the typically dark-complexioned sons and daughters of the old industrial working class; others emerge directly from the old colortocracy, the professional class that was traditionally educated in black colleges and practiced medicine or law or ran businesses in the segregated black community. Largely indifferent to earlier rules of the color caste, darker- and lighter-complexioned blacks commonly socialize with and marry one another, while some take white or Asian spouses. Now, the black elite are often nationally and internationally connected with the white elite and with one another. Early beneficiaries of affirmative action and other equal opportunity policies, they are now often highly visible and wealthy. Some are highly distinguished in their fields and have become local and national celebrities. They are doctors, lawyers, corporate executives, top journalists, politicians, college professors, publishers, entrepreneurs, and foundation heads. Some are professional athletes and famous entertainers. These highly accomplished blacks are sought out by the power structure to represent the black community but also solely for their unique talents and contributions. Refined and elegant in self-presentation, they clearly understand the mores and values of the elite white social world and embody them to a large extent.

Strikingly, they can be said to have a complex approach to social and economic life. They tend to socialize with a diversity of people, including whites, while worshiping in all-black congregations. Some belong to predominantly white social clubs. And most reside in upscale, predominantly white neighborhoods. Yet, as they have become upwardly mobile, for them race tends to be more visible, consequential, and thus more persistent than ethnicity is for, say, many Irish, Italians, or Jews of their social class (Gordon 1964). These black elites live in two worlds: they socially connect with other blacks—with whom they can feel a nurturing connection—at a favorite barbershop, church, social club, or friendship group of their social standing, and they connect socially and professionally with their white counterparts. Most operate quite comfortably in either social world. Their experience brings to mind an affective accommodation to the cultural twoness of which Du Bois spoke so long ago (Du Bois [1903] 1990).

The middle class

Like the elite, the middle class is to a large extent a product of the nation's affirmative action and equal opportunity programs. Also, it is strongly supported by the society's egalitarian ethos of tolerance for diversity and racial incorporation. The presence and advancement of members of this class in so many organizations strongly reflects the support and mentoring of liberal whites as well as blacks who were so inclined (see Anderson 1999b), but also the recent growth in human capital among African Americans (Coleman 1988).

Increasingly, their children take on more general cultural orientations, particularly those attending private and suburban schools; many advance to elite colleges and universities, while some seek out historically black institutions for a uniquely "Black" social and academic experience. But, generally, among their friendship groups, diverse ethnicities are represented, including African, Jewish, Asian, Indian, and white. Strikingly, these children sometimes become a special breed of cultural broker among the increasingly diverse elements of the metropolitan area. Yet, their parents continue to face occasional racial

challenges in the workplace and sometimes complain of having a hard time fitting in.

While many members of this new middle class testify to being well received, some also report the occasional direct insult and other acts of disrespect, which they deeply resent (see Cose 1993). In public places, particularly restaurants, they may become especially alive to slights, and when slighted, will not hesitate to answer in kind. Such experiences generate in them a certain ambivalence about the broader society; they wonder if it holds a generalized contempt for the ordinary black person, particularly black males. Feeling they are not completely welcome, they begin to value a certain insularity. Accordingly, members of this group only rarely attend symphony concerts, theater performances, or Phillies baseball games or visit upscale restaurants, museums, or places such as Longwood Gardens, a popular local arboretum. In Philadelphia, the clientele in such places is always predominantly white.

Today, the members of this class are often the grown children of the Mr. and Mrs. Johnsons of the world. They were often brought up with financial stability and a stable set of community and family values and were poised to take advantage of the opportunities offered with desegregation and affirmative action. Earning from $30,000 to $100,000 a year, many now work in corporations, universities, hospitals, and governmental agencies. Often upwardly mobile, they work in clerical positions or as teachers, social workers, systems engineers, and middle managers.

And many others have become successful entrepreneurs and small-
business owners. As accomplished
and as talented as they are, many of
them believe that without equal
opportunity programs and the egalitarian ethos that inspired them,
their numbers in the workplace
would be far smaller. When they look
around the workplace, they often
still see a paucity of black people and
intuitively understand why—the
department or company or organization has not attempted to recruit
black employees or has turned its
back on affirmative action or equal
opportunity.

With such assessments, members
of the new black middle class remain
ever more ambivalent on the issue of
assimilation. As just noted, many
rose in the system largely due to
organized efforts toward racial incorporation. But these efforts, along
with that of full cultural assimilation
with whites, have now been widely
questioned, if not discredited. Many
of them reject assimilation as a goal
or at least do not support it fully. Yet,
ironically, they are already largely
assimilated, particularly with regard
to family names, language, lifestyle,
and core cultural values. Still, their
socioeconomic position is weak in
comparison with that of middle-class
whites both because their mobility
has been sponsored by the wider
political system and because they are
still working to establish their position in the system (see Oliver and
Shapiro 1995; Conley 1999).

Well educated and often with
well-paying jobs, members of the
black middle class have mostly chosen to live away from the ghetto in
racially mixed communities, though
many continue to reside in the old
inner-city neighborhoods. So often,
in the past when blacks moved into
formerly all-white neighborhoods, it
was a signal for the whites to leave,
and this is often exactly what happened. For some, interracial encounters in these residential communities
become trials and tests of whether
whites will be stereotypically true to
form and exhibit prejudicial behavior
toward them. From such a perspective, incidents that may in fact have
been caused by simple negligence or
color-blind incivility easily become
racialized. As the store of such incidents grows in public and private
memories, many middle-class blacks
find themselves unable to forget the
country's troubled racial past and
the likelihood of its return, and this
thought erodes expectations of fair
treatment from whites in authority.

Sometimes society reinforces
these diminished expectations.
When the police shoot an unarmed
black man, when a Rodney King incident occurs, when institutionalized
practices of discrimination such as
those at Texaco are exposed, middle-
class blacks are reminded of the pre-
cariousness of their position. This
reality works to organize the community around the issue of race and
develop among middle-class blacks
a strong bond with all other
blacks. In this way, the communal
memory can become a polarizing
force in both local and national black
communities.

One consequence is that middle-
class blacks will sometimes gravitate
toward segregated communities,
thereby signaling that they have given

up on the wider system. Acknowledging the twoness Du Bois spoke of, they adapt to a double life, one in the white community and one in the black community, returning to the ghetto neighborhoods to attend church, a wedding, or a funeral.

Members of this group are keenly aware that today's younger blacks may take for granted much of the social progress of the past 30 years. Working downtown or in the suburbs, lunching with diverse co-workers with whom they have professional relations, and earning a respectable income—these are a part of the new reality. At the same time, it is clear that this is a group on the move, collectively building stores of human and social capital (Coleman, 1988). On weeknights, the most ambitious in this respect may be found in Center City taking foreign-language classes or attending evening university courses for formal degrees or for self-improvement. Others take opera lessons or even play in classical music ensembles in recitals for predominantly white audiences. Moreover, their children can sometimes be found at the Settlement Music School, taking flute or piano or singing lessons taught by an ethnically diverse international faculty. Yet, in the broader society, incidents of discrimination, or their expectation, continue to unnerve them, thus undermining feelings of comity and goodwill that should prevail in their lives. But in general, with a positive attitude, they press on.

At the same time, while many do not look back, some members of the new black middle classes are at times bothered by feelings of ambivalence about their successes. Having sometimes rapidly climbed the ladder of socioeconomic status, they may feel guilt about those left behind and may feel obligated to reach back and offer help; at times, this is expressed in calls for race unity and activism. Extended families and childhood friends in the ghetto with whom many middle-class blacks maintain close relations remain vulnerable to the problems of the ghetto—such as crime, welfare difficulties, and lack of health care—and lack the resources to address them. As a result, receiving an occasional call for help in the middle of the night because a member of their extended family requires financial assistance for legal or medical problems is not uncommon for successful blacks. They are not so far removed from the inner-city ghetto.

The working class and the underclass

Because of historic racial segregation, the working class and the underclass tend to reside interspersed among one another. In these circumstances, both groupings are exposed—though not equally—to the "neighborhood effects" of concentrated urban poverty (Wilson 1987). Hence, the inner-city, or "the 'hood," is home to diverse elements, which, however, are often not distinguished by people from the wider community who lack familiarity with the inner city and therefore paint the community with a broad brush.

In this community, local residents divide themselves into social categories of "decent" and "street," which amount to value orientations. The result of so many social contests, these labels have moral connotations, but there is a sense in which they inform local distinctions of social class. It is important to point out that, objectively speaking, a decent person can be poor, but typically the people who are judged to be decent in fact more clearly embody the work ethic. They are marginally better off financially, attend church regularly, and are known to treat people with respect.

Mr. and Mrs. Johnson are the icons of the inner-city working class of old. Now retired, they have tried, not always successfully, to distance themselves from the problems of the ground-zero neighborhood, including crime, violence, drugs, and so many suffering people.

After working a lifetime to buy and pay for a home, they now have little ability to move away. In such inner-city communities, they try as best they can to make do and to get along with their neighbors, to make the best of a difficult situation. One strategy is to "see but don't see," as they try to mind their own business in public. Another is to limit their activities and shut themselves in after dark. They bond most closely with those with whom they have the most in common, often others of the same age, who used to work in the factories, but who are now retired and on pensions. Here they engage in a rich cultural life, trading favors and friendship and looking out for one another. Among their working-class neighbors are men and women who are employed as convenience

store cashiers, night watchmen, janitors, nurses' aides, construction workers, schoolteachers, factory workers, car wash workers, taxi drivers, and pensioners.

But Mr. and Mrs. Johnson also share the streets and local stores with drug dealers, drug addicts, ex-convicts, mothers on welfare, grandmothers raising children—in a word, people barely coping with conditions of persistent urban poverty. They have become disdainful of the welfare mother next door, who now lives there only because of Section 8, whose four unsupervised children "are taking the old house apart," who is "ignorant" and has little sense of propriety. Their community is besieged by the drug trade, and there is little that the authorities will do.

In these circumstances, Mr. and Mrs. Johnson feel threatened and alienated, but there is really little they can do. In their frustration, they simply sit and wait, unable but wanting to move from ground zero. Gradually, those who were able have moved away, leaving behind an ever greater concentration of the poor and the desperate. They try to negotiate with those remaining, trying to get along with them, hoping they will not be "ganged up" on and robbed or assaulted.

There are also many decent people of working age in the ghetto, but they find themselves unable to achieve the financial stability of Mr. and Mrs. Johnson and are marginally poor. While they hold jobs, these jobs, generally in manufacturing or at the lowest levels of the service economy, are not secure, pay little, and provide few benefits. Generally, people adapt and make do with what they have. Thus, even as the wider economy booms, enabling more people at ground zero to find work, the situation has yet to materially affect the conditions of the neighborhood. Too many local people, although working, remain impoverished, alienated, and socially challenged.

For the most desperate people here, particularly the youth, the underground economy of drugs and crime holds not only a certain fascination but temptation as well. In these circumstances of sometimes profound hopelessness, some are inclined to simply escape their problems through drugs or alcohol. Hence, though many decent people aspire to a better life for their children, one of their biggest obstacles is their limited opportunities for gainful employment (see Anderson 1990, 1999a).

Roughly corresponding to Du Bois's submerged tenth, members of the ghetto underclass are profound casualties of the economic system that characterizes the end of the twentieth century (Auletta 1982; Wilson 1978, 1987). Their forebears like Mr. and Mrs. Johnson performed low-skill jobs in the factories of South Philadelphia, North Philadelphia, and beyond. But today, many of them lack the skills and education, or human capital, to compete on their own in the postindustrial system.

Marvin represents the antithesis of Mr. Johnson. Currently working part-time at a car wash, he has a checkered past that includes robbing people, selling drugs, hustling, and doing time in Graterford Prison. Seven years ago, he had a baby with Sherise, a woman on welfare, and he is now raising his daughter with the help of his mother and his sister, with whom he lives. He tries to take care of his daughter, but his economic position is very weak. He works solely for tips, so if it rains all week, he can make no money and is easily tempted to revert to robbing and preying on the Mr. and Mrs. Johnsons of the neighborhood. Indeed, although he and Sherise may be trying to approximate the values of Mr. and Mrs. Johnson, they do so poorly. Yet it is their confused version of the old working-class life that now dominates the neighborhood.

In the local community, people like Mr. and Mrs. Johnson are very often looked up to as the "decent" people. In turn, they look down on others like Marvin and Sherise, whom they readily label "street," and in this connection, consider them ignorant, loud, boisterous, and lacking in decorum. In fact, many though not all of the street oriented are more often demoralized, jobless, persistently on welfare, and sometimes homeless. Though one may argue that the institutions of the wider society have failed these people, their working-class neighbors and others readily hold them to blame. This stance allows those who are better off to maintain faith in the system, especially the work ethic, while morally legitimating their own position in the local system of stratification. So, members of the local underclass or street group are viewed and treated as convenient objects of scorn, fear, and embarrassment. In this way, the street group can serve as a critical social yardstick that allows those judged to be decent to compare themselves favorably with those of the street (see Anderson 1990, 1999a).

All too often, those of the street or the local underclass are caught up in abusive conditions, either as perpetrators or as victims. Drug and alcohol addiction, unsafe sex and AIDS, domestic and street violence, high levels of crime and run-ins with the police—all are commonly found in this group. Their existence is very much dog-eat-dog, and many live from hand to mouth, sometimes begging on the streets. Many have become socially invested in the welfare culture, as they have become accustomed to getting by without working. The prospect of welfare reform generates in them much anxiety. At the same time, out of concern for their community and social environment as well as for their families and loved ones, many of the local residents become anxious about the neighborhood effects of welfare cutbacks, worrying about what the absence of welfare sanctions in the form of payments to their impoverished neighbors will mean for their own safety, security, and general quality of life.

The inner-city ghetto of today is home to a wide diversity of people, but it is the street element who so often control its public spaces, particularly at night, and therefore its image. Many outsiders too easily associate its residents with poverty and crime, and a subset of residents is indeed close to the criminal element. Nevertheless, most ghetto residents embody decency and actually approximate and enact their own version of the most honorable ethics of the broader society, a reality too often missed by outsiders, black and white. Others, particularly alienated young people, have made a virtue of the street and derive a measure of pride from their association. Much of the inner-city community, however, is threatened by and fearful of the street element and has difficulty embracing it. Parenthetically, blacks residing outside the ghetto are often stereotyped in the street image, and this is a confusion that particularly disturbs such people who work hard to organize themselves and their behaviors around being socially distant from the culture of the street.

Within the working class, there are people with more or less human and social capital. It is this that most clearly divides the decent people from the street people. It is not just a matter of how much money a person here has, but of how they spend their money. Some people have been able to buy things of lasting value, such as a house or education, while others spend what they get on fleeting pleasures, such as expensive clothes and jewelry, electronic equipment, flashy cars, and drugs and alcohol. Some people have a sense of propriety and decorum, while others do not. And those who do not are more often connected with the street.

Another factor in the decency orientation seems to be age. Youths are more likely to be of the street than are older people, while some of the most stable Mr. Johnsons were involved in street-oriented activities when young. The possibility of effecting such a change speaks to the general social changes that have occurred over the past two generations. Although the working class and the underclass are not that different structurally from their counterparts in Du Bois's time, deindustrialization is leaving the ghetto in the lurch while the underground economy takes up the slack. Without the prospect of finding a steady job once they outgrow their youthful hustling, men remain stuck in their hustles, preying on people who are marginally better off. As a result, the problems of the ghetto are likely to become more acute as we move into the twenty-first century.

At the other end of the social structure, however, the class categories are dramatically different from those Du Bois described. The elite and the middle class have been transformed from a colortocracy to a more egalitarian group. Despite ambivalence and continued instances of racism, their members are now acknowledged to be full citizens of American society. Yet the legacy of past exclusion continues to haunt blacks at all levels of the class structure.

CULTURAL ASSUMPTIONS, PERSPECTIVES, AND BEHAVIOR

The shifts in class stratification in the black community in the context of the continuing importance of race as an identifying characteristic have allowed for the emergence of another kind of internal division between blacks, one that is based on racial perspective and that crosses class lines. The country's refusal to truly address the race issue, as Du Bois insisted, has led to the profound marginalization as well as alienation of the black community but, as noted above, particularly residents of the inner-city ghetto. Such political and social factors as white militia movements, economic depression, severe cutbacks in welfare, the ghetto drug economy, the availability of guns, the high rate of black male incarceration, police brutality—especially high-profile cases such as the police killing of African immigrant Amadou Diallo in New York City or of Dante Dawson, an unarmed black motorist in Philadelphia—and the broad rolling-back of affirmative action have given rise in the black community to a peculiar but complex racial orientation toward the wider white society. For many blacks, race becomes ever more an organizing principle, with the persistent assumption that blacks are commonly victimized and oppressed by the broader system and its agents.

Among many blacks, racial particularism has acquired positive value and meaning. In making sense of this with respect to the emerging black class structure, I use the concepts "type A" and "type B" to refer to attitudes or orientations black people have toward whites and the cultural assumptions and behavior that result from them. Generally, type A people focus on characteristics of ascription (such as skin color), and type B people balance such traits with those of achievement (such as education and experience). These views appear to govern racial conduct in the black community and how individuals define themselves and others. For conceptual purposes, these perspectives can be thought of as social types, though in practice they are of course not mutually exclusive. Individual blacks may take one position or the other or both simultaneously, or they may move between them depending on the situation (see Anderson 1990).

Both types can be found up and down the class structure, but there are some class correlations between them and there is a class component in how they operate. Generally, type A attitudes are strongly associated with the ethnic particularism of the working and lower classes. These individuals tend to emerge from a highly segregated or racially particularistic background. To many, the white man historically was often a cheat and a devil, the epitome of evil. Generally, the ethos of black separatism is based on such observations, and it has made important inroads in the inner-city black community. Many type A blacks are quite suspicious of whites in general. Some of them manifest an extreme version of the type A perspective, believing that the white community has a plan that ultimately includes the destruction of the black community.

The South Philadelphia neighborhood of Gray's Ferry exemplifies a place in which type A behavior predominates among both blacks and whites. A mostly working-class to poor community, the area is a mix of blacks and ethnic whites (mainly Irish). It experiences day-to-day racial tension that occasionally erupts into shootings or other forms of violence, some of which make local and even national news. Blacks and whites here generally see each other as outsiders, as people they cannot relate to.

Such adversarial relations between racial groups are in part a function of class and social isolation. As Massey and Denton argue in *American Apartheid* (1993), much of America continues to be segregated, and that encourages the type A orientation (Feagin and Sikes 1995; Hacker 1995). Only blacks who are upwardly mobile or in an assimilationist setting are type B. Middle-class mixed neighborhoods thus experience less tension, as seen in the northwest neighborhoods of Mount Airy and Chestnut Hill. As blacks move up the class structure, they encounter whites with more cosmopolitan views, and both blacks and whites more easily find points of engagement. The ethnic particularism of whites also diminishes as they move up the social ladder. However, type A behavior appears to be more persistent among blacks because of the racism they continue to encounter all through American society. In the middle class, blacks experience less hostility, but they remain to a certain degree alienated from the system. So with upward mobility, both blacks and whites develop a more tolerant racial perspective, but type A attitudes continue to exert a pull. Type B attitudes are more readily found in the emerging middle class, among people who may expect a cultural payoff from adopting dominant cultural and behavioral codes that let them move more easily in mainstream society; to be mobile, blacks have had to assume a type B orientation. Both of the types are represented in Philadelphia's black middle class and in all of the classes.

Because the type A perspective on the social world is mainly in terms of ethnicity and color, emphasizing these characteristics in all important relationships, a central problem for individuals with this perspective is retaining their racial identity, or blackness, in a predominantly white socioeconomic class context that they perceive as threatening. All whites are considered suspect on the race question, and selective experiences of many type A blacks bear this out. Therefore, prejudice against whites is understandable and tolerable, if not totally acceptable. Type A people are generally resigned to the notion that whites are unalterably prejudiced against blacks. Hence, they believe that almost any relationship with whites that is not clearly instrumental is fundamentally a waste of time. Moreover, they observe a racial etiquette based on these assumptions.

Such people's primary group relations are exclusively with other blacks. They tend to decline social invitations from whites or accept out of politeness, curiosity, or to serve a particular purpose, and their own social gatherings are almost always totally black. In support of these actions, they recall the history of the black experience, citing white racism and persistent black social inequality or simply their discomfort in the social presence of whites. They continue to perceive racial prejudice as rampant, particularly noting the treatment of black males in public.

The type B perspective presupposes a somewhat more cosmopolitan outlook. Confronting issues of racial caste—on the streets, in the schools, and in the workplace—blacks holding this view generally assume there is persistent racism in society, and because of this and the etiquette surrounding it, most of their close friends are black. Yet in everyday life, social class generally outweighs racial influences; they move comfortably in both white and black middle-class circles. They are prepared to play down the importance of color in their own lives and are open to an array of friends from a variety of ethnic backgrounds. At social gatherings, type B blacks mingle with middle-class Jews, Italians, and others—people somewhat estranged from their ethnic ghettos. In these settings ethnicity is usually ignored.

Accordingly, type B blacks are inclined to see themselves as individuals and thus to choose their friends not so much by color as by apparent social attitudes, interests, and affinities, such as sports, community organizing, home and school association participation, and politics. On political issues, these people are moderate to liberal, but they may surprise some of their white friends, particularly former civil rights activists, with pro-life stands on abortion, conservative views on the work ethic, or intolerance toward the black poor.

In their work in technical and service-related jobs, middle-class blacks of either perspective gain exposure to the wider culture and may come to accept the need to get along with professional peers. Moreover, because of their middle-class position, their child care arrangements, including their children's play groups, tend to be predominantly white. And because of such associations they may come to know the parents of white children socially, as individuals and not simply as members of a racial category. On occasion, they may attend the symphony or the theater with white friends; some even take up pastimes traditionally exclusive to whites such as golf or tennis.

Most of the black elite tend to be type B; relatively few seriously embrace type A behavior. Due to their experiences with upward mobility, they are generally open to a more diversified social life. In fact, because of the social stratification previously noted, particularly the etiquette of the color line and the limited number of middle-class blacks in many settings, at parties and social affairs hosted by their white friends they may be the only blacks present.

A further distinction within both type A and type B can be made in terms of an active and passive mode. Some people are type A in large part because they have been exposed to nothing else. The social isolation they experience as a result of the segregated, castelike system of race relations held over from Jim Crow makes them feel that the wider system is unreceptive to them. This orientation can be distinguished from that of the active, more chauvinistic type A's who actively reject assimilation (see Patterson 1977). Similarly, type B people can be divided into those who are actively so, genuinely desiring to be part of the wider system, and those who are passively

integrationist, whose orientation is mainly instrumental.

CONCLUSION

A great deal has occurred in the black community of Philadelphia since Du Bois's time, reconfiguring the strict castelike system of racial exclusion. That class structure has largely broken down. Black people now operate at all levels in the social system, and achievement has partly replaced ascription in determining how they will fare, especially at the upper levels. The class structure of the black urban community is in some respects much more complex than it was in Du Bois's day. Factors like the type A and type B racial perspectives cut across class boundaries. Yet, as Du Bois indicated, there is still an elite, and there is still a submerged tenth, but both of these have changed radically since his day.

At the same time, within the black community a mini-diaspora has occurred. When Du Bois wrote *The Philadelphia Negro* ([1899] 1996), the Philadelphia black community was concentrated around Sixth and Lombard streets in the old Seventh Ward. It has now spread out significantly, with concentrations in various parts of the city, including sections of Southwest, West, South, and North Philadelphia. Deep in these pockets is the black ghetto, characterized by concentrated poverty. As black people become well-to-do, they move out of these areas and into white areas. The white residents fear that blacks will bring with them the problems of the ghetto, so they typically flee the areas into which the blacks have moved. The result is that the ghetto tends to follow black migration (see Massey and Denton 1993).

Despite their social and economic success, middle-class blacks still often suffer prejudice and discrimination at the hands of whites. This situation alienates many middle-class blacks, discourages assimilation, and encourages indifference to and cynicism about the wider society.

Recent political and legal attacks on affirmative action pose a threat to the black middle class. It is not clear whether the attacks are strong enough to stop the momentum of progress for this group, but it is clear that these attacks contribute to alienation and make it difficult for middle-class blacks to maintain a type B perspective. The progress made up to this point would not have been possible without political pressure for government policies of incorporation. It remains to be seen whether this progress can be sustained with the withdrawal of this pressure.

Following Du Bois's prescient observations, the problem of the twenty-first century is still the problem of the color line, a color line made ever more problematic by issues of inequality, structural poverty, joblessness, alienation, and the resulting social pathologies that are readily and erroneously blamed on the victims themselves. The reconfiguration of the class structure of the black community has not changed the fundamental nature of this problem in American society.

References

Anderson, Elijah. 1990. *Streetwise: Race, Class, and Change in an Urban Community*. Chicago: University of Chicago Press.

———. 1997. The Precarious Balance: Race Man or Sellout? In *The Darden Dilemma*, ed. Ellis Cose. New York: HarperCollins.

———. 1999a. *Code of the Street: Decency, Violence, and the Moral Life of the Inner City*. New York: Norton.

———. 1999b. The Social Situation of the Black Executive. In *Cultural Territories of Race*, ed. Michele Lamont. Chicago: University of Chicago Press.

Appiah, K. Anthony, and Amy Gutman. 1996. *Color Consciousness: The Political Morality of Race*. Princeton, NJ: Princeton University Press.

Auletta, Ken. 1982. *The Underclass*. New York: Random House.

Blumer, Herbert. 1958. Race Prejudice as a Sense of Group Position. *Pacific Journal of Sociology* 1(1):3-7.

Coleman, James. 1988. Social Capital in the Creation of Human Capital. *American Journal of Sociology* 94:S95-S120.

Collins, Sharon M. 1997. *Black Corporate Executives: The Making and Breaking of a Black Middle Class*. Philadelphia: Temple University Press.

Conley, Dalton. 1999. *Being Black, Living in the Red: Race, Wealth and Social Policy in America*. Berkeley: University of California Press.

Cose, Ellis. 1993. *The Rage of a Privileged Class*. New York: HarperCollins.

Davis, Allen F. and Mark H. Haller. 1998. *The Peoples of Philadelphia: A History of Ethnic Groups and Lower-Class Life, 1790-1940*. Philadelphia: University of Pennsylvania Press.

Domhoff, G. William and Richard L. Zweigenhaft. 1998. *Diversity in the*

Power Elite: Have Women and Minorities Reached the Top? New Haven, CT: Yale University Press.

Drake, St. Clair and Horace R. Cayton. 1945. *Black Metropolis: A Study of Negro Life in a Northern City.* New York: Harper & Bros.

Du Bois, W.E.B. [1899] 1996. *The Philadelphia Negro.* Philadelphia: University of Pennsylvania Press.

———. [1903] 1990. *The Souls of Black Folk.* New York: Vintage Books.

Feagin, Joe R. and Melvin P. Sikes. 1995. *Living with Racism.* Boston: Beacon Press.

Franklin, Vincent P. 1979. *Education of Black Philadelphia: Social and Educational History of a Minority Community, 1900-1950.* Philadelphia: University of Pennsylvania Press.

Frazier, E. Franklin. 1939. *The Negro Family in the United States.* Chicago: University of Chicago Press.

———. 1957. *Black Bourgeoisie.* New York: Free Press.

Glazer, Nathan. 1989. *Affirmative Discrimination: Ethnic Inequality and Public Policy.* Cambridge, MA: Harvard University Press.

Gordon, Milton M. 1964. *Assimilation in American Life: The Role of Race, Religion, and National Origins.* New York: Oxford University Press.

Graham, Otis. 1998. *Our Kind of People: Inside America's Black Upper Class.* New York: HarperCollins.

Hacker, Andrew. 1995. *Two Nations: Black and White, Separate, Hostile, Unequal.* New York: Ballantine Books.

Hughes, Everett C. 1945. Dilemmas and Contradictions of Status. *American Journal of Sociology* 50:353-59.

Ignatiev, Noel. 1996. *How the Irish Became White.* New York: Routledge.

Kilson, Martin L. 1983. Black Bourgeoisie Revisited. *Dissent* (Winter): 85-96.

Landry, Bart. 1988. *The New Black Middle Class.* Berkeley: University of California Press.

Lane, Roger. 1986. *Roots of Violence in Black Philadelphia.* Cambridge, MA: Harvard University Press.

Lewis, David Levering. 1994. *W.E.B. Du Bois: Biography of a Race.* New York: Henry Holt.

Lieberson, Stanley. 1981. *Piece of the Pie: Black and White Immigrants Since 1880.* Berkeley: University of California Press.

Massey, Douglas S. and Nancy A. Denton. 1993. *American Apartheid: Segregation and the Making of the Underclass.* Cambridge, MA: Harvard University Press.

Morris, Aldon. 1984. *The Origins of the Civil Rights Movement: Black Communities Organizing for Change.* New York: Free Press.

Myrdal, Gunnar. [1944] 1964. *An American Dilemma,* 2 vols. New York: McGraw-Hill.

National Advisory Commission. 1968. *Report of the National Advisory Commission on Civil Disorders.* Washington, DC: U.S. Government Printing Office.

Oliver, Melvin and Thomas M. Shapiro. 1995. *Black Wealth, White Wealth: A New Perspective on Racial Inequality.* New York: Routledge.

Omi, Michael and Howard Winant. 1994. *Racial Formation in the United States: From the 1960s to the 1990s.* New York: Routledge.

Patterson, Orlando. 1977. *Ethnic Chauvinism: The Reactionary Impulse.* New York: Stein and Day.

Pettigrew, Thomas. 1980. *The Sociology of Race Relations, 1900-1980.* New York: Free Press.

Sitkoff, Harvard. 1981. *The Struggle for Black Equality.* New York: Hill and Wang.

Spear, Allan H. 1967. *Black Chicago: The Making of a Negro Ghetto, 1890-1920*. Chicago: University of Chicago Press.

Wacquant, Loic J. D. and William J. Wilson. 1989. The Cost of Racial and Class Inclusion in the Inner City. *The Annals* of the American Academy of Political and Social Science 501:8-25

Williams, Juan. 1988. *Eyes on the Prize: America's Civil Rights Years, 1954-1965*. New York: Penguin.

Wilson, William J. 1978. *The Declining Significance of Race*. Chicago: University of Chicago Press.

———. 1987. *The Truly Disadvantaged*. Chicago: University of Chicago Press.

Rising Inequality and the Case for Coalition Politics

By WILLIAM JULIUS WILSON

ABSTRACT: Income and wage inequalities in the United States have increased significantly since 1973. This article documents these changes and argues that an organized national multiracial political constituency is needed for the development and implementation of policies that will help reverse the trends of the rising inequality and ease the burdens of ordinary families. However, a vision of American society that highlights racial differences rather than commonalities makes it difficult for Americans to see the need for and appreciate the potential of mutual political support across racial lines. Accordingly, this article explains why the idea of a national multiracial coalition should be seriously considered. It also spells out the theoretical conditions that facilitate the formation of such a coalition. Finally, it discusses a current network of community grassroots organizations—the Industrial Areas Foundation—that demonstrates how obstacles to sustained interracial cooperation can be overcome.

William Julius Wilson is the Geyser University Professor at Harvard. He has been elected to the National Academy of Sciences, American Academy of Arts and Sciences, American Philosophical Society, and National Academy of Education. He was awarded the 1998 National Medal of Science. His books include Power, Racism and Privilege *(1973);* The Declining Significance of Race *(1978);* The Truly Disadvantaged *(1987);* When Work Disappears *(1996); and* The Bridge over the Racial Divide *(1999).*

NOTE: This article is derived from a larger study by the author, *The Bridge over the Racial Divide: Rising Inequality and Coalition Politics* (Berkeley: University of California Press, 1999).

H ARVARD economist Richard B. Freeman recently stated that America is approaching a two-tiered society. He argues that American ideals of political "classlessness" and shared citizenship are threatened by falling or stagnating real incomes and rising inequality. This could eventually create a society in which "the successful upper and upper-middle classes live lives fundamentally different from the working classes and the poor" (Freeman 1999, 4).

Whereas Americans experienced broadly and rapidly rising real income from the end of World War II through 1973, after 1973 average wages adjusted for inflation either declined or stagnated for most workers through 1996. Moreover, income inequality which had stabilized through the mid-1970s began to grow rapidly (see Figure 1). Whereas each of the bottom four quintiles' share of aggregate income declined from 1975 to 1997, the share of the highest quintile increased significantly, and the share of the top 5 percent rose considerably above that of the bottom three-fifths. Indeed, what is particularly striking is that the top 5 percent's increase in income exceeded the entire income of the bottom 20 percent of families.

These trends are associated with the rate of productivity growth and the level of skill bias in the economy, but they can also be related to the strength of what MIT economist Frank Levy calls "the nation's equalizing institutions," referring to "the quality of education, the welfare state, unions, international trade regulations, and the other political structures that blunt the most extreme market outcomes and try to insure that most people benefit from economic growth" (Levy 1998, 3). As Levy points out, "We cannot legislate the rate of productivity growth and we cannot legislate the economy's level of skill bias in technological change and trade. That is why equalizing institutions are important" (4).

Signs indicate that this rising inequality has slowed in the last two years due to the continued strong economic recovery and may enter a period of remission as long as the economy remains strong. However, except for a recent increase in productivity growth, there is little evidence to suggest that the basic shifts in the economy that have been associated with the rise in inequality are changing (Ellwood 1998). Accordingly, I see the need for a national multiracial political coalition with a broad-based agenda to strengthen our equalizing institutions. A large, strong, and organized political constituency is essential for the development and implementation of policies necessary to reverse the trends of the rising inequality and to ease the burdens of ordinary families.

Political power is disproportionately concentrated among the elite, most advantaged segments of society. The monetary, trade, and tax policies of recent years have arisen from and, in turn, deepened this power imbalance. And, although elite members of society have benefited, ordinary families have fallen further behind. However, as long as middle- and lower-class groups are fragmented along racial lines, they will fail to see how their combined efforts could change the political

FIGURE 1
**SHARE OF AGGREGATE INCOME RECEIVED BY EACH
FIFTH AND TOP 5 PERCENT OF ALL FAMILIES, 1975-1997**

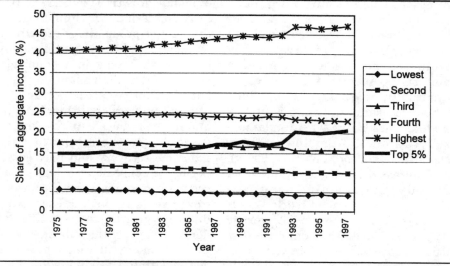

SOURCE: U.S. Bureau of the Census 1998.

imbalance and thus promote policies that reflect their interests. Put another way, a vision of American society that highlights racial differences rather than commonalities makes it difficult for us to see the need for and appreciate the potential of mutual political support across racial lines.

Accordingly, as the new millennium dawns, the movement for racial equality needs a new political strategy. That strategy must appeal to America's broad multiracial population while addressing the many problems that afflict disadvantaged minorities and redressing the legacy of historic racism in America. But in the last decade, the nation seems to have become more divided on issues pertaining to race. Affirmative action programs are under heavy assault, and broad public sympathy for those minority individuals who have suffered the most from racial exclusion has waned.

Today, it seems imperative that the concerns of both the larger American population and the racial minority population be simultaneously addressed. However, political strategies designed to ease the economic problems that confront the majority of Americans will not be found until whites, African Americans, Latinos, Asians, and Native Americans begin thinking less about their differences and more about the things they have in common—including problems, aspirations, and hopes.

I believe that proponents of racial equality can pursue policies that unite rather than divide racial groups, thus opening the way for the formation of a multiracial progressive coalition in national politics.

THE CHALLENGES
OF AMERICAN RACISM

Racial tolerance, as expressed in national attitudinal polls, has increased significantly in the last several decades (Patterson 1997; Thernstrom and Thernstrom 1997). However, the idea that the federal government "has a special obligation to help improve the living standards of blacks because they have been discriminated against so long" was supported by only one in five whites in 1991 (Bobo and Kluegel 1993).

Several decades ago, efforts to raise the public's awareness about the plight of African Americans helped the enactment of civil rights legislation and, later, affirmative action programs. By the 1980s, however, African American leaders' assertion that black progress was a "myth," rhetoric used to reinforce arguments for stronger race-based programs (compare Hill 1978), ironically played into the hands of conservative white critics. Although the leaders' assertion may have increased sympathy among some whites for the plight of black Americans, it also created the erroneous impression that federal antidiscrimination efforts had largely failed. And it overlooked the significance of the complex economic changes that have affected the black population since the early 1970s. Perhaps most pernicious of all, arguments for more and more government race-based programs to help African Americans fed

growing concerns, aroused by demagogic messages, that any special effort by politicians to deal with black needs and complaints were coming at the expense of the white majority (Greenberg 1995; Fine and Weis 1998).

Meanwhile, from the early 1970s through the first half of the 1990s, national and international economic transformations placed new stresses on families and communities—stresses hardly confined to blacks. Along with African Americans, large segments of the white, Latino, Asian, and Native American populations also experienced growing economic insecurities, family breakups, and community stresses. Such conditions could hardly fail to breed racial and ethnic tensions.

In this social climate, some conservatives have attempted to unite white Americans around anger at the government and racial minorities. Their political messages seem plausible to many white taxpayers, who see themselves as being forced to pay for programs perceived as benefiting primarily racial minorities. For example, focus group discussions among blue-collar whites reveal that they direct some of their anger concerning high taxes at black welfare recipients (Greenberg 1995). Another study reveals that even whites who have received public assistance expressed the same anger. In an interview of working-class men and women in the cities of Buffalo and Jersey City, Michelle Fine and Lois Weis found that "although many, if not most, of the white men interviewed have themselves been out of work and have received government benefits and at times welfare benefits (including food stamps), they see themselves as deserving of such benefits, in contrast to blacks whom they see as freeloaders" (Fine and Weis 1998, 21).

Many liberals maintain that such findings reflect underlying feelings of American racism and that the conservative political messages during the first half of the 1990s were effective because they spoke to such feelings. Accordingly, these American liberals are pessimistic about efforts to bring blacks, whites, and other racial groups together in a progressive political coalition. They contend that racist sentiments among many in the society at large will severely hamper such efforts. This argument is pervasive and widely shared. But it is based on an inadequate understanding of the changing nature and dynamics of racial antagonism in this society.

ECONOMIC ANXIETY,
POLITICAL RHETORIC,
AND RACIAL ANTAGONISMS

The degree of support for social policies to address racial inequality is in no small measure related to feelings of economic anxiety. When affirmative action programs were first discussed in the 1960s, the economy was expanding and incomes were rising. It was a time of optimism, a time when most Americans believed that their children would have better lives than they had. During such times, a generosity of spirit permits consideration of sharing an expanding pie.

In the decades immediately after World War II, all income groups experienced economic advancement, including the poor. A rising tide did indeed lift all boats. In fact, between 1947 and 1973, the lowest quintile in family income experienced the highest growth in annual income, which meant that the poor were becoming less poor not only in relative terms but in absolute terms as well (Bronfenbrenner et al. 1996). This pattern changed, however, in the early 1970s (see Figure 2). Economic growth slowed and the distribution of inflation-adjusted income became more unequal. Whereas average income gains from 1974 to 1997 continued for the higher quintiles, especially the top fifth, the lowest quintile actually experienced annual declines in income during this period and the second lowest stagnating incomes.

Data on individual wages from 1974 to 1996, based on deciles instead of quintiles, show a pattern in which the bottom of the distribution fell even more (see Figure 3). In general, the wages of those at the top continued to climb through this period, while the wages of those below the eighth decile cutoff, the overwhelming majority of workers, declined steadily.

In the 1990s, the bottom of the wage distribution stopped its downward plunge, due in large measure to four increases in the minimum wage (Krueger 1997). On the other hand, the middle of the distribution started to sag (see Figure 4). The sagging middle of the distribution, which represents a substantial portion of American workers, "is a major

FIGURE 2
REAL AVERAGE FAMILY INCOME GROWTH BY QUINTILE, 1947-1973 AND 1974-1997

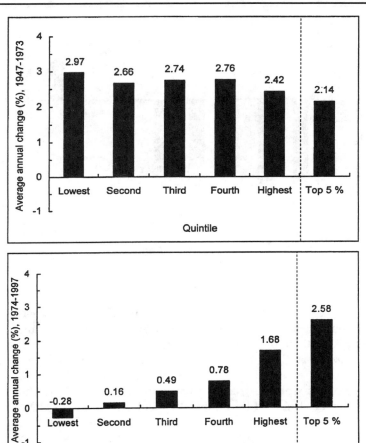

SOURCES: Figures for 1947-1973 are from U.S. Bureau of the Census 1975; 1993. Figures for 1974-1997 are from U.S. Bureau of the Census 1997. Annual change is calculated using 1997 CPI-U adjusted dollars.

reason for the subdued wage growth in the 1990s" (Krueger 1997, 3).

Since 1979, the median wage for Americans overall, after adjustments are made for inflation, has dipped 10 percent, and the hardest hit have been workers without a college degree—a category that represents three-quarters of the labor force. For example, male high school graduates with five years' work experience have lost an average of almost 30 percent in real wages since 1979. If the economic trends in place before 1973 had continued, argued economic analyst Jeff Faux in

FIGURE 3
WAGE GROWTH FOR ALL WORKERS, 1974-1996

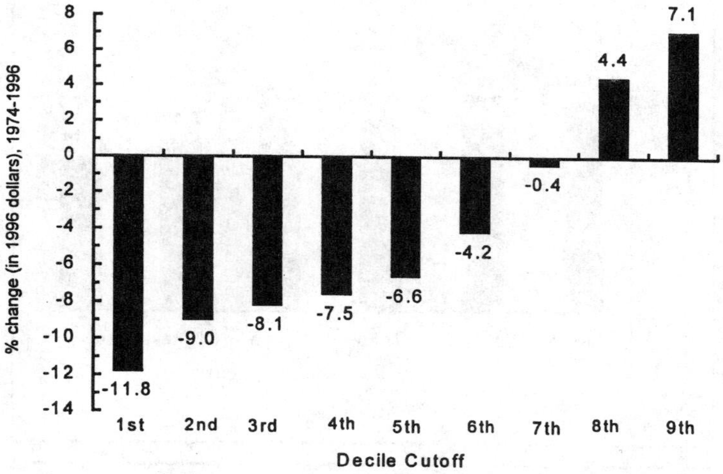

SOURCE: Bernstein and Mishel 1997.

1977, "a young male high school graduate would be making an annual income of $33,000, as opposed to his current income of $13,000" (Faux 1997, 25).

Many families were unwilling to accept the lower standard that their real income implied. Women therefore flooded the labor market, many out of choice, but a sizable percentage out of necessity. "And household debt increased from 58.9% of disposable income in 1973 to an astonishing 94.8% in 1997" (Richmond 1997, 12).

Thus, the downward trend in wages during the past two decades has lowered the incomes of the least well-off citizens. Throughout the first half of the 1990s, this trend was accompanied by a growing sense among an increasing number of Americans that their long-term economic prospects were bleaker. And they would not be reassured to learn

that the United States has had the most rapid growth of wage inequality in the Western world. In the 1950s and 1960s, the average earnings of college graduates were only about 20 percent higher than those of high school graduates. By 1979, it had increased to 49 percent, and then it rapidly grew to 83 percent by 1992.

Across the board, high-skill groups—college graduates, professionals, managers, older workers—have obtained greater pay increases than low-skill groups. The pay of professional men, for instance, increased by 6 percent while that of laborers fell by 21 percent and that of machine operators fell by 16 percent. The only low-paid group whose wages increased were women whose pay rose relative to men (though there still remains a male-female pay gap). (Freeman 1999, 8)

Although the ratio of earnings of the median college graduate worker

FIGURE 4
REAL EARNINGS GROWTH, SELECTED DECILES AND PERIODS

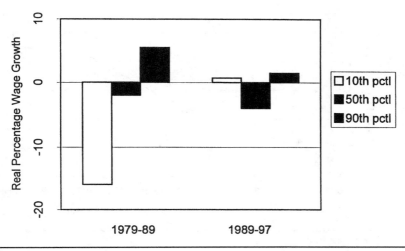

SOURCE: Krueger 1997.

to the median high school graduate may have reached a plateau in the latter half of the 1990s, in the late 1980s and early 1990s the payoff to education climbed to record levels (see Figure 5). Nearly half the rise in wage dispersion in the 1980s was due to education and experience. "Other breakdowns by skill level (e.g., based on occupational categories) also show that skilled workers have experienced an increase in earnings while less-skilled workers have suffered real declines in the last 20 years" (Krueger 1997, 7).

Less skilled workers also have faced less favorable employment circumstances. Occupations that typically require higher education have had much stronger job growth. For example, between 1984 and 1994, while the fraction of the employed male population increased by 1 per-

cent for college graduates, it fell by 3 percent for high school graduates and 10 percent for high school dropouts. The share of total working hours contributed by college graduates grew from 20 percent of the workforce in 1980 to 26 percent in 1994 (Krueger 1997). Thus, the trends, including the decline of real wages (that is, wages adjusted for inflation), that had begun in the early 1970s continued uninterrupted through the first half of the 1990s.

Working-class Americans felt economically pinched, barely able to maintain current standards of living even on two incomes. Seven and a half million workers held two or more jobs in 1996, an increase of 65 percent since 1980 (Hewlett and West 1998). Lawrence Mishel and Jared Bernstein of the Economic Policy

FIGURE 5
RISING PAYOFF TO EDUCATION, 1978-1996

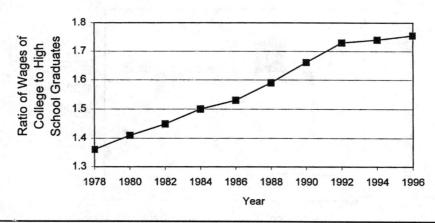

SOURCE: Krueger 1997.

Institute examined national data on the explanations respondents give for holding more than one job. They reported that "'economic hardship,' the need to meet regular expenses or pay off debts," was the primary reason. Indeed, three-fourths of the roughly 1.17 million additional multiple-job holders between 1979 and 1989 said that they were working at more than one job because of economic hardship (Mishel and Bernstein 1993).

Commenting on this situation, Richard Freeman states:

Falling incomes and rising inequality have occurred despite U.S. success in generating jobs and a huge work effort by Americans. Since 1974, the U.S. employment/population ratio has grown from 65 percent to 71 percent while Organization of Economic Cooperation and Development (OECD) Europe's has fallen from 65 percent to 60 percent. Americans work considerably more hours and take less vacation than Europeans; according to the newest OECD data, we even work more than the Japanese. The experience of prolonged earnings declines and rising inequality in the context of job growth and economic expansion is unprecedented in U.S. economic history. (Freeman 1999, 8-9)

Many workers were insecure about keeping their jobs. For example, a 1994 nationwide poll revealed that 40 percent of the workers in America worried that that they might be laid off or have their wages reduced (Bronfenbrenner et al. 1996). Many feared that they would never be able to afford to send their children to college. Many believed that despite all their hard work, their children's lives would be worse than theirs. A 1995 Harris poll conducted for *Business Week* revealed that only half of all parents expected their children to have a better life than theirs; nearly 7 out of 10 believed that the American dream has been more difficult to achieve during the past 10 years; and three-quarters felt that the dream would be even harder to achieve during the next 10 years (Bronfenbrenner et al. 1996).

The economic anxiety evident during the first half of the 1990s lingered on through the more robust economic period in the second half of the 1990s, albeit in a reduced form. Perhaps this explains why so much worker restraint occurred during the mid- to late 1990s in the face of a prolonged economic recovery. Since 1993, the U.S. economy has added more than 14 million jobs. And the unemployment rate declined to 4.2 percent in March 1999, the lowest in 30 years. Yet prices have not increased very much, in part because wages, the main element of costs, have not (except in the last two years) increased much either.[1]

Despite high levels of employment and labor shortages in some areas, workers have been surprisingly hesitant to demand higher wages. Few would have predicted that kind of behavior in such a favorable job market. "Apparently the recession and initially jobless recovery left a deep mark on the national psyche" (Krugman 1997, 21). Workers' confidence has been shaken by downsizing and the specter—real or imagined—that many of their jobs can be done for a fraction of their salaries by workers in third world countries (Krugman 1997).

A recent survey of a random sample of the American public revealed an expressed concern about the sending of jobs overseas by American companies among 68 percent of the respondents overall and 72 percent of the noncollege graduates (Krueger 1997). Commenting on this finding, Krueger states, "The fact that the public is so scared of globalization may mean that wage demands have been moderated as a result." Workers in the United States feel that they cannot rely on weak unions to bargain effectively for higher wages, and if they lose their jobs they feel compelled to take other employment soon on whatever terms they can get. "With such a nervous and timid workforce," states Krugman, "the economy can gallop along for a while without setting in motion a wage/price spiral. And so we are left with a paradox: we have more or less full employment only because individual workers do not feel secure in their jobs. . . . The secret of our success is not productivity, but anxiety" (1997, 21).

Unfortunately, during periods when people are beset with economic anxiety, they become more receptive to simplistic ideological messages that deflect attention from the real and complex sources of their problems. These messages increase resentment and often result in public support for mean-spirited initiatives. Candidates for public office and elected officials advance arguments that hinge on the apprehensions of families, including arguments that associate the drop in their living standards with programs for minorities, immigrants, and the welfare poor (Wilson 1987). During periods of economic duress, it is therefore vitally important that leaders channel citizens' frustrations in more positive or constructive directions.

During the first half of the 1990s, a period of heightened economic anxiety as the country was staggering from the effects of the 1990-1992 recession, just the opposite frequently occurred. The poisonous rhetoric of certain highly visible spokespersons (such as Pat Buchanan, Louis Farrakhan, Al Sharpton, David Duke, Rush Limbaugh, Governor Pete Wilson, as well as former House Speaker Newt Gingrich and several other House members who framed the 1994 Personal Responsibility Act in the Republican "Contract with America") increased racial tensions and channeled frustrations in ways that divided groups in America. Instead of associating citizens' problems with economic and political changes, these divisive messages encouraged them to turn on each other—race against race, and citizens against immigrants. Perhaps economist Jeff Faux sums it up best:

Health care and pension coverage for the typical family has shrunk, full-time permanent jobs are disappearing, and families are putting in longer working hours. As the slowdown in economic growth reduced tax revenues, the public sector's ability to respond to the squeeze on working families has been undercut. Finally, the staggering loss of access to reasonably well-paid jobs for the non-college educated has knocked the rungs out of the ladder of upward mobility, the traditional route through which minorities and immigrants have been integrated into American society. As a result, economic competition among middle- and lower-income workers has intensified, heightening racial and ethnic tensions. And it has fanned the embers of nativist politics while dampening those of the American dream. (Faux 1997, 26)

We must understand that racial antagonisms are products of situations—economic, political, and social. Average citizens do not fully understand the complex forces that have increased their economic woes—the slowing of economic growth and the declines in annual real family income and changes in the global economy and the rise in wage dispersion. They are looking for answers as they cope with their own anxieties.

The answers that most recently proved to be the most powerful and persuasive to the general public have come not from progressives, who are more likely to associate economic and social problems with the complex changes of the late twentieth century. Rather, they have come from conservative spokespersons who utter effective, often mean-spirited sound bites that deflect attention from the real sources of our problems.

Sadly, these sound bites include messages directed against minorities and affirmative action, immigrants, and welfare recipients. The effectiveness of these messages was demonstrated in the months leading up to and following the congressional election of 1994, when conservative Republicans gained control of the U.S. Congress. However, since 1996 the frequency and intensity of these messages have noticeably decreased. I think that we can thank continued improvement in the economy for that. Ordinary Americans are still economically anxious and continue to be worried about their future, and with good reason, but various Harris polls conducted in 1997 and 1998 reveal that they are more satisfied today than they were in 1994 when the Republicans took over Congress and in 1995 when conservative political leaders perceived that their pronouncements about the adverse effects of affirmative action, welfare, and immigration would resonate with the general population. I believe that now is the time for proponents of multiracial coalitions to build on this shift in the public's mood.

TOWARD AN EFFECTIVE
MULTIRACIAL POLITICAL
COALITION

Despite the persistence of racial antagonisms, if we develop a new public dialogue on how our problems should be defined and how they should be addressed, we can create a climate in the United States that bridges the divide among groups and lay the foundation for multiracial political cooperation. It is important to appreciate, first of all, that the poor and the working classes of all racial groups struggle to make ends meet and that even the middle class has experienced a decline in its living standard. And unlike the top 20 percent of the U.S. population, these groups are struggling. Indeed, "virtually all of the past decade's economic growth has gone to the upper 5 percent of families. Since the early 1970s, while the income of the top 1 percent of households has doubled, family and household incomes have

stagnated or declined for 80 percent of the population" (Freeman 1999, 8). Thus, despite improvements in the economy, these Americans continue to worry about unemployment and job security, declining real wages, escalating medical and housing costs, the availability of affordable child care programs, the sharp decline in the quality of public education, and crime and drug trafficking in their neighborhoods.

Furthermore, inequality in the labor market is growing at the same time that new constraints on the use of federal resources to address social inequities have emerged. The retirement of the baby boomers over the next 20 to 30 years will increase the burden on Medicare and social security, with powerful consequences for overall tax and spending decisions. Programs earmarked for the poor could undergo sharper cuts and even elimination. In addition to new time limits on the receipt of welfare benefits, public housing and food stamp programs have been cut for impoverished Americans. Eroding public sector support for the poor seems destined to increase pressures for economic survival in the low-wage labor market. Millions of the jobless poor now receiving welfare assistance are slated to enter the labor market, where they will compete with the working poor for available jobs. And, to repeat, even substantial segments of the middle class have experienced a decline in their living standards.

Also, changes in the American family structure have increased the need for social and family support among all racial groups. When I speak of the need for a multiracial coalition to address the problems of ordinary families, it should be noted that a large segment of such families feature a lone parent. One-quarter of all families and 6 of every 10 black families today are lone-parent families, and most of these single parents are never-married mothers (U. S. Bureau of the Census 1997). Today, one-half of all marriages end in divorce, and only one-half of divorced fathers make the payments that they owe by law in support of their children. If current trends continue, one-half of the children in the United States will experience at least part of their childhood in a lone-parent family (Luker 1996). "Families with multiple earners rise toward the top of the family income distribution, while families with just one earner fall toward the bottom," observes economist James K. Galbraith. "As the number of single-headed households rises, so too will inequality. This pattern is compounded in the real world by the grim fact that single-headed households also comprise, to a large extent, those with the most unstable employment experiences at the lowest hourly wages" (Galbraith 1998, 12).

These changes in family structure have been accompanied by significant changes in work and family responsibilities. Since the 1940s, the proportion of women in the labor force has increased, especially since 1970, when women's rates of labor force participation began to accelerate. In 1950, only one-third of high-school-educated women were employed; today two-thirds are working. More than half of women

with young children are also working, twice as many as two decades ago. And working women tend to do most of their family's housework despite their employment outside the home (Greenberg 1997; Robinson and Godbera 1997).

In addition to these burdens, women have taken on increasing responsibility for the care of older relatives. "In the past decade, such caregiving has increased threefold," states Stanley Greenberg. "Almost three-quarters of those caring for the elderly are women, two-thirds of whom work outside the home. This is why ordinary Americans are starting to demand a serious debate about social and family support, even as the country's elite are pressing ahead with a long-term bipartisan agenda centered on deficit reduction, entitlement reform, and free trade" (Greenberg 1997, 292).

Despite being officially race neutral, programs created in response to these concerns—programs that increase employment opportunities and job skills training, improve public education, promote better child and health care, strengthen supports for working lone-parent families, and reduce neighborhood crime and drug abuse—would profoundly benefit the minority poor, but they would also benefit large segments of the remaining population, including the white majority.

The results of national opinion polls suggest the possibility of a new alignment in support of a comprehensive social rights initiative that would include such programs (Wilson 1999; Hochschild and Rogers forthcoming). If such an alignment is attempted, it should feature a new public rhetoric focused on problems that plague broad segments of the American public—from the jobless poor to the struggling working and middle classes—and emphasize integrative programs that would promote the social and economic well-being of all groups. But these groups will have to be effectively mobilized in order to change the current course taken by policy makers. I believe that the best way to accomplish this is through coalition politics.

Because an effective political coalition in part depends upon how the issues to be addressed are defined, I want to repeat that it is imperative that the political message underscore the need for economic and social reform that benefits all groups, not just America's minority poor. The framers of this message should be cognizant of the fact that changes in the global economy have increased social inequality and enhanced opportunities for antagonisms between different racial groups. They also should be aware that these groups, although often seen as adversaries, are potential allies in a reform coalition because they suffer from a common problem: economic distress caused by forces beyond their control.

Supporters of a multiracial political coalition would certainly be aided by a broader vision of American race relations. This vision would acknowledge the existence of racial ideology and its past and present impact on the lives of minority individuals and families, but it would also recognize other important social processes that affect the quality of race relations in society and the life chances of individuals and families.

GENERATING INTERRACIAL
COOPERATION AND
COALITION BUILDING

The case for a progressive multiracial political coalition must be made in political messages that resonate with broad segments of the American population. How this is accomplished will partly depend upon how we define the issues to be addressed. The political message calling for change and outlining the need for a multiracial coalition ought to emphasize the benefits that would accrue to all groups who are struggling economically in America, not just poor minorities. The message should encompass the idea that changes in the global economy have enhanced social inequality and created situations that have heightened antagonisms between different racial and ethnic groups and that, although these groups are seen as social adversaries, they are potential allies in a reform coalition. Why? Because they are all negatively affected more or less by impersonal global economic changes.

Given the racial friction that has marred intergroup interaction in urban America, the formation of a multiracial reform coalition presents a challenge. Indeed, the contemporary emphasis on racial division and racial ideology make it difficult to promote the idea of a multiracial political coalition to develop and pursue a mass-based economic agenda.

TABLE 1

**ARE THE PROBLEMS OF PEOPLE LIKE YOU
(OR FAMILIES LIKE YOURS) GETTING WORSE?**

| | Percentage Saying "Worse" or "Harder" | | | |
Problem	Whites	African Americans	Latinos	Asian Americans
Public schools	55	57	45	47
To get good jobs	56	60	50	56
To find decent, affordable housing	55	49	55	48
For families like yours to stay together	45	48	40	34
Health care	44	39	30	30
Number of respondents	802	474	252	353

SOURCE: Hochschild and Rogers forthcoming.

Beginning with the riots in Los Angeles in 1992, and especially after the 1995 O. J. Simpson murder trial, media attention to racial matters has highlighted those factors that divide us.

Although it is important to acknowledge the racial divisions in America so that they can be meaningfully addressed, the incessant attention given to these gaps has obscured the following fact: blacks, whites, Latinos, Asians, and Native Americans share many concerns, are besieged by many similar problems, and have important norms, values, and aspirations in common. Take the issue of values. An analysis of the responses to questions that were variously asked in national surveys conducted by the National Opinion Research Center's General Social Survey since 1982 reveals only marginal racial differences in core values pertaining to work, education, the family, religion, law enforcement, and civic duty. For example, in a 1982 survey, 90 percent of whites and 89 percent of blacks felt that one's own family and children were

very important; in a 1984 survey, 88 percent of whites and 95 percent of blacks felt that the obligation of American citizens to do community service was very or somewhat important; and in a 1993 survey, 95 percent of whites and 92 percent of blacks felt that hard work in life outcomes was either important or very important, and 97 percent of blacks and 88 percent of whites supported the view that being self-sufficient was either very important or one of the most important things in life (National Opinion Research Center 1982, 1984, 1993).[2]

Also consider the perception of problems. Survey questions about whether problems pertaining to public schools, jobs, affordable housing, families, and health care were getting worse or harder for the people with whom the respondents identified ("people like you or families like yours") elicited considerable agreement across racial and ethnic groups (see Table 1).

Furthermore, consider views on major policy issues. Except for affirmative action and abortion, no

TABLE 2
POLICY PREFERENCES FOR CONGRESSIONAL ACTION

Policy Issue	Whites	Percentage Saying "Strongly Feel Congress Should Do"		
		African Americans	Latinos	Asian Americans
Limit tax breaks for business	39	41	41	30
Balance the budget	82	79	75	75
Cut personal income taxes	52	50	55	46
Reform the welfare system	83	73	81	68
Reform Medicare	53	58	59	58
Put more limits on abortion	35	32	50	24
Limit affirmative action	38	25	30	27
Number of respondents	802	474	252	353

SOURCE: Hochschild and Rogers forthcoming.

notable differences are detected across racial and ethnic groups on reported strong preferences for congressional action—with overwhelming support for balancing the budget and changing the welfare system, less enthusiasm for cutting personal income taxes and reforming Medicare, and even less for business tax breaks (see Table 2). Finally, as Jennifer Hochschild and Reuel Rogers point out, there is considerable convergence in views across racial and ethnic groups with regard to policy preferences for solving particular problems, including education, crime, gang violence, and drugs (Hochschild and Rogers forthcoming).

The development and articulation of an ideological vision that captures and highlights commonalities in basic core values and attitudes are paramount in establishing the case for a progressive multiracial political coalition and defusing the opposition of pessimists who promote the more limited advantages of group-specific political mobilization (Sonenshein

1990). Social psychological research on interdependence reveals that when people believe that they need each other, they relinquish their initial prejudices and stereotypes and are able to join in programs that foster mutual interaction and cooperation. Moreover, when people from different groups do get along, their perceptions about and behavior toward each other undergo change (Johnson, Johnson, and Maruyama 1984). Under such circumstances, not only do participants in the research experiment make efforts to behave in ways that do not disrupt the interaction but they also make an effort to express consistent and similar attitudes and opinions about an issue that confronts and concerns them (Johnson, Johnson, and Maruyama 1984).

These conclusions are based mainly on David W. Johnson, Roger Johnson, and Geoffrey Maruyama's review and analysis of 98 experimental studies of goal interdependence and interpersonal attraction. They revealed support in the research literature for the idea that interpersonal attraction among different racial and ethnic groups is enhanced by cooperative experiences. One reason for enhanced cooperation is that "within cooperative situations participants benefit from encouraging others to achieve whereas in competitive situations participants benefit from obstructing others' efforts to achieve" (Johnson, Johnson, and Maruyama 1984, 199). Accordingly, promotive interaction is greater within situations that are cooperative than in those that are competitive. The research reported considerably more interaction across ethnic lines in cooperative situations and more cross-ethnic helping in such situations as well. In addition, the research indicated that cooperative situations enhance social perspective taking—"the ability to understand how a situation appears to another person and how that person is reacting cognitively and emotionally to it" (200). Finally, the research revealed that within cooperative situations, "participants seemed to have a differentiated view of collaborators and tended to minimize perceived differences in ability and view all collaborators as being equally worthwhile, regardless of their performance level or ability" (202).

This research suggests the need for effective leadership to develop and articulate an ideological vision that not only highlights common interests, norms, values, aspirations, and goals, but also helps individuals and groups appreciate the importance of interracial cooperation to achieve and sustain them. This does not mean that group differences are not acknowledged in this vision. As Harvard sociologist Marshall Ganz has pointed out, "Acknowledging differences is essential to collaborating around common interest. . . . It is important not to pretend that we are all the same." He notes that racial and ethnic groups have important differences, "but these become resources rather than liabilities if we come up with ways to [build] on our commonalities" (Ganz 1998).

Visionary group leaders, especially those that head strong community organizations, are essential for articulating and communicating this vision as well as for developing and sustaining this multiracial political coalition. According to Sonenshein, the most effective coalitions are those that begin building in communities with strong political organizations already in place (Sonenshein 1990).

Nonetheless, there is a common perception that, given America's history of racial division and its current racism, it is naive to assume that a national multiracial coalition with a mass-based economic agenda could ever materialize. Many who share this perception do not consider seriously the possibility of creating the conditions of perceived interdependence needed to promote interracial cooperation and coalition building. Nor do they entertain the idea that given the right social circumstances, including the presence of creative, visionary leaders, such conditions could emerge.

However, there are cases from historical and contemporary America that would not support such pessimism. A comprehensive study of interracial unionism during the Great Depression, for example, reveals that the United Auto Workers in Detroit and the Steel Workers Organizing Committee and the United Mine Workers, both primarily in Pennsylvania, were "able to organize a racially mixed labor force in settings where past racial antagonisms and minority strike-breaking had been sources of labor defeat" (Brueggemann and Boswell 1998, 437). The interracial solidarity was facilitated by a number of factors that relate to some of the general principles about perceived interdependence and that represent structural conditions conducive to interracial cooperation. These include racial convergence of orientations toward the labor market, a favorable political context featuring legislation (for example, the Wagner Act) that facilitated organizing activities, and changes in organizing tactics "that institutionalize racial inclusiveness in the union structure" (Brueggemann and Boswell 1998, 442).

Moreover, on the current scene, multiracial grassroots community organizations whose institutions, actions, and belief systems exemplify the very conditions of perceived interdependence do in fact exist in this country. These groups benefit from the presence of forward-looking leaders who have effectively mobilized groups in their communities to achieve local goals. A notable example is the national community organization networks of the Industrial Areas Foundation.

CASE STUDY OF AN EFFECTIVE
GRASSROOTS MULTIRACIAL
POLITICAL COALITION

More than 50 years ago, Saul Alinsky founded the Industrial Areas Foundation (IAF) in conjunction with his efforts to organize Chicago's marginalized poor. Alinsky envisioned a team of professional organizers who could identify committed individuals, assemble them for group action, and instruct them in effective methods of community improvement. Through this method, the IAF could help individuals organize into potentially powerful coalitions; IAF professionals could move from place to place in their mission of education and development, while the work of community development and improvement could be carried out by the people with the greatest stake in its success.

Today, dynamic IAF organizations are active in a national network of 40 communities from California to Massachusetts. To achieve this success, IAF professional organizers have worked within faith-based organizations—in most cases, Christian churches—to identify experienced leaders and to assemble them into nonsectarian coalitions devoted to community development. An important feature of the IAF approach is that, even though the members of the coalition are drawn from faith communities, the IAF assembly constitutes an independent organization that is not tied to the participants' respective churches.

IAF organizations are known by many names—Greater Boston Interfaith Organization; Tying Nashville Together; East Brooklyn Churches, New York; Baltimoreans United in Leadership Development; and Valley Organized Community Efforts, in Los Angeles County—and each reflects the distinctive needs of its community. The agenda of each organization is determined by its leaders and members, not by the IAF.

Some of the IAF's most successful organizations are in Texas, where 11 IAF institutions are active across the state. Included among these is the San Antonio-based Communities Organized for Public Service (COPS), the largest, longest-standing IAF institution in the country and generally regarded as one of the strongest community organizations in the nation. COPS initiatives have resulted in hundreds of millions of dollars of infrastructural improvements in poor inner-city neighborhoods of San Antonio through the upgrading or repair of streets, sidewalks, public lighting, and sewer drainage and the establishment or construction of parks and libraries. In addition, COPS has been responsible for the construction or rehabilitation of thousands of units of housing (Cortes 1994).

In Texas, the IAF has created a model statewide network that has effectively influenced political decisions in municipal governments, the state legislature, and the governor's mansion. Furthermore, the network has brought together whites, African Americans, Mexican Americans, Catholics, and Protestants for mutual support in addressing matters of common concern and interest.

In mobilizing leadership in Texas, the IAF has been able to generate and sustain interracial cooperation in three related ways. First, in initially establishing its multiracial organization, the Texas IAF relies on its members' shared commitment to broad religious principles to generate trust and a sense of common identity. Second, Texas IAF issues originate from local consensus and thus are not divisive. The issues are always framed in a race-neutral manner, "emphasizing the potential benefit of its campaigns to all Americans" (Warren 1996). And third, Hispanic, African American, and white leaders are united into single local organizations but retain significant autonomy in continuing to serve in other organizations or enterprises that address race- and neighborhood-specific issues that are not part of the Texas IAF agenda, "as long as they remain within the broad unitary framework of the IAF" (Warren 1996).

CONCLUSION

Adequate political solutions to the global economic problems confronting the majority of Americans will not be found until whites, African Americans, Latinos, Asians, and Native Americans begin thinking more about what they have in common and less about their differences. To clear the path for the formation of a national progressive, multiracial political coalition, it is important that proponents of social equality pursue policies that unite rather than divide racial groups.

Although elites invariably have a say in the leadership of the nation, the voice of the people can be muffled by fragmenting the masses into competing, divisive race-based groups. A sustained upward trend in the economy improved conditions in the late 1990s. The lessening of the social tensions that come with such an economic improvement allows us room to discuss our country's future and to drive home the point that the needs of ordinary, working Americans can best be met by multiracial, broad-based coalitions.

Notes

1. In addition to the stability of wages, other factors have kept prices from rising significantly. As Uchitelle points out, a rise in the productivity rate since 1997 has also kept prices in check. Workers are producing more goods and services per hour on the job, and the extra revenue from the sales of these "additional goods and services has helped maintain profits without price increases." He also notes that the economic crisis in Asia is helping to hold prices down "in two ways. Asian currencies are falling in relation to the dollar, making American products more expensive in those currencies. To compete, United States exporters are cutting their prices in dollars. Imports from Asia, on the other hand, are less expensive in dollars, also dampening inflation" (Uchitelle 1997, 4).

2. Considering the prevailing stereotypes, the findings on self-sufficiency are counterintuitive. Although there is a 9 percent racial gap, an overwhelming majority of respondents from both races strongly supported the idea of self-sufficiency. Another finding that should be mentioned pertains to views on the importance of being married. Whereas 43 percent of the black respondents felt that being married was very important or one of the most important things in life, 53 percent of the white respondents felt this way.

References

Bernstein, Jared and Lawrence Mishel. 1997. Has Wage Inequality Stopped Growing? *Monthly Labor Review* Dec.:3-16.

Bobo, Lawrence and James R. Kluegel. 1993. Opposition to Race Targeting: Self-Interest, Stratification Ideology, or Racial Attitudes. *American Sociological Review* 58:443-64.

Bronfenbrenner, Urie, Stephen Ceci, Phylliss Moen, Peter McClelland, and Elaine Wethington. 1996. *The State of Americans: This Generation and the Next*. New York: Free Press.

Brueggemann, John and Terry Boswell. 1998. Realizing Solidarity: Sources of Interracial Unionism During the Great Depression. *Work and Occupations* 25(Nov.):436-81.

Cortes, Ernesto, Jr. 1994. Reweaving the Social Fabric. *Boston Review* June-Sept.:12-14.

Ellwood, David. 1998. Winners and Losers in America: Taking Measure of the New Economic Realities. Paper presented to the Aspen Domestic Strategy Group Meeting, July, Aspen, CO.

Faux, Jeff. 1997. You Are Not Alone. In *The New Majority*, ed. Stanley Greenberg and Theda Skocpol. New Haven, CT: Yale University Press.

Fine, Michelle and Lois Weis. 1998. *The Unknown City: Lives of Poor and Working-Class Young Adults*. Boston: Beacon Press.

Freeman, Richard B. 1999. *The New Inequality: Creating Solutions for Poor America*. Boston: Beacon Press.

Galbraith, James K. 1998. *Created Unequal: The Crisis in American Pay*. New York: Free Press.

Ganz, Marshall. 1998. Private communication, 16 Oct., Cambridge, MA.

Greenberg, Stanley B. 1995. *Middle Class Dreams: The Politics and Power of the New American Majority*. New York: Times Books.

———. 1997. Popularizing Progressive Politics. In *The New Majority*, ed. Stanley B. Greenberg and Theda Skocpol. New Haven, CT: Yale University Press.

Hewlett, Sylvia Ann and Cornel West. 1998. *The War Against Parents*. New York: Houghton Mifflin.

Hill, Robert B. 1978. *The Illusion of Black Progress*. Washington, DC: National Urban League Research Department.

Hochschild, Jennifer L. and Reuel Rogers. Forthcoming. Race Relations in a Diversifying Nation. In *New Directions: African Americans in a Diversifying Nation*, ed. James Jackson. Washington, DC: National Policy Association.

Johnson, David W., Roger Johnson, and Geoffrey Maruyama. 1984. Goal Interdependence and Interpersonal Attraction in Heterogeneous Classrooms: A Meta-Analysis. In *Groups in Contact: The Psychology of Desegregation*, ed. M. Miller and M. B. Brewer. Orlando, FL: Academic Press.

Krueger, Alan. 1997. What's up with Wages? Mimeo. Princeton, NJ: Princeton University, Industrial Relations Section.

Krugman, Paul. 1997. Superiority Complex. *New Republic*, 3 Nov., 20-21.

Levy, Frank. 1998. *The New Dollars and Dreams: American Incomes and Economic Change*. New York: Russell Sage Foundation.

Luker, Kristin. 1996. *Dubious Conception: The Politics of Teenage Pregnancy*. Cambridge, MA: Harvard University Press.

Mishel, Lawrence and Jared Bernstein. 1993. *The State of Working America 1992-1993*. Armonk, NY: Sharpe.

National Opinion Research Center. 1982-93. General Social Surveys. University of Chicago.

Patterson, Orlando. 1997. *The Ordeal of Integration: Progress and Resentment in America's Racial Crisis*. Washington, DC: Civitas.

Richmond, Henry R. 1997. Program Design: The American Land Institute. Manuscript. N.p.

Robinson, John P. and Geoffrey Godbera. 1997. *Time for Life: The Surprising Ways Americans Use Their Time*. University Park: Pennsylvania State University Press.

Sonenshein, Raphael J. 1990. Biracial Coalitions in Big Cities: Why They Succeed, Why They Fail. In *Racial Politics in American Cities*, ed. Rufus P. Browing, Dale Rogers Marshall, and David H. Tabb. New York: Longman.

Thernstrom, Stephan and Abigail Thernstrom. 1997. *America in Black and White*. New York: Simon & Schuster.

Uchitelle, Louis. 1997. As Asia Stumbles, U.S. Stays in Economic Stride. *New York Times*. 7 Dec.

U.S. Bureau of the Census. 1975. *Historical Statistics of the United States: Colonial Times to 1970*. Washington, DC: Government Printing Office.

———. 1993. *Money Income of Households, Families, and Persons in the United States: 1992*. Current Population Reports P60-184. Washington, DC: Government Printing Office.

———. 1997. *Current Population Reports*. Series P-20. Washington, DC: Government Printing Office, Mar.

———. 1998. Table F-2. Share of Aggregate Income Received by Each Fifth and Top 5 Percent of Families (All Races): 1947-1997. Available at http://www.census.gov:80/hhes/income/histinc/f02.html.

Warren, Mark R. 1996. Creating a Multi-Racial Democratic Community: Case Study of the Texas Industrial Areas Foundation. Paper presented to conference on Social Networks and Urban Poverty, 1-2 Mar., Russell Sage Foundation, New York.

Wilson, William Julius. 1987. *The Truly Disadvantaged: The Inner City, the Underclass, and Public Policy*. Chicago: University of Chicago Press.

———. 1999. *Bridge over the Racial Divide: Rising Inequality and Coalition Politics*. Berkeley: University of California Press.

ANNALS, *AAPSS*, **568**, March 2000

Du Bois as Social Activist:
Why We Are Not Saved

By MARY FRANCES BERRY

ABSTRACT: W.E.B. Du Bois completed most of his 1898 agenda, and much of the remainder has been accomplished since. And yet we are not saved. We need to reclaim race relations studies about power and institutions. Agency is only part of the story. We should remember Du Bois's emphasis on the increasing importance of black, "brown, and yellow" men and women because of "sheer numbers and physical contact." As we enter the twenty-first century, we need more studies of other people of color replicating those Du Bois proposed concerning African Americans. If scholars have any interest in being like Du Bois, they must be devoted to research but not as onlookers in the struggle for social justice. They must act to "raise" not just themselves but the race. This is the work that must be done if we want one America in the twenty-first century to be more than just a cliché but a reality.

Mary Frances Berry is Geraldine R. Segal Professor of American Social Thought at the University of Pennsylvania and chairperson of the U.S. Commission on Civil Rights. A lawyer and historian, educated at Howard University and the University of Michigan, she is a member of the District of Columbia Bar. Her most recent book is The Pig Farmer's Daughter and Other Tales of American Justice: Episodes of Racism and Sexism in the Courts *(1999).*

AMIRI Baraka describes Du Bois in *Black Renaissance* as the "first voice of the 20th century Afro-American intellectual, no longer able to be sweetly patronized by so-called friends or immediately strangled by sworn enemies, based on the formal educational subtraction created by slavery" (Baraka 1998, 18). For scholars, W.E.B. Du Bois's life provides both an inspiration and a cautionary tale. He fought unceasingly for full citizenship for blacks, from founding the Niagara movement, to leading the 1917 Silent Protest Parade in New York, to maintaining such a radical stance in *The Crisis* during World War I that the attorney general seized one of the issues, to joining William Patterson and others in bringing *We Charge Genocide* (Patterson 1970) to the United Nations in 1951.

OPPOSING BOOKER T. WASHINGTON

The Du Bois–Washington controversy over how African Americans should be educated is the most taught subject concerning Du Bois. Students often know little else, even if they learn that much. I am concerned, however, with his broad policy influence. Du Bois in the early 1900s quickly became an effective challenger of Booker T. Washington's power to decide what should be the black agenda, to control black access to presidents and other public officials, to decide whether and how black civil liberties should be defended, to stand astride most routes for advancement, and to determine the dispensation of almost all philanthropic monies. Washington could essentially make and unmake men's careers. Du Bois escaped Washington's clutches because he did not define success as other men did. He had intellectual ambitions. Du Bois might ask, "What do you think, Washington, what do you want?" In short, Washington was a player and the young Du Bois was not. Du Bois was not interested in controlling the abilities and access to power of others. "Cast down your buckets where you are," spoken by Washington at the Atlanta Exposition in 1895, and "[We will take not] one jot or tittle less than our full manhood rights," spoken by Du Bois at the second Niagara meeting at Harper's Ferry in 1906, both resonated with African Americans at the time. But, in retrospect, Washington, although he lived into the twentieth century, was a late-nineteenth-century man—a transitional leader between Frederick Douglass and Du Bois. Du Bois was the voice of black twentieth-century middle-class and middle-brow aspirations.

There were many very ignoble aspects of Du Bois's personality. He was so self-consciously elitist as to appear a snob. He was a misogynist and a sexist; a cold, indifferent, absent husband and father. He was also a philanderer, although (unlike Washington) he was apparently not a frequenter of prostitutes. He surely and as arrogantly as Washington had his own ideas about how to advance the race, although he adapted and changed his ideas over time like the good social scientist he was.

BECOMING A WORLD-CLASS SCHOLAR

Du Bois went public with his ideas at an early age, beginning with his 1880s contributions to the *Springfield Republican* and T. Thomas Fortune's *New York Globe* before he even finished high school in Great Barrington, Massachusetts. He was a public intellectual who soared as high as his wings could carry him in a lifetime of commitment, despite spending his existence in the stifling cages of Jim Crow. His article, "The Study of the Negro Problems" (Du Bois 1898), expressed the political and intellectual commitment he first embraced in writing on his twenty-fifth birthday in Berlin, where he was a graduate student. In his diary he promised to "work for the rise of the Negro people, taking for granted that their best development means the best development of the world." He outlined his plan "to make a name in science, to make a name in literature and thus to raise my race. . . . I wonder what will be the outcome?" (Du Bois 1985, 29; Lewis 1993, 38, 47).

Du Bois surely deserves his reputation as a world-class scholar. The circumstances under which he worked make his scholarly productivity all the more remarkable. The research he organized and pursued and the schedule he kept without graduate assistants or amanuenses is incredible. The Du Boisian scholarly legacy is the work of his own hands and mind. There stood or sat Du Bois thinking and writing for years, for the most part bereft of foundation grants, sabbaticals, or any of the other paraphernalia that most scholars insist is essential to their work. In 10 years, by the time he was 35, Du Bois had taught every term, written two books, a dozen monographs, and numerous articles, and laid the groundwork for much of twentieth-century scholarship on African Americans. Except for the fact that he lived so long and had multiple careers, we could ask what a reporter shouted to me years ago on the day when I became the first African American woman head of a research university (chancellor at the University of Colorado), "Don't you think you've peaked too early?"

Du Bois had a great deal of trouble adjusting to the color consciousness that pervaded American life then and still does. A 1998 poll found that people of color share negative attitudes toward whites, but they express even more bigoted views toward each other than whites do (National Conference 1998). These attitudes evolving from the long-term effects of color consciousness cause conflict between and among people of color and whites along the next frontier of the rapidly moving color line today. Early on, Du Bois seemed not entirely comfortable inside his own beige skin. This was the period when the mulatto ancestry of which he and Booker T. Washington both partook as products of that "spurious race mixture" was supposedly a sign of greater intelligence than that possessed by ordinary blacks. He would emphasize his French and German ancestry and point out that the "so-called American Negro is probably less than 25% of pure African descent" (Wintz 1996, 143-44).

Despite his racial anxieties, Du Bois later emphasized the importance of the time he spent at Atlanta University benefiting from the influences and networks of African Americans with whom he was engaged. He owed his intellectual development not just to Fisk and Harvard and his training in Germany but also to his interactions with Alexander Crummell, William Scarborough, and John Hope. He grew to understand the importance of economic factors and class analysis and to discard his emphasis on negative black behavior. He learned to place an understanding of social and economic factors at the center of his analysis. As Francille Wilson concludes in her pathbreaking work on black labor scholars, he realized that some black workers may have had "bad character" but that was not the whole story. The parched, cramped, segregated existence in the South made it necessary for him to escape to engage in serious research (Wilson 1988, 105-6, 109-11, 114-15, 141-55).

Psychologically comfortable with African Americans in the American Negro Academy and engrossed in his studies at Atlanta University, Du Bois also became an accepted participant in white mainstream organizations. His participation helped to bring about some change. In *The Annals* after 1906, for example, fewer articles invoked heredity and more cited social and economic causes for key indicators of problems among African Americans (Wilson 1988, 69-93).

LEAVING THE
ACADEMY BEHIND

Du Bois migrated from the academy to the world beyond when it was high time for the transition. In a sense, he became a social activist because he had to. The very nature of his intellectual vision, his published work and evolving ideology, and his jousting with Washington kept him and his university under constant financial stress. We may lament that there were no endowed chairs at Harvard or Penn for him or not even the assistant school superintendency in the District of Columbia that might have kept him solvent. And we may ask what he could have produced with adequate support. But in 1910, as he embarked on the even riskier enterprise of the NAACP, he knew the significance of the transition: "Stepping therefore in 1910 out of my ivory tower of statistics and investigation, I sought with my bare hands to lift the earth and put it in the path in which I ought to go" (Lewis 1993, 407). He broadened his search for solutions to the problem of social and economic inequity—and race as one of its markers. The intellectual as social activist, he remained directly in the arena from then on, wherever he worked, whether in academia or outside, unlike those who huddled in the academy, never experiencing the taste of public policy victory or defeat.

Du Bois consistently believed in the power of education. People would remain in chains unless they understood that they need not be. The centrality of this fact was brought home to me as the Dalit leadership in India explained to me in January 1999 that their greatest problem was the illiteracy of Dalits, which renders them unable to understand why they need not remain at the bottom of the heap in conformity within the rigors of caste. When they become educated, they immediately understand why they had such difficulty gaining an education. Du Bois never abandoned his elite conception of the "talented tenth," but years later he concluded that many of the talented rejected the idea of being in the social change vanguard. His disaffection increased when in 1951 he was indicted for supposedly being a Communist sympathizer. Although acquitted, he saw the talented tenth distance themselves from him. In their almost unanimous rejection of him, he was disconsolate and he bent "but did not break" (Du Bois 1968, 390-95).

Perhaps we might judge Du Bois's criticism of the talented tenth for refusing social activism as too imperiously precipitous. After all, there was his own example and that of his Niagara movement and his NAACP fellows who tried to engage in uplift activities. We might note also that three years after his experience of rejection, events in Montgomery, Alabama, and the freedom rides involved intelligent educated blacks and whites who were not immoral on the question of legal segregation. We might conclude that he died too soon when on 28 August 1963 his passing

was announced in the midst of the March on Washington during music and speeches at the Lincoln Memorial. He missed the rest of the civil rights movement, the Black Panthers, and the rebellions in the cities and the responses thereafter. Furthermore, still standing are Marian Wright Edelman and the Children's Defense Fund, Farrakhan and black solidarity movements, concerned black men and women, and divergent currents of inclusion and alienation. There was also more to come from progressives on the international front, including the antiwar protests during the Vietnam War and later the free South Africa movement, led by African Americans who surely fit his definition of the talented tenth.

On the other hand, Whitney Young and Roy Wilkins criticized the nonviolent civil disobedience movement for not working within the system, and Martin Luther King, Jr., was a pariah by 1966, not even invited to a White House conference on civil rights. Even more significant is the fact that educated blacks scattered to political office and the suburbs, and academics fled to predominantly white institutions once the opportunity arose. Economic opportunity for poor people as a major goal with activism by the talented tenth—or the talented twentieth or talented thirtieth—did not arise again from the mud of Resurrection city during the Poor People's Campaign. Whatever happened, by the way, to the Poor People's Campaign?

W.E.B. Du Bois looked at the problem of race from every imaginable angle. He evolved from an integrationist, who found Garveyism to be anti-intellectual crackpotism and pungently offensive, to a race man, to a pan-Africanist, to an economic black nationalist, to ultimately a Socialist or Communist living in Ghana and writing an *Encyclopedia Africana*. However confused he may have appeared at times, the Du Boisian epic is entirely comprehensible if we understand that his problem was our problem but worse. He lived in America, caught not just in two-ness as an African American and an American, but threeness as an intellectual adhering to the "standards" of the academy.

As inspiring as the Du Boisian epic is, it also contains a cautionary tale in assessing his scholarly achievements. Du Bois accomplished much of the work in his 1898 agenda, and in the years since, much of the remainder has been accomplished. And yet, if Derrick Bell were here, Jeremiah-like, he would surely remind us that we are not saved. Du Bois's goal that the history of race relations and African American history become legitimized was long ago accomplished. Every imaginable state and local study and synthesis has been published or is being prepared. Gender as a category of analysis, which surely Du Bois would have included if he had decided to write the agenda again in his later years, has also found an appropriate place.

The field of statistical investigation has been routinized in Census Bureau population studies and studies from the Bureau of Labor Statistics. Other government agencies including the U.S. Commission on Civil Rights have voluminously documented race discrimination.

Studies from the Urban Institute, the National Opinion Research Center (at the University of Chicago), and the Survey Research Center (at the University of Michigan) abound. Foundation-supported research from the National Academy of Sciences has proliferated. There are also Lou Harris and Gallup polls and news reports from investigative journalists.

The study of diseases beyond sickle cell anemia remains an under-researched area, although disparities and differences are well understood to exist. The propensity for high blood pressure, heart disease, diabetes, and other ills is being researched. However, research is in an incipient stage on the disparate health care African Americans receive. In the social sciences, the work of sociologists is voluminous. There also has been a virtual flood of work in folklore, music, literature, the arts, and philosophy. If Du Bois's agenda has been mostly accomplished, then why are we not saved?

ON THE WORK
YET UNDONE

We need to reclaim race relations studies about institutions and power from journalists and policy analysts in search of proving the marginal effect, if any, of racial exclusion. With our valid concern for showing the agency of African Americans, we forget that agency is only part of the story. Du Bois said in 1935 that some educated Negroes believe that the way to solve the problem of race is by "ignoring it and suppressing all reference to it." He pointed out that they think the future lies in "having their more educated and wealthy classes gradually and continually escape from their race into the mass of the American people." Since the "age-old process of raising a group is through the escape of its upper class into welcome fellowship with risen peoples, the Negro intelligentsia would submerge itself if it bent back to the task of lifting the mass of people." However, he stated, "If the leading Negro classes cannot assume and bear the uplift of their own proletariat, they are doomed for all time. It is not a case of ethics; it is a plain case of necessity" (Wintz 1996, 164).

Studies of agency should be combined with an analysis of the impact on African Americans of institutions and power centers that impede agency. However, the future lies in raising questions of race, class, gender, power, self-help, individualism, and whatever comes to hand and in avoiding a single category of analysis.

Most studies done on blacks have reflected Du Bois's 1898 faith that more research and the dissemination of information will improve opportunities and lessen the racial divide. Du Bois, however, despairing after so much time and energy spent on this approach, said,

For many years it was the theory of most Negro leaders that this attitude was the insensibility of ignorance and inexperience, that white America did not know or realize the continuing plight of the Negro. Accordingly, for the last two decades, we have striven by book and periodical, by speech and appeal, by various dramatic methods of agitation, to put the es-

sential facts before the American people. Today there can be no doubt that Americans know the facts; and yet they remain for the most part indifferent and unmoved. (Wintz 1996, 161)

Faith in the power of knowledge has necessarily inspired many studies of race relations since Du Bois's 1898 agenda. This faith received one of its highest expressions in Gunnar Myrdal's *An American Dilemma*, published in 1944. Finding a raging conflict between the American creed of democracy and racism, Myrdal ratified an approach which greatly emphasized the role of educating Americans about race, setting out the facts and defining racism as a moral issue. He concluded that if the nation became educated enough to practice its creed, then the problem of race would dissipate to the benefit of everyone (Myrdal 1944). In President Clinton's Race Initiative, the issue is again defined primarily as the need to educate Americans about race—but this time about Indians, Asian Americans, and Latinos. This information-healing approach was the driving force behind President Clinton's position on race relations in the twenty-first century that Christopher Edley, Jr., a lawyer and policy wonk and not a social scientist or humanist, was tasked to write.

Du Bois was always a big thinker who asked big questions, even though ethnocentric lists of big thinkers usually still ignore him. His big question in 1935 was, "What shall be the place of the Negro in the new industrial order?" Our big question today should be, What shall be the place of black Americans in the new technological order? (Wintz 1996, 160).

He also made big statements, like the one at the 1900 Pan African Congress that "the problem of the 20th century is the problem of the color line." He underscored the problem correctly, but as we enter the twenty-first century, the next words he uttered are more prescient:

The millions of black men in Africa, America and the Islands of the Sea, not to speak of the brown and yellow myriads elsewhere, are bound to have great influence upon the world in the future, by reason of sheer numbers and physical contact. (Lewis 1993, 250-51)

His inclusion of people of color generally, which he repeated when he later named the NAACP, is the demographic fact of the United States in the twenty-first century. We are in the midst of expanding interest in studies of individual communities of color replicating the kinds of history and social science studies Du Bois proposed in 1898 that have already for the most part been executed concerning African Americans. Scholars from different groups of people of color are already eagerly joining in the work and demanding that foundations, universities, and government support such efforts. The rationale is the same as the one Du Bois established in 1898 and in his 1893 diary—truth and objectivity will uplift the race or national origin group.

This is part of a historical process that must occur in the lives of any group of people. They want to know about themselves and hope that others will respond more favorably once they have more information. When I was in Australia recently, I noted that the Aborigines were still in the recognize-our-heritage stage and were just entering the more-information-will-set-us-free stage. It was like being in South Africa before the beginning of the end of apartheid and feeling what it might have been like in the American South in the 1940s or 1950s. The Dalits and tribals in India also appear to be at a just beginning stage. They seem to believe they had skipped over the earlier stages but discovered that having equality enshrined in a constitution is not enough.

Also we need a new focus on the impact of color consciousness and how to address it. I do not mean positing some simplistic misleading notion that the nation is color-blind and we all should forget what color people are and the race problem will disappear. Examining our research and experiences concerning interactions between African Americans and whites can provide an angle of vision for understanding that the essence of racism is color consciousness, which serves as a marker for social and economic inequality. Whenever Europeans have encountered darker people, this phenomenon has existed, and it continues to influence race relations and economic opportunity, and how we see ourselves and how others see us. Among American Indians, redness serves as a marker of conquered status, a target for extermination and subordination. As a consequence, the Indian claim of tribal sovereignty to profit from casinos or to maintain fishing rights is necessarily unpalatable to those whites who see them as becoming empowered and therefore accuse Indians of wanting "special rights." Among African Americans, blackness has marked our inferior status from the beginning.

In Latin American and Caribbean countries with large black and/or Indian populations, a fair-skinned elite perpetuated by race mixing or immigration holds power, and darker people are poorer and discriminated against. Deference to white privilege is also a well-known phenomenon in Asian societies. Among Hispanics or Latinos and Asian Americans in the United States, the darker ones are generally the more subordinated and deprived and less likely to be literate in English. They may not be literate even in their own indigenous languages.

Scholars, including David Roediger in *The Wages of Whiteness* (1991), and Noel Ignatiev in *How the Irish Became White* (1995), have explained how color consciousness has played out in every group to live in this country or reach these shores. They discuss the phenomenon of how immigrants from Europe overcame powerlessness to become white and distance themselves from blackness. Camille Cosby's discussion (1998) of how her son Ennis's murderer, Mikail Markhasev, was infected with racism needs modification only to point out that the virus is so pervasive that immigrants may be infected regardless of whether their home country has a black population. Becoming white means distancing oneself from blackness, which means

overcoming inequality and legal exclusion and moving up the political and economic ladder from powerlessness. African Americans as the quintessential purveyors of blackness find it difficult to make the leap. Exceptions such as Michael Jordan and Sammy Sosa, because of their celebrated achievements, only prove the rule. They can come closer to white privilege and more easily transcend color boundaries and avoid some of the burden of race.

Adding this dimension to the social science and humanistic studies can help us figure out how to address gaps and disparities in social and economic opportunity. It can also help us to avoid policies which will worsen the inequality marked by color that solidifies class distinctions within communities of people of color. For any group, getting its share must include leaving no person behind in the chance for opportunity. It requires understanding the role of color—and its extreme signifiers black and white—in undergirding inequality not only in America but globally. Otherwise we unfairly reduce the chances for everyone to become productive citizens and consign them to deprivation and dependency. We also risk more contention between various groups of people of color instead of cooperation—creating an atmosphere that politicians can eagerly exploit.

LEARNING FROM DU BOIS

We do not have to replicate Du Bois's migration and evolution as a scholar, public intellectual, and activist. We can learn from the total fabric of his experiences. We can begin with understanding not only that activism is more important to social change than scholarship but that scholarship can inform activism. In the free South Africa movement, we consciously analyzed other movements and tried to avoid the traps of failure and to replicate successes (see Robinson 1998). Also, instead of slowly coming to broaden our focus from race or national origin to gender, class, and internationalism, we can start there. We can also realize that "truth" often serves rather than uproots power and that the question is whose truth.

We are at a stage now where we need to translate the research on African Americans into useful policy. We need policy formed on the history of the coverage of African Americans under social security and of how blacks were ready, willing, and able to seek government contracts, but the contracts were given to a white male elite—a system that perpetuated itself until affirmative action made a few dents (which might help to explain why affirmative action is under attack). We need an exhaustive policy focused on the history of standardized testing—the measurement mystique and race and how standardized testing arose and how sorting is a device related to the exclusion of African Americans. We need a systematic study of why public education since the end of de jure segregation has remained largely segregated. Such a history might help us to understand the impact of a policy to just "educate black children where they are." We need a serious analysis of Harlan's dissent in *Plessy* and the opinion in *Brown* so that we may understand why color-blindness fell easily on the ears but became a cudgel used against blacks. Lawyers need this scholarship for their briefs and arguments, and teachers need it to dilute the distortion abroad in the land.

If we have any interest in being like Du Bois, instead of just writing and talking about Du Bois, we must understand that following his example means much more than being a public intellectual who writes for mainstream publications and graces an occasional meeting or dinner at the White House. It means a commitment to act for social change, to rub shoulders with activists on a regular basis, and to rejoice when attacked for being too radical. It also means understanding that Du Bois was not just a complicated man who possessed an inquiring analytical mind and became an activist. He tediously taught himself to articulate his ideas and goals publicly, with passion, felicity, and grace. He believed that there is a public debate that must be engaged. He thought it too important for scholars to remain onlookers if they shared his vision of helping to "raise" not just themselves, but the race. This is the work that must be done, if we want one America in the twenty-first century to be more than just a cliché but a reality.

References

Aptheker, Herbert, ed. 1982. *Writings in Non-periodical Literature Edited by Others*. Millwood, NY: Kraus-Thomson.

Baraka, Amiri. 1998. Paul Robeson and the Theater. *Black Renaissance* 2(Fall/Winter):12-34.

Cosby, Camille. 1998. Camille Cosby: America Taught My Son's Killer to Hate Blacks. *USA Today*, 8 July.

Du Bois, W.E.B. 1898. The Study of the Negro Problems. *The Annals of the American Academy of Political and Social Science* Jan.:1-23.

————. 1968. *The Autobiography of W.E.B. Du Bois: A Soliloquy on Viewing My Life from the Last Decade of the First Century*. New York: International.

————. 1985. Celebrating His Twenty-fifth Birthday (1893). In *Against Racism. Unpublished Essays, Papers, Addresses 1887-1961*, ed. Herbert Aptheker. Amherst: University of Massachusetts Press.

Ignatiev, Noel. 1995. *How the Irish Became White*. New York: Routledge.

Lewis, David Levering. 1993. *W.E.B. Du Bois: Biography of a Race 1868-1919*. New York: Henry Holt.

Myrdal, Gunnar. 1944. *An American Dilemma: The Negro Problem and Modern Democracy*. New York: Harper.

National Conference. 1998. Taking Our Nation's Pulse. Poll.

Patterson, William L., ed. 1970. *We Charge Genocide: The Historic Petition to the United States for Relief from a Crime of the United States Government Against the Negro People*. New York: International.

Robinson, Randall. 1998. *Defending the Spirit: A Black Life in America*. New York: Dutton.

Roediger, David. 1991. *The Wages of Whiteness: Race and the Making of the American Working Class*. New York: Verso.

Wilson, Francille. 1988. *The Segregated Scholars: Black Labor Historians, 1895-1950*. Ph.D. diss., University of Pennsylvania, Philadelphia.

Wintz, Cary D. 1996. *African American Political Thought, 1890-1930: Washington, Du Bois, Garvey and Randolph*. Armonk, NY: M. E. Sharpe.

ANNALS, *AAPSS*, **568**, March 2000

Race, Poverty, and Welfare:
Du Bois's Legacy for Policy

By MICHAEL B. KATZ

ABSTRACT: This article discusses Du Bois's analysis of poverty, charity, and relief in Philadelphia, and places it in the context of his research methods and agenda. It uses this consideration of method and agenda as a framework for an overview of the relations between race and the American welfare state. After describing the structure of the American welfare state, the article limns some of the themes in the historic imbrication of race in social welfare. The article then turns to the implication for African Americans of the post-1980 redefinition of the welfare state by the three great forces of dependence, devolution, and markets. These forces not only redefine benefits; they also recast the idea of citizenship and what it means to be an American.

Michael B. Katz is Sheldon and Lucy Hackney Professor of History at the University of Pennsylvania. He has written on the history of American education, the history of nineteenth-century urban social structure and family organization, and the history of poverty and welfare. He is co-editor of W.E.B. Du Bois, Race, and the City: The Philadelphia Negro and Its Legacy *(1998). He is completing a book on the redefinition of the American welfare state.*

I N 1896, when W.E.B. Du Bois wanted to assess the extent of poverty among African Americans in Philadelphia's Seventh Ward, he observed "a vast amount of almsgiving," much of which remained "unsystematic," riddled with "duplication," and reported with records "so meagre . . . that the real extent of pauperism and its causes are hard to study." As a result, he found it "very difficult to get any definite idea of the extent of Negro poverty." Nonetheless, Du Bois used what he could find: records of the city's almshouse, outdoor relief, and police station lodgings; arrests of vagrants; his own survey of the Seventh Ward; and reports of the Children's Aid Society and the Charity Organization Society. He fleshed out the statistics with case histories that offered insight into the causes of poverty, which he grouped into "sickness and misfortune," "lack of steady employment," "laziness, improvidence and intemperate drink," and "crime"—artificial single categories that, he knew, masked the complex nature of poverty's etiology: "crime causes sickness and misfortune; lack of employment causes crime; laziness causes lack of work, etc." (Du Bois [1899] 1973, 18, 269-75).

Du Bois anchored the rhythms of black poverty in the economic dislocations of the 1890s—"a period of financial stress and industrial depression" that bore most heavily on "the poor, the unskilled laborers, the inefficient and unfortunate, and those with small social and economic advantage." Although increases and decreases in poverty among blacks

and whites tended to move in tandem, with the trends accentuated among blacks, unique problems "which can rightly be called Negro problems" arose "from the peculiar history and condition of the American Negro." The consequences of slavery and emancipation ranked first among special problems. Emancipation, with an impact parallel to "any sudden social revolution," registered in "a strain upon the strength and resources of the Negro, moral, economic, and physical, which drove many to the wall," and shaped "the rise of the Negro in this city" into a "series of rushes and backslidings rather than a continuous growth." The immigration of great numbers of blacks into Philadelphia interacted with the legacy of slavery and emancipation to fuel the growth of poverty. This "great number of raw recruits . . . shared" the "small industrial opportunities" of Philadelphia's existing black population and "made reputations which, whether good or bad, all their race must share" (Du Bois [1899] 1973, 282-83).

But the greatest source of "Negro problems"—"possibly greater in influence than the other two"— remained the ubiquitous discrimination that surrounded black Philadelphians. Du Bois called it "the world of custom and thought in which he must live and work, the physical surrounding of house and home and ward, the moral encouragements and discouragements which he encounters." The vague term "color prejudice" failed to capture this quality of the social environment whose study demanded attention not to "thought and feeling" but to "concrete manifestations." The social environments of "a young white lad, or a foreign immigrant who comes to this great city to join in its organic life" were well known; but the full portrait of the social environment surrounding blacks remained to be drawn. "That this environment differs broadly from the environment of his fellows, we all know, but we do not know just how it differs." At its core, he thought, the difference resulted from the persistent refusal of white Americans to accept blacks as citizens. "The real foundation of the difference is the widespread feeling all over the land . . . that the Negro is something less than an American and ought not to be much more than what he is" (Du Bois [1899] 1973, 282-84).

Because Du Bois remained too honest and rigorous a scholar to exaggerate, he drew some unexpected conclusions from his study of poverty among Philadelphia's African Americans and of the response it evoked. Blacks, about 4 percent of the population, composed at least 8 percent of Philadelphians more or less permanently stuck in poverty. Many others "from time to time just receive temporary aid, but can usually get on without it." At moments of great "stress as during the year 1893 this class is very large." Poverty showed itself in "especial suffering and neglect among the children" of the poor. What seemed to surprise him, however, was not the severity of black poverty but its relative modesty. With the "economic difficulties of the Negro" in mind, he concluded, "we ought perhaps to expect rather

more than less of this" (Du Bois [1899] 1973, 273).

In part, the relative modesty of black poverty reflected high black employment rates. Unlike the situation late in the twentieth century, miserable jobs and low wages rather than joblessness characterized the situation of African Americans in cities. Du Bois found 78 percent of blacks in Philadelphia's Seventh Ward in "gainful occupations" compared to 55.1 percent of the whole population. In three articles he wrote for the *New York Times* in 1901, he compared the consequences of economic discrimination for blacks in Boston, Philadelphia, and New York. The result, he argued, offered convincing evidence that African Americans as "a race are not lazy. The canvass of the Federation of Churches in typical New York tenement districts has shown that while nearly 99 per cent. of the black men were wage earners, only 92 per cent. of the Americans and 90 per cent. of the Germans were at work." Despite their high rate of employment, blacks remained excluded from opportunities for advancement and were confined to menial jobs that paid low wages. This was the indisputable message of *The Philadelphia Negro* and the finding that struck readers with greatest force (Du Bois [1901] 1969, 6; Du Bois [1899] 1973, 29-30; Katz and Sugrue 1998, 26-30).

White Philadelphians, for all their prejudice, showed surprising sympathy for their impoverished black neighbors. Only they failed to act intelligently on their better instincts or to extend the kind of help that would set impoverished blacks on the road to independence. Philanthropy, in short, remained mired in the contradictions of racism.

Prejudice and apparent dislike conjoined with widespread and deep sympathy; there can, for instance, be no doubt of the sincerity of the efforts put forth by Philadelphians to help the Negroes. Much of it is unsystematic and ill-directed and yet it has behind it a broad charity and a desire to relieve suffering and distress. The same Philadelphian who would not let a Negro work in his store or mill, will contribute handsomely to relieve Negroes in poverty and distress. (Du Bois [1899] 1973, 355).

Philadelphia's public charities—its outdoor relief and almshouse—dispensed aid to both blacks and whites. Fourteen private charitable agencies devoted themselves exclusively to blacks and 59 to whites. Another 51 "profess not to discriminate, but in some cases do," while 57 "make no statements, but usually discriminate." About half the city's charities, concluded Du Bois, helped blacks with various kinds of aid. Surprisingly, blacks received "far more than their just proportion" of "direct almsgiving, the most questionable and least organized sort of charity," while "protective, rescue, and reformatory work" was "not applied to any great extent among them." As a result, blacks found "actual poverty and distress . . . quickly relieved" but "only a few agencies to prevent the better classes from sinking or to reclaim the fallen or to protect the helpless and the children." Blacks bore some of the responsibility for the ineffectiveness of white benevolence "because the classes on whom it has been showered have not appreciated it, and because there has been no careful attempt to discriminate between different sorts of Negroes." Du Bois approvingly quoted the motto of the Charity Organization Society—the leader of the era's "scientific charity" movement—the "need of the Negro, as of so many unfortunate classes, is 'not alms but a friend'" (Du Bois [1899] 1973, 357-58).

DU BOIS AND SOCIAL RESEARCH

Du Bois's great report on social and economic conditions in Philadelphia's Seventh Ward—unprecedented in American social science—led him to formulate an ambitious research agenda that would extend his study from the Seventh Ward to the nation. In his 1898 essay in *The Annals*, "The Study of the Negro Problems," Du Bois, drawing on his earlier work on the African slave trade and his Philadelphia study, set out this research agenda and explained his methods. Du Bois thoroughly and painstakingly canvassed all available sources, searched imaginatively for evidence, handled empirical data with meticulous care, refused to accept simple or monocausal explanations, and blended historical, quantitative, and qualitative methods. At the core of his research strategy lay history. Commentators (and Du Bois included himself in this criticism) usually spoke of "the Negro problem as though it were one unchanged question" when, in truth, it "had a long historical development"; had "changed with the growth and evolution of the nation"; and represented "not one problem, but rather a plexus of social problems" joined "in the act that they group themselves about those Africans whom two centuries of slave-trading brought into the land" (Du Bois 1898, 3).

For Du Bois, blacks' imperfect incorporation into public life constituted the "Negro problems" that remained after 275 years "of evolution." Blacks found themselves "a definitely segregated mass of eight millions of Americans" not "wholly" sharing "the national life of the people . . . not an integral part of the social body." While Du Bois deplored the refusal of white Americans to accept blacks as full citizens, he argued that blacks failed to "reach the social standards of the nation" in "economic condition," "mental training," or "social efficiency." Naming problems, however, constituted only a first step that served "little purpose unless we can say to what extent each element enters in the final result." Did the situation of blacks "arise more largely from ignorance than from prejudice, or vice versa?" This, he observed, was where "every intelligent discussion of the American Negro comes to a standstill." Thomas Jefferson had complained that the lack of real study of slaves had left all "general conclusions about them extremely hazardous." Two centuries later this situation remained scarcely improved (Du Bois 1898, 7-9).

The failure to mount credible and extensive studies of blacks con- stituted more than a gap in early social science. It reinforced stereotypes, popular misunderstandings, and bad public policy. So "vast and intricate" were "Negro problems" that they demanded "trained research and expert analysis, touching questions that affect the very foundation of the republic and of the human progress, increasing and multiplying year by year." Research on blacks, moreover, offered an unparalleled opportunity to advance "the cause of science in general. No such opportunity to watch and measure the history and development of a great race of men ever presented itself to the scholars of a modern nation." Du Bois did not mean to imply that few people had written about "American Negroes." To the contrary, a torrent of published opinions littered magazines, journals, and books. But almost all of it was unscientific and worthless. "Thus we possess endless final judgments as to the American Negro emanating from men of influence and learning, in the very face of the fact known to every accurate student, that there exists to-day no sufficient material of proven reliability, upon which any scientists can base definite and final conclusions" about the eight million black Americans (Du Bois 1898, 9-10, 15).

A sophisticated appreciation of the relation between social science and social action underlay Du Bois's call for a massive research project. Social research shared with other sciences one overriding goal: "the discovery of truth." All attempts to give social research "a double aim, to make social reform the immediate instead of the mediate object" would "inevitably defeat both objects." Sociological research too frequently had allied itself "with various panaceas and particular schemes of reform," with a "good deal of groundless assumption and humbug in the popular mind" as a result. Nonetheless, Du Bois retained great faith in the outcome of social science. We must insist, he emphasized, "that if we would solve a problem we must study it, and that there is but one coward on earth, and that is the coward that dare not know." Like other social scientists of the Progressive Era, Du Bois early in his career believed that facts gathered impartially with scientific methods would lead—ineluctably—to conclusions that evoked only one legitimate response (Du Bois 1898, 16-17, 23).

Du Bois's proposed massive study of "the Negro" fell "naturally into two categories," difficult to separate in practice but necessarily distinct for analytic purposes. These were, first, "the study of the Negro as a social group," and, second, "the study of his peculiar social environment." The first he divided in his customarily multidisciplinary fashion into four divisions: historical study, statistical investigation, anthropological measurement, and sociological interpretation. The second he defined as "the reaction of the surroundings." Du Bois called for a massive and dynamic project that focused on the interaction of races and on the boundaries to black progress set by whites. He proposed always holding in exquisite tension what today would be termed structure and agency (Du Bois 1898, 18-20).

THE LEGACY OF
DU BOIS FOR RESEARCH
ON POVERTY AND WELFARE

Du Bois has left a rich legacy for current-day students of race, poverty, and the welfare state. First, his work highlights the need to anchor research on poverty and the welfare state (as well as on race) in history. The study of the American welfare state demands attention to history because it consists of an accretion of institutional and ideological layers deposited over the entire span of American history. What today we call welfare—public assistance in the form of "outdoor relief"—originated in the colonies which adapted British poor laws. Despite the best efforts of generations of reformers to abolish it, outdoor relief remained ubiquitous and despised, but essential, throughout American history. In the nineteenth century, the creation of institutions (poorhouses, mental hospitals, general hospitals, penitentiaries, reformatories, orphanages) responded in part to the limits of outdoor relief. The legacy of the institutional landscape and modes of public-private relations set in place in the nineteenth century reverberates today while the periodic wars on outdoor relief find echoes in regularly recurring public policy struggles, notable recently in the 1996 congressional debates on welfare reform. Social insurance, another great component of the welfare state, emerged with a great burst in the 1930s while in the postwar years the cooperation of employers with trade unions constructed a massive parallel private welfare state of employee benefits. The initiatives of the Great

Society, such as Medicare and Medicaid, and the tax code, especially the earned income tax credit, added other layers without superseding and modifying the existing structures in any fundamental way (Katz 1996).

Just as the welfare state cannot be comprehended without history, it cannot be understood through one disciplinary lens or an exclusive focus on either its clients or officials. The study of the welfare state constitutes a multidisciplinary project that demands attention to both of Du Bois's two categories: groups and the "social environment." One task concentrates on groups: their beliefs and behaviors, the reasons for their dependence, and their use of programs and institutions. The other task starts with programs and institutions. It calls for explicating their political construction, organization, and interaction. Efforts to explain the relations of the welfare state to race demand attention to both tasks.

Although the history of the American welfare state is not primarily a story about race, race remains deeply imbricated in its origins and development—something Du Bois certainly would have expected. Like Philadelphia's charities, the programs and agencies of America's public and private welfare states have served African Americans both identically to and differently from whites. The original structure of some key programs guaranteed blacks different treatment while debased images of African Americans have dominated discourse around welfare reform—issues to which I will turn shortly.

But there remains one other part of Du Bois's legacy that calls for attention: his warning about the use of social science in social reform. Bad social science, like the turn-of-the-century social research to which he objected, has misinformed both the politics of the welfare state and popular views. Indeed, the experience of a century's worth of social science casts doubt on Du Bois's early faith in objective truth and the capacity of good data to shape public policy and reform public opinion. Not only postmodernism but the stubborn persistence of stereotypes about poverty, welfare, and race in the face of credible social science calls into question the capacity of research to lead where public opinion and political will are not ready to follow. The use of social science in the debates surrounding the 1988 Family Support Act (FSA) highlights the ambiguous uses of social science in welfare reform. In one prominent story, welfare reform languished in the early 1980s because reformers lacked credible evidence that welfare-to-work programs produced measurable results whose benefits exceeded their costs. The results of demonstration programs studied by the Manpower Demonstration Research Corporation (MDRC) broke the logjam by showing the success of programs allegedly analogous to ones proposed in the FSA. Armed with this data, congressional proponents, backed by governors, overcame all remaining opposition and passed a historic welfare reform bill. Unfortunately, a close examination of the MDRC results undercuts this tale of social science's triumph. By no means were the MDRC results unambiguous. The demonstration programs did not target the most difficult-to-serve populations or the category of people most affected by the new legislation. Nor did the programs lift women with children out of poverty or remove them permanently from welfare. Politicians found in the results nuggets they could use to support their case, not powerful evidence that proposed programs would succeed. Social science became the handmaiden of politics, not its teacher (Katz forthcoming).

It has been politics, of course, much more than social science that has shaped America's welfare state with its complicated relation to race. Indeed, no simple generalizations characterize those relations. Race has worked differently in each of the welfare state's multiple tracks. Even along the same tracks, relations between race and the welfare state remain fluid, shifting and re-forming continuously in response to influences outside the welfare state as well as to changes within it.

America's vast and complicated welfare state consists of two sides—public and private—intimately related but distinct. The three tracks that divide the public welfare state are public assistance (for instance, Temporary Assistance for Needy Families [TANF] and food stamps), social insurance (social security, Medicare, unemployment insurance, workers' compensation, disability insurance), and taxation (the earned income tax credit and many other programs, which have become increasingly important

means for delivering benefits). The two tracks that comprise the private welfare state are the enormous system of employee benefits and the world of charity and social service. Charities and social services, of course, receive a large share of their funding from public coffers, and a massive compendium of laws and rules regulate employee benefits. In truth, its mixed economy distinguishes America's welfare state, which is not usefully described as either public or private.

The history of each of the welfare state's tracks reads partly as a story about race. The exploitation, discrimination, mutuality, protest, and forms of poverty that wind through African American history shaped relations between race and the history of relief—the older term—and social welfare. Books have been written about these relations, and the subject remains far from exhausted. A short essay cannot do justice to this long and complicated story. It only can sketch some of its main lines (Brown 1999; Quadagno 1994; Lieberman 1998; Gordon 1994, 111-44).

RACE AND THE HISTORICAL
ARCHITECTURE OF THE
AMERICAN WELFARE STATE

Before the New Deal

Very few historians have examined the relations between race and relief prior to the New Deal. Indeed, outdoor relief and poorhouses, ubiquitous and contentious throughout American history, remain the most understudied components of America's history of social welfare. (There is no American counterpart to the vigorous historical controversies over poor laws in Britain.) As a result, little can be said with any confidence about how fairly they dealt with African Americans. The story differs, we can be sure, in the North and South. Slavery "solved" the problem of dependence for most southern blacks and kept them off the public assistance roles. Where they did enter poorhouses, they remained segregated. After the Civil War, the Freedmen's Bureau, in the best traditions of the scientific charity of the age, tried to discourage outdoor relief while the funds and institutions for relieving dependence remained less developed in the South than in the North. In the North, at least in Philadelphia, as Du Bois showed, African Americans received outdoor relief from public and private sources. Little reason exists to suspect the situation differed greatly in other cities. Whether they received assistance in proportion to their share of the population or their level of need remains another matter, which awaits research (Bellows 1983; Cohen 1991, 58-59).

Public assistance consisted of institutional support as well as relief because dependent persons found help in hospitals, mental hospitals, and orphanages. By overlooking this institutional help, claims that Americans provided little public assistance in the past make a great mistake. Major institutions originated as part of the structure of public welfare, and during their early history they served primarily the very poor with forms of assistance essential to survival. Although early institutions admitted African Americans, facilities remained by and large segregated, very likely inferior, and even more poorly funded than those serving whites. Again, no one has tried to assess the relative proportion of need among whites and blacks met by the institutions of social welfare. Whether different groups turned to institutions with more or less reluctance also remains unknown. The greater prevalence of fostering among blacks—that is, sharing child-rearing among relatives—at least hints that they may have fallen back on orphanages less often than whites. But this remains pure speculation (Grob 1973, 243-56; Rosenberg 1987, 301-3; Schneider 1992, 71, 217-29; Miller 1995).

One important exception stands out in the story of mean and discriminatory public assistance in the late nineteenth and early twentieth centuries: Civil War pensions for veterans expanded greatly from the 1870s to the 1910s, and veterans pensions constituted the first great federal welfare system. Theda Skocpol has told the story of their growth and imbrication in patronage politics and of the reaction of reformers appalled at what appeared to be their excessive generosity and corruption. Skocpol argues that the award and administration of veterans pensions showed far less racial bias than other public benefits and that black veterans remained eligible on the same basis as whites. Indeed, in the late nineteenth century, the U.S. Pension Bureau helped "former slave veterans or widows establish their eligibility," and "African American eligibility for Civil War benefits persisted over many decades, even as black voting rights and other progressive legacies of the Civil War petered out." The federal welfare state that succeeded veterans pensions only partly retained this legacy (Skocpol 1995).

The New Deal and the federal welfare state

During the New Deal, southern influence shaped the charter of the federal welfare state in ways that disadvantaged African Americans. Part of the price for winning passage of old-age insurance (social security) and unemployment insurance consisted of excluding agricultural and domestic labor—the industries employing most African Americans. New Deal legislation created Aid to Dependent Children (what we today call "welfare") as a federal-state program that allowed states great latitude in setting eligibility standards. Southern states responded with "suitable home" requirements used to exclude black women who thereby remained conveniently available as cheap domestic labor (Quadagno 1988, 99-151; Davies and Derthick 1997; Bell 1965).

In Shifting the Color Line, political scientist Robert Lieberman provides a useful set of distinctions for systematically analyzing the relations between race and the history of the welfare state programs created during the New Deal. Lieberman focuses on three federal or federal-state programs that originated with the Economic Security Act of 1935: old-age insurance (social security), Aid to Dependent Children, and unemployment insurance. Each fol-

lowed a different trajectory with respect to race.

Old-Age Insurance [OAI] progressed from statutory exclusion of African-Americans to administrative inclusion and finally to statutory inclusion. Aid to Dependent Children regressed . . . from statutory inclusion to administrative exclusion of African-Americans. . . . Unemployment Insurance began with the same statutory exclusion as OAI, but it did not grow toward greater racial inclusion as OAI did. (Lieberman 1998, 8)

Some programs, such as old-age insurance and unemployment insurance, offered benefits to everyone who met their criteria—but the criteria discriminated. In the social insurances, eligibility rested on work for a specified length of time in "covered" industries which, originally, excluded the occupations followed by most African Americans. In time, Congress removed most of the industrial exclusions from old-age insurance; more restrictive rules for unemployment insurance remain in place. Unlike unemployment insurance, Aid to Dependent Children allowed local rules and local administrative determination of eligibility. With "a weak, decentralized, and parochial institutional structure," the implementation of Aid to Dependent Children "discriminated against African-Americans, first denying them benefits and then making them the central focus of bitter political disputes over benefits, leading to crackdowns, retrenchment, and ever more race-laden welfare policies" (Lieberman 1998, 9).

Lieberman shows a steady increase after the mid-1950s in the proportion of the nonwhite population receiving old-age insurance benefits. Nonwhites received lower benefit payments because they had earned less, but the benefit formulas tilted slightly toward redistributing income toward lower-income workers. As a result, the ratio of nonwhite to white benefits remained higher than the ratio of nonwhite to white income. Aid to Dependent Children (which became Aid to Families with Dependent Children [AFDC] in 1962 and TANF in 1996) followed a different trajectory. By the late 1930s, all southern states with Aid to Dependent Children programs awarded aid to proportionally fewer black than white families, and the grant amounts were less. In the North and Midwest, the pattern varied. A number of states—notably Pennsylvania, Ohio, and Indiana—awarded African Americans "relief at much higher rates than their proportion in the population," and in some states they received higher payments. Other states—New Jersey, for example—awarded them lower benefits. Over time, the African American proportion of AFDC rolls rose steeply—far exceeding the white proportion. The reason did not reflect generosity or a willingness to counteract discrimination. Rather, it grew out of two other sources: the structure of local political patronage and the removal of dependent whites to the more generous social insurance programs. Its association with blacks added to the historic stigma of relief that tainted AFDC. In AFDC, race, gender, and relief fused into a powerful and degraded image that dominated attacks on the program

and its participants from the 1960s through its abolition by Congress in 1996 (Lieberman 1998, 88-89, 174-76).

The early history of unemployment insurance, claims Lieberman, showed little direct discrimination against African Americans. They received less benefit from the program because they worked more often in occupations not covered and because their longer unemployment spells left them at greater risk of exhausting their benefits. Nonetheless, those African Americans who did work in covered industries "stood to benefit more than others precisely because of their greater probability of being unemployed and suffering long spells of unemployment." "By all accounts," concludes Lieberman, African Americans received "what they deserved" under the program's rules (Lieberman 1998, 192-94).

Lieberman does not analyze the racial dynamics of old-age assistance (OAA), the largest early welfare program. No one received social security (old-age insurance) until 1940, and then it phased in slowly as more and more people reached eligibility. OAA, by contrast, began at once. Funded half by the federal government and half by the states, it provided means-tested relief to the needy elderly. OAA was a massive program; until 1955 the number of its beneficiaries exceeded the number receiving Aid to Dependent Children, and it was the program most people had in mind when they referred to relief or welfare. Did African Americans receive their fair share? Presumably, they were subject to the same local discriminations as under Aid to Dependent Children. Without detailed research of the sort Lieberman undertook for other programs, no definitive answer is possible, but the rough, preliminary data that follow point to some intriguing patterns.

The Social Security Act made OAA contingent on need, whose definition was left to the states. Many states defined need as "insufficient income to provide reasonable subsistence compatible with decency and health"—a loose definition further qualified by property limitations and open to widely varying interpretations. Without a uniform federal standard, individual grants varied widely from state to state (Sterner 1943, 272).

The sheer magnitude of poverty among the elderly leaps out from even a cursory look at estimates based on the 1940 census (see Table 1).[1] For whites, the lowest rate among the states studied was 52 percent in New York; for blacks, the lowest rate also existed in New York, 61 percent. With few exceptions, the rate of black poverty exceeded white poverty. In the South, almost all elderly blacks and around three-quarters of whites remained poor. OAA reached only a small fraction of these elderly poor and addressed only the extremes of poverty. Like Aid to Dependent Children (and its successor AFDC), it aimed at survival, not at an exit from poverty. In 1939 and 1940, in the 25 states studied by social scientist Richard Sterner, the proportion of the elderly black poor who received OAA benefits varied from a low of 1.3 percent in Georgia to a high of 26.9 percent in Pennsylvania. In 13

TABLE 1

POVERTY RATES FOR BLACKS AND WHITES AGE 65 AND OVER, 1940

State	White	Black	Ratio
NY	52.40	60.50	1.15
PA	56.30	62.70	1.11
OH	63.30	68.30	1.08
IL	59.20	74.30	1.26
MI	61.90	60.30	0.97
MD	55.40	73.20	1.32
VA	68.10	82.70	1.21
WV	73.20	71.80	0.98
NC	71.10	90.90	1.28
SC	64.30	95.00	1.48
GA	67.90	93.40	1.38
FL	74.70	92.00	1.23
KY	74.30	80.50	1.08
TN	75.50	92.00	1.22
AL	72.60	93.00	1.28
MS	78.10	97.20	1.24
AR	84.40	97.70	1.16
LA	70.10	94.50	1.35
OK	82.00	90.80	1.11
TX	76.50	91.60	1.20

SOURCE: Ruggles et al. 1997.

states, the proportion was less than 10 percent (see Table 2).

Nonetheless, in 22 of the 25 states, the proportion of elderly blacks among OAA recipients exceeded their proportion of the population. Although the disproportion tilted strongly in blacks' favor in the North (with the highest ratio of 2.60 in Michigan), it remained high in several southern states as well—for instance, 1.48 in Georgia and 1.44 in Texas (see Table 3). With the exception of Texas, the average OAA payment to elderly blacks remained close to the payment for whites. In all cases, however, the amount was pathetically low, ranging from a monthly high of $24.55 for blacks in New York to a low of $5.70 in Georgia (see Table 4).

TABLE 2
POOR BLACKS AGE 65 AND OVER WITH OLD-AGE ASSISTANCE BENEFITS, 1940

State	Number with Benefits	Number of Poor	Percentage of Poor with Benefits
NY	1,049	9,710	10.8
PA	3,441	12,785	26.9
OH	1,551	10,812	14.3
IL	1,569	15,214	10.3
MI	79	3,306	2.4
MD	1,030	9,223	11.2
VA	2,523	24,352	10.4
WV	187	2,828	6.6
NC	2,252	28,512	7.9
SC	1,057	24,920	4.2
GA	549	42,150	1.3
FL	1,044	18,235	5.7
KY	1,064	11,355	9.4
TN	5,053	22,488	22.5
AL	2,433	32,286	7.5
MS	1,904	38,633	4.9
AR	1,463	17,502	8.4
LA	3,017	33,544	9.0
OK	862	8,888	9.7
TX	2,089	36,576	5.7

SOURCES: Sterner 1943; Ruggles et al. 1997.

Sterner qualified the overrepresentation of blacks among OAA beneficiaries; the "high proportion of dependency among aged Negroes" made "their need for old-age assistance . . . greater" than whites'. Given their greater need, Negroes remained unlikely to find themselves "disproportionately aided in terms of their economic situation." Indeed, in 1938 to 1939, the Social Security Board suggested that "the number of Negroes to whom aid was granted during the year was low in proportion to the number who needed assistance" (Sterner 1943, 274). For one thing, elderly blacks may have fallen further below the poverty line than

elderly whites. Among 65- to 69-year-olds, moreover, whites more often than blacks received benefits because, Sterner observed, "welfare agencies are more inclined to consider Negroes under 70 years of age as able to support themselves by odd jobs than whites." In the South a "general belief" that "Negroes can get along on less than whites" also limited the distribution and amount of benefits (Sterner 1943, 274, 277).

Despite variations among states, limited coverage, inadequate benefits, and discriminatory administration, Sterner concluded that "the old-age assistance program has brought about a very considerable improvement in the economic position of the aged Negro" (Sterner 1943, 277). His is probably a fair verdict on OAA and on most of the rest of the welfare state. Poverty, as Mark Stern has shown, fell dramatically between 1940 and 1980, and about half the decline resulted from government transfer programs (Stern 1995). Even though the elderly proved the greatest winners, poverty dropped remarkably among all groups. African Americans received lower benefits from social security, qualified less often for unemployment insurance, and remained stuck more frequently in the inadequate and stigmatized public assistance track of the welfare state. But social security transformed the economics of aging for blacks as well as whites; Medicare and Medicaid brought unprecedented access to health care; unemployment insurance surely proved crucial for very large numbers of African Americans; and with unprecedented regularity the

TABLE 3
BLACKS AND OLD-AGE
ASSISTANCE, 1939-40

State	Percentage of Black OAA Recipients	Percentage of Black Population Age 65 and Over	Ratio of Black OAA Recipients to Entire Age 65 and Over Population
NY	4.60	2.00	2.30
PA	8.80	2.80	3.14
OH	7.60	3.10	2.45
IL	8.20	3.10	2.65
MI	5.20	2.00	2.60
MD	30.30	11.80	2.57
VA	39.90	21.80	1.83
WV	6.30	4.70	1.34
NC	32.10	25.60	1.25
SC	39.00	42.00	0.93
GA	49.00	33.00	1.48
FL	33.20	18.40	1.80
KY	13.60	8.40	1.62
TN	25.30	17.30	1.46
AL	39.70	33.80	1.17
MS	42.60	47.10	0.90
AR	23.00	23.20	0.99
LA	51.80	35.70	1.45
OK	8.90	9.30	0.96
TX	19.70	13.70	1.44

SOURCE: Sterner 1943.

combination of AFDC, Supplemental Security Income, and food stamps brought the resources essential for survival to millions of the poorest African Americans. As this welfare state threatens to erode, its accomplishments weigh more heavily than ever in assessments of its successes and failures.

RACE AND THE REDEFINITION
OF THE WELFARE STATE

In the years since 1980, the American welfare state has sustained an attack that has not only rolled back some benefits but, even more important, redefined the principles on which it rests. This redefinition, which threatens to fall most heavily on African Americans and other minorities, results from three forces that I call dependence, devolution, and markets. A war on dependence, notably but far from exclusively on young unmarried mothers; the devolution of authority from the federal government to states, from states to localities, and from public to private agencies; and the application of market models to social policy: these three forces course through all the corners of America's welfare state (Katz forthcoming). Fewer Americans receive health insurance through work, and a smaller share of the unemployed earn unemployment insurance. Congress reduced funds for public housing, increased the retirement age for social security, threw disabled children off supplemental social insurance, cut food stamps for adults, and time-limited public assistance; state governments abolished or severely curtailed general assistance.

All these actions exemplify how the forces redefining the welfare state manifest in practice. That they threaten to fall harshly on African Americans (and Latinos, too) is obvious. Because they remain more concentrated in low-skill, service sector jobs, African Americans less often qualify for health benefits or unemployment insurance. Because they die younger, increasing the retirement age decreases their return from social security and shortens their retirement. The abolition or reduction of general assistance and cuts in

TABLE 4
AVERAGE MONTHLY OLD-AGE ASSISTANT PAYMENTS TO BLACKS AND WHITES, 1939-40

State	Monthly Payment to Blacks	Monthly Payment to Whites	Ratio
NY	$24.55	$22.88	1.07
PA	24.23	21.14	1.15
OH	23.27	22.16	1.05
IL	22.11	21.26	1.04
MI	n.a.	n.a.	n.a.
MD	15.32	16.50	0.93
VA	8.86	9.65	0.92
WV	12.58	12.75	0.99
NC	8.87	10.25	0.87
SC	7.60	9.80	0.78
GA	5.70	7.13	0.80
FL	9.37	12.36	0.76
KY	8.38	8.82	0.95
TN	9.00	9.61	0.94
AL	16.81	20.30	0.83
MS	7.17	11.09	0.65
AR	6.36	6.78	0.94
LA	10.61	13.76	0.77
OK	16.77	17.40	0.96
TX	7.17	11.09	0.65

SOURCE: Sterner 1943.

food stamps have fallen heavily on young African American men unable to find work in the regular labor market. A very large share of the women who will find themselves disqualified from public assistance by time limits will be African American and Latino.

The redefined welfare state not only threatens to reduce benefits disproportionately among African Americans; it pushes them further toward the margins of American society. For the great forces of dependence, devolution, and markets are also redefining the meaning of citizenship. Increasingly, only work for pay in the regular labor market qualifies for the full benefits

associated with membership in the American nation. More and more, full citizenship rests on participation in the market, not birth.[2] This marketization of citizenship threatens to reinvigorate the condition Du Bois found most responsible for retarding black progress—"the widespread feeling all over the land . . . that the Negro is something less than an American."

As we assess the damage, Du Bois would not allow us to overlook or explain away the very real reduction in poverty among African Americans, the increased rate of high school graduation and college attendance, the growth in home ownership, progress in pursuit of income parity, and the expanding black middle class. He would emphasize, as he had a century earlier, poverty's complex etiology and the inadequacy of simple single-causal models, whether advanced by the political right or left. He would echo his earlier call for research that would hold in tension the forces of structure and agency by focusing on both the characteristics of groups in need and their "social environment"—the political economy of the welfare state.

His archeological dig into the foundations of black economic support and social advance, however, would uncover its underlying fragility. He would find poverty still showing itself in "especial suffering and neglect among the children of the poor." He would turn up, as he had before, racial discrimination as well as national trends in poverty and inequality accentuated among blacks who also confront problems that arise "from the peculiar history and condition of the American Negro." He would discover an emergent definition of citizenship that labels many African Americans "something less than an American." At the end of the twentieth century, he would add to the list of special problems confronting African Americans the institutional racism built into the architecture of the welfare state (and, of course, many corporate and educational structures). He would confront the paradox that a welfare state scarred by institutional racism remains essential to the survival of millions of African Americans with minimal comfort and dignity, and he surely would worry about the impact of its transformation.

Notes

1. Poverty estimates for blacks age 65 and over were calculated by Professor Mark Stern at my request. My great thanks to Professor Stern for these data. For an explanation of how he derives poverty estimates for the 1940s, see Stern 1991 and Stern 1995, 231-34, nn. 13, 16-18. Calculation of the standard error shows estimates of poverty among whites and blacks age 65 and over to be reliable, with the exception of blacks in Michigan, where the numbers in the sample were very small. An analysis of variance shows the difference in poverty rates for individuals age 65 and over between the states to be greater than the differences within them; the F statistic is significant at the 0.000 level.

2. The most articulate exposition of this view of citizenship is Mead 1986.

References

Bell, W. 1965. *Aid to Dependent Children*. New York: Columbia University Press.

Bellows, B. L. 1983. *Tempering the Wind: The Southern Response to Urban Poverty, 1850-1865*. Columbia: University of South Carolina Press.

Brown, M. K. 1999. *Race, Money, and the American Welfare State*. Ithaca, NY: Cornell University Press.

Cohen, W. 1991. *At Freedom's Edge: Black Mobility and the Southern White Quest for Racial Control 1861-1915*. Baton Rouge: University of Louisiana Press.

Davies, G. and M. Derthick. 1997. Race and Social Welfare Policy: The Social Security Act of 1935. *Political Science Quarterly* 112:217-35.

Du Bois, W.E.B. 1898. The Study of the Negro Problems. The Annals of the American Academy of Political and Social Science 11(Jan.):1-23.

——. [1899] 1973. *The Philadelphia Negro: A Social Study*. Millwood, NY: Kraus-Thomson.

——. [1901] 1969. *The Black North in 1901: A Social Study*. New York: Arno Press and *New York Times*.

Gordon, L. 1994. *Pitied But Not Entitled: Single Mothers and the History of Welfare*. New York: Free Press.

Grob, G. 1973. *Mental Institutions in America: Social Policy to 1875*. New York: Free Press.

Katz, Michael B. 1996. *In the Shadow of the Poorhouse: A Social History of Welfare in America*. New York: Basic Books.

——. Forthcoming. *Market Price or Social Justice? Redefining America's Welfare State*. New York: Metropolitan Books.

Katz, Michael B. and Thomas J. Sugrue. 1998. Introduction. In W.E.B. Du Bois, *Race, and the City: The Philadelphia Negro and Its Legacy*, ed. M. B. Katz and T. J. Sugrue. Philadelphia: University of Pennsylvania Press.

Lieberman, R. C. 1998. *Shifting the Color Line: Race and the American Welfare State*. Cambridge, MA: Harvard University Press.

Mead, L. M. 1986. *Beyond Entitlement: The Social Obligations of Citizenship*. New York: Free Press.

Miller, A. T. 1995. Social Science, Social Policy, and the Heritage of African-American Families. In *The "Underclass" Debate: Views from History*, ed. M. B. Katz. Princeton, NJ: Princeton University Press.

Quadagno, J. 1988. *The Transformation of Old Age Security: Class and Politics in the American Welfare State*. Chicago: University of Chicago Press.

———. 1994. *The Color of Welfare: How Racism Undermined the War on Poverty*. New York: Oxford University Press.

Rosenberg, C. 1987. *The Care of Strangers: The Rise of America's Hospital System*. New York: Basic Books.

Ruggles, S. et al. 1997. Integrated Public Use Microdata Series: Version 2.0. Minneapolis: University of Minnesota, Historical Census Projects. Available at http://www.ipums.umw.edu

Schneider, E. C. 1992. *In the Web of Class: Delinquents and Reformers in Boston, 1810s-1930s*. New York: New York University Press.

Skocpol, T. 1995. African Americans in U.S. Social Policy. In *Classifying by Race*, ed. P. E. Peterson. Princeton, NJ: Princeton University Press.

Stern, M. J. 1991. Poverty and the Life Cycle, 1940-1969. *Journal of Social History* 24(3):521-40.

———. 1995. Poverty and Family Composition Since 1940. In *The "Underclass" Debate: Views from History*, ed. M. B. Katz. Princeton, NJ: Princeton University Press.

Sterner, R. 1943. *The Negro's Share: A Study of Income, Consumption, Housing and Public Assistance*. New York: Harper & Brothers.

ANNALS, *AAPSS*, **568**, March 2000

Identity and Economic Performance

By GERALD D. JAYNES

ABSTRACT: Reductions in the employment of less-skilled Americans during recent decades are often attributed to a deterioration in work values. That view is challenged. The key determinants have been deteriorating earnings opportunities and the poor's assimilation of mainstream values. Urbanization facilitates less-skilled workers' assimilation of preferences for high standards of living and egalitarian interpersonal relations found in advanced economic democracies. The rewards received in the competition for jobs become major affirmations or denials of the validity of self-perceptions. Demand for public respect induces people to avoid jobs perceived to be demeaning even as the proportion of such jobs increases. Traditional scientific data are combined with personal documents (autobiography and rap music) to construct subject-centered analyses of behavior. The data enrich the contextual basis for explaining behaviors of low-status men labeled the "malcontented."

Gerald D. Jaynes is professor of economics and of African and African American studies, Yale University. His current research examines the interaction of values and ideology with the structure of social institutions in the production of behavior and the perpetuation of poverty.

But they [whites] should not keep these prizes . . . some, all, I would wrest from them . . . by reading law, by healing the sick, by telling the wonderful tales that swam in my head, some way. With other black boys the strife was not so fiercely sunny: their youth shrunk into tasteless sycophancy, or into silent hatred of the pale world about them and mocking distrust of everything white; or wasted itself in a bitter cry.

—W.E.B. Du Bois (1903)

In *The Philadelphia Negro* (1899), W.E.B. Du Bois devotes only a few pages to the dialectical relationship between a person's self-image and his social position. This dialectic, a major determinant of social behavior, is a problem particularly acute for African Americans and one Du Bois would give a brilliant but laconic statement in his most famous essay.

The Hegelian formulation of the dialectic of Negro identity and social status that forms the theoretical basis of the first chapter of *The Souls of Black Folk* (Du Bois 1903) is implicated in several sections of the earlier book. There, issues of self-image and social behavior are most evident in discussions of employment and criminal behavior. The black streetcorner men and women of whom Du Bois writes in 1899 had a pervasive presence throughout American history, North and South, in cities and small towns. That presence is attested to in myriad historical studies and contemporaneous research monograms, not the least of which is Du Bois's own *The Negro American Family* (1908).

Bitter resentment of severely blocked opportunities to employment disappointed ambitions and bred a sullen and easily offended black laboring class with minimal incentives to labor industriously. The resultant atmosphere of rebellion and discontent fueled conditions supporting rationalization of personal failures and listless despair. These forces, argued Du Bois, turned "black boys and girls into gamblers, prostitutes, and rascals" (Du Bois 1899, 138, 351).

The diagnosis locates the economic subject, who is generally unemployed and alienated from the occasional job offer, betwixt a personal demand for self-respect and a nonaffirming social structure. That subject, constrained by perceptions of an environment vacant of opportunity, may with dogged resignation accept his fate as a low-status worker; he may sink into despair and apathy, or he may learn in the company of similarly situated subjects that projection of a self-chosen oppositional identity is among the most basic and empowering forms of human agency possible.

Such identic agencies span a range of identities from the constructive rebellion of those who pursue prizes reserved for the other to the wasted and bitter cry of the street hustlers, criminals, and no-accounts. Social outcomes are neither structural inevitabilities nor behavioral destinies fated by genes or pathological cultures. Social outcomes are mediated by human choices interacting with experience. That mediation occurs within social institutions, the family, schools, labor markets, churches. When institutions fail to affirm an individual's self-image, his response to the status discrepancy corresponds to identity formation.

To interpret what motivates these agencies, we must discover how social identity is related to social institutions that affirm or deny a self-image. By centering on the subjects' own views of the motivations, attitudes, and beliefs undergirding their behavior, we may construct interpretations derived from the meaning social actions have for the actors themselves. Such subject-centered interpretations, although derived from the actor's perspective, should not be held hostage to it. The goal is to interpret behavior in terms of the entire constellation of underlying motives, not merely the motives recognized by the actor.

The articulation of a point of view represents a subjective viewpoint. Frequently, the communication of a subjective viewpoint reveals information that is incompatible with that viewpoint. Acceptable interpretations of behavior cannot be based on self-undermining data. The social scientist must deconstruct the subjective viewpoint to uncover motivations hidden from the actor but relevant to his actions.

DISCURSIVE LOCATION

Combining the subject's explanations with objective measures of his social position reveals a discursive location. A discursive location is the vantage point an external observer ascribes to an agent whose subjective viewpoint has been deconstructed. This vantage point is an analytical construct that resituates the deconstructed subjective viewpoint and the agent's observed social location into a more general discursive space where interpretation of the agent's actions remains subject centered but is not necessarily subject determined.

In ongoing research, I combine traditional social science data (for example, census and other survey data and ethnographic research) with autobiography, letters, historical documents, and a subgenre of rap music I label testimonial rap to construct subject-centered analyses of the behavior of the urban poor. This article applies this methodology to the question of labor market behavior among young low-status men whose discursive location is labeled the "malcontented."

The vantage point of the malcontented is defined with respect to a discursive space that is structured on three topics of discourse: the value the labor market confers on the subject, the subject's self-valuation, and the subject's evaluation of the distributive principles of the labor market.

The malcontented's location is constituted by the following verbalizations: they are valued low by social institutions, they verbalize a high self-valuation, and they disparage the distributive principles of the social institutions that devalue them. Jaynes (1999a, 1999b) shows that the defense mechanisms malcontents use to cope with the social psychological pressures of status discrepancy disclose their articulated point of view to be self-undermining.

IDENTITY AND
LABOR SUPPLY

It is a common observation that during the past quarter century joblessness among less-skilled Americans has increased dramatically. This labor supply response supports a much richer interpretive field than the common practice of labeling the chronically jobless as lazy and/or bereft of positive values. Labor market behavior cannot be compartmentalized into a purely economic decision; the rewards received in the competition for jobs are major affirmations or denials of the validity of men's and women's self-perceptions.

Less-skilled Americans have assimilated the nonnegotiable preferences for high standards of living and egalitarian interpersonal relations found in the world's advanced economic democracies. This demand for public respect induces many less-skilled people to avoid jobs perceived to be demeaning even as the proportion of such jobs available to the bottom quarter of wage earners in the postindustrial economy is increasing. To gain access to deeper interpretations of labor supply behavior, we must examine the malcontented's discursive location.

Nothing conveys the labor market alienation of the malcontented better than their use of the term "slave" and its semantic equivalents to describe certain types of employment. Contrary to the belief that this term represents an attitude toward any employment and that it indicates the development of a relatively recent "poor work ethic" among the late-twentieth-century inner-city poor,

referring to certain types of jobs as "slaves" invokes a complex metaphor with a long history. That history manifests a continuity in the discursive locations of many working-class urbanized blacks throughout the twentieth century. Moreover, it has similarities among descendants of other agrarian immigrants to American cities (Jaynes 1999a).

Explication of the social meaning of this concept clarifies the relation between discursive location, identity, and labor supply. To refer to a job as a slave is to make several highly repugnant claims about the job and its occupant. If the metaphor is taken seriously, then being employed in a slave brands one, by self-admission, if not a slave precisely, then at least slavelike. Thus, to work in a slave is likely to severely undermine one's identity and damage self-esteem. Among persons whose discursive location admits the term, a slave is clearly something to be avoided.

Slave does not refer to all employment. A slave is defined in opposition to a "good job" (this allows its characteristics to change with the social standard of living). The most important characteristics of a slave job are that it entails repellent interpersonal relations; it involves demeaning and close supervision; it does not offer a career—longtime employees are doing the same work, under the same demeaning conditions, as those newly hired; and it does not pay well or at least not well enough given its other characteristics.

Use of the term is not restricted to hustlers, to men, or to recent generations of the poor. Women working as domestics in New York at least as early as the 1930s spoke of these same negatives when discussing the jobs to be had at the "Bronx slave market" (the corner of 174th Street and Sedgwick Avenue) where whites would drive by and hire workers.

The malcontented will have great difficulty accepting the kinds of jobs that are offered to them. Moreover, they will refer to the existence of such jobs as proof that their criticism of the purported distributive principles of the labor market is confirmed; that their own low valuation by such an unjust institution should be ignored; and, finally, to carry the entire metaphor to its logical conclusion, that as fugitives evading slavery they are justified in adopting any means necessary to ensure their personal survival.

THE TROPE OF FORCED AGENCY AND SUSPENDED VALUES

The malcontented's verbalized point of view is similar to the viewpoint articulated by the slave girl Harriet Jacobs (pseudonym Linda Brent) who to escape the repugnant sexual advances of her master chose to enter a love affair and conceive children with another white man (Brent 1973). This desperate act of free agency, exercised within the limits of a constrained situation, caused Harriet Jacobs considerable moral anguish. We may say that the contemporary malcontented, like Jacobs, choose to lose public respect in order to gain self-respect. The point is illustrated nicely in the following rap poem delivered by a Baltimore street hustler during the mid-1960s:

A hustler is a very wise person, but yet he's lost, he's a person who refuses to "eight," (for Charlie) the white boss. His life consists of heartaches, a little pleasure and no pity at times I hesitate to believe that hustlers are very witty. His profession ranges from dealing seconds to controlling the cue from conning, pimping and cheating at crap and sometimes after making a misplay, he'll gladly confess that being a backstreet hustler is his own mishap. This cat is cool, smooth, sharp, handsome, dashing and neat except his eyes are always red because he doesn't get very much sleep. Now with the exception of his red eyes a normal face will remain but then his nose is always raw, from snorting the best of cocaine. He possesses a lively tongue, the instant gift of gab he's a liar and an actor and to the ladies never a drag. Now when this man has a good day, you'll see him smile, hear him say "All bona fide hustlers come forward, all suckers stay away." The moral of this poem is very sad but true a hustler's life is not all roses most of it is blue and chumps you be glad the title "hustler" doesn't mean you. There will come a time, when great things will seem quite normal not unique at all. Something standing strong and erect will eventually someday fall. The tall black stallion will get corralled or stumble to its own end over a stone, well The Backstreet Hustler is sure to die broke, unmarried, unwanted and most of all alone. (Hudson 1977, 415-16)

This rap poem illustrates several aspects of the hustler's philosophy and value system. His discursive location is that of the malcontented. The underlying point of view emphasizes values of independence, self-determination of the work/leisure choice, hard work, maintenance of social dignity, and freedom from white control. While the rap poem provides evidence of pride in the life-style chosen, much of this pride is lodged in the negative act of refusing to slave—"eight"—under white supervision. About his actual lifestyle there is great ambivalence, even regret. The backstreet hustler's message is shaped by a gritty realism; he entertains no prospects for a really satisfying life, and his lifestyle would not be chosen under more favorable circumstances. The backstreet hustler is doomed by his own chosen lifestyle and he knows it.

The tragic irony dominating these lyrics renders an implicit statement of the malcontented's most central ideological stance, the trope of forced agency and the phenomenon of suspended values. Stated briefly, the trope of forced agency is a commonly articulated argument that rationalizes the commission of negative and immoral acts. Such acts are said to be forced because the actor is confronted with an extremely restricted range of noxious alternatives from which he must choose. Implicit in the trope of forced agency is the inference that the agent would not violate the relevant values if he or she were given real choices. The trope implies suspended values.

To verbalize the trope of forced agency is to demonstrate a commitment to the values in question. Confronted by limited, even determining, choices, the agent fails to abide by the values in practice. But that practice is merely a suspension of the values, not an abandonment in principle—if constraints circumscribing behavior were relaxed, the subject claims he would adhere to the values. From a policy perspective, the importance of suspended values is that agents who verbalize them may change their behavior if environmental choices are appropriately expanded.

Jaynes (1999a, 1999b) demonstrates that a subgenre of rap music labeled testimonial gangsta rap articulates the discursive location of lower-working-class African American malcontents. Thus, contemporary rap contains some of the clearest explications of the trope of forced agency, suspended values, and the social meaning of the word "slave." In "A Bird in the Hand," from his 1992 album *Death Certificate*, Los Angeles rapper Ice Cube, formerly with NWA (niggas with attitude) and among the founders of gangsta rap, defines slave by example in a testimonial that utilizes the trope of forced agency to rationalize why poor youths sell drugs.

While the narrator would prefer to work in a black organization (preferably one with a black nationalist orientation such as the Nation of Islam), he finds that the black economy offers too few good jobs. Nonetheless, because he believes corporate employers like AT&T is turned down. Moneyless, in desperation, he accepts what he calls a slave job only as a last resort. The narrator clearly implies that slave jobs are in plentiful supply, being readily available to people just like him. The good jobs, however, are rationed and African Americans are placed at the bottom of the hiring queue due to discrimination..

That last sentiment is an implicit introduction of the trope. Since blacks are denied access to good jobs, the narrator is about to resign himself to his fate, selling drugs, an activity commonly referred to as "clocking gs." However, he introduces moral tension by implying that he is not ready to surrender his moral worth by dealing drugs, even if it means working as a slave. Even so, the driving force of the trope has been activated. Although the economy contains good employment opportunities, those jobs are for others. For people in his social location, the opportunity structure of the American economy is narrowed to a stark Manichaean choice—become a slave or sell drugs.

In the rap, McDonald's is a synecdoche for any job in a fast-food restaurant or equivalently any "slave." The rap offers a negative critique of the political-economic structure that offers people jobs that fail to pay a living wage and then has the gall to extract taxes from those sub-subsistence wages. The rap states the trope of forced agency clearly by framing a rhetorical question that, from the narrator's perspective, needs no response: given the inadequate standard of living available to lower-wage workers, do they have to push illegal drugs to house and feed their families?

He argues that for young men near the social location implied by the narrative, poor urban black men, the drug economy provides the only opportunity to obtain a decent standard of living. To political elites who argue with political scientist Lawrence Meade (1989) that the poor earn public assistance by deporting themselves as such elites require, he

demurs; passive acquiescence to marginal economic survival in an unresponsive political system with weak black support structures is no social contract. A reference in the rap to then President George Bush, is a synecdoche for the entire political-economic system, and that system needs a radical cleansing. If the narrator waits for help from the government or black middle-class-oriented self-help organizations, he could starve.

The final strophe of "A Bird in the Hand" exemplifies further the process of suspended values. The narrator justifies his drug dealing as forced agency to ensure his survival. And he rationalizes that agency further by reminding the listener that drug use is a common activity throughout society, even among well-known celebrities. The rap ends with an uncompromising argument. The words of political elites trying to cajole people through moral suasion (a government campaign of the period was "just say no to drugs") are worth little to poor people confronting survival in a nonremunerative labor market.

In the end, he admits that dealing drugs is morally wrong but insists people trapped in his social location have no viable alternatives. This rationalization illustrates how internalized moral values can be suspended in practice but not abandoned in principle.

The Geto Boys out of Houston, Texas, provide another testimonial rap based on the trope of forced agency and suspended values, "I Ain't with Being Broke" (1991). One of the final strophes gives a detailed explication of the social meaning of "slave."

Their compact statement makes some points implicitly, but the major characteristics that differentiate a good job from a slave are stated clearly. The narrator explains that he attempted to ready himself for legitimate employment by getting his high school equivalency diploma but was unable to obtain a good job. His doubt that any employer will offer someone in his social location a good job suggests he is aware of both class and racial limitations on his employment opportunities. That interpretation is consistent with other material from this group and with the overwhelming tenor of rap lyrics. McDonald's is again a synecdoche for any "slave."

Note again the contrast in the narrator's treatment of the employment dynamics involved. The good jobs, for which he earned a G.E.D. in the hopes of obtaining, present a demand-side problem; he applies but cannot find a position. Nonemployment at a slave, however, is a supply-side problem; he implies he could get such jobs but does not want them. Slave jobs, like a poorly tailored suit of clothes, do not conform to the shape of the wearer. In such jobs, employees are worked liked animals, are spoken to line menials, and are not paid enough to compensate for the poor working conditions. To the narrator, working in these jobs is analogous to going through life in a deathlike state. No wonder, he tells his listeners that ghetto men push drugs.

The malcontenteds' discursive location is shaped by the discrepancy between their self-image and the value placed on them. Low-pay service work is rejected because as the "slave" metaphor suggests, the status and self-esteem of adult occupants of such jobs would be demeaned by the package of conditions coming with the employment: hard working conditions and subordinate role behavior for wages that are too low to compensate for the conditions of employment.

FROM TESTIMONIAL
RAP TO ETHNOGRAPHY

These well-articulated perspectives contextualize the meaning of the term "decent" job in the remarks of a 35-year-old interview respondent to the Chicago Urban Poverty and Family Life Study conducted during 1987-88. The respondent makes an argument basically identical to that offered by the testimony of the rappers and explicitly invokes suspended values and the trope of forced agency.

I'm a cocaine dealer 'cause I can't get a decent-ass job. So, what other choices do I have? I have to feed my family. . . . I work. I been working since I was fifteen years old . . . can't nobody bring me that bullshit about I ain't looking for no job. (Wilson 1996, 58)

Kenneth Clarke reported similar justifications from the drug-dealing warlord of a Harlem gang during the early 1960s:

You want me to go down to the garment district and push one of those trucks through the street and at the end of the week take home $40 or $50 if I'm lucky?

They don't have animals doing what you want me to do. There would be some society to protect animals if anybody had them pushing them damn trucks around. I'm better than an animal, but nobody protects me. Go away, mister. I got to look out for myself. (Clarke 1965, 13)

Claude Brown's brilliant autobiographical and ethnographical account of life in Harlem during the period 1940-65 confirms both the ubiquity of the last attitude expressed and my explication of the social meaning of slave. About employment in the garment center (a major employer of black New Yorkers during most of this century), which he tried and quit, he had this to say:

A guy who worked in the garment center wouldn't say he had a job; he'd say, "Man, like, I got a slave." That was what it amounted to. It was a real drag. I had seen old men down there, old colored cats. . . . They looked like they were about sixty years old, but they were still pushing trucks through the snow. I knew I didn't want to be doing that kind of shit. I'd rather be in jail or someplace. (Brown 1965, 184)

It is an error to assume that these men and women were avoiding jobs because they were lazy. To the contrary, significantly, these testimonials imply that the hustlers' value system does not reject work so much as it rejects work that requires the assumption of servile attitudes and demeanor and low social prestige. The work life of the street hustler is exceedingly demanding with long hours. In Malcolm X's first hustle, his mentor instructed him, "Get here early . . . everything in place . . . you

never need to waste motion" (Haley 1965, 46). And at the height of his criminal activity in Harlem, he, like other hustlers, was working long, desperate hours, selling reefer, avoiding police, constantly moving:

I kept turning over my profit, increasing my supplies, and I sold reefers like a wild man. I scarcely slept . . . a roll of money was in my pocket . . . I felt for the first time in my life, that great feeling of free! . . . I was the peer of the other young hustlers. (Haley 1965, 99)

Nathan McCall, referring to his experiences as a criminal hustler during the 1970s in Portsmouth, Virginia, discovered the demanding work ethic required to become successful:

I quickly discovered that dealing wasn't as easy as it seemed. Selling reefer was a round-the-clock hustle that required more time and energy than I wanted to invest. . . . Guys . . . were always looking for me . . . all hours of the day and night. Dudes always wanted me to meet them in out-of-the-way places to deliver the goods. . . . I had to rough it, work the streets and stay there most of the time. . . . I finally had to admit that I lacked the discipline to be a good dealer. Dealing drugs is harder than any job I've had, then or since. (McCall 1994, 121-23)

McCall's avoidance of the mainstream labor market represents a classic real-world testimonial to the ubiquitous presence of the trope of forced agency and suspended values. As a young boy observing the race relations on jobs held by his parents' generation, seeds of malcontent sprouted within him:

I wasn't sure how Country got his money. . . . All that mattered to me was that he chose not to earn his living slaving at the shipyard or bowing to white folks on some other gig. Turkey had an older brother who was definitely a hustler. He and his friends gave me my first inside look at those blacks who live and operate almost completely outside the white man's system. (McCall 1994, 80-81)

Black avoidance of white-controlled employment networks is crucial to any understanding of the political economy of labor supply. Historically, African Americans' major defense against demeaning treatment in interracial relations has been avoidance of whites. Such avoidance continues to be a significant determinant of black labor supply.

SELF-RESPECT AND AVOIDANCE OF RACIALIZED LABOR MARKETS

I argue that social scientists researching labor market inequality have overlooked workplace race relations as a contributing factor (Jaynes 1998). Despite significant movement toward equal treatment of minorities with respect to wage and hiring practices, interracial relations at the workplace continue to inflict public humiliation on black employees. Blacks are subjected to rude and exclusionary treatment and confronted with attitudes of condescension from white coworkers and supervisors.

Moreover, wage deterioration, increased immigration of less educated workers willing to accept harsh and authoritarian working conditions, and spatial movement of jobs out of central cities has increased the proportion of jobs deemed undesirable. These changes have accentuated reductions in labor supply.

Across class status, blacks voicing disaffection from employment in white-owned firms make similar complaints. To succeed, they must mask their black identity and assimilate a persona acceptable to white coworkers and supervisors. Consequently, many blacks continue to avoid social institutions such as the labor market.

But access to means of avoidance and its costs are differentiated by class. Middle-class African Americans working in mostly white organizations are compensated generously for any stress they suffer. Among low-pay workers, more blatant affronts to self-worth must be endured for remuneration inadequate to escape poverty. For many, the labor market has not met their price for adjustment and conformity. Such avoidance invariably leads to oppositional identities and crime.

CONCLUSION

The deterioration in wage opportunities occurring during the past few decades supports the belief (when viewed from the bottom of the class structure) that for poor African Americans little has changed since 1970. Many of today's black poor sit in a racialized class position from which they perceive themselves to be limited to social locations similar to those that constrained African American identities before the

1960s. This backward-looking perspective does not describe African Americans' situation generally. Indeed, one way of understanding the altered race relations affecting American society since the 1970s is to observe that blacks are no longer (categorically) constrained to historical social locations. But important analyses of the negative effects of residential segregation on the socioeconomic status of blacks show that improved opportunities exist much more for the middle class than for the poor (Massey and Denton 1992; Wilson 1987). Given that reality, the black deeply poor's social isolation veils their vision of society with hues of the past, as the identity choices and the discursive locations they occupy reenact scenarios scripted by earlier generations.

This line of analysis complicates our understanding of the relation between joblessness and social disorganization. I believe we have gone too far in stressing the ability of work per se to rejuvenate communities devastated by postindustrial joblessness and poverty. If the vast majority of those in deep poverty were the apathetic carriers of cultural deficits, as presumed by the 1996 welfare reforms, those reforms might make sound policy; if all of the deeply poor (not just a strong majority) were pure archetypes of the structural poor, then creating jobs of any kind would put most of the poor to work. But a significant subset of the postindustrial poor, especially young men, are malcontents and will not accept the kinds of employment currently available or likely to be made available under the kinds of social policies currently being discussed.

Reaching future generations of the malcontented will require serious and massive private sector and public interventions into the education, training, and job opportunities available to the poor. Our tasks as scholars, social scientists, and activists are to ascertain the facts as clearly as we can, endeavor to understand how and why individuals make the social choices they do, and then, recognizing that life is highly complex, in sober humility prescribe policies designed to expand agents' perceptions of their available choices so that they may improve their own lives and ours.

References

Brent, Linda. 1973. *Incidents in the Life of a Slave Girl*. New York: Harcourt Brace.

Brown, Claude. 1965. *Manchild in the Promised Land*. New York: Signet.

Clarke, Kenneth. 1965. *Dark Ghetto*. New York: Harper & Row.

Du Bois, W.E.B. 1899. *The Philadelphia Negro*. Philadelphia: University of Pennsylvania Press.

———. 1903. *The Souls of Black Folk*. New York: Signet.

———. 1908. *The Negro American Family*. Atlanta University Study no. 13. Atlanta, GA: Atlanta University Press.

Haley, Alex. 1965. *The Autobiography of Malcolm X*. New York: Ballantine.

Hudson, Julius. 1977. The Hustling Ethic. In *Rappin' and Stylin' Out*, ed. Thomas Kochman. Urbana: University of Illinois Press.

Jaynes, Gerald D. 1998. Race and Class in Postindustrial Employment. *American Economic Review* May.

———. 1999a. Deep Poverty: Social Existence Under Postindustrial Poverty. Manuscript, Yale University, New Haven, CT.

———. 1999b. Rap: Freedom and Identity in Urban America. Manuscript, Yale University, New Haven, CT.

Massey, Douglas S. and Nancy Denton. 1992. *American Apartheid*. Cambridge, MA: Harvard University Press.

McCall, Nathan. 1994. *Makes Me Wanna Holler*. New York: Random House.

Meade, Lawrence. 1989. The Logic of Workfare: The Underclass and Work Policy. *The Annals* of the American Academy of Political and Social Science 501(Jan.):156-69.

Wilson, William J. 1987. *The Truly Disadvantaged*. Chicago: University of Chicago Press.

———. 1996. *When Work Disappears*. New York: Vintage.

Anthropology: From Bones
to the Human Genome

By JAMES E. BOWMAN

ABSTRACT: Race is an interminable subject of controversy. Nevertheless, people do differ and once were classified on the basis of skin color. With the advent of genetic markers, and more recently DNA differences, with myriad intragroup variability, many geneticists view race as an anachronism. Unfortunately, prejudice permeates human classifications. In the United States, a black mother cannot have a white baby, but a white mother can have a black baby. An African American could be in one of 40 categories in Brazil; in South Africa be classified black, coloured, or white; but in the Middle East be perceived as a member of a local population. In the early 1970s, African Americans were selectively tested for sickle hemoglobin and discriminated against in sports, employment, and health and life insurance as a result of misinformation distributed by the federal government and African American community programs. The Lawrence Berkeley Laboratory (supported by the U.S. Department of Energy) was recently sued for selectively testing African Americans for sickle hemoglobin and syphilis.

James E. Bowman is professor emeritus in the Departments of Pathology and Medicine and is senior scholar for the MacLean Center for Clinical Medical Ethics at the University of Chicago. He has held fellowships at St. Luke's Hospital, Chicago (pathology); University College London (genetics); and the Center for Advanced Study in the Behavioral Sciences, Stanford. He has conducted research in and consulted on population genetics in several countries. He has authored two books and over 90 articles.

MOST human and medical geneticists, human population geneticists, and some physical anthropologists maintain that "race" is out of fashion. Rarely do we see references to Negroid, Caucasian, Mongoloid, and Australoid races. In Africa, peoples of African origin resent being referred to as Negro, for they look upon Negroes as being descendants of slavery in the Americas (Bowman and Murray 1990). Even so, peoples do differ, and although race today may be viewed as a continuum, peoples are still classified. Even a 3-year-old child can delineate physical differences between a Nigerian Yoruba and a Swede. Unfortunately, however, centuries of prejudice and discrimination based on physical differences are apparently immutable.

COMPLEXITIES OF DIVERSITY

Peoples of African origin are quite diverse—perhaps more diverse than Europeans (Bowman and Murray 1990). As one example, both the tallest people in the world (the Tutsi and Nuer) and the shortest people (pygmies) live in Africa. Hammerschmidt (1999), editor of the *Journal of Laboratory and Clinical Medicine* (the official journal of the Central Society for Clinical Research) developed, with other editors of scientific journals, fairly strict criteria for accepting papers that use racial classification of patients and population subjects. He states,

"Black" subjects, for example, may include slave descendants, whose ancestors were from West Africa, but may also include recent immigrants from South Asia, the horn of Africa, South Africa, certain Pacific Islands, and even Australia. The genetic diversity between some of these groups (as estimated from a number of DNA homology studies) is as great as the disparity between some groups of "blacks" and "whites." (Hammerschmidt 1999, 11)

I add to this group some Southern Asian Indians. Descendants of the Veddoids in India have darker skin than most African populations south of the Sahara. On the other hand, many Asian Indians from Kashmir may be indistinguishable physically from Northern Europeans. In short, race based on physical appearance is not a precise enough concept to be used as a categorical variable in science (Hammerschmidt 1999).

Accordingly, Hammerschmidt and many other science and medical editors will reject a paper if human categories are not precisely defined, even to the point of a general category. For example, a category of "a black Chicago population" would be imprecise according to the new criteria. The editors argue if the population is only described as black or white, how may the study be replicated?

Today we know that even though genetic variation is used to delineate populations and ethnic groups, often there is more intragroup variance than intergroup variance. No matter what, we are all the same species (Homo sapiens), for whenever divers peoples have met, mating between dissimilar peoples has produced fertile offspring.

Cavalli-Sforza (1997) stated unequivocally that "races do not exist"

(53). He asserted that there is such continuity in variation from place to place that it is practically impossible to define race, except in very general terms. Cavalli-Sforza also maintained that in order to be precise, there would have to be thousands of races. Cavalli-Sforza was one of the main instigators of the Human Diversity Project. Bob Murray and I assert that there are as many racial classifications as there are investigators (Bowman and Murray 1990). The vagaries of classification of peoples of African origin are numerous.

THE LAW OF HYPODESCENT

In the United States, a black mother cannot have a white child, but a white mother can have a black child. This anachronism arose to perpetuate slavery, for if a black mother could have a white child, her offspring could no longer be slaves, which would have been an economic disaster to slave owners. According to D'Souza (1995), exceptions to this rule have occurred if the mother is white, but such is not current practice.

Classifications of peoples of African descent in the United States are as changeable as the moon. In the early days of the United States, African Americans were known by various pejorative terms, which need not be repeated here. African Americans have been variously classified as mulatto, colored, Negro, black, and African American. (Interestingly and pejoratively, the word "mulatto" is derived from "mule," an offspring of a horse and a donkey.) Today, however, African Americans could be called black in the United States and 1 of at least 40 classifications in Brazil, for in Brazil, money "whitens." Pelé, the Brazilian football (soccer) star, was born black, but Pelé has a master's degree and he is wealthy. Today, he is white. An African American in South Africa may be categorized as white, coloured, or black. In the Middle East, classifications include Arab, Egyptian, or Iranian. Some African Americans insist that children of a black-white parentage should be classified as mixed. And why not? Other children of matings between members of different ethnic groups also insist on being categorized as mixed.

In the United States, untold thousands of descendants of Africans are lost within European American and other populations. "Passing" has long been in vogue. Several of my African American colleagues in college and medical school ignore me on the street and in national conferences. They are passing. One former classmate of mine is now passing and moved far away from home. Her father had blond hair and blue eyes but her mother could be identified externally as African American. (But, of course, she could resemble many other ethnic groups.) When her father died, she only allowed her mother to live with her as her maid.

Even so, as Cornel West asserted, "race matters" (West 1993). And it does unless one has lived in a cave all of one's life. Sociologists, political scientists, historians, and other scholars use race in diverse publications, but D'Souza (1995) obfuscates the picture in *The End of Racism*. He, like most geneticists, insists on "ethnic groups" in preference to race. I will not quibble, because I also use this category, but he goes too far. He maintains that Asian Indians, or Chinese, or Japanese do not practice racism because they are not races. Nevertheless, there is no society that practices more blatant discrimination among its own peoples than Asian Indians.

Keown (1987) pointed out that, in contrast to most Western ethical principles, the same moral rules should apply to all, but with respect to the caste system such an idea is nonsense, because caste determines the rightness of actions. For example, the same act may be acceptable for a Brahmin but wrong for an outcast. Gandhi tried to eliminate the pernicious caste system in India but failed. Chinese and Japanese historically looked upon peoples other than their own group as barbarians. But D'Souza claims that since they are not races they cannot be called racists.

Black activists also obfuscate the notion of race by asserting that blacks cannot be racists because they are victims of racism, but whites can be racists. Nonsense. Blacks also have long practiced intragroup racism, usually based on skin color. Witness my previous example of a former classmate of mine who practiced racism against her own mother. Her form of racism is far more pernicious than racism of one group against another.

Many years ago at a sickle cell disease conference in Canada, my black colleagues in Canada were upset because the Canadian census did not use racial classifications. They believed, and perhaps rightfully so, "How could they document the inequities in Canada if there were no statistics on race?" The outstanding scholarship of my former colleague at the University of Chicago, William Julius Wilson, and others would be remiss if it did not have the advantage of the U.S. national health, census, and other population statistics in addition to reports of private foundations and state statistics, all of which use racial categories (Wilson 1987, 1996). Voting patterns would be indiscernible without this important information. We must know who we are, even though some of us decry the one-drop rule, which admittedly is also a racist peculiarity of our culture.

Williams (1976), cited by Bowman and Murray (1990), quoted a Sumerian legend: " 'What became of the Black people of Sumer?' the traveler asked the old man, 'for ancient records show that the people of Sumer were Black. What happened to them?' 'Ah,' the old man sighed. 'They lost their history, so they died.' "

CRANIAL NONSENSE

A most important way to subjugate peoples is to make them feel inferior so they will not challenge the ruling classes. What better way to do so than to make oppressed peoples believe that they have subnormal intelligence? The literature is replete with assertions that blacks have smaller brains than Europeans (Bowman and Murray 1990). On the other hand, since most of the anthropological literature on the subject is written by Europeans and their descendants, it would be odd if the results were skewed in favor of blacks.

Interestingly, however, a white South African wrote the article that punctured the brain-size myth (Tobias 1970). Tobias showed that brain size varies with sex, age at death, nutritional state in early life, source of sample, occupational group, cause of death, lapse of time after death, and many other parameters. He also asserted that unless corrections have been made for differences in body height and comparisons of mean brain sizes of different populations, valid statements cannot be made on interracial differences. Because no studies have made these corrections, all reported comparisons are invalid. Tobias also concluded that he could not substantiate that the cerebral cortex of blacks is thinner than that of whites.

Here, I will not contribute to the logjam in libraries on IQ differences. Academic and racist "poverty pimps" make tenure and fortunes by analyzing why poor homeless black children have lower IQ scores than affluent white children. Others are far more expert on the IQ scientific weapon than I am.

SKIN PIGMENTATION

The early classification of peoples was on the basis of skin color. Darker-skinned peoples live in tropical or desert climates, and light-skinned peoples live in temperate zones. Differences in skin color are explained by natural selection (Post and Rao 1977). As populations moved out of Africa into temperate zones, dark skin was at a disadvantage. If the diet did not contain vitamin D, darker-skinned peoples developed rickets and the pelvis of women became deformed; as a result, the infant mortality of darker-skinned peoples was higher than for those who were selected for light skin. Light skin is at a disadvantage in the tropics.

RACIAL ADMIXTURE

Various studies have estimated the extent of admixture of African Americans with European Americans (Politzer 1958; Bowman et al. 1967; Reed 1969; Cavalli-Sforza and Bodmer 1971; Chakraborty and Smouse 1988). These estimates range from a low of 4 percent in South Carolina to a high of 31 percent in Baltimore, further evidence that there is considerable intragroup genetic variation among African Americans. Accordingly, editors are quite correct in insisting that whenever "race" is used in scientific publications, authors be specific about the source or sources of their data.

SICKLE HEMOGLOBIN: SENSE AND NONSENSE

In the early days of the sickle hemoglobin screening fiasco in the United States, discrimination was rampant because of misconceptions (Bowman 1977, 1983). First, it was believed that sickle hemoglobin was confined to Africans and their descendants. Rather, sickle hemoglobin is found in appreciable frequency not only in Africans and their descendants but also Greeks,

Southern Italians (particularly Sicilians), Arabs, Egyptians, Southern Iranians, and Asian Indians.

Another misconception was the confusion of sickle cell trait, hemoglobin AS (the carrier state), with sickle cell anemia (hemoglobin SS) or sickle cell disease. Even the National Institutes of Health perpetuated this misinformation in the early 1970s. Such misinformation resulted in increased insurance premiums for African Americans with sickle cell trait even though their life expectancy and health were comparable with those who did not have sickle cell trait. Restrictions in sports activities for persons with sickle cell trait was rampant, even though some of our best athletes have sickle cell trait and performed well at the 1968 Olympics in the highlands of Mexico (altitude 7,000 to 9,000 feet) and on the football field in Denver, Colorado (altitude 5,000 feet). Believing the misinformation about sickle cell trait, many black community groups advocated the passage of mandatory sickle hemoglobin screening laws in at least 12 states. These laws were selective for blacks. Eventually, some peoples other than those of African descent with high frequencies of sickle hemoglobin threatened states to screen everyone for sickle hemoglobin, which, of course, they did not want to do. We also had our scientific weapon, but this time against discrimination.

Community pressure and allegedly politics resulted in the passage of the National Sickle Cell Anemia Control Act (1972), which was later modified to the Omnibus Genetics Bill (1976), and then the Health Services Amendments (1978). The title of the Sickle Cell Anemia Control Act was unfortunate because the "control" of sickle cell anemia—and most serious genetic disorders—is only possible today with eugenics practices reminiscent of Nazi Germany.

Sickle hemoglobin misinformation even infiltrated the first line of the Sickle Cell Anemia Control Act, which stated that over 2 million blacks in the United States have sickle cell anemia, rather than correctly stating that they have sickle cell trait. Federal legislation inaugurated a National Sickle Cell Disease Program, which supported community education, testing, and counseling programs; Comprehensive Sickle Centers with education, testing, counseling and research components; and Program Projects, which were limited to research. Federal guidelines for education, testing, and counseling programs were developed. The equation of sickle cell trait with sickle cell disease was rebutted. The National Sickle Cell Disease Program and the Hematology Section of the Centers for Disease Control also set standards for appropriate hemoglobin testing by various electrophoresis techniques and discouraged the use of a solubility test as the primary screening device (Bowman 1977).

The federally supported screening and education clinics were directed, unfortunately, to mass population screening of up to 20,000 subjects per year—an unrealistic goal because the personnel to appropriately administer the educational, counseling, and psychosocial needs of the target populations was not available, and still is not today.

Ostensibly, the major objective of these programs was to enable the community to make informed decisions about reproduction. This is nonsense. Since 1972 more than $260 million has been spent on federally sponsored sickle hemoglobin screening programs. Members of Congress would not have allocated these funds unless they believed that these screening programs would lead to a reduction in the number of children with sickle cell disease. If the programs were only informational, then there are much higher health priorities in the African American community. Counseling was allegedly nondirective, which is a standard caveat in genetic screening programs. But what were the options before the advent of prenatal diagnosis? They were all somewhat distasteful: abstinence, artificial insemination, genetic roulette, or abortion in the event of accidental pregnancy. But these programs were initiated before 1973, when abortion was available legally in only a few states.

NEWBORN SCREENING OF SICKLE CELL DISEASE

The development of reliable techniques for newborn screening and prenatal diagnosis of sickle cell disease, first through sampling of fetal blood and then by amniocentesis and now chorionic villous biopsy, ushered in a new phase of hemoglobin screening. Newborn screening was important because it was found that

morbidity and mortality in patients with sickle cell disease could be reduced by newborn diagnosis and the initiation of penicillin prophylaxis to prevent a major cause of death in infancy and early childhood, infections, particularly those of pneumococcal origin (Gaston et al. 1986). Unfortunately, important issues raised by newborn screening will be only alluded to in this article, because a proper discussion of the problems of newborn hemoglobinopathy screening diverts from prenatal diagnosis, to which I now turn.

PRENATAL DIAGNOSIS

The National Association for Sickle Cell Disease, under the leadership of its president, Dr. Charles F. Whitten, developed a position on prenatal diagnosis of sickle cell anemia (National Association 1990). On the first prenatal visit, all black mothers should be tested to determine whether they are carriers of the sickle cell gene. (Whitten's program emphasizes sickle hemoglobin, and not hemoglobinopathies, and only black pregnant women are screened.) Second, each mother who is a carrier should be counseled that the father should be tested to determine whether he is also a carrier, and that if both are carriers, tests can be conducted to determine whether the fetus has sickle cell anemia. If the partners elect to continue the pregnancy, their decision must be supported. Post-abortion counseling should also be offered. No mention was made of options if the father refuses testing or is unavailable. The potential of sickle cell disease in the fetus other than sickle cell anemia was not mentioned.

Rowley and coworkers (Rowley et al. 1991; Loader et al. 1991) investigated the feasibility of prenatal education, testing, and counseling of pregnant women for hemoglobinopathies in blacks, whites, Asians, and other ethnic groups. Providers of prenatal care—from obstetricians in private offices to public health care providers to health maintenance organizations—were enlisted. All pregnant women were screened for hemoglobinopathies at the first visit. The health care provider was given the option of obtaining informed consent for hemoglobinopathy screening; however, obstetricians in only 1 of 19 centers elected to inform their patients. The others asserted that they had their patients' implied consent for relevant diagnostic tests. Patients who tested positive were notified by telephone or by certified mail with return receipt. Women who had a positive result were offered counseling, but prenatal diagnosis was offered to only those women whose partners agreed to be tested and were found to be positive and if the couples agreed to learn through counseling the risks and their options. The cost of amniocentesis, however, was included.

Of the women coming for counseling, 50 percent were not living with the father, and 62 percent were single. Significantly, 75 percent of the pregnancies were of less than 18 weeks. Of 453 women counseled during the first screened pregnancy, 86 percent wanted their partners tested, but only 55 percent had their partners tested. In 77 pregnancies at risk, 12 women were too late in their pregnancy to be offered prenatal diagnosis; in another 12 pregnancies the condition for which the fetus was at risk was considered too mild to offer prenatal diagnosis. Prenatal diagnosis was offered to the remaining 53 pregnancies and was accepted by only 25 couples.

Several important issues were uncovered by Rowley's studies. First, should programs for prenatal testing for hemoglobinopathies include only populations at high risk, such as blacks, peoples of Mediterranean origin, Middle Easterners, Asians, or Southeast Asians? Apparently not. The first article pointed out that 7 percent of the subjects with sickle cell trait were not black, and 22 percent of the beta-thalassemia trait individuals were not Mediterranean, black, or Asian. The authors concluded that these findings indicated the need for prenatal screening of all women, rather than only those of high-risk groups.

Second, will prenatal programs for pregnant women in black communities result in a significant number of abortions of affected fetuses? Rowley's group concluded that black women often asserted that they would not terminate a pregnancy for any reason, but Southeast Asians frequently accepted abortion. These findings were in keeping with a survey (Rowley 1989) of prenatal diagnostic services for sickle cell disease at 12 centers in the United States. The induced abortion rate for fetuses with sickle cell anemia in the centers was 39 percent and 23 percent for hemoglobin sickle cell disease. Interestingly, however, induced abortion has been consistently far more frequent in blacks than in whites in the United States (National Center for Health Statistics 1990). There were 17.5 abortions per 100 live births in 1973 and 30 in 1987 in the white population. Blacks were classified in an "all other" group and undoubtedly constituted the vast majority. This group included 28.9 per 100 live births in 1973 and 55.7 in 1987.

Should women whose partners refuse testing or are unavailable be offered prenatal diagnosis? The National Association for Sickle Cell Disease did not address this issue, but partner decision-making was emphasized in that program. Rowley's program terminated the options of approximately one-half of the pregnant women. Of 463 black women who were counseled during pregnancy, the partner was not tested in 209 instances, and prenatal diagnosis was not offered.

Nevertheless, if a black women has sickle cell trait and if her partner is black, the odds are about 1 in 40 that she will have a child with sickle cell disease—more commonly sickle cell anemia (hemoglobin SS), hemoglobin SC, or hemoglobin S/β-thalassemia. A recalcitrant or unavailable partner in Rowley's program subjects a woman to a high risk of having a child with sickle cell disease that she may not want, even though prenatal diagnosis is performed for many disorders with much lower odds of having an affected child. Should not the pregnant women be allowed to make a choice? Yes. Is her autonomy compromised? Yes. Should a genetic counseling program conceal important

reproductive options? No. The choice is between autonomy and paternalism. Here, paternalism adversely affects those who can least afford it, and this, I believe, is a major drawback of this program.

Along these lines, an editorial in the *New York Times* (1988) stated that the Department of Health and Human Services issued regulations banning federal funds to clinics that offer abortion counseling. It was pointed out that should these rules take effect, 4 million (mainly poor) women who depend on federally supported family planning clinics would suffer. These women would be denied access not only to abortion but also to medical information that would keep them from becoming pregnant. The question was asked how can a physician, forbidden under the regulations even to mention the word "abortion," help a woman make an informed choice about family planning. Further, "and how cruel that a poor woman can't be told that an abortion is a legal option—and given a referral if she requests one—compared with the woman who can afford a private doctor." It was also asserted that in the United States there are two kinds of family planning counseling: one for the affluent (and the middle class) and one for the poor. Rowley's prenatal screening program is in the latter category.

In regard to hemoglobinopathy testing, considerable evidence suggests that the screening of pregnant women and other adults will detect a significant number of individuals who do not know that they have sickle cell disease. Rowley and colleagues found similarly unsuspecting patients (Rowley 1989; Rowley et al. 1991). Accordingly, pregnancy screening for hemoglobinopathies offers both reproductive and crucial medical information. Thus, if obstetricians do not screen for hemoglobinopathies, they could be at risk for medical malpractice if a pregnant woman with sickle cell disease is overlooked and has complications from the disease. Further, there are many precedents for successful wrongful birth lawsuits against obstetricians and other health workers who fail to inform or counsel, or who use improper techniques to detect genetic variation disorders in groups who are at high risk (Capron 1979; Shaw 1984).

The research of Rowley and colleagues opens the door for an additional discussion of some crucial issues. First, is a public policy just that offers public support for newborn screening and prenatal diagnosis of hemoglobinopathies and other disorders but renounces public support for abortion of affected fetuses (Bowman 1983)? It may not be just, but such a policy is legal. The Supreme Court has repeatedly (in *Harris* v. *McRae*, 48 Law Week 4941 [1980], and *Maher* v. *Roe*, 432 U.S. 464 [1973]) upheld the denial of public support for abortion, if the state so chooses.

But in its wisdom, the Supreme Court in the case of *Dandridge* v. *Williams* (397 U.S. 471, 485 [1970]) also upheld the legality of a maximum welfare grant imposed by the state of Maryland. This regulation restricted total state Aid for Dependent Children to a maximum of $250 per month per family, no matter how large the family. If a limitation on public support for potentially healthy children is the law of the land, surely there will be restrictions on public support for children with severe genetic disorders if the state so chooses. Thus, unfortunately, the specter of *Dandridge* may haunt us as health care costs escalate. There are many back doors to eugenics and this is one of them.

OUT-OF-WEDLOCK BIRTHS

Lamentably, high rates of out-of-wedlock births in the black community are frequently ignored in federal and community programs and in premarital sickle hemoglobin state testing mandates (Bowman 1983). Genetics programs usually are constructed on the basis of the classical description of the family. The testing of couples before marriage and of marriage partners is emphasized, but reality is ignored. Wilson's investigation of out-of-family patterns and out-of-wedlock births in the black community found that the proportion of women married and living with their husbands decreased from 52 percent in 1947 to 34 percent in 1980. Tragically, the jobless rate for black males has also contributed to the out-of-wedlock birth rate, because black women see little advantage in marrying a man who has poor prospects for contributing to family support (Wilson 1987). The lessons are obvious. A genetics program that depends on the cooperation of putative fathers and partners who are readily available places the pregnant woman who does not wish to have a child with sickle cell disease in an untenable position. Recall that 62 percent of all women were single in Rowley's program, and their partners were usually uncooperative. Nationally, the out-of-wedlock black birth rate in 1970 was 37.4 percent and in 1987 62.2 percent (National Center for Health Statistics 1990).

Though disturbing, it should be mentioned that arguments for mandated pregnancy screening for hemoglobinopathies could be more persuasive than mandated newborn screening. But even if pregnancy screening is not mandated, indirect coercion of pregnant women by the state, insurance companies, employers, family, or friends may be just as effective.

"DÉJÀ VU ALL OVER AGAIN" (YOGI BERRA)

Is discriminatory sickle hemoglobin testing a thing of the past? No. The U.S. Department of Energy recently violated its own ethical precepts despite a plethora of bioethical commissions, all of which have been loudly silent. The handout "To Know Ourselves" (1996), developed by the U.S. Department of Energy and the Human Genome Project, has a chapter entitled "Ethical, Legal, and Social Implications: An Essential Dimension of Genome Research," which emphasizes that, although the Human Genome Project is rich with promise, it also is fraught with social implications: that genetic information might be used to predict sensitivities to various industrial or environmental agents and, most important, that the dangers of mis-

use and potential threats to personal privacy should not be taken lightly. Interestingly, it was emphasized that genetic information, if handled carelessly, could lead to discrimination by potential employers and insurers.

I was asked by Vicki A. Laden, Esq. (Boxer, Elkind & Gerson, Attorneys at Law, Oakland, California) in 1997 to submit an amicus curiae brief for plaintiff employees against the University of California Lawrence Berkeley Laboratory, which I did (Bowman 1998). Other physicians and the American Public Health Association, the American Civil Liberties Union, the Council for Responsible Genetics, the National Employment Lawyers Association, and the Lawyers Committee for Civil Rights also filed briefs. Prominent medical and human genetics organizations were not participants in the brief for the employees.

The Lawrence Berkeley Laboratory is part of the University of California, Berkeley, but most important, the lab is supported by the U.S. Department of Energy. The appeal from the United States District Court for the Northern District of California to the United States Court of Appeals for the Ninth Circuit involved the question of whether a clerical or administrative worker who undergoes a general employee health examination may, without his or her knowledge, be tested for highly private and sensitive medical and genetic information such as syphilis, sickle cell trait, and pregnancy. Only black employees were tested for sickle cell trait, and only black and

Hispanic employees were repeatedly tested for syphilis—without their knowledge. Sadly, the repeated testing of only black and Hispanic employees for syphilis has distinctive racial overtones.

The employees' complaint asserted that the testing violated Title VII of the Civil Rights Act of 1964, the Americans with Disabilities Act (ADA), and their right to privacy as guaranteed by both the United States and State of California Constitutions. The district court granted the defendants-appellees' motion for dismissal judgment on the pleadings and summary judgments on all of the plaintiffs-appellants' claims. In other words, the employees lost the case.

The Ninth Court of Appeals concluded that the district court erred in dismissing the federal and state constitutional privacy claims and the Title VII claim. The district court's dismissal of the ADA claims was deemed proper. However, none of Secretary of the Department of Energy Federico Peña's arguments with respect to the claims brought against him in his official capacity had merit. The court thus affirmed in part, reversed in part, and remanded. Today, the Department of Energy, a cosponsor of the Human Genome Project and the Ethical, Legal and Social Issues Program, and a distinguished university are repeating the tragic history of sickle hemoglobin screening.

Having served on the Ethical, Legal, and Social Issues Working Group of the National Institutes of Health / Department of Energy National Human Genome Program and on many sickle hemoglobin and other genetics study sections and advisory groups, I believe that, if a grant applicant had submitted or defended what was done at the Lawrence Berkeley Laboratory, it would have been unanimously summarily rejected by any committee with which I am familiar. Nevertheless, former secretaries of the Department of Energy, Federico Peña and Hazel O'Leary, defended the actions of the Lawrence Berkeley Laboratory. Interestingly, however, the Department of Energy document (To Know Ourselves 1996) is replete with cautions about informed consent and invasion of privacy in genetic testing programs.

Anthropology and anthropological genetics have come a long way since the days of W.E.B. Du Bois. These disciplines are now the province of not only anthropologists and geneticists but also lawyers, the courts, ethicists, political scientists, sociologists, historians, economists, health care providers, and experts in federal and state governments and many other disciplines and organizations. It is most important that we all be involved in discussions about the revolutionary discoveries that will result from the Human Genome Program. Nevertheless, scientists on all continents are making revolutionary discoveries outside of the Genome Program. Witness the advent of the clone Dolly in Scotland and her mouse and goat successors in other countries. We humans may be next. Scientific discovery is endless and has never been successfully suppressed despite numerous efforts by politicians, popes, and other theologians to do so throughout history.

The past 45 years have produced remarkable discoveries in science and medicine. Poverty, no health insurance for more than 43 million Americans, racism, homelessness for several million Americans in this most affluent of countries, with disgraceful pockets of de-development persist. One hundred years from now we will have conquered most if not all diseases, genetic and otherwise, including, perhaps, even death. I speak as an authority on this subject because none of us will be here to dispute me. Nevertheless, I also predict that although these advances may come to fruition, I can state unequivocally that our inhumanity to each other and to peoples who are different from ourselves will not be conquered. Every time my wife and I go to Egypt we visit the sound and light display at the Pyramids. Five thousand years of history are revealed. We have the same foibles as the ancient Egyptians. It also has been estimated that 5 billion years from now the sun will explode and die. Unless our ancestors can escape our solar system, life here will not even be history. But that will be no problem, because unless we can acknowledge our inhumanity to each other and act on it, our ancestors may not last even the next 100 years.

References

Bowman, James E. 1977. Genetic Screening Programs and Public Policy. *Phylon* 38:117-42.

———. 1983. Is a National Program to Prevent Sickle Cell Disease Possible? *American Journal of Pediatrics Hematology / Oncology* 5:367-72.

———. 1998. Minority Health Issues and Genetics. *Community Genetics* 1: 142-44.

Bowman, James E., Henry Frischer, Franco Ajmar, Paul E. Carson, and Miriam E. Gower. 1967. Population, Family, and Biochemical Investigations of Human Adenylate Polymorphism. *Nature* 214:156-58.

Bowman, James E. and Robert F. Murray, Jr. 1990. *Genetic Variation and Disorders in Peoples of African Origin.* Baltimore, MD: Johns Hopkins University Press.

Cavalli-Sforza, L. L. 1997. Race Differences: Genetic Evidence. In *Plain Talk About the Human Genome Project.* Tuskegee, AL: Tuskegee University, College of Agricultural, Environmental and Natural Sciences.

Cavalli-Sforza, L. L. and Walter F. Bodmer. 1971. *The Genetics of Human Populations.* San Francisco: W. H. Freeman.

Chakraborty, Ranjit and Peter E. Smouse. 1988. Recombination of Haplotypes Leads to Biased Estimates of Admixture Proportions in Human Populations. *Proceedings of the National Academy of Sciences* (U.S.A.) 85:3071-74.

D'Souza, Dinesh 1995. *The End of Racism.* New York: Free Press.

Gaston, Marilyn H., Joel I. Verter, Gerald Woods, Charles Pegelow, John Kelleher, Gerald Presbury, Harold Zarkowsky, E. Vishinsky, Rathi Iver, Jeffry S. Lobel, Steven Diamond, C. Holbrook, Gill Tate, M. Frances, Kim Ritchy, and John M. Falletta. 1986. Prophylaxis with Oral Penicillin in Children with Sickle Cell Anemia. *New England Journal of Medicine* 314:1593-99.

Hammerschmidt, Dale E. 1999. It's as Simple as Black and White! Race and Ethnicity as Categorical Variables. *Journal of Laboratory and Clinical Medicine* 133:10-12.

Health Services Amendments. 1978. Section 205 of Pub. L. 95-626.

Illinois Department of Public Health. 1990. *Newborn Screening: An Overview of Newborn Screening Programs in the United States*. Springfield: Illinois Department of Public Health.

Keown, Damien. 1987. *Buddhism and Ethics*. New York: St. Martin's Press.

Loader, S., C. J. Suters, M. Walden, A. Kozyra, and P. T. Rowley. 1991. Prenatal Screening for Hemoglobinopathies II: Evaluation of Counseling. *American Journal of Human Genetics* 48:447-51.

National Association for Sickle Cell Disease. 1990. Position of the National Association for Sickle Cell Disease on Prenatal Diagnosis of Sickle Cell Anemia. Los Angeles: National Association for Sickle Cell Disease.

National Center for Health Statistics. 1990. *Health United States, 1989*. Hyattsville, MD: Public Health Service.

National Institutes of Health. 1971. *HEW NEWS*. National Heart and Lung Institute, 9 Nov.

National Sickle Cell Anemia Control Act. 1972. Pub.L. 92-294.

Omnibus Genetics Bill. 1976. Title IV of Pub. L. 84-278, National Sickle Cell Anemia, Cooley's Anemia, Tay-Sachs, and Genetic Diseases Act.

Politzer, William S. 1958. The Negroes of Charleston (S.C.): A Study of Hemoglobin Types, Serology, and Morphology. *American Journal of Physical Anthropology* 16:241-63.

Post, Peter W. and D. C. Rao. 1977. Genetic and Environmental Determinants of Skin Color. *American Journal of Physical Anthropology* 47:399-402.

Reed, T. Edward 1969. Caucasian Genes in American Negroes. *Science* 165:762-68.

Rowley, Peter T. 1989. Prenatal Diagnosis for Sickle Cell Disease: A Survey of the United States and Canada. *Annals of the N.Y. Academy of Sciences* 565:48-52.

Rowley, Peter T., Starlene Loader, Carol J. Sutera, Margaret Walden, and Alyssea Kozyra. 1991. Prenatal Screening for Hemoglobinopathies, I: A Prospective Regional Trial. *American Journal of Human Genetics* 48:439-46.

Tobias, Philip V. 1970. Brain Size, Grey Matter and Race-Fact or Fiction. *American Journal of Physical Anthropology* 32:3-26.

To Know Ourselves. 1996. U.S. Department of Energy and the Human Genome Project, July.

West, Cornel. 1993. *Race Matters*. Boston: Beacon Press.

Williams, Charles. 1976. *The Destruction of Black Civilization: Great Issues of Race from 4500 B.C. to 2000 A.D*. Chicago: Third World Press.

Wilson, William Julius. 1987. *The Truly Disadvantaged: The Inner City, the Underclass, and Public Policy*. Chicago: University of Chicago Press.

———. 1996. *When Work Disappears*. New York: Vintage.

Anthropological Measurement:
The Mismeasure of African Americans

By FATIMAH L. C. JACKSON

ABSTRACT: W.E.B. Du Bois's prophetic century-old statements on America's unwillingness to fairly assess its citizens of African descent still provide important insights into the continuing philosophical and methodological problems of Western anthropology and biology. Too frequently, the bias of a "problem of the color line" mentality undermines the accurate measurement, analysis, and valid scientific interpretations of human variation. The history of biological anthropology is replete with instances of "virtual science" being used to camouflage a political and social agenda. Today, as the post-genome era approaches, arbitrary and often capricious evaluations of Africans and African Americans still abound, as Du Bois had predicted. New paradigms such as ethnogenetic layering are proposed to disentangle cultural identity from genetic identity and provide an alternative to static, stereotype-dependent racial models of traditional anthropology and biology. Ethnogenetic layering has been applied in ecological risk assessment studies and has already revealed significant regional biodiversity (genetic substructuring) among African Americans.

Fatimah L. C. Jackson is professor of anthropology and affiliate professor of biology at the University of Maryland. She is an active researcher and has published over 80 scientific articles. She currently serves the National Academy of Sciences Institute of Medicine as a member of the Committee for Genetics Health and Behavior. Her research has been highlighted in the Chronicles of Higher Education, *the Wonderwise Science Project, the World Wildlife Fund, and on the Discovery Channel, the British Broadcasting Corporation, and the Canadian Broadcasting Corporation.*

The problem of the 20th century is the problem of the color line.
—W.E.B. Du Bois ([1903] 1996)

As one of the more famous quotations from W.E.B. Du Bois, it is noteworthy that, at the turn of the twentieth century, anthropology still struggles with the concept of the "problem of the color line." The analysis of human variation and biodiversity, impeded by this unresolved problem, continues to confound many in the scientific community and in the larger cultural groups with which these scientists are affiliated. While Du Bois spoke of the problem of segmenting or partitioning a continuum in the context of the European and European American fixations of the time, it is clear that the pathology he identified is, at least today, not limited culturally, temporally, or geographically.

As late as January 1999, Chinese physical anthropologists had significant difficulty accepting both an African origin for all modern humans (monogenesis) and, by extension, China's inexorable link to Africa and Africa's (more recent) descendants.[1] They had a "problem of the color line." However, a recent large genetic analysis of Chinese citizens and others, the Chinese Human Genome Project, provides data that are consistent with the only hypothesis for human origins that explains the striking continuity, the lack of meaningful segmentation, and the absence of racial divergence within modern humanity. The Chinese Human Genome Project (Cavalli-Sforza 1998) findings support the hypothesis that modern humans, originating in Africa, migrated across Asia in a southeasterly direction before heading north into what is now China (Chu et al. 1998). This challenges the long-standing view favored by Chinese anthropologists and paleontologists and is based on limited fossil evidence that a separate East Asian branch of *Homo erectus* evolved on its own into *Homo sapiens*, independent of any significant African connection. Careful measurement is producing new data that have begun to successfully challenge old assumptions.

The "problem of the color line" is a cultural construct, deeply rooted in the philosophical underpinnings of international Western science. Whether this science is practiced in China or in the United States, the recurring presence of the color line paradigm reflects the saturation of modern science by Western historical obsessions and the failure of practicing scientists to identify, examine, and extricate themselves from this important source of bias. The mindset referenced in Du Bois's encapsulated statement is an expected outgrowth of the construction of privileged whiteness and the universalization of European and European American norms. The same norms that entitle "whiteness" also fundamentally debase all persons, places, or things labeled "black."

However, progress in reconceptualizing human variation and biodiversity, particularly recognizing African and African American patterns, and then reorienting our models is evident in many branches of anthropology. Indeed, the data will not allow us to continue to do otherwise (see Agulnik et al. 1998). An increasing number of scholars recognize the importance of critiquing the resilient but erroneous cultural need to bifurcate and juxtapose, to compartmentalize, to make the dynamic static, to distort in order to understand. Slowly, with some trepidation, researchers are constructing new perspectives that are compatible with anthropology's inherent dependence upon Africa and African human variations to illuminate world patterns of human biodiversity (Relethford and Jorde 1999; Lahr and Foley 1998; Kidd et al. 1998; Tishkoff et al. 1998; Foley 1998; Hammer et al. 1998; Stoneking et al. 1997; Ayala and Escalante 1996). Yet these efforts are still in their infancy, and there is still room for much improvement and for the development of new, more accurate and more explanatory paradigms. Indeed, we still find that at a basal level, the "problem of the color line" mind-set remains a conceptually vexing distraction to good science and meaningful measurement, as it was in an earlier, less technologically robust era.

The solution to the Negro problem is a matter of systematic investigation. Ignorance alone is the cause of race prejudice and scientific truth can dispel it.

—W.E.B. Du Bois at the University of Berlin ([1903] 1996)

Anthropology, as a discipline that straddles the life sciences and the social sciences, purports to study systematically both biological and cultural aspects of human variation. Yet the discipline continues to debate the meaning and significance of human variation and diversity (see the September 1998 issue of *American Anthropologist*).[2] Among physical or biological anthropologists, that debate is couched in the context of measured, quantifiable assessments of difference, be these data anatomical, physiochemical, or molecular. The debate and its outcome are linked to interpretations of the origins of modern humans and the notion of primacy. The debate is tied to evaluations of human and nonhuman primate behaviors and the relationship of artifact-inferred behaviors to cognitive maturity and "modern" anatomy in the earliest (African) *Homo sapiens*. The debate is associated with the traditions, among peoples of European descent, of being the taxonomic template. Indeed, the debate and its outcome challenge many of our previously held concepts of what it means to be human. The outcome of the debate is critical; the stakes are high. The importance of human variation, particularly non-European diversity, is also intimately tied to the stated rationales for the design, scope, and applications of Human Genome Project data in the rapidly approaching postgenome era.

For although humans are a single species, *Homo sapiens*—in fact, a single race or subspecies, *Homo sapiens sapiens*—we are indeed a polytypic species. Visible differences are evident and unappreciated. In the past, our species' inherent biodiversity has been given profound, usually wrong, and often devastating social, political, and economic interpretations.

The "problem of the color line" in America has been fundamentally the question of the Negro problem: who is the Negro, what is the Negro, and where is the Negro. African Americans have been systematically defamed in the biomedical and psychosocial literatures, in particular, as defective, deficient, or deformed, relative to an unspoken alien (non–African American) norm. As we approach the post-genome era of the twenty-first century, the prevailing question is this: will Du Bois's prediction for the twentieth century be a premonition for the twenty-first? Will human variation, particularly the range and depth of diversity exhibited among African Americans, continue to be presented, albeit framed in molecular jargon, as "labels of shame," deviations from a European human norm, and relics from a premodern past?

This article explores the roots of anthropological measurement and, in so doing, evaluates the very real potential that the structure of these measurements inadvertently (or perhaps, in some cases, advertently) functionally promotes the mismeasure of peoples of African descent, indeed the mismeasure of humanity. My argument rests upon certain lines of evidence: the historical context of anthropological measurement, the specific assignment given African Americans in general anthropological inquiry, and recent developments that provide insight into how African Americans and other non-European peoples will be evaluated in the molecular genetic age.

HISTORICAL CONTEXT OF ANTHROPOLOGICAL MEASUREMENT

Overwhelmingly, the scientific study of human variability and human biodiversity remains Eurocentric in its structure and functional benefit. Stanford geneticist Cavalli-Sforza and his colleagues (Cavalli-Sforza, Menozzi, and Piazza 1994), in *The History and Geography of Human Genes*, have correctly reported that our current repertoire of disease genes and genetic polymorphisms in general is highly biased toward European patterns of diversity, especially those observed among North Atlantic European groups. This, of course, is symptomatic of a research agenda mainly informed by a "problem of the color line" mind-set. If the unstated scientific goal has been to delimit the Negro and expand the European, then the most powerful variables for study are those traits presumed to be expressed most exclusively in one group and not the other.[3] However, even with this acknowledged, built-in bias, African biodiversity and, by extension, African American variability, still exceed the level of variation observed among non-Africans.

Some anthropologists and biologists have begun to recognize the generic liability of not truly knowing African biodiversity. The most important recent countermeasure designed to overcome this bias and address the existing paucity of knowledge was the Human Genome Diversity Project. Yet it was so ill-formulated and poorly presented that researchers alienated many of the indigenous groups whom they sought to study. In any event, African American diversity was not considered worthy of study within the original research design of the Human Genome Diversity Project for reasons I will elaborate shortly. More recently, the larger and more extensively funded Human Genome Project has declared its interest in the study of human genome sequence variation (NHGRI 1998a, 1998b). However, whether this will just be a new molecular forum for the unending stream of black-white comparisons that already plague the biomedical, epidemiological, and psychosocial literatures (for example, see Tershakovec et al. 1999; Gheiler et al. 1999; Fritzsch et al. 1999; Grisso et al. 1999) remains to be seen.

Given the historical overdominance of the "problem of the color line" mentality and its associated baggage, it remains a serious "radical" proposition to deconstruct Eurocentric, temperate-zone interpretations in the assessment of human adaptation and evolution and to replace them with more origin-oriented, diversity-inclusive, evolutionarily perceptive approaches. We have yet to internalize that science is a human endeavor that predates the accomplishments of the ancient Romans, Greeks, or Egyptians. We are taught, and we teach, that true science begins with post-Renaissance European endeavors and discoveries. In this mind-set, valid anthropological measurements likewise begin with *Systema Naturae*

(1735), where the most familiar and accessible communities to Linnaeus established the reference group for a species, even though a primitive awareness of intraspecies diversity existed. Certainly, until very recently this unacknowledged assumption was an underlying theme in the research design of the Human Genome Project. In producing the "molecular periodic table" for our entire species, Human Genome Project scientists still overwhelmingly based their identifications of the locations of various genes and the sequences characterizing these genes on a limited number of North Atlantic European–derived lineages (Jackson 1998). Ironically, each of these lineages had been initially transformed into cell lines because they exhibited genetic diseases. Also ironic is that normal, nonpathological variation was not to be considered in establishing the reference sequences for the species.

THE SEARCH FOR LAWS IN ANTHROPOLOGICAL MEASUREMENT

Toward the end of the nineteenth century and midway through the beginning of the twentieth century, the quantification of human biodiversity was strongly influenced by the intellectual hegemony of physics and mathematics and the desire to identify the laws governing natural phenomena. In *The Growth of Biological Thought: Diversity, Evolution, and Inheritance*, Ernst Mayr (1982), a professor emeritus at Harvard University and one of the fathers of modern evolutionary thought, traces this misapplication of physical science research designs and goals in the life sciences. Physical anthropology was not immune to these influences, particularly since so many of the early physical anthropologists were anatomists. Michael Blakey, a professor of anthropology at Howard University and director of the African Burial Ground Project, has written perceptively on the inherent biases in such practices and how measurements were concocted to quantify the "color line" and concretize certain injustices (Blakey 1996).

In the history of anthropology, too few scholars have questioned the practice of producing mountains of comparative, often highly speculative, "virtual genetic" group data on traits that magnify the differences between "blacks" and "whites." Most of the assessed traits ultimately prove to be highly malleable by environmental circumstances, to demonstrate variability throughout the life span, or to be themselves the product of complex gene-gene interactions. Even today, few studies document within-group variability. In the post–World War II era, there was a call for a new anthropology, particularly a new physical or biological anthropology, more in line with the new appreciation of diversity resulting from the genetic study of natural populations of more short-lived organisms. Studies by Dobzhansky (1975)—on the population biology of fruit flies—and others, for example, indicated the importance of genetic variation in retaining the viability of

a species. These studies promoted the ecological and evolutionary value of polymorphisms and provided an important theoretical break with a previous, more reactionary commitment to static, typological thinking. It was this paradigm that had facilitated the association of anthropological measurement with the eugenics movement and with the Nazi agenda. By the 1950s and 1960s there was enough momentum in physical anthropology to begin the break with this dishonorable past. Now, 50 years later, we seem to again be in need of another paradigm shift. This is particularly urgent given our significantly improved technical abilities to characterize variation at the level of the DNA (rather than the inferred "virtual genetics" of the past) to study specific gene sequences and to tie genomic structure to specific phenotypic functions.

THE AFRICAN AMERICAN
IN PHYSICAL ANTHROPOLOGY

We seldom study the condition of the Negro to-day honestly and carefully. It is so much easier to assume that we know it all. Or perhaps, having already reached conclusions in our own minds, we are loath to have them disturbed by facts. And yet how little we really know of these millions—of their daily lives and longings, of their homely joys and sorrows, of their real shortcomings and the meaning of their crimes.

—W.E.B. Du Bois ([1903] 1996)

Anthropological measurement was initially a search for anatomical regularities that would form the template for the identification of laws that permitted prediction, rapid diagnosis, and efficient control. Early physical anthropology was an offspring of medicine (primarily anatomy and physiology). The search in medicine was for the "norm," while physical anthropology sought to expand this search to articulate several norms, each appropriate for the relevant "racial" group in question as well as one that was suitable for the species as a whole. Ideally, it was thought, measurements should be made on "pure," unadmixed groups, known entities, each with their own norm, a collection of true breeders.

In this conceptual model, the African American was problematic. The scientists' dilemma in using the Negro as subjects in anthropological measurement was their suspicious origins, their apparently high morphometric variability (owing to the application of the "one-drop rule"), their undetailed lineage, and their fundamental illegitimacy. And yet the Negro was available, accessible, unprotected, and phenotypically different enough from the stereotypical European American to be an interesting contrast.

Since anthropology is (still) primarily interested in indigenous populations, African Americans were technically out of the loop. As weak surrogate Africans,[4] they are still relegated by some researchers today as a post-1492 C.E. creation (Cavalli-Sforza, Menozzi, and Piazza 1994), without history, and unsuitable for inclusion in studies designed to link language, genetics, geography, and environment. Perhaps it is this double-edged sword of illegitimacy that continues to inhibit the systematic, serious anthropological study of African Americans and peripheralize what research results do exist.[5]

The concept of admixture, a prevalent yet undoubtedly erroneous concept in human population genetics because it implies preceding genetic uniformity, further works against the proper comprehensive anthropological measurement of African Americans. African Americans are thought of being (detrimentally) unevenly admixed with non-Africans. Uneven admixture levels in various African American lineages (see Parra et al. 1998) mean that researchers wishing to make sweeping generalizations of the diversity encountered in the Negro would have to actually investigate other aspects of individual African American identities. Such studies would have to focus on, for example, African American regional histories, their likely African origins, and the specific sources of non-African gene flow into regional groups. But this would mean coming face-to-face with the circumstances of the actual lives of African Americans, as Du Bois had recommended.

Such efforts would require contact with uncomfortable considerations of the residential implications of the history of post-Reconstruction chain migrations. These studies would demand recognition of the true genetic consequences of America's domestic slave trade. Such studies might reveal the historical fact of the targeted procurement and enslavement strategies to collect skilled Africans from particular ecological zones and geographical areas to meet the specific demands of European American slave owners. Such investigations would require recognizing a level of personhood that had not traditionally been acknowledged or afforded the Negro. Scholarly attention to this level of nuance in a much maligned group might suggest structure and purpose in the existence of the Negro, rather than the prevailing thesis of chaos.

If African Americans were to have a role in anthropological measurement, it would be as a foil to the measurement of Europeans and European Americans. To play this vital role, African Americans must be considered homogeneous and monomorphic, both uniform and distinct in the variables of interest from the non–African Americans with whom they were being compared. Otherwise, the African American would provide an irregular contrast to European and European American norms. And so, anthropology, in conjunction, perhaps in collusion, with epidemiology, medicine, sociology, and psychology, used the measurement of African Americans to serve as the foil, the other, a role still evident in 2000. Measurements of the African American serve most consistently as the anatomical and physiochemical contrast against which European Americans might find solace, reaffirm their centrality in the human story, reiterate their geographical expansiveness, and restate their dominance and unity. As the attention now shifts, in molecular genetic studies at least, to Africa, it is interesting to see how old concerns are being carried forward in interpretations of the new database.

We now know though that African genetic diversity may hold the key to understanding all human origins and that the bulk of human biological (including genetic) variability is found among African peoples. The "problem of the color line" is now being reformulated: the problem is not who, what, and where is the Negro, for the Negro is in everyone and thus is everywhere.

We have been handicapped by our ignorance of African and African American biodiversity and its ecological and evolutionary implications for far too long. Genetic diversity among Africans and their American descendants is extremely high, even between closely related or geographically located groups.[6] This diversity suggests a recent African origin for modern humans. It also suggests that discerning the historical, geographical, ecological, and sociocultural nuance of this variation among Africans and African Americans may be essential for making sense of the origins and affinities of non-African diversity.[7]

Yet something else is happening to remind us how refractory the "problem of the color line" paradigm is to truly radical reconfiguration. As more voices in the molecular anthropological sciences recognize and respond to the primacy of the African database, the discussion is often concentrated on which Africans are the progenitors of non-Africans in general and Europeans in particular. Since Northeast Africa (including Egypt and Ethiopia) has long been (mis)characterized as non-Negroid, was anyone surprised when the search for the earliest African ancestors of European peoples focused on the Falasha peoples of Ethiopia (a genetic isolate) and the Egyptian Arabs while neglecting indigenous Nilotic groups such as the Nubians?

ANTHROPOLOGICAL
MEASUREMENT IN THE
POST-GENOME ERA

Even to-day the masses of the Negroes see all too clearly the anomalies of their position and the moral crookedness of yours. You may marshal strong indictments against them, but their countercries, lacking though they be in formal logic, have burning truths within them which you may not wholly ignore.

—W.E.B. Du Bois ([1903] 1996, 85)

*Anatomical and
physiological measurements*

Molecular biology, particularly molecular genetics, exerts an overwhelming impact in science today. Still, other measurement criteria are in use. However, the scientific accuracy, reproducibility, and statistical power of many of these traditional anthropological measures are currently being questioned (Jantz, Hunt, and Meadows 1995; Williams and Bale 1998; Shaner et al. 1998).

In craniometry, it is now recognized that the long-studied neurocranial surface is actually void of biologically meaningful landmarks (Valeri et al. 1998). Fuzzy landmarks are proposed to broaden the scope of these measurements, although these are associated with increased measurement error. Fuzzy landmarks are also proposed for other anatomical sites. The plasticity of human anatomy reduces the reliability of many of the traditional measures of biodiversity.

In skinfold anthropometry, it is recognized that this widely practiced anthropological technique has a huge error component (Beddoe and Samat 1998). Since there is nonconstancy of the ratio of subcutaneous to total body fat across diverse populations, this dramatically increases the residual error in such measurements (see Goran 1999). Beddoe and Samat (1998) suggest an alternative gold standard. Shaner et al. (1998) report that using specific landmarks decreased the variance somewhat (that is, increased the accuracy) when they compared photogrammetric versus caliper-derived measurements.

In osteological measurements, it is evident that important variation exists between individuals and groups in bone mineral content, density, and apparent density. The relationships of these differences to diet, activity, and other factors must be disentangled before meaningful comparative measurements can proceed. Perhaps the underexplored origins of this variability contribute to the reported long-standing mismeasurement of the tibia reported by Jantz, Hunt, and Meadows (1995).

Genetic measurements

The typological, racial divergence perspective is one that reflects and responds to static, stereotypical views of humanity's variability. Nowhere have genetic measurements been more convoluted to reproduce demarcation lines along the continuum of world human genetic variation than in molecular forensic studies. For example, the wealth of mitochondrial DNA (mtDNA) heterogeneity in Africans is still frequently studied, with the aim of eventually fitting human biodiversity into neat typological forensic boxes (see Comas, Reynolds, and Sajantila 1999). However, as the range of molecular anthropological measurements increases, it becomes more difficult to racially compartmentalize contemporary human biodiversity, particularly among continental Africans and African Americans.

Furthermore, it also appears that most of the forensic and population genetic models used to analyze mtDNA, Y-chromosome microsatellites, and nuclear DNA data often fail to reflect important features of genomic evolution. Most of the models that compare DNA sequences between geographical groups are two-dimensional and do not reflect the dynamic potential for genome-level selection, special population migration effects, or alternative mutation mechanisms. Individuals may be pooled based upon existing sociocultural criteria and then treated as if these aggregates were biologically (and forensically) real. This practice goes right to the heart of the limitations of typological thinking.

A forensic study may measure and find a "pool" of genes frequently encountered among, for example, Louisiana Creole peoples. However, it would be a mistake to biologically limit the Louisiana Creole, a geographic and sociocultural subset of African Americans, to the presence or absence of a particular genetic constellation of traits. Genes, and individuals carrying those genes, that do not fit preconceived patterns of group variability are seen by many forensic anthropologists as being external to the group, introduced from elsewhere, and as evidence of phyletic substructuring. However, as more genetic data are amassed on African Americans in general and various geographical and sociocultural subgroups of African Americans in particular, it is clear that static models of intra- and intergroup variability are of limited utility.[8] To know African Americans anthropologically, African Americans must be studied more intensely, not less. We do not know enough about diversity in African (and African American) mtDNA, Y-chromosome microsatellites, or nuclear DNA (for example, beta globin haplotypes), but it is already clear that West and Central Africans, the African ancestral gene pool for many African Americans, maintain high levels of heterogeneity for many traits (Armour et al. 1996; Jorde, Bamshad, and Rogers 1998; Tishkoff et al. 1998). Light must be shed on the nuances of African American biodiversity through the accurate, appropriate, and comprehensive measurement of this complex group, genetically and biohistorically. Otherwise, their measurement becomes a mismeasurement.

NEW PARADIGMS: TURNING
THE "PROBLEM OF THE
COLOR LINE" ON ITS HEAD

At the turn of the twentieth century, we are awakening (through our increased molecular insights) to the truth that W.E.B. Du Bois proposed a century ago. African Americans are a highly heterogeneous, exceptionally variable subset of the general American population. Their health/disease conditions are determined by the complex interplay between many factors, such as environmental exposures to chemicals, growth and development, and genetic susceptibilities. Rapid advances in molecular genetic technologies are providing scientists with new opportunities for better identifying and understanding the implications of human biodiversity. We can now genetically identify individuals with traits that affect their responses to environmental toxicants. We can use molecular genetic measurements to identify traits that may influence their suitability for organ and tissue transplantation. We can identify ancestral biomarkers that may link certain African American lineages to particular geographical and ecological zones in continental Africa and elsewhere. Additionally, the introduction of sophisticated computer software programs, such as the Geographic Information System, allows anthropologists to map and characterize measurable differences between African Americans, with a level of comprehensiveness heretofore unknown. At the University of Maryland, we have developed a unique ethnogenetic layering method that can be used to identify and evaluate human variation across ethnic groups.

Ethnogenetic layering (applied to the U.S. context) relies on the historical fact that, as different ethnic groups have occupied various regions of the country and as genes and culture have flowed between resident groups, the United States has become a mosaic over geographical space. Over the last 500 years, waves of different groups from various specific parts of the world have come to particular U.S. geographical regions, established residence, interacted with each other, and been acted upon by the existing biotic and abiotic environments. The major ancestral groups contributing to the U.S. gene pool are Western and Northern Europeans, Western and Central Africans, Native American Indians, and East Asians. However, among specific regional groups of Americans, both the percentage and specific allelic contributions of these ancestral groups vary. Over the generations, each part of the country developed different constellations of ethnic origins, creating a mosaic over geographical space and through time. By carefully documenting the genetic aspects of this mosaic, a framework emerges for identifying pockets of particular types of variation. Studies of the molecular genetics of various groups of Americans have revealed that some of these pockets of variation provide insights into the ancestral origins and extent of variability within the nation. Ethnogenetic layering provides a dynamic, interactive, and highly flexible model for anthropological reconstructions.

Our most recent application of ethnogenetic layering has been in the identification of regional differences in the disease susceptibility of African Americans and others to environmental toxicants. Significant variation exists in the incidence of many disorders by ethnicity and geographic location (Kue Young 1993; Gilliland 1997; Xu et al. 1995). Some of these disorders are of public health importance but require sophisticated anthropological measurements to locate the most vulnerable lineages. Recent environmental health studies of human molecular genetics have begun to identify diversity in susceptibility biomarkers among different regional groups of African Americans. Indeed, some of these polymorphic traits allow risk assessors to subdivide various groups of African Americans who had otherwise been lumped into macroethnic (racial) groups. This resolution power is important because it now helps researchers correlate local ethnicity, genetics, and susceptibility more precisely, especially when the phenotypes produced are clinically similar.

Each day, our list lengthens of genetic conditions that affect environmental risk and that display variability both between and within macroethnic groups. Frequently, polymorphisms in biomarkers show regional clines. This means that biomarkers derived from studies of African Americans living in one part of the country may not be most relevant for identifying susceptibility in other groups of African Americans living elsewhere or with slightly different ancestral genetic backgrounds. We are just beginning, with the help of this new paradigm, ethnogenetic layering, to explore the contribution of this variation to differential individual and group susceptibility to, in this case, adverse environmental

agents.[9] Among African Americans, we are finding important regional variation that might explain, in part, regional diversity in the expression of certain chronic disorders such as hypertension and diabetes.

Ethnogenetic layering is also a valuable alternative to the static, stereotype-dependent, racial models usually employed when anthropologists attempt to reconstruct human origins and historical migrations. As alluded to earlier, the accuracy and inferential power of anthropological measurements is significantly handicapped by the numerous gaps in the African genetic database. Given the centrality of Africa to understanding the story of *Homo sapiens*, completing the African database would seem to be a necessary prerequisite to understanding the ancestral roots and ancient migration histories of all peoples (see Watson et al. 1996; Comas et al. 1997; Francalacci et al. 1996; Jorde et al. 1997). For anthropology to correctly measure African Americans, as Du Bois called for a century ago, this African database needs to be well documented. To date, there are few published molecular studies of human genetic diversity in the parts of Africa most relevant for African American ancestral studies. Inferences made about a lack of molecular variability in West Africa (Cavalli-Sforza, Menozzi, and Piazza 1994) are unfounded, and certainly untested.

Ethnogenetics has also been applied ecologically (Jackson 1997b) as a way of measuring variability in diverse, biologically heterogeneous, and culturally complex societies in

Africa. Throughout the continent, we have been evaluating the interrelationship of ecological variation with cultural diversity to develop a model for predicting where in Africa certain kinds of genetic variability might be most frequently encountered.

CONCLUSION

Du Bois bequeathed an invaluable legacy of honest scholarship, perceptive inquiry, bold vision, and hope. Rereading *The Souls of Black Folk* and other great works by this intellectual giant encouraged me to try to contribute to the path he laid down. Asserting our humanness, challenging mismeasurement, defying exclusion, holding ourselves, our colleagues, and our disciplines accountable to a truth greater than any of us are all by-products of contact with and respect for the work of W.E.B. Du Bois. May the intellectual and moral leadership he provided continue to inspire current and future generations of scholars.

Notes

1. Systematic assessments of the genetic relationships among 28 of China's 56 official ethnic groups, including the majority Han population, were evaluated using short DNA segments or microsatellites. Over time, microsatellites accumulate varying numbers of repeated sequences of DNA nucleotides, and these can be compared to reconstruct group origins and affinities. Researchers used a computer program to construct an evolutionary tree of genetic relationships based on 30 microsatellites per person among 14 East Asian populations, 3 populations from Africa, and 8 from elsewhere in the world. Researchers then constructed a second genetic tree, based on 15 microsatellites, for 32 East Asian populations (including the 28 Chinese groups) and the 11

non-Asian populations. Both reconstructions indicated that East Asian populations derived from a single lineage in Southeast Asia (Chu et al. 1998). This result is consistent with the existence of a prior genetic source in Africa, and not with the notion of a separate emergence of modern humans in East Asia, which many Chinese scientists had preferred. The East Asian findings fit with the theory that humans migrated out of East Africa around 100,000 years ago, traveling across short stretches of sea along Asia's southern coast, then migrating into East Asia.

2. The American Anthropological Association's official journal *American Anthropologist* devoted most of the September 1998 issue to a discussion of race in anthropology. Guest editor Faye Harrison recruited anthropologists from various subfields to address this topic. Race was presented in this special issue as the most contentious topic in contemporary American society, a complex combination of social reality, historical fact, and scientific misunderstanding. Audrey Smedley wrote about the social construction of race, Alan Templeton discussed the DNA evidence indicating that there are no distinct race-based lineages, Charles Orster, Jr., presented the archaeological emphasis on ethnicity rather than race, and Matt Cartmill wrote that racial categories are biologically incoherent and misleading.

3. It is interesting that while the scientific paradigm defining who is Caucasoid has expanded, the legal definition of who is white (and therefore entitled to certain political, social, and economic advantages) has constricted and increasingly been restricted to fewer and fewer of the world's populations. A listing of the legal racial prerequisite cases is presented in Lopez (1996), excerpted at http://www.udayton.edu/~race/white05.htm.

4. The "problem" of African American admixture surfaced in early criticisms of the mitochondrial Eve hypothesis of Allan Wilson and Rebecca Cann (1992). These pioneer studies indicated an African molecular genetic origin for the maternal ancestry of all humanity. However, the sample used to represent Africa was derived from African Americans. Critics complained vigorously that the mtDNA of these African Americans might not be truly African and sought to discredit the work and its implications. Subsequent studies using

various indigenous African sources of mtDNA reinforced the validity of these earlier findings (and the legitimacy of using these particular African Americans' mtDNA as reflective of African variants).

5. It is interesting, in the context of the history of modern human taxonomy, to remember that the ancient Greeks referred to all black Africans as Ethiopians (Brues 1990). In 1781, Johann Blumenbach, a German physician and comparative anatomist, continued this tradition, dividing humanity into five "races": Caucasian, Mongolian, Ethiopian, Malayan, and American (Stein and Rowe 2000, 435). However, with the rise of colonization and the continued enslavement of African people, the name shifted to Negro. One of the strongest rationales for the enslavement of Africans was that they were not Christian and were therefore uncivilized and inferior in character and intellect. Many ethnic Amhara peoples from Ethiopia, however, had developed extensive material evidence of civilization and accepted Christianity before it had come to dominate Europe. Ethiopian could no longer be considered a suitable race name for an enslaved and degraded people. The term Negro, on the other hand, was tied to nothing but skin color. In contrast to Caucasian, Mongolian, Malay, or American, it was an empty category, unlinked to geography, language, history, or culture. It, and the people so classified, had no past.

6. At the University of Maryland, the Genomic Models Research Group has identified regional variation in the African, European, and Native American ancestral backgrounds of African Americans from three major importation sites for enslaved Africans: Chesapeake Bay, Carolina Coast, and Mississippi Delta (Jackson et al. 1995; Jackson 1997a, 1997b).

7. Africa has been greatly underrepresented in studies of genetic diversity, compared with European and Asian populations. This is important not only in determining where, when, and how modern humans evolved but also in understanding genetic diseases of Africans and African Americans and in identifying potential treatments for disease. Evaluating samples of three different DNA loci from 13 to 18 populations in Africa and 30 to 45 populations in the remainder of the world, Tishkoff and her colleagues (1998) found an enormous amount of diversity within

and between the African populations, and they identified much less diversity in non-African populations. Since only a small subset of the diversity in Africa is found in Europe and the Middle East, and an even narrower set is found in American Indians, it is illogical to base the human molecular taxonomic norm on non-Africans.

8. Among molecular forensic scientists, particularly those responding to the requests of the law enforcement community for quick and reliable ethnic/racial genetic profiles, ethnic group genetic reference pools have been established to facilitate the identification of crime suspects and victims. However, the correspondence between an individual African American and the established reference sequence for the group is fairly low (about 76 percent), reflecting the inherent diversity of the group. In contrast, the correspondence for European Americans is quite reliable (about 98 percent). The correspondence for any Native American individual to the Native American reference pool is extremely low (about 26 percent), reflecting the nation's long history of reproductive isolation and genocide against these peoples.

9. Regional differences in genetic susceptibilities define, to some extent, the identity and toxicity of harmful environmental agents. Something which may be highly toxic for a significant segment of one local regional group may be essentially nontoxic for another (otherwise similar) regional group. For example, American infants and children (including African Americans) with partial ancestry in the northern and highland part of Atlantic Europe (the British Isles, Norway Isles, and much of Sweden and Denmark) have an increased frequency of HLADQ2+ phenotypes. The genotypes underlying these phenotypes, for example HLADQ beta 1*0201, demonstrate clear sensitivity to wheat gliadin and susceptibility to the cell-mediated immunity disorder, celiac disease (Rocher et al. 1995; Sturgess et al. 1994). For these infants and children, wheat gliadins and as yet unknown compounds in rye, barley, oats, and triticale (Campbell 1992) can provoke often fatal sensitivities and are, for these youth, clearly environmental toxins. Many studies now identify other regional and ethnic differences in susceptibility for other environmentally linked diseases such as the

leptin (OB) locus and hypertension, vitamin D receptor gene (BsmI and polyA markers), and glucose-6-phosphate dehydrogenase, asthma-linked genes.

References

Agulnik, A. I., A. Zharkikh, H. Boettger-Tong, T. Bourgeron, K. McElreavey, and C. E. Bishop. 1998. Evolution of the DAZ Gene Family Suggests That Y-linked DAZ Plays Little, or a Limited, Role in Spermatogenesis but Underlies a Recent African Origin for Human Populations. *Human Molecular Genetics* 7(9):1371-77.

Armour, J.A.L., T. Anttinen, C. A. May, E. E. Vega, A. Sajantila, J. R. Kidd, K. K. Kidd, J. Bertranpetit, S. Paabo, and A. J. Jeffreys. 1996. Minisatellite Diversity Supports a Recent African Origin for Modern Humans. *Nature Genetics* 13:154-60.

Ayala, F. and A. A. Escalante. 1996. The Evolution of Human Populations: A Molecular Perspective. *Molecular Phylogenetics and Evolution* 5(1): 188-201.

Beddoe, A. H. and S. B. Samat. 1998. Body Fat Prediction from Skinfold Anthropometry References to a New Gold Standard: In Vivo Neutron Activation Analysis and Tritium Dilution. *Physiological Measurement* 19(3): 393-403.

Blakey, M. L. 1996. Skull Doctors Revisited: Intrinsic Social and Political Bias in the History of American Physical Anthropology, with Special Reference to the Work of Ales Hrdlicka. In *Race and Other Misadventures: Essays in Honor of Ashley Montagu in His Ninetieth Year*, ed. Larry T. Reynolds and Leonard Lieberman. Dix Hills, NY: General Hall.

Brues, A. M. 1990. *People and Races.* Prospect Heights, IL: Waveland Press.

Campbell, J. A. 1992. Dietary Management of Celiac Disease: Variations in the Gluten-free Diet. *Journal of the Canadian Dietetics Association* 53(1):15-18.

Cavalli-Sforza, L. L. 1998. The Chinese Human Genome Diversity Project. *Proceedings of the National Academy of Sciences* 95(Sept. 29):11501-3.

Cavalli-Sforza, L. L., P. Menozzi, and A. Piazza. 1994. *The History and Geography of Human Genes.* Princeton, NJ: Princeton University Press.

Chu, J. Y., W. Huang, W. Q. Kuang, J. M. Wang, J. J. Xu, Z. T. Chu, Z. Q. Yang, K. Q. Lin, P. Li, M. Wu, Z. C. Geng, C. C. Tan, R. F. Du, and L. Jin. 1998. Genetic Relationship of Populations in China. *Proceedings of the National Academy of Sciences* 95(Sept. 29):11763-68.

Comas, D., R. Reynolds, and A. Sajantila. 1999. Analysis of mtDNA HVRII in Several Human Populations Using an Immobilized SSO Prove Hybridization Assay. *European Journal of Human Genetics* 7(4):459-68.

Comas, E., F. Calafell, E. Mateu, A. Perez-Lezaun, E. Bosch, and J. Bertranpetit. 1997. Mitochondrial DNA Variation and the Origin of the Europeans. *Human Genetics* 99:443-49.

Dobzhansky, T. 1975. Analysis of Incipient Reproductive Isolation Within a Species of Drosophila. *Proceedings of the National Academy of Sciences* 72(9):3638-41.

Du Bois, W.E.B. [1903] 1996. *The Souls of Black Folk.* New York: Penguin.

Foley, R. 1998. The Context of Human Genetic Evolution. *Genome Research* 8(4):339-47.

Francalacci, P., J. Bertranpetit, F. Calafell, and P. A. Underhill. 1996. Sequence Diversity of the Control Region of Mitochondrial DNA in Tuscany and Its Implications for the Peopling of Europe. *American Journal of Physical Anthropology* 100:443-60.

Fritzsch, R. J., R. Ford, R. Thomas, H. Huffman, and C. G. Roehrborn. 1999. Serum Prostate Specific Antigen (PSA) and the Ratio of PSA to Prostate Volume (PSAD) in African American and Caucasian Men. *Journal of Urology* 161(4 Suppl.):95.

Gheiler, W. L., R. Tiguert, I. Powell, M. Banerjee, J. E. Pontes, and D. P. Wood. 1999. Impact of Positive Surgical Margins on Disease Free Survival Between African American and Caucasian Men Following Radical Prostatectomy. *Journal of Urology* 161(4 Suppl.):246.

Gilliland, F. D. 1997. Ethnic Differences in Cancer Incidence: A Marker for Inherited Susceptibility? *Environmental Health Perspectives* 205(4 Suppl.):897-900.

Goran, M. 1999. Visceral Fat in Prepubertal Children: Influence of Obesity, Anthropometry, Ethnicity, Gender, Diet, and Growth. *American Journal of Human Biology* 11(2):201-7.

Grisso, J. A., E. W. Freeman, E. Maurin, B. Garcia-Espana, and J. A. Berlin. 1999. Racial Differences in Menopause Information and the Experience of Hot Flashes. *Journal of Genetics and Internal Medicine* 14(2): 98-103.

Hammer, M. F., T. Karafet, A. Rasanayagam, E. T. Wood, T. K. Altheide, T. Jenkins, R. C. Griffiths, A. R. Templeton, and S. L. Zegura. 1998. Out of Africa and Back Again: Nested Cladistic Analysis of Human Y Chromosome Variation. *Molecular Biology and Evolution* 15(4):427-41.

Jackson, F.L.C. 1997a. Concerns and Priorities in Genetic Studies: Insights from Recent African American Biohistory. *Seton Hall Law Review* 27(3):951-70.

———. 1997b. Correlation of Geographic Patterns of Ecological Diversity and Ethnic Variation in Africa: Implications for Identifying Gene X Environment Interactions and Patterns of Human Genetic Heterogeneity. *American Journal of Human Biology* 9(1):129.

———. 1998. Scientific Limitations and Ethical Ramifications of a Nonrepresentative Human Genome Project: African American Responses. *Science and Engineering Ethics* 4:155-70.

Jackson, F.L.C., D. L. Foster, M. G. Franke, and T. L. Goodrich. 1995. Identification of Potential Marker Genes and Gene Products for Geographical Mapping of Intra-African Diversity and Affinity. *American Journal of Physical Anthropology* 22(3):110.

Jantz, R. L., D. R. Hunt, and L. Meadows. 1995. The Measure and Mismeasure of the Tibia: Implications for Stature Estimation. *Journal of Forensic Sciences* 40(5):758-61.

Jorde, L. B., M. Bamshad, and A. R. Rogers. 1998. Using Mitochondrial and Nuclear DNA Markers to Reconstruct Human Evolution. *Bioessays* 20(2): 126-36.

Jorde, L. B., A. R. Robers, M. Bamshad, W. S. Watkins, P. Krakowiak, S. Sung, J. Kere, and H. C. Harpending. 1997. Microsatellite Diversity and the Demographic History of Modern Humans. *Proceedings of the National Academy of Sciences USA* 94:3100-3103.

Kidd, K. K., B. Morar, C. M. Castiglione, H. Zhao, A. J. Pakstis, W. C. Speed, et al. 1998. A Global Survey of Haplotype Frequencies and Linkage Disequilibrium at the DRD2 Locus. *Human Genetics* 103(2):211-27.

Kue Young, T. 1993. Diabetes Mellitus Among Native Americans in Canada and the United States: An Epidemiological Review. *American Journal of Human Biology* 5(4):399-413.

Lahr, M. M. and R. A. Foley. 1998. Toward a Theory of Modern Human Origins: Geography, Demography, and Diversity in Recent Human Evolution. *Yearbook of Physical Anthropology* 41:137-76.

Linnaeus, C. 1735. *Systema Naturae*. Leiden: University of Leiden.

Lopez, I. H. 1996. *White by Law: Legal Construction of the White Race*. New York: New York University Press.

Mayr, E. 1982. *The Growth of Biological Thought: Diversity, Evolution, and Inheritance*. Cambridge, MA: Harvard University Press, Belknap Press.

NHGRI. 1998a. National Human Genome Research Institute Resources for Detecting Genetic Variations. A Resource for Discovering Human DNA Polymorphisms. Available at http://www.nhgri.nih.gov.80/98plan/resource_report.html.

———. 1998b. National Human Genome Research Institute Workshop on Human DNA Sequence Variation, (31 Mar. and 1 Apr. 1997. Available at http://www.nihgri.nih.gov.80/98plan/variation_report.html.

Parra, E. J., A. Marcini, J. Akey, J. Martinson, M. A. Batzer, R. Cooper, T. Forrester, D. B. Allison, R. Deka, R. E. Ferrell, and M. D. Shriver. 1998. Estimating African American Admixture Proportions by Use of Population-Specific Alleles. *American Journal of Human Genetics* 63:1839-51.

Relethford J. H. and L. B. Jorde. 1999. Genetic Evidence for Larger African Population Size During Recent Human Evolution. *American Journal of Physical Anthropology* 108(3):251-60.

Rocher, A., F. Soriano, E. Molina, G. Gonzalez-Limas, and E. Mendez. 1995. Characterization of Distinct Alpha- and Gamma-type Gliadins and Low Molecular Weight Components from Wheat Endosperm as Coeliac

Immunoreactive Proteins. *Biochimica at Biophysica Acta* 1247(1):143-48.

Shaner, D. J., J. S. Banforth, A. E. Peterson, and O. B. Beattie. 1998. Technical Note: Different Techniques, Different Results: A Comparison of Photogrammetric and Caliper-Derived Measurements. *American Journal of Physical Anthropology* 106(4):547-52.

Stein, P. L. and B. M. Rowe. 2000. *Physical Anthropology*. 7th ed. Boston: McGraw-Hill.

Stoneking, M., J. J. Fontius, S. L. Clifford, H. Soodyall, S. S. Arcot, N. Saha, et al. 1997. Alu Insertion Polymorphisms and Human Evolution: Evidence for a Larger Population Size in Africa. *Genome Research* 7(11):1061-71.

Sturgess, R., P. Day, H. J. Ellis, K.E.A. Lundin, H. A. Gjertsen, M. Kontakou, and P. J. Ciclitrira. 1994. Wheat Peptide Challenge in Coeliac Disease. *Lancet* 343:758-61.

Tershakovec, A., B. Zemel, M. Watson, and V. Stallings. 1999. Resting Energy Expenditure (REE) of Obese Pre-menarchal African American and White Girls. *FASEB Journal* 13(4 pt. 1):A597.

Tishkoff, S. A., A. Goldman, F. Calfell, W. C. Speed, A. S. Deinard, B. Bonne-Tamir, et al. 1998. A Global Haplotype Analysis of the Mytonic Dystrophy Locus: Implications for the Evolution of Modern Humans and for the Origin of Myotonis Dystrophy Mutations. *American Journal of Human Genetics* 62(6):1389-1402.

Valeri, C. J., T. M. Cole III, S. Lele, and J. T. Richtsmeier. 1998. Capturing Data from Three-Dimensional Surfaces Using Fuzzy Landmarks. *American Journal of Physical Anthropology* 107(1):113-24.

Watson, E., K. Bauer, R. Aman, G. Weiss, A. von Haeseler, and S. Paabo. 1996. mtDNA Sequence Diversity in Africa.

American Journal of Human Genetics 59(2):437-44.

Williams, C. A. and P. Bale. 1998. Bias and Limits of Agreement Between Hydrodensitometry, Bioelectrical Impedance and Skinfold Calipers Measures of Percentage Body Fat. *European Journal of Applied Physiology and Occupational Physiology* 77(3):271-77.

Wilson, A. and R. Cann. 1992. The Recent African Genesis of Humans. *Scientific American* 266(4):68-73

Xu, W., B. Westwood, C. S. Barsocas, J. J. Malcorra-Azpiazu, K. Indrk, and E. Beutler. 1995. Glucose-6-Phosphate Dehydrogenase Mutations and Haplotypes in Various Ethnic Groups. *Blood* 85(2):256-63.

Deracializing Social Statistics: Problems in the Quantification of Race

By TUKUFU ZUBERI

ABSTRACT: Race is usually defined as an individual attribute fixed at birth and is employed by researchers as a variable with potential for causing change in some other aspect of that same individual. When an individual's race can change (as in Brazil), race is not an attribute but a dynamic characteristic dependent on other social circumstances. In the United States, an individual's race cannot change and thus is considered an individual attribute. As such, social statisticians may have measured racial classification correctly. The major error is in how race has been interpreted. The author suggests a new language to express things that our current language handles inadequately. This new language attempts to increase the efficiency of communication about the statistical analysis of race.

Tufuku Zuberi is associate professor of sociology and director of African studies at the University of Pennsylvania. He is an expert on the sociology and demography of African and African diaspora populations. He is the author of Swing Low, Sweet Chariot: The Mortality Cost of Colonizing Liberia in the Nineteenth Century *(1995) and* Thicker Than Blood: An Essay on the Quantification of Race *(2000). He also has published several articles on the sociology and demography of African and African diaspora populations.*

This study should seek to ascertain by the most approved methods of social measurement.

—W. E. Burghardt Du Bois (1898)

In scholarly circles, demographic and statistical interpretation of racial differences has taken on an almost sacred quality. As a result, demographers and other scholars have forgotten—or perhaps have never realized—that the social concept of race affects how we interpret quantitative representations of racial reality. Moreover, many quantitative studies of racial differences fail to place race within a social context, thus allowing the faulty assumption that the existence of race relations could be benign.

In the beginning of the twentieth century, empirical social scientists took a eugenic perspective toward race. Du Bois's idea was an exception to the accepted view about race among empirical social scientists. Du Bois was of the opinion that the best minds should study the problem of race according to the best methods. He thought that statistical analysis could help us gain a concrete understanding of the social status of the African American population. He formulated the first empirical refutation of eugenic and social Darwinist thought. After conducting an empirical study of African American life in a modern city in *The Philadelphia Negro*, Du Bois illustrated how biological notions of African inferiority were grounded only in ideology. However, Du Bois's contribution has been ignored by most sociologists, and its theoretical significance to understanding modern society

continues to be underplayed. This article demonstrates the theoretical significance of Du Boisian thought for understanding modern society, particularly his contributions to the understanding of quantitative data in societies where race is an "essential" variable.[1]

Unfortunately, among social statisticians, including demographers, there has developed an implicit tendency to accept the underlying logic of racial reasoning. In part, the statistical logic of justifying racial stratification has resulted from a lack of critical theory among social statisticians and a tendency to avoid reflexive discourse with statisticians in general and other areas of the social sciences, such as African and African diaspora studies in particular. This essay describes the scientific birth of racial reasoning in statistical analysis, what I have learned from reading statistics and practicing demography, and how this shapes a new logic for the quantitative study of racial stratification that has developed between Du Bois's *Philadelphia Negro* and the reflexive discourse among statisticians.

BIRTH OF SOCIAL STATISTICS

Francis Galton was a key intellectual power behind the modern statistical revolution in the social sciences (Stigler 1986, chap. 8; Kevles 1985, chap. 1). His imaginative ideas lay the conceptual foundation of eugenic thought and inspired much of the early work in social statistics. Galton's research in *Hereditary Genius* (1869), *English Men of Science* (1874), and *Natural Inheritance*

(1889) suggests that genius and success are inherited and that this process could be measured statistically.

Galton used statistical analysis to make general statements regarding the superiority of different classes within England and of the European-origin race, statements that were consistent with his eugenic agenda. In the 1892 edition of *Hereditary Genius*, he outlined that

the natural ability of which this book mainly treats, is such as a modern European possesses in a much greater average share than men of the lower races. There is nothing either in the history of domestic animals or in that of evolution to make us doubt that a race of sane men may be formed, who shall be as much superior mentally and morally to the modern European, as the modern European is to the lowest of the Negro races. (Galton 1892, 27)

Although this statement may be considered insignificant in the context of Galton's overall statistical contribution, it is fundamental in understanding the direction and purpose of his causal explanations and placing Du Bois's empirical response in a historical context (Zuberi 2000).

In 1875, Galton wrote an article, "Statistics by Intercomparison, with Remarks on the Law of Frequency of Error," which suggested that measurement of two values—the median and the quartile—was sufficient to characterize or compare populations. For Galton, this meant different populations could be represented in a bell curve of all populations.

In 1885, Francis Ysidro Edgeworth developed a test to ascertain whether different populations existed within the bell curve (Edgeworth 1885). Edgeworth's test adapted the bell curve to assess the "significance" of differences between the subpopulations. He used Galton's 1875 formulation as a vehicle to employ classical statistical theory in understanding social statistics.

Around the same time, in 1889, statistician Karl Pearson met W.F.R. Weldon, the chair of zoology at University College, London. Weldon was attempting to adapt Galton's methods to the study of evolution in wild populations. Weldon turned to Pearson with a series of questions to which Pearson responded in a series of articles known as *Contributions to the Mathematical Theory of Evolution*. Published between 1894 and 1916, the series was retitled *Mathematical Contributions to the Theory of Evolution*, after the second in what became a series of about 19 articles.[2] Pearson's elaboration of Edgeworth's theorems advanced correlation theory into the mainstream of social statistics.[3] In Pearson's third and fourth papers of the *Mathematical Contributions to the Theory of Evolution*—"Regression, Heredity and Panmixa" and "On the Probable Errors of Frequency Constants and On the Influence of Random Selection on Variation and Correlation" (co-authored with L.N.G. Filon)—he provided a basic formula for estimating the correlation coefficient and a test of its accuracy.

In 1897, George Udny Yule provided the conceptual and statistical expression that completed Galton's project to apply statistics to the study of society.[4] Yule was one of the first social statisticians to demonstrate the relationship between regression and least-squares estimates. Yule was exceptional in that his application of statistics focused on causation in social sciences. Yule extended the application of regression in one of the first regression analyses of poverty. Interestingly, Yule's analysis provided support for the conservative position advocated by Malthus at the beginning of the century (Yule 1899; Stigler 1986, 355-57). He argued that providing income relief outside the poorhouse increased the number of people on relief. By 1920, Yule's approach to multiple correlation and regression predominated in social science research.

Social statistics took another intellectual leap when Ronald A. Fisher published *Statistical Methods for Research Workers* in 1925 and *The Design of Experiments* in 1935. Both books had a tremendous impact on the teaching and practice of statistics. His work clarified the distinction between a sample statistic and population value, and he emphasized the derivation of exact distributions for hypotheses testing. He is also credited with introducing the modern experimental design and statistical methods to social sciences. These innovations remain as the basis of social statistics (Fisher 1925, 1935).

CAUSAL REASONING
AS RACIAL REASONING

The experimental notion of causal inference is the implicit guide in the selection of observations in quasi-experimental research and in the model selection, design, and statistical analysis of nonexperimental data from sample surveys and samples from census data. Most researchers, however, seem not to appreciate the consequences of adopting the experimental model as a guide in the design, collection, analysis, and interpretation of social science data. Most social scientists use experimental language when interpreting empirical results, thereby entailing a commitment to the experimental mode of analysis introduced by Fisher (Holland 1986; Cox 1992; Sobel 1995; Smith 1990). I am intentionally explicit in this section so that I can present the fundamental elements of the causal process in statistical modeling.

Because most social science researchers study causal effects for the purpose of making inferences about the effects of manipulations to which groups of individuals in a population have been or might be exposed, causes are only things that can, in theory, be manipulated or altered. This recognition forces us to consider the individuals or units we study and our ability to alter or treat them. This type of clarity is essential yet absent in most policy-oriented social research in which decisions to manipulate the real world often depend on social researchers' causal inferences. A lack of clarity in the statistical analysis of racial processes has contributed in great measure to the confusion about how to resolve issues of racial stratification.

Cultural studies in anthropology, history, literary criticism, sociology, philosophy, and African studies have questioned and criticized the concept of race. Statisticians are in the process of an important discussion on the issue of using attributes like race in social statistics (see Holland 1986; Cox 1992; Sobel 1995; Rosenbaum 1984). This discussion has not focused on the issue of the conceptualization of race. It nevertheless places a considerable theoretical burden on social statisticians who use race as a variable in their statistical analyses to predict social outcomes. Most social statisticians have not yet integrated the latest statistical research in their statistical analyses of race.

Statistical populations consist of observed measures of some characteristic; yet no observational record can capture completely what it is to be a human being. Researchers employ observational records to define abstract concepts like race. The researchers or the subject (as in self-administered surveys or censuses) can make the observation; however, the researchers and the purpose of their study determine the meaning of the record. This is how empirical research reifies race. If we have records of racial classification, the population of races rather than the population of persons is open to statistical investigation; yet in social statistics it is always a mistake to think of a population of races as a genetic population.

A population of races in this sense is a statistical concept based on a politically constructed measure. Deriving a statistical model of social relationships requires an elaborate theory that states explicitly and in detail the variables in the system, how these variables are causally interrelated, the functional form of their relationships, and the statistical quality and traits of the error terms. Once this theoretical model is achieved, it is possible to estimate a regression model.[5] Rarely, however, does social science research provide the level of theoretical detail necessary to derive a statistical model in this manner.

The alternative is a data-driven process. To derive a statistical model from data, we assume the model is a black box and "test" it against our empirical results. Both the theory- and data-driven statistical models attempt to provide a parsimonious and generalizable account for the phenomenon under investigation. Statistical models attempt to provide a rigorous basis—rooted in abstract statistical theory—for determining when a causal relationship exists between two or more variables in a model. However, unless we start with prior knowledge about the causal relationship, the calculation of the regression equation refers to a regression model and its system of equations, not to the "real" world the model purports to empirically define.

The language of causation originates in the experimental framework of modeling causal inference (Holland 1986; Cox 1992; Sobel 1995; Rosenbaum 1984). Statistically, causation has a particular meaning. Measuring the effects of causes is done in the context of another cause, hence X causes Z relative to some other cause that includes everything but X. In the context of causal inference, each individual in the population must be potentially exposable to any of the causes. And, as statistician

Paul Holland notes, "the schooling a student receives can be a cause, in our sense, of the student's performance on a test, whereas the student's race or gender cannot" (Holland 1986, 946). For example, being an African American should not be understood as the cause of a student's performance on a test, despite the fact that being African American can be a very reliable basis for predicting test performance. The logic of causal inference itself should give every nonpartisan scholar reason to avoid flamboyant rhetoric about the genetic-based cognitive causes for racial and gender stratification.

To see this point of view in a social context, consider the following non-experimental study, in which causation assumes only two causes, denoted by t (private school) and c (public school). Now let P be a variable that indicates the cause to which each individual in the population, U, is exposed. In this case, $P = t$ indicates that the individual is exposed to t (private school).

In social statistics, P is generally determined by factors beyond the researchers' control. The point here is that the value of P_u could have been different for each individual in the population. That is, in this example, the researcher does not determine who attended private school; yet each individual theoretically could have attended private school.

The response variable Y (test scores) measures the effect of the cause and has values that are theoretically determined after exposure to the cause. Causes have effects for the reason that the particular cause, t or c, to which each individual has been exposed, potentially affects the values of Y. The potential responses are denoted as Y_t and Y_c. For any given individual in the population, denoted as u, we interpret the response variable $Y_t u$ as the value of the response that would be observed if the student attends private school and $Y_c u$ as the value of the response that would be observed if the same individual attended public school.

Finally, the effect of the cause public versus private school on each individual as measured by Y (test scores) and related to the cause of not attending private school is the difference between $Y_t u$ and $Y_c u$, and is expressed by the algebraic difference $Y_t u - Y_c u$. This represents the causal effect of private school relative to public school on each individual in the population as measured by the test scores.

In social statistics, inferences about causal effects are statistical inferences about effects on collections of individuals in the population. For our example, the average causal effect of private school relative to public school is denoted as T over the population U, and is the expected value of the difference $Y_t u - Y_c u$ over the individual u in the population U.[6]

This experimental model contains three variables P, $Y_t u$, and $Y_c u$; however, only P and Y_p are observed. Remember, it is P that determines which value—$Y_t u$ or $Y_c u$—is observed for a given individual. If $P_u = t$, then $Y_t u$ is observed; or if $P_u = c$, then $Y_c u$ is observed, and the observed response on individual u is $Y_{pu} u$.

Inferences in social statistics employ (usually implicitly) a model that corresponds to the experimental model. To further illustrate these points, consider the example. To estimate the effect, we can compute the mean difference in subsequent test scores between private school and public school students. This is "true" when T is independent of subsequent test scores (under either treatment).[7]

Race and gender as unalterable characteristics of individuals are inappropriate variables for inferential statistical analysis. Statisticians have questioned and criticized the use of such attributes—unalterable properties of individuals—in inferential statistical models (Holland 1986; Cox 1992; Rosenbaum 1984).

Most social statisticians, however, continue to treat race and sex as individual attributes in their inferential models. Statistical models that present race as a cause are really statements of association between the racial classification and a predictor or explanatory variable across individuals in a population. To treat these models as causal or inferential is a form of racial reasoning.

Most statisticians agree that in social statistical analysis (observational studies, quasi experiments, social surveys, etc.), only those variables that can conceptually be manipulated are eligible to represent causal processes. It must make sense in the context under examination that for any individual the causal variable might have been different from the value actually taken. Thus, race is not a causal variable but rather an intrinsic property of the individual. The study of racial change (that is, passing from black to white in the United States or from *preta* [black] to *parda* [brown] in Brazil), of racial prejudice, and of possible racial discriminatory employment or payment practices are exceptions.

The statistical definition of causation is limited by the lack of an explicit notion of an underlying process at the observational level stating how the variables in the system are causally related and the form of this relationship beyond that involved in the data under analysis. Such explanations are not the "true" underlying process but rather relate the phenomenon under study to knowledge at a different level (for example, relating a demographic finding to some biological process, or, as David Cox notes, it relates "an epidemiological finding to some biochemical or immunological process" [Cox 1992, 297]).

We can distinguish between causal effects and causal theories. Causal effects can be observed in a random experiment, although in principle, causal effects can be estimated in observational studies (see Smith 1990; Rosenbaum 1984). A causal effect is a comparison of two or more potential responses that are observed from each individual in the population. A causal theory "is a scientific theory describing aspects of the various biological, chemical, physical, or social processes by which the treatment produces its effects" (Rosenbaum 1984, 42). Causal effects refer to the effect of a factor on a given response variable, Y, whereas causal theories consider how and why the effect operates. Causal effects are more important in experimental studies, where causal theories can be called into question if they contradict the results of the study.

The causal theory serves a more fundamental purpose in social statistics. If the causal theory is contradicted by the results of a well-designed study, and the causal theory is supported by evidence from other studies and well-developed arguments or perspectives, questions can arise regarding the assumption of the independence of the treatment and the response variable and the positive probability of receiving each treatment.[8]

The problem with race as a variable in social statistics might be clearer in a hypothetical example.[9] Consider an example that involves two causal statements:

1. She did well on the test because she is of African origin.

2. She did well on the test because of the affirmative action taken by her teachers and the university.

The meaning of "because" is different for each of these statements. The effect, "did well on the test," is the same in each statement. In (1) the cause is assigned to an attribute she possesses. In (2) it is assigned to an activity performed by others. The first causal statement suggests that African women do better on the test, in some sense, than non-African women. The second causal statement means that had she not had the advantage of affirmative action, she would not have done as well as she did. This statement presents a comparison between the responses to two

causes. In (1) all that can be discussed is association. In (2) we can measure the causal effects.

FROM CAUSATION TO
ASSOCIATION AS
AN ASPECT OF
DERACIALIZED STATISTICS

An unalterable characteristic cannot be a cause in inferential statistical models. Causal statements involving unalterable characteristics are really statements of association between the values of an attribute and a response variable across individuals in the population.

I begin with a population-based model of associational inference involving race.[10] This statistical model relates two variables over a population. Again, I am explicit in this section so that I can present the fundamental elements of the suggested clarification of race in statistical modeling.

A population-based statistical model starts with a population of units. An individual in a population is denoted by u. Individuals are the basic objects of investigation. In this discussion, human subjects are the basic units. A variable is a characteristic or function defined on every u in the population U. The basic elements of social statistical models are a population of units and variables defined on these units.

For example, suppose for each unit u in U there is an associated value of Yu of a variable Y. Also suppose that Y is a variable of interest and we want to understand why the values of Y vary over the units in the population. Y is the variable to be explained. In associational inference, we discover how the values of Y are associated with the values of other variables defined on the units in the population. Now let race be R—another variable defined on the population. I distinguish R from Y by referring to it as an attribute of the units in u. In a more general sense, R could be any unalterable characteristic of units in the population, such as sex. However, unlike sex, race is a socially based characteristic, and, as mentioned previously, in some societies actually may be alterable. In this context, the meaning of race takes on added importance. Both race and Y are on equal footing, since they are both variables defined on the population. Race is analogous to variable P mentioned previously, but with the essential difference that R_u indicates a property or characteristic of u, whereas P_u refers to exposure to a specific cause. In this example, the value of R could not have been different, whereas the value of P_u for each individual could have been different.

Probabilities, distributions, and expected values of the variables race or Y are computed over the population. A probability in this case is equal to a proportion of units in the population. The expected value of a variable is the average value over all of the population. And the conditional expected values are averages over subsets of units, where each subset is defined by conditioning in the values of variables. In this sense, social statistical models are population based.

If we let Y equal some variable of interest (such as intelligence or income) and R equal race, then the most detailed level of measurement we can have in this model is the values of Y and R for all the individuals in the population. The joint distribution of Y and R over the population is specified by $Pr(Y = y, R = r)$ and equals the proportion of individuals, u, in the population for which $Y_u = y$ and $R_u = r$.

The conditional distribution of Y given R is specified by $Pr(Y = y \mid R = r) = Pr(Y = y, R = r)/Pr(R = r)$. This describes how the distribution of Y values changes over the population as race varies. In the social sciences, a typical associational parameter is the regression of Y on R—that is, the conditional expectation $E(Y \mid R = r)$.

Associational inference involves descriptive statistics and consists of making statistical inferences (estimates, tests, posterior distributions, etc.) about associational parameters relating Y and R on the basis of data gathered about Y and R from individuals in the population.

For example, it is usually a mistake to use the association between race and intelligence as evidence of a "causal link" between them. The data involved in this debate are purely associational. Most of these studies ascertain only racial status and test results on sets of subjects. Researchers on both sides of the debate argue that race measures certain genetic differences between racial groups and that these genetic differences could be related to test results. They argue that a prima facie case has been made for further study.

I am suggesting that in this case race be considered an individual attribute rather than something that can be manipulated. In the context of research on intelligence, one cannot be more or less of one race; such a notion is impossible to measure, because race is thought to be an unalterable characteristic.

Examples of the confusion between attributes and causes fill the social science literature. Paul L. Menchik gave the following example of a causal conclusion:

Table 3 depicts the association between ethnic group and mortality. Blacks face greater mortality risks than whites, as is shown in Column 1; in fact, the effect of being black on mortality is equivalent to over five years of increased age. Controlling for background by using p_t results in a small reduction of the "black" coefficient, but the effect of being black is still equivalent to over five years of increased initial age. (Menchik 1993, 435)

I chose for illustration an article that I think has an important finding to which I am sympathetic but that nevertheless presents a problematic conclusion. In general, my concern with the author's article pertains to the language he used to interpret his results, not his results per se. The author clearly intended for this interpretation of his logit regression results to state that the race of a man could affect his mortality. However, an individual trait such as race cannot determine another trait of the individual. The problem is determining when race is viewed as an unalterable characteristic of an individual and when it is seen as a cause that can act on individuals in the population under investigation. As an unalterable characteristic, race can be discussed only as an association

(which is what the author does in the first sentence); as a causal statement, it is at least possible to contemplate measuring causal effects (as the author does in the remainder of the paragraph). From my perspective, it is difficult to conceive of how race could be a treatment in a social survey and, therefore, a cause. The problem is not in the findings but in Menchik's interpretation of the results. He assumes that we can use race as a cause.

I suggest that we reconsider the notion of causation in the study of race. It is better to interpret these impacts of race as the association of racial stratification on an individual's mortality outcome. In this context, the attenuation of the race variable that occurred via the introduction of wealth into Menchik's model would imply the way that race interacts with wealth in its association with mortality.

Menchik's model might be useful for predicting the results of interventions into health or of changing circumstances or to provide a better understanding of the racial stratification process. But this interpretation of his results must be based on a theory in order to connect the statistical calculations to the process.

In terms of measuring causal effects, the other extreme can be found in statement (2) of the earlier example. The interpretation is that had she not had the advantage of affirmative action taken by her teacher and the university, she would not have done as well as she did. It implies a comparison between the responses to two causes and is appropriate for causal inference. In the second statement, neither sex nor race is an issue. Yet, as seen in our substantive example, it is not unusual for individuals to look at hypotheses like those in statement (1) and treat them like those in statement (2).

Association may not prove causation; however, it may provide the basis for support of a causal theory. Association is evidence of causation when it is buttressed with other knowledge and supporting evidence. When we discuss the "effect of race," we are less mindful of the larger world in which the path to success or failure is routinely influenced by other contingencies or circumstances.

CONCLUSION

Some argue that causal models are the best way for social scientists to make public policy statements, because statistical models used in this way allow us to elaborate on how and what produces particular effects. This may be true, but human knowledge is uncertain and imperfect, and it is not clear how statistical models contribute to this uncertainty (Freedman 1987). Interpreting the results of a causal inference is validated by an underlying causal theory. If the theory is rejected, the interpretations have no foundation. Decision makers may like causal models that appear to support their position on important questions, but it is the continued misuse of the models by scholars that makes the process respectable.

Some argue that the causal language used by many social scientists does not reflect an unarticulated

causal model but is simply the careless use of language. However, this tendency has significant implications for how results are interpreted in policy circles and within the professional discursive mode.

Race, or more specifically the process of racialization, may be the stimulus of how other individuals respond or interact with persons so characterized. The examination of discrimination and prejudice provides a solution to the trap of racial reasoning. One example of such research is the study of racial attitudes (see Bobo, this volume). Du Bois was aware of this process and gave it direct attention in his work. Another example of research on this process is found in the economic study of statistical racism and the demographic study of environmental racism.[11] The causal factors in statistical racism are discriminatory practices by employers, not the races of the people involved. The causal factors in environmental racism are discriminatory practices by institutions in determining the location of hazardous wastes cites.

The solution to the problem in the analysis of unalterable characteristics such as race and sex in inferential statistics requires a shift in perspective. We should describe race and sex as events that represent the acquisition of the attributes for each individual. Thus, being classified one way or another might have a particular impact. As our understanding of what race or sex means changes, so too does our statistical analysis.

The national liberation movements to decolonize Africa, Asia, and Latin America; the civil rights movement to deracialize civic society in the United States; and the anti- apartheid movement in South Africa all questioned the Eurocentric division of humanity. We would benefit by continuing to question the racialization of identity. Using racialized census, survey, or other social data is not in and of itself problematic. But the racialization of data is an artifact of both the struggles to preserve and to destroy racial stratification. Before the data can be deracialized, we must deracialize the social circumstances that created race. Statistical research can go beyond racial reasoning if we dare to apply the methods to the data appropriately.

Notes

1. For a more extensive examination of the social statistical analysis in *The Philadelphia Negro: A Social Study*, see my article on this classic community study (McDaniel 1998). Here, I will not repeat the detail covered in that article; rather, I focus my attention on the logical implications of the Du Boisian perspective for social statistical analysis within the context of recent advances in statistical methods.

2. The long series of memoirs entitled *Mathematical Contributions to the Theory of Evolution* was reissued by the Trustees of Biometrika in 1948 in a single volume. The selected papers consist of articles published in the *Philosophical Transactions of the Royal Society*, in the *Drapers' Company Research Memoirs*, and in *Philosophical Magazine*. Most of these articles cover Pearson's *Mathematical Contributions to the Theory of Evolution* series. The article published in *Philosophical Magazine*, "On the Criterion That a Given System of Deviations from the Probable in the Case of a Correlated System of Variables Is Such That It Can Be Reasonably Supposed to Have Arisen from Random Sampling," presents the first derivation of the distribution referred to as the chi-square. The

chi-square test, a goodness-of-fit test, is considered Pearson's most significant contribution to statistical theory. In this work, Pearson greatly expanded social statistics. He also expanded on Edgeworth's significance test by measuring difference in terms of standard deviations (see Pearson 1948; Stigler 1986).

3. Pearson's correlation coefficient, r, continues to be the most commonly used measure of correlation. When the term "correlation" is used with no other specification, it is assumed to be Pearson's r.

4. Yule's article "On the Theory of Correlation" reconciled the theory of correlation with the method of least squares from the traditional theory of errors (Yule 1897). See Stigler (1986, 348-58) for an excellent discussion of the importance of this article for social statistics. Linking least squares and regression made the developments in simplifying the solutions of normal equations and the calculation of the probable errors of coefficients by astronomers and geodesists available to regression analysis among social statisticians.

5. I use the term "regression" in a broad sense to include logistic regression, regression analysis, regression analysis of survival data, ordinary least-squares regression, and so on.

6. An unbiased estimator of the average effect of public school in the population is $E(Y_t u - Y_c u) = T$. T is the average causal effect. In probabilistic terms, $T = E(Y_t u) - (Y_c u)$, where $E(\bullet)$ is the expectation in the population. For an estimate of the average effect of t, we would calculate $E(Y_t u)$—that is, $\overline{Y}_t u$—as the sample mean among individuals receiving treatment t. In our example, this would refer to individuals attending private school. Likewise, we would use data on individuals receiving treatment c—public school—to estimate $E(Y_c u)$. In practice, these are estimates of $E(Y_t u \mid T = t)$ and $E(Y_c u \mid T = c)$. Yet these quantities are not equal to the respective unconditional expectations unless our sample is random and the population is randomly divided into treatment and control groups. Randomization allows the assumption that $Y_1 \ldots, Y_t \times T$ is statistically reasonable and allows us to estimate the average effect of attending private school, t, versus c by $\overline{Y}_t u - \overline{Y}_c u$.

7. If T is not independent of subsequent test scores, the researcher would have a good estimate of $E(Y_t u \mid T = t)$ but not $E(Y_t u)$. In this

case, the mean difference in test scores between public and private school students estimates the actual average difference between the two groups, and not the average effect. We would have what economists call "selection bias" (see Heckman 1976).

8. These two assumptions are referred to as the assumption that treatment assignment is strongly ignorable (see Rosenbaum 1984).

9. Note the similarity between my examples and those presented by Holland (1986, 954-55).

10. For more general presentations of the model of associational inference, see Holland (1986) and Rosenbaum (1984).

11. It is important to distinguish between the "statistical" reasoning by an employer and the statistical reasoning discussed in this article that focuses on social scientists engaged in a very different sort of statistical reasoning. The econometric "theory" of statistical racism maintains that racial preference of an employer for a "white" job candidate over a "black" job candidate who is not known to differ in other respects might stem from the employer's previous statistical experience with the two groups (Phelps 1972). This analysis has been extended to the examination of the impact of affirmative action on employer beliefs and worker productivity (see Lundberg 1991; Coate and Loury 1993). According to my argument, statistical racism is a difficult process to examine. An employer's assessment of the expected productivity of employees in less favored groups may be wrong in a way that a longitudinal study could effectively demonstrate; however, such a study is still prohibitively expensive. We might argue that an employer's perspective is invalid because it does not incorporate certain systemic mechanisms of other types of prejudice, such as the effect of higher rewards for the productivity of employees in a less favored "race."

The analysis of environmental racism examines whether facilities for treatment, storage, and disposal of hazardous wastes are located disproportionately in communities of the less favored race (see Bullard 1990; Anderton et al. 1994). Although the study of statistical racism focuses on intentional prejudice and the study of environmental racism focuses on dumping prejudice, both depend on inequitable distributions as evidence of intentional prejudice.

References

Anderton, Douglass L., Andy B. Anderson, John Michael Oakes, and Michael R. Fraser. 1994. Environmental Equity: The Demographics of Dumping. *Demography* 31(2):229-48.

Bullard, R. D. 1990. *Dumping in Dixie: Race, Class, and Environmental Quality*. Boulder, CO: Westview Press.

Coate, Stephen and Glenn C. Loury. 1993. Will Affirmative-Action Policies Eliminate Negative Stereotypes? *American Economic Review* 83(5):1220-40.

Cox, David R. 1992. Causality: Some Statistical Aspects. *Journal of the Royal Statistical Society* A 135(pt. 2):291-301.

Du Bois, W. E. Burghardt. 1898. The Study of the Negro Problems. *The Annals* of the American Academy of Political and Social Science Jan.:1-23.

Edgeworth, Francis Ysidro. 1885. Methods of Statistics. *Jubilee Volume of the Statistical Society* 181-217.

Fisher, Ronald A. 1925. *Statistical Methods for Research Workers*. London: Oliver and Boyd.

———. 1935. *The Design of Experiments*. London: Oliver and Boyd.

Freedman, David A. 1987. As Others See Us: A Case Study in Path Analysis. *Journal of Education Statistics* 12(2):101-28.

Galton, Francis. 1869 [1892]. *Hereditary Genius: An Inquiry into Its Laws and Consequences*. 2d ed. Gloucester, MA: Peter Smith.

———. 1874. *English Men of Science: Their Nature and Nurture*. London: Macmillan.

———. 1875. Statistics by Intercomparison, with Remarks on the Law of Frequency of Error. *Philosophical Magazine*, 4th ser., 49:33-46.

———. 1889. *Natural Inheritance*. London: Macmillan.

Heckman, James J. 1976. The Common Structure of Statistical Models of Truncation, Sample Selection and Limited Dependent Variables and a Simple Estimator for Such Models. *Annals of Economic and Social Measurement* 5:475-92.

Holland, Paul W. 1986. Statistics and Causal Inference. *Journal of the American Statistical Association* 81(396):945-70.

Kevles, Daniel J. 1985. *In the Name of Eugenics: Genetics and the Uses of Human Heredity*. Berkeley: University of California Press.

Lundberg, Shelly J. 1991. The Enforcement of Equal Opportunity Laws Under Imperfect Information: Affirmative Action and Alternatives. *Quartile Journal of Economics* 106(1):309-26.

McDaniel, Antonio. 1998. The "Philadelphia Negro" Then and Now: Implications for Empirical Research. In *W.E.B. DuBois, Race, and the City: The Philadelphia Negro and Its Legacy*, ed. M. B. Katz and T. J. Sugrue. Philadelphia: University of Pennsylvania Press.

Menchik, Paul L. 1993. Economic Status as a Determinant of Mortality Among Black and White Older Men: Does Poverty Kill? *Population Studies* 47:427-36.

Pearson, Karl. 1948. *Karl Pearson's Early Statistical Papers*. Cambridge: Cambridge University Press.

Phelps, Edmund S. 1972. The Statistical Theory of Racism and Sexism. *American Economic Review* 62(4):659-61.

Rosenbaum, Paul R. 1984. From Association to Causation in Observational Studies: The Role of Tests of Strongly Ignorable Treatment Assignment. *Journal of the American Statistical Association* 79(38):41-47.

Smith, Herbert L. 1990. Specification Problems in Experimental and Non-Experimental Social Research. *Sociological Methodology* 20:59-91.

Sobel, Michael E. 1995. Causal Inference in the Social and Behavioral Sciences. In *Handbook of Statistical Modeling for the Social and Behavioral Sciences*, ed. Gerhard Arminger, Clifford C. Clogg, and Michael E. Sobel. New York: Plenum Press.

Stigler, Stephen M. 1986. *The History of Statistics: The Measurement of Uncertainty Before 1900.* Cambridge, MA: Harvard University Press, Belknap Press.

Yule, George Uduy. 1897. On the Theory of Correlation. *Journal of the Royal Statistical Society* 60:812-54.

———. 1899. An Investigation into the Causes of Changes in Pauperism in England, Chiefly During the Last Two Intercensal Decades, I. *Journal of the Royal Statistical Society* 62:249-95.

Zuberi, Tukufu. 2000. *Thicker Than Blood: An Essay on the Quantification of Race*. Chicago: University of Chicago Press.

ANNALS, *AAPSS*, **568**, March 2000

Reclaiming a Du Boisian Perspective on Racial Attitudes

By LAWRENCE D. BOBO

ABSTRACT: This article asserts that Du Boisian sociology included a strong role for racial prejudice in analyzing the conditions and dynamics of African American social life. The article examines Du Bois's empirical social scientific legacy with a special focus on *The Philadelphia Negro* and how he treated racial prejudice in this seminal work. It then examines the turn away from a concern with racial prejudice in modern sociological analysis and identifies the necessity of returning to the theoretical holism exemplified by Du Bois if sociological theory on race and racism are to advance.

Lawrence D. Bobo is professor of sociology and Afro-American studies at Harvard University. He is co-author of Racial Attitudes in America: Trends and Interpretations *(1998) and* Racialized Politics: The Debate on Racism in America *(2000). He has been a fellow at the Center for Advanced Study in the Behavioral Sciences at Stanford University and a visiting scholar at the Russell Sage Foundation in New York.*

The American Negro, therefore, is surrounded and conditioned by the concept which he has of white people and he is treated in accordance with the concept they have of him.
—W.E.B. Du Bois ([1940] 1995)

W.E.B. Du Bois is most widely known as an essayist, biographer, social commentator, and activist. His life's project involved an interrogation of the problem of race and the pursuit of freedom for African Americans (indeed the pursuit of freedom for all those trapped on the wrong side of the color line in a colonial, imperialistic, and capitalistic world order). In what is surely his most oft quoted passage, Du Bois declared,

The problem of the twentieth century is the problem of the color line—the relation of the darker to the lighter races of men in Asia and Africa, in America and the islands of the sea. (Du Bois [1903] 1997, 45)

Deep and timeless social insights of this kind, including his discussion of double-consciousness, life behind the veil, and his broad visionary humanism constitute the universally recognized aspects of Du Bois's legacy.

Yet, for much of Du Bois's long and productive life he was an empirical social scientist. He pioneered in the conduct of comprehensive community social surveys, in the documentation of black community life, and in the theoretically grounded analysis of black-white relations. Were it not for the deeply entrenched racism in the United States during his early professional years, Du Bois would be recognized alongside the likes of Albion Small, Edward A. Ross,

Robert E. Park, Lewis Wirth, and W. I. Thomas as one of the fountainheads of American sociology. Had not racism so thoroughly excluded him from placement in the center of the academy, he might arguably have come to rank with Max Weber or Emile Durkheim in stature.[1] Today, urban anthropologists, historical economists, political scientists, social psychologists, and sociologists all attempt to claim a piece of the Du Boisian legacy (Bay 1998).

My purpose here is to add to the growing stream of scholarship reclaiming and building upon the contributions of W.E.B. Du Bois the empirical social scientist. At core, I argue that Du Bois's sociological analysis of the status of African Americans reflected a foundational concern with prejudice and racial attitudes. It is essential to reconsider and resuscitate this aspect of Du Boisian sociology. Modern sociologists have abandoned, more often implicitly but sometimes quite explicitly so, a perspective on racial inequality that embraces a role for racial identities, attitudes, and beliefs. The result has been energy misspent in well-worn race versus class polemics and a failure to understand the social underpinnings of a changing but durable racial divide.

My argument begins with a consideration of Du Bois the social scientist. This discussion draws heavily on his magisterial work, *The Philadelphia Negro: A Social Study* (1899). From this I extract several ideas about the epistemology of Du Bois and his specific theoretical formulation regarding the dynamics of race. Next, I review the turn in sociology away from aspects of the type of approach that Du Bois epitomized. Finally, I provide modern examples of the role of racial attitudes and beliefs in the status of African Americans.

RACIAL ATTITUDES IN DU BOISIAN ANALYSIS

Du Bois as scientist

Du Bois was a committed empirical social scientist. He was openly critical of sweeping generalizations and the sort of grand theorizing common in the emerging field of sociology:

The biological analogy, the vast generalizations, were striking, but actual scientific accomplishment lagged. For me an opportunity seemed to present itself. I could not lull my mind to hypnosis by regarding a phrase like "consciousness of kind" as scientific law.... I determined to put science into sociology through a study of the condition and problems of my own group. I was going to study the facts, any and all facts concerning the American Negro and his plight, and by measurement and comparison and research, work up to any valid generalization which I could. (Du Bois [1940] 1995, 51)

His inductive approach and zeal for gathering facts had been sparked during his years at Harvard by Albert Bushnell Hart and were subsequently nurtured by the German political economist Gustav Schmoller during Du Bois's studies at the University of Berlin (Rudwick 1974; Bulmer 1991; McDaniel 1998). He shared Schmoller's belief that sensible social reform would flow from complete understanding of the relevant social facts and dynamics.

To be sure, Du Bois's career shifted decisively in the direction of activism and political commentary after 1910. His belief in the power of facts and knowledge to persuade dimmed. Yet his regard for scientific investigation, measurement, and evidence continued long after the era in which he completed The Philadelphia Negro. Thus, in 1944 in his essay for Rayford Logan's edited volume What the Negro Wants, Du Bois summarized his own life work as having three stages, with scientific research a critical ingredient of the first and third stages. The third stage, which stretched from 1928 to 1944, Du Bois dedicated to "scientific investigation and organized action among Negroes, in close co-operation, to secure the survival of the Negro race, until the cultural development of America and the world is willing to recognize Negro freedom" (Du Bois 1944a, 70). Hence, some 40 years after The Philadelphia Negro, Du Bois reasserted the need for scientific evidence in his project of pursuing black freedom. He struck a similar note in a 1948 essay for Phylon assessing change in race relations in the United States (Du Bois 1948).

In The Philadelphia Negro, Du Bois set out to provide a comprehensive analysis of Philadelphia's Seventh Ward, then the largest concentration of blacks in the city. He developed six interview and enumeration protocols. He rejected the reigning ideas in social science which would have faulted basic black capabilities for the impoverished condition of most blacks. Instead, he crafted a historically grounded portrait of blacks whose circumstances, by and large, had clear social or environmental roots. Although this is necessarily a compacted treatment, his analytical framework stressed the interplay of six factors: (1) a history of enslavement, servitude, and oppression; (2) demographic trends and compositional factors (for example, disproportion of women to men); (3) economic positioning and competition with free whites both native born and European immigrants; (4) racial prejudice and discrimination; (5) the resources, internal structure, dynamics, and leadership of the black community itself; and (6) moral agency and black self-determination. Of all these, the burden of slavery and the weak position of blacks in the economic structure were surely the primary factors in Du Bois's model. Du Bois was thus careful to not make prejudice the central or most important variable in his analysis. Yet the force of prejudice was ubiquitous and of unavoidable consequence in his analysis of the dynamics of race relations in Philadelphia.

Du Bois on the role of prejudice

Du Bois saw racial prejudice as a constituent factor in the structural placement of blacks in the labor and housing markets. Consider first the labor market. An early chapter on occupations in *The Philadelphia Negro* asserts the critical role of prejudice in erecting a color bar to economic opportunity for blacks:

In the realm of social phenomena the law of survival is greatly modified by human choice, wish, whim, and prejudice. . . . Now it is sufficient to say in general that the sorts of work open to Negroes are not only restricted by their own lack of training but also by discrimination against them on account of their race; that their economic rise is not only hindered by their present poverty, but also by a widespread inclination to shut against them many doors of advancement open to the talented and efficient of other races. (Du Bois [1899] 1996, 98)

Du Bois documented the extent to which blacks were locked into the most menial and low-wage positions. He concluded that "the cause of this peculiar restriction in employment of Negroes is twofold: first, the lack of training and experience among Negroes; second, the prejudice of the whites" (Du Bois [1899] 1996, 111).

Du Bois saw racial prejudice as acute among working-class whites and as operating in lockstep with the economic interests and ambitions of working-class whites. Prejudice was an element of his account of why white workers strove to displace black workers:

Partially by taking advantage of race prejudice, partially by greater economic efficiency and partially by the endeavor to maintain and raise wages, white workmen have not only monopolized the new industrial opportunities of an age which has transformed Philadelphia from a colonial town to a world-city, but have also been enabled to take from the Negro workman the opportunities already enjoyed in certain lines of work. (Du Bois [1899] 1996, 127)

Prejudice and economic motives both contributed to whites' efforts to seal off opportunities from blacks. "To repeat, then," Du Bois wrote, "the real motives back of this exclusion are plain: a large part is simple race prejudice, always strong in working classes and intensified by the peculiar history of the Negro in this country. Another part, however, and possibly more potent part, is the natural spirit of monopoly and the desire to keep up wages" (129).

Du Bois was careful not to reduce prejudice to economic motives. Indeed, he suggested that quite irrational actions might be undertaken in service of anti-black prejudice. His discussion of black occupational and job opportunities concludes:

All these considerations are further complicated by the fact that the industrial condition of the Negro cannot be considered apart from the great fact of race prejudice—indefinite and shadowy as that phrase may be. It is certain that, while industrial co-operation among the groups of a great city population is very difficult under ordinary circumstances, that here it is rendered more difficult and in some respects almost impossible by the fact that nineteen-twentieths of the population have in many cases refused to co-operate with the other twentieth, even when the co-operation means life to the latter and great advantage to the former. In other words, one of the great postulates of the science of economics—that men will seek their economic advantage—is in this case untrue, because in many cases men will not do this if it involves association, even in a casual and business way, with Negroes. And this fact must be taken account of in all judgments as to the Negro's economic progress. (Du Bois [1899] 1996, 146-47)

For this reason, economic historian Jacqueline Jones (1998, 104) rightly

stresses that Du Bois does not develop an economically deterministic analysis.

Du Bois was equally forceful about the role of prejudice in restricting black options in the housing market. This too has bearing on fundamental quality-of-life experience issues since where one lives immediately affects exposure to a variety of potentially unwanted or even hazardous social conditions. Although the level of segregation had not reached anything like it would in later years, Du Bois concluded that blacks faced discrimination in seeking housing and in what they paid for housing. Thus, he reported that

three causes of even greater importance . . . are the limited localities where Negroes may rent, the peculiar connection of dwelling and occupation among Negroes and the social organization of the Negro. The undeniable fact that most Philadelphia white people prefer not to live near Negroes limits the Negro very seriously in his choice of a home and especially in the choice of a cheap home. Moreover, real estate agents knowing the limited supply usually raise the rent a dollar or two for Negro tenants, if they do not refuse them altogether. (Du Bois [1899] 1996, 295)

He went on to note that proximity to potential job opportunities also influenced where blacks lived as did a desire to be near traditional black community institutions.

Prejudice and racial attitudes were so central to Du Bois's descriptive assessment and analytical framework that he devoted an entire chapter to "The Contact of the Races"—with sections on color prejudice, benevolence, and the intermarriage of the races. That the reason for the chapter and the thread holding together its sections was racial prejudice—the ideas, beliefs, feelings, and consequent patterns of behavior of whites toward blacks—he declared at the very outset:

Incidentally throughout this study the prejudice against the Negro has been again and again mentioned. It is now time to reduce this somewhat indefinite term to something tangible. Everybody speaks of the matter, everybody knows that it exists, but in just what form it shows itself or how influential it is few agree. (Du Bois [1899] 1996, 322)

Although Du Bois never posited a clear conceptual definition of racial prejudice, he systematically recounted its dynamics and effects. He identified six specific types of effects of prejudice: (1) restriction of blacks to menial work roles; (2) vulnerability to displacement due to competition from native whites or white immigrants; (3) resentment of black advancement and initiative; (4) vulnerability to financial exploitation; (5) inability to secure quality education for children or to shelter them from societal prejudice and discrimination; and (6) a wide array of discourteous and insulting treatment in "social intercourse."

Although Du Bois mainly describes actual forms of discrimination, he explicitly invokes an underlying individual mind-set and larger social climate of prejudice as the root of the discrimination. For example, without directly using the term "stereotypes," he describes how general images and beliefs about blacks

come to constrain all blacks: "Being few in number compared with the whites the crime or carelessness of a few of his race is easily imputed to all, and the reputation of the good, industrious and reliable suffer thereby" (Du Bois [1899] 1996, 323). Similarly, he refers to the expectations and tastes of whites as constraining black advancement. Accordingly, "men are used to seeing Negroes in inferior positions; when, therefore, by any chance a Negro gets in a better position, most men immediately conclude that he is not fitted for it, even before he has a chance to show his fitness" (324).

Du Bois recounts 20 cases of blacks capable in the skilled trades, such as book binders, typesetters, carpenters, and stone-cutters, who were excluded from work in their respective fields. His research identified numerous blacks with training in the skilled trades who were unable to secure appropriate employment or who had been driven out of suitable positions:

In the matter of the trades, however, there can be no serious question of ability; for years the Negroes filled satisfactorily the trades of the city, and to-day in many parts of the South they are still prominent. And yet in Philadelphia a determined prejudice, aided by public opinion, has succeeded nearly in driving them from the field. (Du Bois [1899] 1996, 329)

He identified several exceptional instances in which blacks achieved employment in a skilled trade. But in Du Bois's analysis, the extraordinary intervention required in each case proved the general rule of an almost absolute color bar against blacks in access to employment in the skilled trades. He was quite unequivocal about the importance of prejudice to this color line:

The chief agency that brings about this state of affairs is public opinion; if they were not intrenched, and strongly intrenched, back of an active prejudice or at least a passive acquiescence in this effort to deprive Negroes of a decent livelihood, both trade unions and arbitrary bosses would be powerless to do the harm they now do; where, however, a large section of the public more or less openly applaud the stamina of a man who refuses to work with a "Nigger," the results are inevitable. (332-33)

The nature and effects of the prejudice varied by gender and by class in Du Bois's analysis. Black women were stereotyped into a highly restrictive set of roles:

At a time when women are engaged in bread-winning to a larger degree than ever before, the field open to Negro women is unusually narrow. This is, of course, due largely to the more intense prejudices of females on all subjects, and especially to the fact that women who work dislike to be in any way mistaken for menials, and they regard Negro women as menials par excellence. (Du Bois [1899] 1996, 333-34)

He goes on to recount nine instances of black women completely turned away from work or closed out of more skilled positions and instead made to scrub or wash.

These indignities, rebuffs, and profound constraints on one's own life chances and those of one's children Du Bois argued were acutely felt among the most talented segment of the black population:

Besides these tangible and measurable forms there are deeper and less easily described results of the attitude of the white population toward the Negroes: a certain manifestation of a real or assumed aversion, a spirit of ridicule or patronage, a vindictive hatred in some, absolute indifference in others; all this of course does not make much difference to the mass of the race, but it deeply wounds the better classes, the very classes who are attaining to that which we wish the mass to attain. (Du Bois [1899] 1996, 350)

He noted a deep irony here. Rather than creating the sort of blacks they ideally wanted, white prejudice served to depress the most talented and to profoundly alienate the most marginal within the black community. Thus, white prejudice and discrimination contributed to crime, illicit behavior, and social disorder rather than to success, mobility, and harmony. In a manner disturbingly analogous to the "modern incarceration state," as Du Bois saw it,

the class of Negroes which the prejudices of the city have distinctly encouraged is that of the criminal, the lazy, and the shiftless; for them the city teems with institutions and charities; for them there is succor and sympathy; for them Philadelphians are thinking and planning; but for the educated and industrious young colored man who wants work and not platitudes, wages and not alms, just rewards and not sermons—for such colored men Philadelphia apparently has no use. (352)

He concludes the section on color prejudice by calling on the "best conscience" of white Philadelphia to realize its duty to the black citizens of the city.

His final substantive chapter discusses the "duty of the whites." Here again, he stressed the need for new attitudes:

We need then a radical change in public opinion on this point; it will not and ought not to come suddenly, but instead of thoughtless acquiescence in the continual and steadily encroaching exclusion of Negroes from work in the city, the leaders of industry and opinion ought to be trying here and there to open up new opportunities and give new chances to bright colored boys. (Du Bois [1899] 1996, 395)

Du Bois tried to craft a final word on the role of prejudice that did not paint most white Philadelphians as deliberate oppressors:

Again, the white people of the city must remember that much of the sorrow and bitterness that surrounds the life of the American Negro comes from the unconscious prejudice and half-conscious actions of men and women who do not intend to annoy. (396-97)

Black progress required action on both the economic and the attitudinal front.

Du Bois's analytical concern with prejudice lasted long after his completion of *The Philadelphia Negro*. In an essay in the *American Journal of Sociology*, where his ambit was global, he still employed prejudice as a central concept (Du Bois 1944b). Likewise, a concern with racial attitudes and prejudice appears repeatedly in *Dusk of Dawn* ([1940] 1995), particularly the chapter "The Con-

cept of Race." Du Bois's concern with prejudice was thus by no means a passing phase of his early intellectual career.

Du Bois's understanding of the nature of prejudice seemed to underscore its basis in ignorance and acquiescence to social custom. In this sense, his conceptualization is not far from ways of understanding prejudice still common in the social sciences (Katz 1991; Pettigrew 1982). Later in life, he would come to believe that prejudice had deeper psychological and irrational roots. He would occasionally argue that economic arrangements and interests preceded deep racial prejudice. At some points, he even speculated that there was a special perversity or animus underlying white hostility to African Americans.

A number of pioneering black sociologists shared Du Bois's belief that a full analysis of the status of African Americans required engaging issues of racial attitudes and prejudice. For example, Charles S. Johnson's *The Negro in American Civilization* (1930) devoted an entire chapter to racial attitudes. In a subsequent research monograph, Johnson discussed the importance of stereotypes to black-white relations (Masuoka and Johnson 1946). To be sure, Johnson emphasized the economic and situational underpinnings of prejudice and racial conflict. Yet, like Du Bois, he saw racial attitudes as an essential element in analyzing race relations:

The attitude one holds toward another group becomes an important tool for racial adjustment as well as for researches in the field. The tendency to act, a mental set toward an object—in short, an attitude—is a form of conduct. It is an element in social interactions: it constitutes the core of social institutions and personalities. It is for this reason that one should understand the nature of racial attitudes. (Masuoka and Johnson 1946, 7)

In *Black Metropolis*, Drake and Cayton dedicated several chapters to analyzing the dynamics of the color line. In discussing the difference between southern and northern prejudice, Drake and Cayton made it clear that migration to the Midwest had not eliminated prejudice and discrimination from the experience of African Americans (Drake and Cayton [1945] 1993, 101). Even Cox's *Caste, Class and Race* ([1948] 1970) devoted a chapter to race prejudice, intolerance, and nationalism. Although he saw economic relations as fundamental and racial prejudice as an ideology of exploitation promulgated mainly by and for capitalists, Cox did not dismiss racial prejudice as unimportant epi-phenomena. Instead, he recognized that any full account of racial dynamics, conflict, and antagonism had to engage the question of attitudes and prejudice.

SOCIOLOGICAL DISINTEREST
IN PREJUDICE

With the noteworthy exception of the Chicago School, the founding figures of sociology gave short shrift to matters of race relations. Race prejudice, discrimination, and racism were not central concerns of Marx, Weber, or Durkheim (Blauner 1972; Stone 1985; Omi and Winant 1986). It was the crush of world events—

fascism, nazism, the Holocaust, the collapse of colonial institutions in Africa and India, the establishment of the United Nations, and the emergence of a powerful civil rights movement in the United States—that ultimately compelled sociologists to devote more systematic attention to issues of race, ethnicity, and nationality.

The two decades following World War II witnessed an explosion of research on race and ethnic relations, much of it emphasizing a prejudice-discrimination paradigm. The major works during this era include Myrdal's *An American Dilemma* (1944), Adorno and colleagues' *The Authoritarian Personality* (1950), Allport's *The Nature of Prejudice* (1954), Bettleheim and Janowitz's *Social Change and Prejudice* (1964), Williams, Dean, and Suchman's *Strangers Next Door* (1964), Selznick and Steinberg's *The Tenacity of Prejudice* (1969), as well as countless research articles, edited volumes, and monographs. Although increasingly under challenge from power and conflict models, the prejudice approach to race relations continued its intellectual dominance through much of the era of rioting and civil disorder in the 1960s, as epitomized by such works as Marx's *Protest and Prejudice* (1967), Campbell and Schuman's study for the Kerner Commission (1968), and Sears and McConahay's *The Politics of Violence* (1973). But by this later time, the dominance of the prejudice-discrimination paradigm had passed.

As forms of social protest and turmoil mounted in the 1960s, a younger generation of sociologists turned to power and conflict models to understand race relations. These approaches stressed historical, structural, and economy-centered analyses of race relations. Blauner's *Racial Oppression in America* (1972), which articulated his internal colonialism model, is in some respects the paradigm-establishing work in this genre. To be sure, there had been precursors of such theoretical formulations, especially Cox's *Caste, Class and Race* ([1948] 1970). And strong critiques of the prejudice-discrimination model had been heard earlier. For example, Arnold Rose (1956) and Herbert Blumer (1958) had challenged the emphasis on prejudice, questioning the link between prejudice and discrimination.

But it was Blauner who most centrally articulated a view that race and racism were historical and structural forces in their own right. He insisted that racism had an independent institutional base that did not require prejudice in order to exert effect. His critique of prior research identified four shortcomings of prior sociological models; among these was the focus on prejudice:

The processes that maintain domination—control of whites over nonwhites—are built into the major social institutions. These institutions either exclude or restrict the participation of racial groups by procedures that have become conventional, part of the bureaucratic system of rules and regulations. Thus there is little need for prejudice as a motivating force. Because this is true, the distinction between racism as an objective phenomenon, located in the actual existence of domination and hierarchy, and racism's subjective concomitants of prejudice and other motivations and feelings is a basic one. (Blauner 1972, 9-10)

Issues of privilege, group interests, exploitation, and the routine mobilization of biased institutional arrangements and practices—rather than prejudice—should be at the center of analyses of race.

Although a few have pursued the internal colonialism model as such, Blauner's emphasis on structural arrangements as sufficient analytical foundation for examining race relations has had more lasting effects. Certainly this is seen in Bonacich's work on split-labor market theory (1972). In some ways, it is also seen in Wilson's declining significance of race thesis (1978). His theoretical framework, although taking racial ideologies seriously (see Wilson 1973), stresses the changing economic and political structures of race relations (Wilson 1978). Wilson's argument is organized around three major epochs of race relations that reflect distinctive structural configurations of the economy and the polity.

Certainly the critique of studies of prejudice has not vanished. Stephen Steinberg (1998) identifies a focus on attitudes and prejudice as one of the fundamental flaws of social science analyses of race. For Steinberg, analyses that focused on prejudice and discrimination "were ahistorical abstractions that, if anything, obscured the unique aspects of racial oppression" (Steinberg 1995, 87). Likewise, Bonilla-Silva's (1997) recent efforts to develop an argument about structural racism and racialized social processes is heavily critical of examinations of prejudice (though he is equally critical of the failures of Marxist and other purely material determinist positions). Both arguments are easily shown to be oversimplified and, more important, miss the core idea exemplified by Du Bois: powerful social analysis need not deny the force of prejudice and discrimination in order to show the importance of economic and political factors.

THE MODERN ROLE OF
RACIAL ATTITUDES
IN RACIAL INEQUALITY

Studies of prejudice and efforts to theorize how prejudice influences the status of African Americans have not disappeared from the scene (Tuch and Martin 1997; Schuman et al. 1998). Yet the level of skepticism within the discipline remains high. I suggest that the sort of nuanced and organic view of how racial prejudice relates to and influences the structural positioning of African Americans, as developed by Du Bois in *The Philadelphia Negro*, is sorely needed. There are strong reasons to believe that the modern-day disadvantages of African Americans in the labor market, in the housing market, in politics, in the educational arena, and in myriad forms of interpersonal social interaction with whites are strongly linked to modern forms of racial prejudice. While there are no doubt structural conditions and processes that facilitate the reproduction of racial inequality largely without regard to prejudice—that is,

wealth inequalities (see Oliver and Shapiro 1995)—I follow in Du Bois's footsteps in insisting that prejudice is a constituent element in the modern reproduction of systematic racial inequality.[2]

First, accumulating evidence shows that negative racial attitudes are part of the problem of high unemployment faced by African Americans. Recent in-depth interviews with employers seeking to fill low-skill positions suggest that they often hold very negative stereotypical images of blacks, especially of young black men. Kirschenman and Neckerman (1991) found powerful evidence of racial stereotyping that informed employer preferences and decisions in Chicago. The negative stereotypes not only influenced perceptions and hiring decisions but prompted employers to utilize selective recruitment and other screening mechanisms that had the effect of sorting out many potential black job applicants. Waldinger and Bailey (1991) found that white construction contractors, unions, and workers deliberately kept blacks out of construction work even as the demand for low-skill construction workers grew in the New York area.

As a result, "if the employment problems of blacks result from a mismatch of their skills with the job requirements of urban employers, then construction should be the one industry where there should be black workers aplenty. . . . Jobs requiring little schooling there may be in construction, but few of them go to black workers" (Waldinger and Bailey 1991, 314). Thus, even though blacks were in no sense a wage threat to white workers, they still were effectively excluded from this avenue of well-paying low-skill work. While economic self-interest is no doubt one factor at work here, so is racial prejudice.

A recent carefully designed auditing study conducted by the Urban Institute found clear-cut evidence of discrimination in access to low-skill, entry-level positions. In one out of five audits, the white candidate advanced further than the black applicant, even though each possessed identical credentials except for race. Differential behavior could include not being allowed to submit an application, no offer of an interview, and finally not being offered a job. They did find some occasions of favorable treatment of blacks relative to whites, but the general pattern was that "if equally qualified black and white candidates are competing for a job, differential treatment, when it occurs, is three times more likely to favor the white applicant than the black" (Turner, Fix, and Struyk 1991, 62-63).

Second, negative racial attitudes play a part in the perpetuation of residential segregation by race. Sociologists increasingly recognize spatial mobility as a key aspect of broader socioeconomic mobility (Massey and Denton 1993). Hence, to find that prejudice both affects where whites prefer to live and constrains where blacks feel comfortable living suggests that prejudice exerts effects on black opportunity through the dynamics of the housing market. Farley and colleagues (1994) found that negative stereotypes of African Americans strongly predicted whites' willingness to share integrated neighborhood space with blacks. Bobo and Zubrinsky (1996) found that this effect was not restricted to whites' reactions to blacks. The effect of negative stereotypes on openness to residential integration also applied when whites were reacting to the prospect of Hispanic neighbors or to the prospect of Asian neighbors. Importantly, both studies showed that the effect of negative stereotyping on attitudes toward residential integration was independent of perceptions about the average social class status of blacks or other racial minorities. That is, distinctly racial stereotypes influenced whites' willingness to live in integrated communities. Conversely, apprehension about racial discrimination constrains blacks' willingness to be the first family to enter a traditionally all-white neighborhood. There is some evidence that this sentiment may be on the rise (Farley et al 1993).

Third, a wide body of evidence is accumulating to show that racial prejudice affects politics. Black candidates for office typically encounter a degree of difficulty securing white votes, based partly in racial prejudice (Citrin, Green, and Sears 1990; Pettigrew and Alston 1988). The potency of racial prejudice seems to vary with the racial composition of electoral districts and the salience of race issues in the immediate political context (Reeves 1997). Moreover, it is increasingly clear that white candidates can use covert racial appeals to mobilize a segment of the white voting public under some circumstances. For example, the deployment of the infamous Willie Horton ad during the 1988 presidential campaign heightened the concern with race issues among the voting public and accentuated the impact of racial prejudice on electoral choices (Kinder and Sanders 1996; Mendelberg 1997).

Likewise, recent fundamental reforms of welfare policy have taken place in a highly racialized political climate. Both historical research (Quadagno 1994) and a variety of public opinion studies (Gilens 1999) make it plain that racial divisions and racial prejudice have been one of the central weaknesses in the development of American welfare policy. Indeed, Gilens analyzes a wide array of national sample survey data and finds that anti-black racial attitudes are perhaps the central element of white hostility to certain features of welfare provision (that is, food stamps, AFDC, and general relief).

CONCLUSION

A century ago, Du Bois published *The Philadelphia Negro*, a work now recognized as a sociological classic. He developed a highly detailed portrait of black social life in Philadelphia. Part of the legacy of his analysis has lost the theoretical holism which linked structural issues of the economy and labor market dynamics to more social psychological and microsocial issues of prejudice and interpersonal discrimination. Sociology would do well to revisit the model Du Bois established.

It is worth emphasizing two points that are not parts of the argument I advance here. First, I do not suggest

that Du Bois gave us a brief to emphasize surveys and direct measurement of racial attitudes as the only methodological touchstone for examining prejudice. Indeed, none of the six interview protocols developed in *The Philadelphia Negro* include direct measures of racial attitudes. Although I do believe that direct measurement of such attitudes is possible, necessary, and intellectually productive (Schuman et al. 1998), the central point here concerns theory development and the fundamental elements of any theoretical account of the modern dynamics of the status of African Americans. If Du Bois was right then and continues to be relevant today, as I believe he was and is, then theoretical formulations that deny the relevance of racial attitudes and of prejudice are flawed.

Second, I do not suggest that the nature of prejudice and discrimination today is identical to that observed and analyzed by Du Bois 100 years ago. To the contrary, I have argued elsewhere that the type of essentially emergent or quasi–Jim Crow racist ideology that Du Bois found has increasingly been replaced by a more free market or laissez-faire racist ideology (Bobo 1997; Bobo, Kluegel, and Smith 1997). The new laissez-faire racism involves the acceptance of muted but negative racial stereotypes about black behavior (that is, more violence-prone, lazier, more sexually irresponsible, less intelligent as compared to whites on average). Whereas these differences would have been seen as of constitutional or biological origin in Du Bois's era, laissez-faire racism understands them as reflecting a cultural and volitional distinction: that is, under the new ideological regime, race differences are a matter of degree, not kind, and involve a lack of effort on blacks' part, not human nature. The new racism is more subtle, malleable, and penetrable than that observed by Du Bois—this is a qualitatively different ethos and era. Doors to black participation in society are not completely shut—civil rights law stands as a bulwark against such practices. But an array of subtle hurdles and covert processes repeatedly work to constrain black opportunity and performance.

The effort to erect purely "structural theories of racism" is likely to fail. Although the effort to improve upon earlier research paradigms makes sense, there is no need to recreate the theoretical excesses of a bygone era. Strong and more fully specified analyses of racial inequality will seek to link macrosocial conditions to microsocial process, to show the interplay of social structure and personality, and thereby follow Du Bois's example of linking the status of African Americans to both prejudice and other features of social organization.

Notes

1. Du Bois was one of the few American sociologists of his era to actually take a seminar with Weber. His book *The Philadelphia Negro: A Social Study*, published in 1899, is preceded by Durkheim's *Suicide* (1897) by only two years. Although *The Philadelphia Negro* is now recognized as a classic sociological community survey (Converse 1987, 23; Bulmer 1991; and more generally see Broderick 1974; Rudwick 1974; McDaniel 1998), Du Bois was intellectually ostracized by white sociologists in his own time (Rudwick 1969; Green and Driver 1976; Key 1978). Lacking placement in a mainstream university and the recognition of his peers, "Du Bois was denied that attention, because he was black, because the condition of black Americans was not a matter of major political or scholarly concern around 1899, and because a racially stratified system of higher education gave him no significant opportunities for sustained interaction with his white peers in the academic community" (Bulmer 1991, 185-86).

2. Even in the case of wealth inequality, racial prejudice plays a part, both direct and indirect. Some forms of racial prejudice, such as discrimination in the housing market based in prejudice, affect blacks' capacity to accumulate wealth. More indirectly, the denial of societal responsibility for racial inequality and the clear resistance in public opinion to serious discussion of reparations for slavery to African Americans constitute fundamental barriers to overcoming the gaping racial disparities in accumulated wealth.

References

Adorno, Theodore, Elsie Frenkel-Brunswick, Daniel J. Levinson, and R. Nevitt Sanford. 1950. *The Authoritarian Personality*. New York: Norton.

Allport, Gordon W. 1954. *The Nature of Prejudice*. Garden City, NJ: Doubleday.

Bay, Mia. 1998. "The World Was Thinking Wrong About Race": The Philadelphia Negro and Nineteenth-Century Science. In *W.E.B. Du Bois, Race, and the City: The Philadelphia Negro and Its Legacy*, ed. M. B. Katz and T. J. Sugrue. Philadelphia: University of Pennsylvania Press.

Bettleheim, Bruno and Morris Janowitz. 1964. *Social Change and Prejudice*. New York: Free Press.

Blauner, Robert A. 1972. *Racial Oppression in America*. New York: Harper & Row.

Blumer, Herbert. 1958. Recent Research on Race Relations: United States of America. *International Social Science Bulletin* 10:403-77.

Bobo, Lawrence. 1997. The Color Line, the Dilemma and the Dream: Racial Attitudes and Relations at the Close of the Twentieth Century. In *Civil Rights and Social Wrongs: Black-White Relations Since World War II*, ed. J. Higham. University Park: Pennsylvania State University Press.

Bobo, Lawrence, James R. Kluegel, and Ryan A. Smith. 1997. Laissez-Faire Racism: The Crystallization of a "Kinder, Gentler" Anti-Black Ideology. In *Racial Attitudes in the 1990s: Continuity and Change*, ed. S. A. Tuch and J. K. Martin. Westport, CT: Praeger.

Bobo, Lawrence and Camille L. Zubrinsky. 1996. Attitudes on Residential Integration: Perceived Status Differences, Mere In-Group Preference, or Racial Prejudice? *Social Forces* 74:883-909.

Bonacich, Edna. 1972. A Theory of Ethnic Antagonism: The Split Labor Market. *American Sociological Review* 37:547-59.

Bonilla-Silva, Eduardo. 1997. Rethinking Racism: Toward a Structural Interpretation. *American Sociological Review* 62:465-80.

Broderick, Francis L. 1974. W.E.B. Du Bois: History of an Intellectual. In *Black Sociologists: Historical and Contemporary Perspectives*, ed. J. E. Blackwell and M. Janowitz. Chicago: University of Chicago Press.

Bulmer, Martin. 1991. W.E.B. Du Bois as a Social Investigator: The Philadelphia Negro, 1899. In *The Social Survey in Historical Perspective, 1880-1940*, ed. M. Bulmer, K. Bales, and K. K. Sklar. New York: Cambridge University Press.

Campbell, Angus and Howard Schuman. 1968. Racial Attitudes in Fifteen American Cities. In *Supplemental Studies for the National Advisory Commission on Civil Disorders*. Washington, DC: U.S. Government Printing Office.

Citrin, Jack, Donald Green, and David O. Sears. 1990. White Reactions to Black Candidates: When Does Race Matter? *Public Opinion Quarterly* 54:74-96.

Converse, Jean. M. 1987. *Survey Research in the United States: Roots and Emergence*. Berkeley: University of California Press.

Cox, Oliver Cromwell. [1948] 1970. *Caste, Class and Race*. New York: Modern Reader.

Drake, St. Clair and Horace R. Cayton. [1945] 1993. *Black Metropolis: A Study of Negro Life in a Northern City*. Chicago: University of Chicago Press.

Du Bois, W.E.B. [1899] 1996. *The Philadelphia Negro: A Social Study*. Philadelphia: University of Pennsylvania Press.

———. [1903] 1997. *The Souls of Black Folk*. New York: Bedford Books.

———. [1940] 1995. *Dusk of Dawn: An Essay Toward an Autobiography of a Race Concept*. New Brunswick, NJ: Transaction.

———. 1944a. My Evolving Program for Negro Freedom. In *What the Negro Wants*, ed. R. W. Logan. Chapel Hill: University of North Carolina Press.

———. 1944b. Prospect of a World Without Race Conflict. *American Journal of Sociology* 49:450-56.

———. 1948. Race Relations in the United States, 1917-1947. *Phylon* 9:234-47.

Durkheim, Emile. 1897. *Suicide: A Study in Sociology*. New York: Free Press.

Farley, Reynolds, Maria Krysan, Tara Jackson, Charlotte Steeh, and Keith Reeves. 1993. Causes of Continued Racial Residential Segregation in Detroit: "Chocolate City, Vanilla Suburbs" Revisited. *Journal of Housing Research* 4:1-38

Farley, Reynolds, Charlotte Steeh, Maria Krysan, Tara Jackson, and Keith Reeves. 1994. Stereotypes and Segregation: Neighborhoods in the Detroit Area. *American Journal of Sociology* 100:750-80.

Gilens, Martin I. 1999. *Why Americans Hate Welfare: Race, Media, and the Politics of Antipoverty Policy*. Chicago: University of Chicago Press.

Green, Dan S. and Edwin D. Driver. 1976. W.E.B. Du Bois: A Case in the Sociology of Sociological Negation. *Phylon* 37:308-33.

Johnson, Charles S. 1930. *The Negro in American Civilization*. New York: Holt.

Jones, Jacqueline. 1998. "Lifework" and Its Limits: The Problem of Labor in the Philadelphia Negro. In *W.E.B. Du Bois, Race, and the City: The Philadelphia Negro and Its Legacy*, ed. M. B. Katz and T. J. Sugrue. Philadelphia: University of Pennsylvania Press.

Katz, Irwin. 1991. Gordon Allport's The Nature of Prejudice. *Political Psychology* 12:125-57.

Key, R. Charles. 1978. Society and Sociology: The Dynamics of Black Sociological Negation. *Phylon* 38:35-48.

Kinder, Donald R. and Lynn M. Sanders. 1996. *Divided by Color: Racial Politics and Democratic Ideals*. Chicago: University of Chicago Press.

Kirschenman, Joleen and Kathryn Neckerman. 1991. "We'd Love to Hire Them, But . . . ": The Meaning of Race for Employers. In *The Urban Underclass*, ed. C. Jencks and P. Peterson. Washington, DC: Brookings Institution.

Marx, Gary T. 1967. *Protest and Prejudice: A Study of Belief in the Black Community*. New York: Harper & Row.

Massey, Douglas S. and Nancy A. Denton. 1993. *American Apartheid: Segregation and the Making of the Under-class*. Cambridge, MA: Harvard University Press.

Masuoka, J. and Charles S. Johnson. 1946. *Racial Attitudes*. Social Science Source Documents no. 3. Nashville, TN: Fisk University, Social Science Institute.

McDaniel, Antonio. 1998. The "Philadelphia Negro" Then and Now: Implications for Empirical Research. In *W.E.B. Du Bois, Race, and the City: The Philadelphia Negro and Its Legacy*, ed. M. B. Katz and T. J. Sugrue. Philadelphia: University of Pennsylvania Press.

Mendelberg, Tali. 1997. Executing Hortons: Racial Crime in the 1988 Presidential Campaign. *Public Opinion Quarterly* 61:134-57.

Myrdal, Gunnar. 1944. *An American Dilemma: The Negro Problem and American Democracy*. New York: Harper.

Oliver, Melvin L. and Thomas Shapiro. 1995. *Black Wealth / White Wealth: A New Perspective on Racial Inequality*. New York: Routledge.

Omi, Michael and Howard Winant. 1986. *Racial Formation in the United States: From the 1960s to the 1980s*. New York: Routledge.

Pettigrew, Thomas F. 1982. Prejudice. In *Dimensions of Ethnicity*, ed. S. Thernstrom, A. Orlov, and O. Handlin. Cambridge, MA: Belknap Press.

Pettigrew, Thomas F. and Denise Alston. 1988. *Tom Bradley's Campaign for Governor: The Dilemma of Race and Political Strategies*. Washington, DC: Joint Center for Political and Economic Studies.

Quadagno, Jill. 1994. *The Color of Welfare: How Racism Undermined the War on Poverty*. New York: Oxford University Press.

Reeves, Keith. 1997. *Voting Hopes or Fears? White Voters, Black Candidates, and Racial Politics in America*. New York: Oxford University Press.

Rose, Arnold M. 1956. Intergroup Relations vs. Prejudice: Pertinent Theory for the Study of Social Change. *Social Problems* 4:173-76.

Rudwick, Elliot. 1969. Note on a Forgotten Black Sociologist: W.E.B. Du Bois and the Sociological Profession. *American Sociologist* 4:303-6.

———. 1974. W.E.B. Du Bois as Sociologist. In *Black Sociologists: Historical and Contemporary Perspectives*, ed. J. E. Blackwell and M. Janowitz. Chicago: University of Chicago Press.

Schuman, Howard, Charlotte Steeh, Lawrence Bobo, and Maria Krysan. 1998. *Racial Attitudes in America: Trends and Interpretations*. Rev. ed. Cambridge, MA: Harvard University Press.

Sears, David O. and John B. McConahay. 1973. *The Politics of Violence: The New Urban Blacks and the Watts Riot.* New York: Houghton Mifflin.

Selznick, Gertrude J. and Stephen Steinberg. 1969. *The Tenacity of Prejudice: Anti-Semitism in Contemporary America.* Westport, CT: Greenwood Press.

Steinberg, Stephen. 1995. *Turning Back: The Retreat from Racial Justice in American Thought and Policy.* Boston: Beacon Press.

———. 1998. The Role of Social Science in the Legitimation of Racial Hierarchy. *Race & Society* 1:5-14.

Stone, Jonathan. 1985. *Racial Conflict in Contemporary Society.* Cambridge, MA: Harvard University Press.

Tuch, Steven A. and Jack K. Martin. 1997 *Racial Attitudes in the 1990s: Continuity and Change.* Westport, CT: Praeger

Turner, Margery Austin, Michael Fix, and Raymond J. Struyk. 1991. *Opportunities Denied, Opportunities Diminished: Racial Discrimination in Hiring.* Washington, DC: Urban Institute Press.

Waldinger, Roger and Tom Bailey. 1991. The Continuing Significance of Race: Racial Conflict and Racial Discrimination in Construction. *Politics and Society* 19:291-323.

Williams, Robin M., Jr., J. P. Dean, and Edward A. Suchman. 1964. *Strangers Next Door: Ethnic Relations in American Communities.* Englewood Cliffs, NJ: Prentice-Hall.

Wilson, William Julius. 1973. *Power, Racism, and Privilege: Race Relations in Theoretical and Sociohistorical Perspective.* New York: Free Press.

———. 1978. *The Declining Significance of Race.* Chicago: University of Chicago Press.

ANNALS, *AAPSS*, **568**, March 2000

W.E.B. Du Bois and
the Encyclopedia Africana, 1909-63

By HENRY LOUIS GATES, JR.

ABSTRACT: In 1901, W.E.B. Du Bois, the African American intellectual and activist, conceived the idea of an encyclopedia Africana. He envisioned a scientific and comprehensive work on Africa and peoples of African descent that would refute the Enlightenment notion of blacks as devoid of civilization and the hallmarks of humanity. Du Bois stood in a tradition of earlier black works seeking to vindicate the race, but World War I and his move from academia to the NAACP postponed his efforts. In 1931, however, Du Bois participated in an encyclopedia project initiated by the Phelps-Stokes Fund. His writing during this period reveals his thinking about the nature and form a pan-African encyclopedia would take. Beset by rivalries and, primarily, lack of support from the established philanthropies, the project died. In 1960, shortly before his death, Du Bois was invited to Ghana to launch an encyclopedia. If any of these attempts had succeeded, the evolution of African and African American studies in the academy would have been significantly different.

Henry Louis Gates, Jr., is the W.E.B. Du Bois Professor of Humanities at Harvard University, where he is also chair of Afro-American studies and director of the W.E.B. Du Bois Institute for Afro-American Research. He is co-editor with K. Anthony Appiah of the encyclopedia Encarta Africana *(1999). He is the author of* Wonders of the African World *(1999), the book companion to the BBC-PBS television series of the same title.*

There is a dangerous and misleading lag between scientific knowledge of the Negro and intelligent interpretation today, and popular conception handed down from the past. The Negro race today, in the minds of most persons, is set apart as a group of unusual and different individuals; and this attitude can be met only by setting forth the facts of the situation and letting the world know that the essential humanity of the black race is today well attested by a body of facts agreed upon, in all essential particulars, by those whose opinions are worth listening to.

—W.E.B. Du Bois
(1945, in Lewis 1995)

On 5 April 1909, W.E.B. Du Bois wrote to the great pan-Africanist Edward Wilmot Blyden and several other scholars about his desire to edit an encyclopedia Africana, a veritable black *Encyclopaedia Britannica*, which could symbolically reassemble the fragments of the African diaspora set in motion by the European slave trade and the turn-of-the-century "scramble for Africa." Through an encyclopedia, Du Bois sought to marshal a mountain of evidence to refute the centuries of aspersion cast upon the character of the African by a racist West eager to justify the economic exploitation of Africa and its Africans. Thirty years later, Du Bois would recall that his first effort to edit his encyclopedia ended because of his involvement in the creation of the NAACP and the time commitment necessitated by his editing of *The Crisis* magazine:

Another project in which I had long been interested was an Encyclopaedia of the Negro. As early as 1909, I had planned an Encyclopaedia Africana and secured on my board of advisors Sir Flinders Petrie, Sir Harry Johnston, Giuseppe Sergi, Dr. J. Deniker, William James, and Franz Boas; and on my proposed board of editors I had practically all the leading Negroes of the United States who were then inclined toward research. My change to New York and the work of starting the *Crisis*, and finally the World War, put this quite out of my mind. (Du Bois [1940a] 1975, 32)

In addition to these scholars, Du Bois wrote to many others, soliciting their collaboration in preparing a multivolume reference work "covering the chief points in the history and condition of the Negro race" (Lewis 1993, 379). While Du Bois had asked Blyden for names of "eminent white scholars" to serve on an international advisory board, "The real work," he confessed, "I want done by Negroes" (379). Although he stressed to his correspondents that his plan was "still in Embryo," his stationery declared that he wanted the first of five projected volumes to be published in 1913, the "Jubilee of Emancipation in America and the Tercentenary of the Landing of the Negro" (380). The remaining four volumes would be published between 1913 and 1919, as he wrote to W.T.B. Williams on 20 May (Aptheker 1973, 146-47). When he wrote to President Charles Eliot at Harvard inviting him to join the board of advisors, he said that 60 other scholars had already accepted his invitation, including the English ethnographers Sir Harry Johnston and Sir Flinders Petrie, Giuseppe Sergi of Italy, Franz Boas at Columbia, and Clark University President Stanley Hall—all of whose names appeared on the project's letterhead. Additional members of the board were Kelly Miller, Archibald Grimke, John Hope, Benjamin Brawley, Bishop William Sanders Scarborough, Henry Ossawa Tanner, Sutton Griggs, Anna Jones, George Edmund Haynes, Richard T. Greener, J. E. Casely-Hayford, William James, Albert Bushnell Hart, and Hugo Munsterberg, the latter three Du Bois's professors at Harvard (Lewis 1993, 479-80). President Eliot declined but not before advising Du Bois to include entries on the influence of Islam in African societies and admonishing him to proceed only if he had secured adequate funding (Eliot 1909). This would turn out to be sound advice.

As he indicated in *Dusk of Dawn*, Du Bois initially planned for the encyclopedia to be "a co-operative and exhaustive scientific study of Negro history and sociology" (Du Bois [1940a] 1975), to be edited by two boards—a board of white advisors and a "Board of One Hundred Negro American, African and West Indian Scholars" (Aptheker 1973, 146). To identify the latter, he solicited nominations from a wide range of correspondents. Du Bois asked W.T.B. Williams to send him the names of "all colored persons in your state who had had thorough university training or its equivalent, and who would, in your opinion, be capable of joining in this work" (147). Later that year, in July of 1909, when J.R.L. Diggs, president of Virginia Theological Seminary and College in Lynchburg, wrote to Du Bois to propose a 10-volume series of books on Reconstruction to be written by

blacks—"The educated Negro owes the world a history of reconstruction"—Du Bois sought to incorporate Diggs's idea into his own project. Diggs's "set of histories of reconstruction from the Negro point of view is excellent, and will fit into my encyclopedia project perfectly. I shall take it up in the fall," Du Bois promised (150-52). Du Bois's own study of Reconstruction, entitled *Black Reconstruction*, would not appear until 1935. Despite a lively and wide-ranging correspondence, Du Bois's desire to publish volume one of his encyclopedia in 1913 would not be realized.

Although Du Bois's announcement of this project in 1909 appeared to arrive like a bolt out of the blue, Du Bois had several encyclopedic antecedents, ranging from 1808 through 1907. Indeed, though he never admitted it, it is highly probable that the publication of *The Jewish Encyclopedia* in 1907—and all of the praise it received—was the determining factor in Du Bois's thinking, leading him to attempt to mount a project equivalent in range and scope for the black world. Despite this more immediate influence, however, the encyclopedic impulse among both African Americans and enemies of anti-black racism was quite strong and proved to be quite insistent throughout the nineteenth century.

TO REDRESS THE
WORLD'S IGNORANCE

The word "encyclopedia," of Greek derivation (*enkyklopaideia*), initially denoted a circle or a complete system of learning. At least since the first decade of the nineteenth century, the publication of compendia of black intellectual attainment has aimed to redress the world's ignorance of or skepticism about individual and collective black accomplishment in the realm of the arts and letters. At least since Hume alleged in 1748 that Africans had invented "no arts, no sciences," the purported absence of the hallmarks of civilization among blacks in Africa and the New World had to be refuted because it was drawn upon to justify the Africans' enslavement. A slave to ignorance was a slave by nature. Ironically, Hume's allegations—shared by Kant, Jefferson, and Hegel—would serve to generate a surprisingly stubborn impulse to restore African culture to its proper place as one of the world's great cultures by documenting the accomplishments of individual writers, artists, orators, scientists, physicians, lawyers, and preachers of African descent in biographical dictionaries and encyclopedias.

Make no mistake about it; these were charges of the utmost seriousness and gravity. Faced with the awesome task of reconciling the discovery of peoples and cultures of color—in the "New World" as well as in the old world of Africa—with received ideas of the nature of the human species, European speculative philosophers selected, over several centuries, various measures of "civilization" by which to place each newly encountered culture in its relation to European civilization on the great chain of being. Of these successive signs and marks of human sophistication, the absence and

presence of "the arts and sciences" by the Enlightenment had come to be the definitive measure. With Gutenberg's invention of the printing press, and that resurrection of classical Greek and Roman texts so fundamental to Renaissance skepticism, it is not surprising that the verbal and written arts assumed a priority among these "arts and sciences." "That which makes man a god to man," wrote Francis Bacon in 1620, "is the knowledge of the arts and sciences" and, more precisely, the mastery of the written arts. Claims of the absence of these commodities implied nothing less than the subhuman status of Africans, a status that had obviously and unalterably been ordained by nature throughout the African continent.

The seriousness of these charges against the African's very humanity demanded comprehensive rebuttals from the friends of the blacks, initially, and from the blacks themselves, ultimately. The complex response to these allegations engendered by the seemingly unassailable intellectual stature of Bacon, Hume, Jefferson, Kant, and Hegel assumed the form of the "encyclopaedic catalogue" listing black men and women, living previously in Europe and America, whose artistic achievements, varying widely from the mundane to the sublime, were offered as proof of the African's intellectual equality. The collecting and cataloguing of even the slightest literary, artistic, or scientific success of the black person might well be said to be the predominant characteristic of early historical scholarship about blacks, at least since Henri-Baptiste

Grégoire published in 1808 his *De la littérature des nègres ou Recherches sur leurs faculties intellectuelles, leurs qualities morales et leur litterature: suivies de notices sur la vie et les auvrages des nègres qui se sont distingués dans les sciences, les lettres et les arts*, and extending well into the first half of the twentieth century.

Grégoire's curious and slim book, translated into English in 1810, attacked vigorously by Tussac (1880) in his hysterical *Cri des Colons*, and purchased in bulk for his court at Port-au-Prince in Haiti by command of King Christoph himself, proved to be a text of monumental import. The book was widely reviewed and discussed. Such was the success of Grégoire's curiously romantic text, rife with wishful thinking yet surprisingly well documented, that it firmly established the encyclopedia genre as the mode of discourse fundamental to any meaningful defense of the African's intellectual parity with the European's.

Indeed, a full list of Grégoire's intellectual descendants could serve rather well as a chart of the texts by which each successive generation of black scholars sought to define its central task of defending "the race"; and this task, as it had been for Grégoire, remained for the following 150 years the encyclopedic, and sometimes hyperbolic, refutation of racist doubts not only about the fundamental nature of the black person's mind but also about the relation that African cultural artifacts bore to those of European civilization. A partial list of these encyclopedias and bio-graphical dictionaries include the following, pregnant titles, which preceded and followed Du Bois's initial 1909 effort:

1. R. B. Lewis's *Light and Truth; Collected from the Bible and Ancient and Modern History; Containing the Universal History of the Colored and Indian Race, from the Creation of the World to the Present Time* (1836);

2. Hosea Easton's *A Treatise on the Intellectual Character of the Colored People of the United States* (1837);

3. Abigail Mott's *Biographical Sketches and Interesting Anecdotes of Persons of Colour* (1826);

4. James W. C. Pennington's *A Text Book of the Origin and History of the Colored People* (1841);

5. James Theodore Holly's *A Vindication of the Capacity of the Negro Race for Self-Government, and Civilized Progress* (1851);

6. H. G. Adams's *God's Image in Ebony; Being a Series of Biographical Sketches, Facts, Anecdotes, etc., Demonstrative of the Mental Powers and Intellectual Capacities of the Negro Race* (1854);

7. Joseph T. Wilson's rather ambitious *Emancipation: Its Course and Progress from 1481 B.C. to A.D. 1875* (1882);

8. George W. Williams's *History of the Negro Race in America from 1619 to 1880* (1883);

9. William J. Simmons's *Men of Mark: Eminent, Progressive and Rising* (1887);

10. Rufus Perry's *The Cushite; or, The Children of Ham (the Negro Race) as Seen by the Ancient Historians and Poets* (1886);

11. James Haley's *Afro-American Encyclopedia* (1895);

12. W. H. Crogman and H. F. Kletzing's, *Progress of a Race* (1897);

13. Booker T. Washington's *A New Negro for a New Century* (1900);

14. D. W. Culp's *Twentieth Century Negro Literature: Or A Cyclopedia of Thought on the Vital Topics Relating to the American Negro by One Hundred of America's Greatest Negroes* (1902);

15. Daniel Murray's *Historical and Biographical Encyclopedia of the Colored Race Throughout the World; Its Progress and Achievements from the Earliest Period Down to the Present Time (25,000 Biographies, 5,900 Musical Compositions by Colored Composers)* (1912);

16. John W. Cromwell's *The Negro in American History; Men and Women Eminent in the Evolution of the American of African Descent* (1914);

17. Kelly Miller and J. R. Gay's *Progress and Achievements of the Colored People* (1917);

18. Edward C. Garrett's "Negro Encyclopedia" (c. 1940, unpublished); and

19. Joel A. Rogers's two-volume *World's Great Men of Color* (1946).

Perhaps because these pioneering encyclopedists of Africana were so successful in preserving the written record of black intellection and artistic achievement, a generation of scholars could eventually turn from the mere collection of biographies and anecdotes to the far more complex matters of analysis and interpretation. The fascination with the African mask after the 1895 Exposition at Paris and the subsequent birth of cubism, anthropological studies of arguments for "cultural relativity" and "the primitive," and Dvorak's valorization of the spirituals are aspects of the growing fascination of Europe with Africa and Afro-America, overlapping precisely with the European conquest and division of the continent south of the Sahara at the end of the century. W.E.B. Du Bois's response to this intellectual curiosity was, perhaps predictably in retrospect, to organize and contain it within the most profound form imaginable to his supremely fertile mind, an encyclopedia Africana. But it was not to be.

IT WOULD MARK AN EPOCH

In 1931, Du Bois received word that the Phelps-Stokes Fund had launched a project it called "The Encyclopedia of the Negro." Neither Du Bois nor Carter G. Woodson had been invited to the initial organizational meeting, held at Howard University on 7 November 1931. After he protested, Du Bois was invited to the project's second meeting on 9 January 1932. A letter (dated 30 November 1931) to James H. Dillard, the founder of the Jeanes Fund for the training of black teachers and of the Southern University Race Commission, reveals Du Bois's ambivalence about attending:

My dear Mr. Dillard:

I am a little puzzled about the matter of the Negro encyclopedia proposed by the Phelps Stokes Fund and others. As you know, I was not invited to the first meeting, but since then, an invitation has come to the second meeting.

I do not want to be over-modest or over-sensitive, but I initiated the scientific study of the American Negro in the United States and contributed something to it. To be left out of the original invitation to consider a Negro encyclopedia came pretty near being a personal insult and a petty one at that. On the other hand, it is a great project. If properly carried out, it would mark an epoch, and I have no right to let any personal feelings between me and the best accomplishment of this work. On the other hand, if I should come in to help in this project, I should have to criticize what seems to now to be its tendency, and under the circumstances, I rather doubt how I should be justified in criticizing even the beginnings already made. On the other hand, I cannot sit in on a proposition of this sort as a figurehead.

As, of course, you realize, I could not for a moment contemplate a Negro encyclopedia dominated and controlled by Thomas Jesse Jones and Mr. Woofter. I do not, of course, want to exclude them or what they represent, but a Negro encyclopedia that was not in the main edited and written by Negroes would be as inconceivable as a Catholic encyclopedia projected by Protestants. (Aptheker 1973, 447-48)

Du Bois concludes his letter to Dillard by saying, "Evidently I was not wanted by those who started it." Nevertheless, Dillard persuaded Du Bois to attend the 9 January meeting.

At that meeting, Du Bois was elected editor-in-chief. Du Bois, in turn, now sought to persuade Woodson to join the board. He wrote to him on 29 January 1932. His line of reasoning with a recalcitrant Woodson bears repeating, if only because Woodson's animosity toward the project—and toward Du Bois—would soon become quite public.

My dear Sir:

I was asked to act as a Committee by the Conference on Negro Encyclopedia to induce you to join us. I had hoped to see you personally but had to rush back to Washington. When I am there again, I shall talk with you. Meantime, as time is passing, I am venturing to write.

I do not doubt but what you have made up your mind on this matter and that nothing I can say will change it. However, perhaps I ought to bring to your attention the motives that influenced me.

I was omitted from the first call, as you were, and for similar reasons. My first impulse on receiving the invitation to attend the second meeting was to refuse, as you did. Then I learned that this invitation did not come from the Phelps Stokes Fund, but was the unanimous wish of the conferees and that if I refused to heed it, I would be affronting them, even more than Stokes, and Jones. Then, in the second place, I had to remember as both of us from time to time are compelled to, that the enemy has the money and they are going to use it. Our choice then is not how that money could be used best from our point of view, but how far without great sacrifice of principle, we can keep it from being misused. By the curious combination of accident and good will, we appointed at the last meeting a Board of Directors and Incorporators, which leave out the more impossible members of the Conference. A place on that Board was left for you. If you do not accept it, that will leave us so much the weaker.

I hope you will see your way open to join us. (Aptheker 1973, 448-49)

Woodson responded on 11 February:

My dear Dr. Du Bois:

I should have answered your confidential letter before I left the city for a long stay. I have nothing to say, however, except that I am not interested. *I never accept the gifts of the Greeks.*

I should add that the Associated Publishers, drawing upon data collected for this purpose since 1922 by the Association for the Study of Negro Life and History, would bring out its *Encyclopedia Africana by the end of 1933.* We welcome competition, because it is the spice of life.

Respectfully yours,

C. G. Woodson (Aptheker 1973, 449, emphasis added)

Woodson's claims that he had invented the idea of an encyclopedia Africana would surface dramatically in 1936.

Woodson's announcement of a rival project notwithstanding, Du Bois went to work organizing *The Encyclopedia of the Negro*, which, like his 1909 plan for an encyclopedia Africana, was pan-African in scope. Between 1932 and 1946, Du Bois worked tirelessly both to fund his project and to organize its editorial structure. In a letter to Edwin R. Embree, president of the Rosenwald Fund, dated 24 April 1935, Du Bois attempted to persuade him to fund the project, but more important for our purpose, Du Bois makes the argument—in response to Embree's objection that perhaps the time was not quite right for such an encyclopedia—for publishing sooner rather than later, despite the incomplete nature of knowledge and research about the Negro:

It seems to me that you forget that an encyclopedia is not a history. A history may have to be postponed in the writing until more source material is known, but even in that case, it should not be postponed until the collection of material is complete, because that would take a very long time. In any case and in the meantime, there should be some authoritative source from which children and the general public could learn as much as there is to be known about the particular period in mind.

With an encyclopedia, however, the case is even more imperative. An encyclopedia is not only a record of history, but also a record of present conclusions and opinions and whatever an encyclopedia gains in factual accuracy by postponement of publication, it more than loses in lessening its grip on current opinion. For that reason encyclopedias are published and then at reasonable periods revised. But at any particular time there ought to be an authoritative collection of the opinion and historical judgements of that particular day. In no case is that more demanded than in the case of the Negro problem.

You recognized the demand when you published "Brown America." What you did needs to be done on a larger scale by a wider group of scholars and public men, so the universities, colleges, schools and general readers will have a body of knowledge to which they can turn with the conviction that however incomplete it may be and it must be incomplete, it nevertheless expresses fairly well the current opinion of the best authorities of the day. In this time of crisis and inquiry to postpone such an undertaking for half a generation or more would be not only unwise but calamitous. We need, of course, further source material, but nothing is likely to be gathered or discovered which is going to change the basic facts concerning the Negro in this country. And in the same way, the loss which the truth concerning the Negro has sustained in having no such authoritative statement, covering for instance the time of Reconstruction, or the day of Booker T. Washington, is irreparable. (Aptheker 1976, 65)

No, the time to move on this grand idea was now, Du Bois insisted, and he implored all and sundry to finance it, from George Foster Peabody, the wealthy philanthropist and friend of Franklin Roosevelt's, and Dixon Ryan Fox, president of Union College, to the WPA and the Federal Writers Project (Aptheker 1976, 65-68, 109-10).

While beating the bushes for funds, Du Bois also was seeking more and more distinguished contributors, writing to H. L. Mencken; Roscoe Pound, the Dean of the Harvard Law School; Margaret Mead, then assistant curator of ethnology at the American Museum of Natural History in New York; Otto Klineberg, professor of psychology at Columbia; Harold Laski, the leader of the British Labour Party; Broadus Mitchell, professor of political economy at Johns Hopkins; and E. Franklin Frazier among others to write articles for *The Encyclopedia of the Negro.*

Pound, Mead, Klineberg, Laski, and Mitchell wrote enthusiastic responses. Only H. L. Mencken and E. Franklin Frazier declined Du Bois's request. Mencken admitted that he was not an expert on the subject, then advised him that the work, "if possible . . . ought to be done principally by Negroes—indeed, it would be best if it could be done wholly by Negroes" (Aptheker 1976, 69). Frazier, on the other hand, admonished

Du Bois for including too many "politicians," "statesmen," "big-Negroes," and "whites of goodwill." Throw out the encyclopedia's outline, disband the board of advisors, he wrote, reconvene an entirely new board consisting of scholars, and perhaps he might reconsider (Frazier to Du Bois, 7 November 1936, Aptheker 1976, 71-72). Despite extremely favorable responses from many of the world's greatest scholars of the Negro in Africa and throughout the New World, Du Bois was finding it difficult to secure the $225,000 that he needed to publish a four-volume 2 million–word encyclopedia, which now would be written by "25 to 100 research aides" and an international body of experts submitting longer interpretive articles.

As if that were not frustrating enough, Carter Woodson in 1936 decided to attack the project, making public the claim that he had invented the idea. On 30 May 1936, the *Baltimore Afro-American* carried a front-page attack by Woodson on the project, on Du Bois, and on literary historian Benjamin Brawley. In an article dated 3 May 1936, entitled "Calls Du Bois a Traitor If He Accepts the Post"—subtitled "He Told Ofays, We'd Write Own History"—Woodson protested Du Bois's decision to solicit work from white scholars:

What the colored man needs is not to aid this misrepresentation of the race by those who view it from without, but to resort to scientific methods to study his race from within and thus enable him to unfold himself to the world.

This is a task which only the colored man himself can do. The white man, even when he is honest and sincere, cannot at his best write the history of colored people and portray their present status, when he does not live and move among them.

Moreover, Woodson continued, at last revealing his real motivation, "This is an effort to supplant me and my work." Woodson, like Du Bois, had taken the Ph.D. in history at Harvard; Brawley received a master's degree in English there in 1908. Rivalry, like politics, can take peculiarly local forms.

Du Bois did not respond publicly, but he did so privately, in a letter to the sociologist Robert Park, dated 3 March 1937:

I am sending herewith a hundred sheets and envelopes of the Encyclopedia letterheads; also I am sending some data about the Encyclopedia Africana. You will find Mr. Woodson's version of his Encyclopedia Africana on page 15 of the January, 1937, issue of the "Journal of Negro History." You will note that he refers to action on the Encyclopedia Africana in 1921, if you will consult, however, the reports in 1921 (*Journal of Negro History*, 1921 Volume VI, pp. 126-130), you will find there is no notice or mention of any such Encyclopedia in the proceedings of the annual meeting of 1920, nor is there any notice in the meeting of 1921 reported in Volume VII, 1922, pp. 121-126. I believe both of these meetings took place during the time you were president of the Association. My project never went far enough to give me any claim to exclusive occupation of the field. It was merely one of my large ideas which never got down to earth or finance. It is barely possible that I should have pushed further had it not been for the World War; but as a matter of fact I didn't. I never heard of Mr. Woodson's project until after the Phelps-Stokes Encyclopaedia movement was started. When he mentioned it I immediately tried to find out when the idea was first made public, but [he] got angry and refused to give any specific answer. In the case of my Encyclopaedia Africana, I conceived the idea in 1909, and in 1911 while attending the Races Congress in London I talked about it with Sir Harry Johnston, Dr. W. M. Flinders-Petrie, and others. Previous to that I had correspondence with Professor William James, President [Charles] Eliot, and all of the Negroes whose names appear on the letter-head. (Aptheker 1976, 141)

Despite this stormy, bitter controversy, Du Bois continued planning the encyclopedia with the able assistance of Rayford Logan, who, like Du Bois and Woodson, had earned the Ph.D. in history at Harvard. Their plan of work and table of contents were quite detailed, as Du Bois indicated in a letter to Anson Phelps-Stokes, dated 19 May 1937; the letter also provides an indication of the encyclopedia's projected structure:

We have finished the following work on the Encyclopaedia: the preparation of a manuscript of about one hundred and twenty-five pages giving a list of possible subjects for an Encyclopaedia of the Negro with a short bibliographical note under each subject. These subjects have been carefully revised from my original list of last year in light of criticism sent in from various scholars, and have been arranged alphabetically.

In addition to that we have made a careful estimate of the space these articles would occupy by the following method: three of the longest articles on Africa, the Negro Race, and the African Slave Trade; five long articles on the Negro in the United States, Negro in the

West Indies, Negro in South America, Race and Miscegenation. These articles will occupy 350 pages and 280,000 words. Then we have allowed space for 250 chief articles occupying a thousand pages with 800,000 words. We have next allowed for 700 biographies covering the world and including Negroes, persons of Negro descent, and white persons connected with their history. This will occupy 560,000 words. In addition to this we have allowed 550 pages and 440,000 words for minor articles and an index of 200 pages or 160,000 words. This makes a total of 2,800 pages and 2,240,000 words. This calculation has been based on the *Encyclopaedia of the Social Sciences* and we have allowed 400 words to a column. (Aptheker 1976, 145)

By this time, May 1937, Du Bois was quite optimistic about possibilities for funding of the project. Du Bois's assistant editor, Rayford Logan, once told me a poignant story about the failure of this project to receive funding. By 1937, Du Bois had secured a pledge of $125,000 from the Phelps-Stokes Fund to proceed with his project—half of the amount needed to complete it. Du Bois had applied to the Carnegie Corporation after a similar proposal had been rejected by the General Education Board, for the remaining half of his budget, with the strong endorsement of Phelps-Stokes. The president of the General Education Board, a group of four or five private foundations that included the Rockefeller Foundation, also lent his support. So convinced was Du Bois that his project, 28 years after he first articulated it, would be funded, that he invited Logan to wait with him at his office at 200 West 135th Street for the phone call that he had been promised immediately

following the Carnegie board meeting. A bottle of vintage champagne sat chilling on Du Bois's desk in a silver bucket, two cut-glass champagne flutes resting nearby.

The phone never rang. Persuaded that Du Bois was far too "radical" to serve as a model of disinterested scholarship, and lobbied by Du Bois's intellectual enemies, such as anthropologist Melville Herskovits, the Carnegie Corporation rejected the project. In addition, Du Bois had been forced to resign his post as editor of *The Crisis* magazine just three years before, so he had a considerable number of intellectual and political enemies.

David Levering Lewis offers a moving account of what transpired at the meeting of the General Education Board, and its subsequent consequences:

Now came a third turning point in Du Bois's career—the fulfillment of a grand idea that had been with him since the turn of the century, the multi-volume *Encyclopedia of the Negro*. "Cruel" is the word for best describing the roller coaster involving Du Bois and the major foundations over the funding of his ambitious project of research and education. His old faith in the power of ideas, scientifically formulated, to make the world better had welled up again after a quarter-century of activism and propaganda. The encyclopedia project generated preliminary endorsements and promises of collaboration from much of the international scholarly community. After his 1935 funding application was rejected by the Rockefeller-dominated combine of four or five private foundations comprising the General Education Board, he greatly revised and elaborated the proposal for resubmission, the Phelps-Stokes Fund providing seed money. Growing national and even international support for Du Bois among the experts began to exert formidable pressures for foundation funding of the encyclopedia. Rather surprisingly, one of the General Education Board's principal officers, Jackson Davis, had become an *Encyclopedia* convert, introducing Du Bois to the right New York notables, stroking his own trustees, and lobbying the Carnegie Corporation for favorable action on the Carnegie portion of the Du Bois grant application. Melville Herskovits, a competitor for foundation funds, began to fret about Du Bois's bagging the $250,000 research budget. He need not have worried. Clearly, an encyclopedia encompassing the full range of race and race relations in America and directed by Du Bois was to say the least troubling to the custodians of social science orthodoxy.

The seven-member executive committee of the GEB—Raymond B. Fosdick presiding and John D. Rockefeller III participating—rejected the *Encyclopedia* at the beginning of May 1937. In his conference a few days later with Carnegie Corporation president Frederick Keppel, GEB's Jackson Davis paradoxically pleaded for favorable Carnegie consideration of the project. "Dr. Du Bois is the most influential Negro in the United States," Davis reminded Keppel. "This project would keep him busy for the rest of his life." Predictably, Carnegie declined. Within a remarkably short time, the study of the Negro (generously underwritten by the Carnegie Corporation) found a quite different direction under a Swedish scholar then unknown in the field of race relations, one whose understanding of American race problems was to be distinctly more psychological and less economic than was Du Bois's.

The precise moment of preemption is recorded in a remarkable September 1939 exchange between President Robert Maynard Hutchins of the University of Chicago and Director Edwin Embree of the Rosenwald Fund: "Ed, somebody tells me that Keppel has rented the forty-sixth floor of the Chrysler Building and turned it over to a Swede named Gunnar Myrdal to make an elaborate study of Negro education. What's it all about?" "Bob, not Negro education, but the whole realm of the Negro in American civilization [to] take the place of the proposed Negro Encyclopedia in which the Phelps Stokes Fund has been greatly interested." When the president of the Phelps-Stokes Fund wrote Du Bois in 1944 at the time of the publication of *An American Dilemma* that "there has been no one who has been quite so often quoted by Myrdal than yourself," Du Bois must have savored the irony. (Lewis 1995, 7-8)

Nevertheless, Du Bois stubbornly persisted, even publishing two putative "entries" from the *Encyclopedia* in *Phylon* magazine in 1940, one on Robert Russa Moton, the principal of Tuskegee Institute between 1915 and 1935 (1940b), the other on Alexander Pushkin (1940c). He even was able to publish two editions in 1945 and 1946 of *Encyclopaedia of the Negro: Preparatory Volume with Reference Lists and Reports*. But the project itself could never secure adequate financial backing.

Du Bois struggled in vain to secure funding over the next several years, but he managed to publish in 1945 a 208-page "Preparatory Volume with Reference Lists and Reports"; a second edition appeared in 1946.

This remarkable volume is extraordinarily valuable as a compendium of secondary sources about African and African American history, culture, and social institutions. But most valuable is Du Bois's statement about "The Need for an Encyclopedia of the Negro":

There is need for young pupils and for mature students of a statement of the present condition of our knowledge concerning the darker races and especially concerning Negroes, which would make available our present scientific knowledge and set aside the vast accumulation of tradition and prejudice which makes such knowledge difficult now for the layman to obtain: A *Vade mecum* for American schools, editors, libraries, for Europeans inquiring into the race status here, for South Americans and Africans.

Our knowledge of the Negro today is not, of course, entirely complete; there are many gaps where further information and more careful study are needed; but this is the case in almost every branch of knowledge. Knowledge is never complete and in few subjects does a time arrive when an encyclopedia is demanded because no further information is expected. Indeed the need of an encyclopedia is greatest when a stage is reached where there is a distinct opportunity to bring together and set down a clear and orderly statement of the facts already known and agreed upon, for the sake of establishing a base for further advance and further study. Under such circumstances it would seem that an encyclopedia of the Negro is necessary.

In the case of the proposed *Encyclopedia of the Negro* these difficulties are increased because the prejudices and memories surrounding the subject have been more intense. There are hurts and fears; there are current controversies, which make a strictly scientific point of view of questions affecting the Negro race, difficult. Notwithstanding this, the body of accumulated knowledge is today so wide and dependable that it becomes all the more necessary that current social thought and discussion should be placed, to as large an extent as possible, upon a basis of accepted scientific conclusion. (Lewis 1995, 18-19)

In 1948, still another challenge to Du Bois emerged, this time initiated—incredibly—by the General Education Board, the Dodd, Mead publishing company, and Dr. Frederick D. Patterson, the president of the Tuskegee Institute, who had agreed to be its editor-in-chief. It was to be called "The Negro: An Encyclopedia," it would consist of 1 million words, and it would sell for $12. (Aptheker 1978, 191-94; "Grapevine" 1948). Two years later, Charles Wesley—still another Ph.D. in history from Harvard—wrote to Du Bois to say that the Association for the Study of Negro Life and History, in the wake of Carter G. Woodson's death, had decided to publish "an Encyclopedia Africana" and did Du Bois have any objections? Du Bois wished Wesley well, but warned him—just as President Eliot had warned Du Bois in 1909—that the project would be an expensive one (Aptheker 1978, 403-4.) Clearly the concept—and proprietorship—of an encyclopedia of the black diaspora had a vexed history in the first half of the twentieth century. Neither of these projects went beyond the planning stage.

On 26 September 1960, Du Bois reported that he had been invited by Kwame Nkrumah to move to Ghana to edit *The Encyclopedia Africana*. After a harried decade during which he ran for the United States Senate, was arrested and tried for being a

Communist sympathizer, and had his traveling privileges suspended, what a relief this invitation must have been. Du Bois and his second wife, Shirley Graham, moved to Ghana in 1961, becoming citizens there in 1963. He described his reasons for accepting the invitation in the *Baltimore Afro-American* on 21 October 1961 and then again in an essay entitled "Ghana Calls" published in *Freedomways* in the winter of 1962 ([1962] 1965). What he neglected to mention, however, was his disappointment and disgust with so many prominent Negro leaders who had failed to support him during his harassment by the government. Du Bois's anger at this would affect his design for the encyclopedia in its third and final incarnation.

On 15 December 1962, Du Bois convened a conference to launch the encyclopedia at the University of Ghana. It would be his last public speech. In his remarks, Du Bois recapitulated the history of his idea since 1909, then argued that "it is logical that such a work had to wait for independent Africans to carry it out," and now was the ideal time to edit "an *Encyclopedia Africana* based in Africa and compiled by Africans" (Lewis 1995, 323). Du Bois then told his audience:

It is true that scientific written records do not exist in most parts of this continent. But the time is *now* for beginning. The encyclopedia hopes to eliminate the artificial boundaries created on this continent by colonial masters. Designations such as "British Africa," "French Africa,"

"Black Africa," "Islamic Africa" too often serve to keep alive differences which in large part have been imposed on Africans by outsiders. The encyclopedia must have research units throughout West Africa, North Africa, East, Central and South Africa which will gather and record information for these geographical sections of the continent. The encyclopedia is concerned with Africa as a whole. (Lewis 1995, 323)

Ultimately, Du Bois argued, "It is African scholars themselves who will create the ultimate *Encyclopedia Africana.* . . . After all, this is where the work should be done—in Africa, sponsored by Africans, for Africa." The completion of this grand project, he concluded, "is of vital importance to Africa as a whole and to the world at large" (Lewis 1995, 324-25). Dramatically curtailed in scope and coverage from its first two manifestations in 1909 and 1932, this *Africana* would have only a continental focus, rather than the diasporic focus of the other two. This *Africana* would serve as a tool in the liberation and consolidation of an emerging continent.

Du Bois died on the eve of the great March on Washington; indeed, Roy Wilkins announced his death during the proceedings. His secretariat for the *Encyclopedia Africana* continued after his death, and published three volumes of biographies in the late 1970s and early 1980s (*Encyclopedia Africana*, 1977, 1979, 1995). Officially, it is still dedicated to fulfilling his dream of an encyclopedia about Africa edited by Africans, and has recently announced a publication date of the year 2009—48 years after Du Bois launched the project in Ghana.

Had any of these attempts to edit the three versions of his encyclopedia been successful, how dramatically different would have been the evolution of African and Afro-American studies in the academy. An encyclopedia establishes a foundation of common knowledge on which subsequent scholarly inquiry can stand. It removes the necessity of reinventing the proverbial wheel each time scholars embark upon a subject unknown to them but one that has already been thoroughly explored by other scholars. Just as important, an encyclopedia makes it possible to disseminate this baseline of knowledge broadly and widely to schools at even the earliest levels, just as the *Britannica* did for millions of households. How much further along would the fields of African and African American studies be at the end of the century had the great Du Bois been funded in 1909 or in 1932 or had he lived beyond 1963 to see his more narrow, Africa-focused version completed? Du Bois's initial 1909 idea for an encyclopedia of the African diaspora would not be published until January 1999, when *Encarta Africana* was released on CD-ROM, 90 years after Du Bois first articulated the idea. *Africana: The Encyclopedia of the African and African American Experience*, the book version, was published in November 1999. Both, appropriately, are dedicated in memory of W.E.B. Du Bois.

References

Adams, H. G. 1854. *God's Image in Ebony; Being a Series of Biographical Sketches, Facts, Anecdotes, etc., Demonstrative of the Mental Powers and Intellectual Capacities of the Negro Race*. London: Partridge and Oakey.

Aptheker, Herbert, ed. 1973. *The Correspondence of W.E.B. Du Bois*. Vol. 1, *Selections, 1877-1934*. Amherst: University of Massachusetts Press.

———. 1976. *The Correspondence of W.E.B. Du Bois*. Vol. 2, *Selections, 1934-1944*. Amherst: University of Massachusetts Press.

———. 1978. *The Correspondence of W.E.B. Du Bois*. Vol. 3, *Selections, 1944-1963*. Amherst: University of Massachusetts Press.

Crogman, W. H. and H. F. Kletzing. 1897. *Progress of a Race*. Atlanta: J. L. Nicols.

Cromwell, John W. 1914. *The Negro in American History; Men and Women Eminent in the Evolution of the American of African Descent*. Washington, DC: American Negro Academy.

Culp, D. W. 1902. *Twentieth Century Negro Literature: Or a Cyclopedia of Thought on the Vital Topics Relating to the American Negro by One Hundred of America's Greatest Negroes*. Naperville: J. L. Nicols.

Du Bois, W.E.B. 1935. *Black Reconstruction: An Essay Toward a History of the Part Which Black Folk Played in the Attempt to Reconstruct Democracy in America, 1860-1880*. New York: Russell and Russell.

———. [1940a] 1975. *Dusk of Dawn*. Millwood, NY: Kraus-Thomson.

———. 1940b. Moton of Hampton and Tuskegee. *Phylon* 1(4):344-51.

———. 1940c. Pushkin. *Phylon* 1(3):265-69.

————. 1945, 1946. *Encyclopedia of the Negro: Preparatory Volume with Reference Lists and Reports.* New York: Phelps-Stokes Fund.

————. 1961. [Reasons for accepting invitation to Ghana]. *Baltimore Afro-American,* 21 Oct.

————. [1962] 1965. Ghana Calls. *Freedomways* Winter:98-101.

Easton, Hosea. 1837. *A Treatise on the Intellectual Character of the Colored People of the United States.* Boston: I. Knapp.

Eliot, Charles. 1909. Letter to W.E.B. Du Bois. 15 July. Harvard University Archives, Cambridge, MA.

Encyclopedia Africana: Dictionary of African Biography, The. Vol. 1. 1977. New York: Reference.

Encyclopedia Africana: Dictionary of African Biography, The. Vol. 2. 1979. Algonac, MI: Reference.

Encyclopedia Africana: Dictionary of African Biography, The. Vol. 3. 1995. Algonac, MI: Reference.

Garrett, Edward. C. 1940. Negro Encyclopedia. Unpublished.

Grapevine. 1948. *Chicago Defender,* 7 Feb.

Grégoire, Henri-Baptiste. 1808. *De la littérature des nègres ou Recherches sur leurs facultés intellectuelles, leurs qualities morales et leur litterature: suivies de notices sur la vie et les auvrages des nègres qui se sont distingués dans les sciences, les lettres et les arts.* Paris: Maradan librairie.

Haley, James. 1895. *Afro-American Encyclopedia.* Nashville, TN: Haley and Florida.

Holly, James Theodore. 1851. *A Vindication of the Capacity of the Negro Race for Self-Government, and Civilized Progress.* New Haven, CT: W. H. Stanley.

Hume, David. 1748. Of National Characters. *Essays Moral and Political.*

Jewish Encyclopedia, The. 1907. New York: Funk and Wagnalls.

Lewis, David Levering. 1993. *W.E.B. Du Bois: Biography of a Race, 1868-1919.* New York: Henry Holt.

————. 1995. *W.E.B. Du Bois: A Reader.* New York: Henry Holt.

Lewis, R. B. 1836. *Light and Truth; Collected from the Bible and Ancient and Modern History; Containing the Universal History of the Colored and Indian Race, from the Creation of the World to the Present Time.* Portland: D. C. Cotesworthy.

Miller, Kelly and J. R. Gay. 1917. *Progress and Achievements of the Colored People.* Washington, DC: Austen Jenkins.

Mott, Abigail. 1826. *Biographical Sketches and Interesting Anecdotes of Persons of Colour.* New York: M. Day.

Murray, Daniel. 1912. *Historical and Biographical Encyclopedia of the Colored Race Throughout the World; Its Progress and Achievements from the Earliest Period Down to the Present Time (25,000 Biographies, 5,900 Musical Compositions by Colored Composers).* Chicago: World's Cyclopedia.

Pennington, James W. C. 1841. *A Text Book of the Origin and History of the Colored People.* Hartford: L. Skinner.

Perry, Rufus. 1886. *The Cushite; or, The Children of Ham (the Negro Race) as Seen by the Ancient Historians and Poets.* Brooklyn, NY: Literary Union.

Rogers, Joel A. 1946. *World's Great Men of Color.* New York: J. A. Rogers.

Simmons, William J. 1887. *Men of Mark: Eminent, Progressive and Rising.* Cleveland: G. M. Rewell.

Tussac, de, F. R. 1810. *Cri des Colons coutre unouvrage de M. L'eveque et senateur Gregoire. . . .* Paris: Delaunay libraire.

Washington, Booker T. 1900. *A New Negro for a New Century.* Chicago: American Publishing House.

Williams, George W. 1883. *History of the Negro Race in America from 1619 to 1880*. New York: G. P. Putnam's Sons.

Wilson, Joseph T. 1882. *Emancipation: Its Course and Progress from 1481 B.C. to A.D. 1875*. Hampton: Normal School Steam Power Press Print.

ANNALS, *AAPSS*, **568**, March 2000

Being an African in the World: The Du Boisian Epistemology

By ANTHONY MONTEIRO

ABSTRACT: W.E.B. Du Bois sought not merely to rewrite the history of Africa but to think in epistemological terms about what it meant to be an African in the modern world and its significance for social research. This becomes apparent in part from his earliest writing—in particular, a 1904 review of *The Souls of Black Folk*—but takes on a more conscious form in later works. Looking at Du Bois in this way locates his intellectual project in an African-centered challenge to European intellectual and civilizational hegemony, a challenge which is wider and more profound than modern-day Afrocentrism. To achieve what is no less than an epistemic break, he sought to reconceptualize Africa from the standpoint of an African in America. This article views the Du Boisian project as a rupture of vast proportions and one which has continuing value to the social and human sciences of the African.

Anthony Monteiro is associate professor of sociology at the University of the Sciences in Philadelphia. He has written and lectured widely on Du Bois and the construction of social scientific knowledge. He currently is preparing a book that is tentatively titled Race and Pan Africanism: The Du Boisian Epistemology. *He views his scholarship on Du Bois as both history of ideas in the West and sociology of knowledge.*

DURING his years at Harvard and the University of Berlin, W.E.B. Du Bois boldly projected the possibility of subjecting to scientific scrutiny the problem of race in the modern world. He contended, more forcefully over succeeding years, that the central object of American sociology should be the study of race. The intellectual core of what became a unique Du Boisian epistemology of race was a reconceptualization of Africa. Du Bois sometimes openly, often quite subtly, sought out ways to reconceptualize the social, cultural, and civilizational universe from an African-centered standpoint. Forthrightly, he insists in a 1904 review of *The Souls of Black Folk*, "One who is born with a cause is predestined to a certain narrowness of view, and at the same time to some clearness of vision within his limits with which the world often finds it well to reckon" (Du Bois [1904] 1996, 304). He concludes the review in a way that locates both his intellectual style and the object of his project. "In its larger aspects," he says, "the style is tropical—African. This needs no apology. The blood of my fathers spoke through me and cast off the English restraint of my training and surroundings. The resulting accomplishment is a matter of taste. Sometimes I think very well of it and sometimes I do not" (305).

In configuring his epistemology, Du Bois rethought the language, methods, historical references, and civilizational assumptions of the social sciences. He made three crucial intellectual moves in this process. His initial move was to engage the central assumptions of European thought vis-à-vis the world, in particular its idea of progress. Looking back over the nineteenth century, Du Bois foresaw the twentieth century. The problem of the new epoch would be the problem of race. To address this problem and challenge white hegemony, a second move was made. Race would denote more than race. It would in its deepest sense reference civilization. Leading social scientists were arguing that races were biologically determined, with separate genetic histories, geographies, and human potentialities. Du Bois transgressively insisted in "The Conservation of Races" that "the differentiation of spiritual and mental differences between great races of mankind" occurred alongside "the integration of physical differences" (Du Bois [1897] 1986, 818). He understood physical and biological race to be so indeterminate as to be of little scientific significance. The matter of races was, then, a matter of cultures and civilizations and thus a matter to be understood through the social sciences. Races as historically constituted civilizations emerged as his central understanding of race. This began what would be a bold, indeed courageous, effort to alter world ideological and civilizational relationships.

To liberate the study of races from white supremacy, a third move was indispensable. Africa figured into his intellectual project as its strategic intellectual center. Du Bois's investment in a reconceptualization of Africa was enormous, and it is here where Du Bois made the crucial rupture with European thought. He, as a result of the last move, set upon a distinct intellectual trajectory, one that created conditions for revolutionizing the social sciences. His studies of race and the Negro literally invented the social sciences of race in their twentieth-century form. However, Africa was the ever-present factor throughout. These three moves refigured, inverted, transfigured, and transformed the European social science project.

What the Renaissance, the Enlightenment, and modern science are to European thought, Africa is to Du Bois. As he insisted in his Harvard valedictory, European thought is but one way and does not represent a universal or superior approach to knowing. In the conflict of ideas, Du Bois proposes another way—an African way of knowing and being in the world. In this liberating project, Africa is viewed as a civilization for itself and Africans a people for themselves. "Always Africa is giving us something new," he proclaims in "The African Roots of the War," or, he continues, "some metempsychosis of a world-old thing" (Du Bois 1995, 642).

In *The Philadelphia Negro* he argues, "The Negro church is the peculiar and characteristic product of the transplanted African, and deserves especial study" (Du Bois [1899] 1996, 201). He continues that, as a social institution, "the Negro church may be said to have antedated the Negro family on American soil; as such it has preserved, on the one hand, many functions of tribal organization, and on the other hand many of the family functions" (201). What he called its "tribal functions"

are its communal functions, which preserve the African tradition of female authority (see also the discussion of African American religion in Du Bois [1903] 1986, chap. 10).

He reminds us in *The Souls of Black Folk* that, even through the storm and stress of slavery, the Negro brought her African contribution to the Americas (Du Bois [1903] 1986). "In origin," he insists in *Black Reconstruction*, "the slaves represented everything African" (Du Bois [1935] 1992, 3). Africa and the transatlantic slave trade were the foundations of the modern world economy. Moreover, the political and moral agency of modernity, Du Bois reasoned, were disproportionately located in the slaves, their culture, and resistance. "The role which the great Negro Toussaint, called L'Ouverture, played in the history of the United States has seldom been fully appreciated" (Du Bois [1896] 1986, 74). Toussaint, Du Bois tells us, represented the age of revolution in America—not Jefferson, but Toussaint. The Haitian Revolution, Du Bois insists, "was Africa in America and Africans led by Toussaint L'Ouverture" (Du Bois [1961] 1996, 298).

Africans, in Du Bois's historical accounts, are a moral force. Africans in America would give the first and most consistent examples of what Marx called the class struggle. "In Europe," Du Bois says, "the organization of the lowest classes of workers and servants, peasants and laborers to gain political power and property was rare and cannot be compared to the corresponding organizations of African slaves in the West Indies and South America. Many European revolts which are pictured as risings of the masses are nothing of the sort" (Du Bois [1961] 1996, 298). He continues, "There were revolts of the suffering masses in Hungary, France and England but they were small compared with the concerted, long continued rebellion of the black Maroons" (298). Chattel slaves were workers; the plantation system after the introduction of Whitney's cotton gin had become "an industrial system"; and the slave labor system, a "slave-labor large farming system"(Du Bois [1896] 1986, 151).

Slave labor brought to the Americas the earliest examples of class struggle. Their principal means of revolt were work stoppages, breaking tools, leaving the plantations, and slave uprisings for freedom. All of this culminates in the Civil War—"a general strike that involved directly in the end perhaps a half million people. They wanted to stop the economy of the plantation system, and to do that they left the plantations" (Du Bois [1935] 1992, 67). "It is astonishing how this army of striking labor furnished in time 200,000 Federal soldiers whose evident ability to fight decided the war" (67).

He would go on to transfigure communism as a conceptual and civilizational category. Communism, he insisted, was inherent to the African mode of thought and social life. In *The Gift of Black Folk* (Du Bois [1924] 1992) and *Black Folk Then and Now* (Du Bois 1939), he explored the civilizational prerequisites that informed African modes of labor and African class consciousness. Finally, not only is the class struggle deeply rooted in the struggle for African American freedom but also communism itself is compatible with the African cultural traditions of communalism.

THE DU BOISIAN AFRICAN
EPISTEMOLOGY OF RACE

Du Bois's radical rejection of European centrism and privileging of Africa would in his construction separate the American and European social scientific and intellectual projects. The social sciences emerged in the nineteenth century as intellectual endeavors to make sense of historical developments in Europe. They were formed from theoretical questions about the European historical experience. Science and reason became their central tropes. Class, social status, prestige, and the relationship of the individual to society and the state emerged as dominant themes. The social universe was viewed as being exclusively European. To be human, and thus worthy of scientific consideration, meant being European. Social scientists in nineteenth-century Europe organized themselves as branches of science and modeled the social sciences on one of the natural sciences. In this respect, positivism, in the Comtean sense of metaphysical or general statements being tested against carefully collected facts, increasingly defined what it meant to be scientific in the social sciences.

Du Bois challenged a fundamental assumption of Eurocentric social thinking: the idea that only Europeans and only European societies were worthy of scientific investigation. Indeed, Africans were civilized. In his 1898 article, "The Study of the Negro Problems," for the American Academy of Social and Political Science, he said, "The Negro is a member of the human race, and as one who, in the light of history and experience, is capable to a degree of improvement and culture, is entitled to have his interests considered according to his numbers in all conclusions as to the common weal" (Du Bois [1898] 1973, 17). "The American Negro deserves study for the great end of advancing the cause of science in general" (10). Africans, in the European mind, were no more than objects of history, having emerged little beyond the state of nature. Social science as a study of human agency was, by definition, not concerned with Africans. Rather, biology was considered the appropriate field for their study.

Science, in the postbellum United States, was the new intellectual fad. In the Progressive Era, it was touted as the answer to most of the extant problems of white civilization. Of his schooling at Fisk, Harvard, and Berlin Du Bois said, "The main result of my schooling had been to emphasize science and the scientific attitude" (Du Bois [1940] 1995, 50). While the natural sciences were well on their way into the twentieth century, the social sciences, Du Bois observed, "were engaged in vague statements" (51). Herbert Spencer's *Synthetic Philosophy* (1889) (the final of 10 volumes, *Social Statics*, was published in 1896) reflected the intellectual and scientific style of the age. Spencer sought to use biology as a methodological analogue for society. He agreed with Darwin that evolution is a process of adaptation of organisms to their environment. The mind, he argued, was a part of natural evolution. Just as biological evolution had produced superior and inferior species and intelligences, social evolution had produced inferior and superior societies, races, and classes with distinct moral, physical, and intellectual capacities. William James, Du Bois's professor and friend at Harvard, passionately disagreed with Spencer's social Darwinism. James believed Darwin's theory implied that the mind's job is to select aspects of the world important for humans to act on and thus assist in our adaptation to the world. James recognized that the core of Darwin's theory was the idea of local adaptation to specific conditions rather than a grand theory of "progress" predicated upon a linear notion of stages of development, wherein each succeeding stage is considered superior to what preceded it (James [1890] 1950).

Francis Galton's discoveries in statistics translated social Darwinism into what would pass for a scientific research program. Statistics were, Galton thought, methods for proving that selective breeding could produce a superior race. *Hereditary Genius* aimed to convince the skeptical public of the superior hereditary endowments of certain eminent British families (Galton 1869). "Arguing that there is a physiological basis for psychological traits, he invented techniques for measuring what he thought was intelligence, along with the bell shaped curve for demonstrating its 'normal distribution' " (Smedley 1993, 266).

Du Bois had experienced an even more lethal form of social Darwinism in Germany in the classes of the German ultranationalist and racist Heinrich von Treitschke. For, along with normal social Darwinism, German academics combined it with the Nietzschean concept of the superman. The nineteenth century's legacy to the twentieth on race was extending the positivist philosophical bent to measurement of human genetic inheritance.

For most white Americans, these views expressed both common sense and experience. They became the dominant ideological and research paradigms on race matters within Anglo-American social science and research of the time. Each actively supported racism, class subordination, and was strongly anti-immigrant. Social structure and social behavior were viewed as the consequences of inherited genetic characteristics. As the official scientific explanation of their age, they dominated political and social discourse. Du Bois early in his career attributed this flawed ideology to society's lack of scientific knowledge, which he traced to the conceptual and methodological poverty of the social sciences—a situation he hoped to change.

Du Bois's ambition was to use science against scientific racism in the interest of reform and uplift, "but nevertheless, I wanted to do the work with scientific accuracy" (Du Bois [1940] 1995, 51). He subsequently turned his gaze "from fruitless word-twisting [to] the facts of [his] own social situation and racial world. [He] determined to put science into sociology through a study of the conditions and problems of [his] own group" (51). Du Bois earnestly sought to discover and then to equip the social sciences with methodologies appropriate to their object of inquiry. In doing so, he rejected the lures of reductionism, solipsism, and the pure objectivism of positivism. This, in the end, placed Du Bois in an irreparable conflict with social Darwinism and the hereditarian research program that accompanied it.

What he failed to see early on in his career was that, rather than science, this research program was ideologically driven. Race and white supremacy were for it what Bourdieu (1977) calls structuring structures. That is to say, white supremacy shaped the intellectual space within which Anglo-American social thought and research operated. In the end, white supremacy is the irreducible element in the equation, both ordering white intellectual space and operating as a springboard for shaping and reshaping its geography. Race and white supremacy, Du Bois discovered, were elemental to the configuration of capitalism itself. Social Darwinism and the hereditarian research program, therefore, while constituting a "science" of race, were ideologically linked to capitalism and its relationships of production. Race, as an ideological category, was a decisive part of the ideological production of the social structure based on race and class inequalities.

As Du Bois strode from Harvard to assume his place in the world, his motto might have been that of a fellow alumnus of Berlin University, Karl Marx: "The philosophers have only interpreted the world in various ways; the point is to change it" (Marx [1845] 1969, 15). The precocious young scholar was no doubt dissatisfied with the ways in which the natural and social sciences were discussing race. To address this situation, a multidisciplinary exploration of knowledge itself as well as the objects of knowledge—in this instance, race and civilization—was required. A great intellectual leap would be called for. A new categorical grid would have to be constructed out of the inadequate European foundations. Africa would have to be introduced as an integral part of world history.

Du Bois explored, in this respect, a wide and complex philosophical terrain. His Harvard and University of Berlin training had allowed him to become conversant in, and acutely sensitive to, the contending philosophical camps of his day. He intellectually engaged the competing claims of pragmatism and European epistemology. Scholars differ in their opinions about Du Bois's philosophy. Robert Gooding-Williams (1991-92), David Levering Lewis (1993), and Shamoon Zamir (1995) argue that Hegel's *Phenomenology of Mind* exerted a strong and enduring influence upon him. Arnold Rampersad (1976) and Cornel West (1989), on the other hand, claim that Du Bois remained a Jamesian pragmatist. Rampersad contends, "The overall

impact of William James was preeminent" (Rampersad 1976, 30).

Du Bois's sociological and historical studies demonstrate, however, what I consider a synthesis of several philosophical and methodological stances. He, nonetheless, brought a specific philosophical and methodological attitude to the understanding of race, one that acknowledged the plebian and existential orientation of pragmatism as articulated by Emerson and William James, along with its sense of contingency and specificity, the phenomenology and dialectics of Hegel, and the inductivist methods of his German professors of economic history, Adolph Wagner and Gustav von Schmoller. Du Bois, at the same time, remained committed to a mild version of positivism; he did not abandon in either sociological or historical research hard data, be they from official censuses, government documents, specific studies, or his own information carefully gathered through well-constructed and thoroughly executed surveys.

Du Bois was also a masterful ethnographer. Through his ethnographic work he sought to discover that uniquely human dimension of behavior and society: the nonmaterial, the psychological, and, if you will, spiritual dimensions. This line of inquiry would bring him into the domain of anthropology and cultural studies. Philosophical questions were handled in relation to issues that came up in the course of social and historical research, not as issues in themselves. Yet Du Bois constructed not merely a distinctive methodological approach to the problems of race but a distinct epistemology, a way of knowing and, for him, changing the world of race relations.

To understand these commitments it is necessary to go beyond his academic influences. Alexander Crummell, his mentor in the American Negro Academy, is one such influence. Crummell was an Anglo-African nationalist with commitments to Christianity, the destiny of Africa, an authoritarian political style, and belief in black separate institutions (Moses 1978, 59). Although Du Bois, unlike Crummell and later Marcus Garvey, was not an Anglophile, he, like them, believed in a single destiny for black people in Africa and the United States.

In large measure, the disputes about where to place Du Bois intellectually and politically emerge from the fact that most commentators have failed to examine his effort in epistemic terms. Thus, without coming to terms with epistemic issues and perspectives inherent to his scholarship and political activity, it is not possible to accurately locate him and his project. Du Bois's epistemology, in its broad outlines, is holistic, maintaining a Hegelian concern with world history combined with an acute awareness of contingency and a sense of the significance of day-to-day events. Something of this synthesis was first revealed in a paper, "The Large and Small-Scale System of Agriculture in the Southern United States, 1840-1890," written for Schmoller and intended to become the thesis for a Ph.D. from the University of Berlin. The paper looked at the land tenure system in the U.S. South from the bottom up. What we see here from a methodological and philosophical point of view are the influences of the German school of historical economics (headed by Schmoller and Wagner) which, according to Du Bois's class notes, "tries as far as possible to leave the *Sollen* [should be] for a later stage and study the *Geshehen* [what is actual] as other sciences have done" (see Lewis 1993, 142). This view that large patterns emerge only after determining the pattern of particular events mirrored what Du Bois had heard at Harvard from his professors, William James and Albert Bushnell Hart.

DU BOIS'S PROLEGOMENON OF
A GENERAL THEORY OF RACES

In 1897, while polishing the research and language of *The Philadelphia Negro*, Du Bois delivered a paper to the American Negro Academy entitled "The Conservation of Races"—a work that can be viewed as a prolegomenon to a general theory of race. It seeks to provide a general concept of races, uniting the general concept of races, or large populations, with the particularity of the African or Negro race (Du Bois [1897] 1986). A deep reading of the work suggests two compatible conceptualizations. First, one finds a populationist definition of races— that is, that races are large groups of people united on the basis of civilization, culture, language, and recognizable phenotypic characteristics. Second, one finds a geno-geographical definition, which suggests that gene populations occupy, generally, certain geographic regions of the planet and that civilization, language, and culture correlate with the histories and geographies of human genes. Moreover, from a genetic or biological point of view, there is significant drift (genetic drift) and integration, while civilizations and cultures are more permanent. They are deep structures as opposed to biology, which is more prone to change, combination (integration), and recombination. These foundations inform Du Bois's race conceptualizations in later works, especially *Dusk of Dawn* ([1940] 1995) and *The World and Africa* ([1947] 1995).

The Suppression of the African Slave Trade to the United States of America ([1896] 1986) and *The Philadelphia Negro* ([1899] 1996) provide enormous empirical and historical data to demonstrate the reality of race, and "The Conservation of Races" ([1897] 1986) seeks to generalize upon that data. In a concrete sense, we witness Du Bois working from the concrete to the general, from specific knowledge to general explanation. Races as he articulated them are constituted on the basis of geography, genes, history, and culture. Race is a type of supranational community of people. The object of "The Conservation of Races," however, was to assert the civilizational equality of the Negro race with other great races. Africans were one of his eight major races. The article was to become the basis of scientific research and political agitation for civil and political rights. It used as its foundational assumption that Africans were civilized, and indeed Africa was where human civilization originated. From the standpoint of the Du Boisian oeuvre, this article should be viewed as an initial approximation to a more general theory of race and race construction and not his final statement.

"The Conservation of Races" helps us to understand Du Bois's oeuvre generally and to understand how each subsequent work was a further approximation to a deeper understanding of social complexity. Starting with "The Conservation of Races," a series of approximations, amendments, additions, revisions, and rethinkings occurs as new evidence and new arguments and explanations come forward. And yet he would always attempt to empirically verify the categories of his thinking. This article was, however, given the time, competitively plausible and generally progressive. It, like all of his scholarly and intellectual work, was profoundly political. Du Bois was responding to the racist and colonialist notions of world history. He declared,

We are the first fruit of this new nation, the harbinger of that black tomorrow which is yet destined to soften the whiteness of the Teutonic today. We are that people whose subtle sense of song has given America its only American music, its only American fairy tales, its only touch of pathos and humor amid its mad money-getting plutocracy. As such, it is our duty to conserve our physical powers, our intellectual endowments, our spiritual ideals; as a race we must strive by race organization, by race solidarity, by race unity to the realization of that broader humanity which freely recognizes differences in men, but sternly deprecates inequality in their opportunities of development. (Du Bois [1897] 1986, 822)

The reactionary political and racial climate that made such a work necessary is suggested in *Dusk of Dawn* (Du Bois [1940] 1995, 98). This context helps explain its political and intellectual strategy. It assumes a militant nationalist voice, not heard in either *The Suppression of the African Slave Trade* or *The Philadelphia Negro*—explained, certainly, by its audience, a Black Nationalist–led group. In *The Souls of Black Folk*, the militant and political tone in "The Conservation of Races" reappears. Du Bois proposes a conceptualization of races which views them as culturally and historically distinct, while each, and significantly Negroes, has contributions to make to civilization. In the graduate schools at Harvard and Berlin, race became a matter of culture and cultural history. The history of the world was paraded before the observation of students, Du Bois tells us in his autobiography (Du Bois 1968). Comparative history was done for the sake of determining superior and inferior races and peoples. The white race, of course, had history and thereby civilization. There was some mention, Du Bois continues, of Asiatic culture, "but no course in Chinese or Indian history or culture was offered at Harvard, and quite unanimously in America and Germany, Africa was left without culture and without history" (Du Bois [1940] 1995, 98).

Commentators have missed in assessing "The Conservation of Races" that Du Bois was arguing for preserving races and peoples as distinct cultural entities but not in a separatist, insular, or invidious ethnocentrist manner. What he was demanding was recognition of both the flowering of and pride among races and peoples on one hand and their coming together to form a better humanity on the other. Revealed here is recognition of a two-sided historical process among races, cultures, and peoples rather than the unilinear notion of progress advanced in European thought.

In both "The African Roots of the War" (1995) and *The World and Africa* ([1947] 1995), Du Bois's conceptualization becomes more strikingly political and ideological. Rather than inventing Africa, Du Bois contests the colonialist and white supremacist conceptualizations of Africa. Africa is in European thought a conundrum, a riddle. "The answer to the riddle we shall find in the economic changes in Europe," he points out (Du Bois 1995, 644). The Africa that emerges after the fifteenth century is gradually and inexorably the Africa of colonialism and imperial domination. Africa becomes central in this epoch to world history because, as Du Bois insists, "the 'Color Line' began to pay dividends" (643). It is upon the color line and African colonization that a "new democracy" is built, a Herrenvolk democracy, a master race democracy, a racialized white democracy, what Du Bois calls "a new democratic despotism." He continues,

"Such nations it is that rule the modern world. Their national bond is no mere sentimental patriotism, loyalty, or ancestor worship. It is increased wealth, power, and luxury for all classes on a scale the world has never saw before. Never before was the average citizen of England, France and Germany so rich, with such splendid prospects of greater riches." This wealth, he asserts, "comes directly from the darker races of the world" (645).

One thing is certain of the world at the beginning of the twentieth century: "Black Africa, prostrate, raped, and shamed, lies at the feet of the conquering Philistines of Europe" (Du Bois 1995, 650). And thus "the white European mind has worked, and worked the more feverishly because Africa is the Land of the Twentieth Century." World War I is rooted in the "desperate struggle for Africa which began in 1877" (646). In *The World and Africa* Du Bois again advances the idea that Africa is the future; however, in this case it is the land of the twenty-first century. We cannot forget, he reminds us, "America was built on Africa." "Despite the crude and cruel motives behind her shame and exposure, her degradation and enchaining, the fire and freedom of black Africa, with the uncurbed might of her consort Asia, are indispensable to the fertilizing of the universal soil of mankind, which Europe alone never would nor could give this aching earth" ([1947] 1995, 227, 260).

According to Du Bois, Africa has the civilizational resources to free itself and advance humanity, especially European or white humanity.

To do so, the ideological and philosophical edifice of white supremacy had to be ruined—a political and intellectual task of world historic significance, especially now that science "was called to help" prop up the myth of European superiority. "Students of Africa," he protests, "especially since the ivory-sugar-cotton Negro complex of the nineteenth century, became hag-ridden by the obsession that nothing civilized is Negroid and every evidence of high culture in Africa must be white or at least yellow" (Du Bois [1947] 1995, 34). Continuing, he says, "The very vocabulary of civilization expressed this idea; the Spanish word 'Negro' from being a descriptive adjective, was raised to the substantive name of a race and then deprived of its capital letter" (34). All in all, he tells us, to many men's minds the Negroes in the United States need "careful watching and ruthless repression" (1995, 646).

But in *Black Reconstruction* he would define race and the problem of race in far more radical terms. "His fight is a fight to the finish," he says of the African American struggle. "Either he dies or he wins. He will enter modern civilization here in America as a black man, or he will enter not at all. Either extermination root and branch, or absolute equality. There can be no compromise. This is the last great battle of the West" (Du Bois [1935] 1992, 703). In *Dusk of Dawn* he looks at African American raciality in robust cultural, historical, political, and ideological terms. He says, "The physical bond is least and the badge of color relatively unimportant save as a badge; the real essence of this kinship is its social heritage of slavery, the discrimination and insult; and this heritage binds together not simply the children of Africa, but extends through yellow Asia and into the South Seas. It is this unity that draws me to Africa" (Du Bois [1940] 1995, 117).

RACE, PHILOSOPHY, AND CULTURE

Du Bois in *The Souls of Black Folk* starts to come to terms with pragmatism. He would not (and did not) countenance self-edifying individualism. He demanded a commitment to the oppressed black masses. While American pragmatists and Hegelians avoid real history, Du Bois confronts it head on and seeks to construct a philosophy of real history and of human action. *The Souls of Black Folk*, when viewed in relationship to the research that preceded it, is part of a Du Boisian challenge to the limits of the social sciences and philosophy of the time. How, Du Bois seems to ask, to construct a social scientific and philosophical discourse on race at the start of the twentieth century? Du Bois understood that the audience for *The Souls of Black Folk* was wide and interracial. However, the text speaks in specific ways to the black talented tenth. He joins the attack upon the compromise policies of Booker T. Washington. He locates the black freedom struggle in the long struggle for democracy and especially the Haitian Revolution.

In drawing upon Hegel's *Phenomenology of Mind* and adapting its categorical grid to understanding the specificities of the United States, Du Bois gives to U.S. social science the intellectual tools to understand the complexities of race. Zamir suggests that Du Bois reworks Hegel's *Phenomenology* (Zamir 1995, 117).[1] Most American nineteenth-century readings of Hegel were upbeat, justifying the idea of an organically united people with a historic mission. Du Bois's critical reading of Hegel is similar to the one that emerges from Marx or Sartre. "What Hegel's idealist philosophy makes available to Du Bois is a complex model for thinking about the relationship of consciousness and history" (117). And Du Bois makes a radical rupture with Hegel by anchoring his enterprise in actual history. Yet, like Hegel, Du Bois acknowledges complexity, contradiction, striving, and movement in history and day-to-day events.

In *The Souls of Black Folk*, Du Bois rejects naive psychologism of the Jamesian and Deweyan types.[2] His examination of the collective souls of black folk is his way of historicizing psychology. He develops a historically contextualized and contingent notion of double consciousness and of black strivings that suggests a social psychology which argues that black folk emerge from a history of oppression and resistance. In the last chapter of *The Souls of Black Folk*, "The Sorrow Songs," Du Bois locates the Negro spirituals within the context of the striving for freedom and justice and the realization of a collective self—a peoplehood. He, however, defines the sorrow songs as the central historical narrative of black folk. "They are," he tells us, "the music of an unhappy people, of the children of disappointment; they tell of death and suffering and unvoiced longing toward a truer world, of misty wanderings and hidden ways." Yet, "through all the sorrow of the Sorrow Songs there breathes a hope—a faith in the ultimate justice of things. The minor cadences of despair change often to triumph and calm confidence. Sometimes it is faith in life, sometimes a faith in death, sometimes assurance of boundless justice in some fair world beyond. But whichever it is, the meaning is always clear: that sometime, somewhere, men will judge men by their souls and not by their skins." And then he asks, "Is such a hope justified? Do the Sorrow Songs sing true?" (Du Bois [1903] 1986, 544).

This engagement with the sorrow songs and locating them as the central narrative of the African American people is also part of Du Bois's locating the role of the talented tenth. Chapter 12, entitled "Of Alexander Crummell," develops a notion of the centrality of the black masses (Du Bois [1903] 1986, 512-20). Crummell, an Anglican priest and ascetic, believed that the essential need of freedmen was moral uplift. Du Bois believed their essential need was freedom, civil rights, the vote, and education. Crummell believed the talented tenth were a civilizing tenth, which would bring Christianity and thus civilization to the former slaves. Du Bois believed the talented tenth were obligated to serve and that the freedmen through the sorrow songs and the anti-slavery resistance had demonstrated they were civilized. Crummell's notion of the sublime personality is thus countered by Du Bois's notion of the sublimeness of a people whose resistance to oppression had elevated them above their oppressors. Here Du Bois emphasizes the mass and calls upon the intellectuals to enter into an organic relationship to them. Here is found, finally, Du Bois's belief in an activist, practical, and engaged social science. Rather than an intellectual gentry, the social scientist has a moral and professional obligation to be part of the mass that he studies.

CONCLUSION

Du Bois is a seminal thinker in the social sciences in large measure due to what I have argued is his African-centered epistemology—one that he worked on throughout his life and that was integral to the theoretical challenges that he made to racism. In this sense, he is the father of African centeredness as a way of thinking and being in the world. His approach to the social sciences emerged from the racially and politically hostile environments within which he worked. This situation is important to understanding the contours of his thinking. In the end, Du Bois makes a historically unique contribution to our understanding of race and modernity and certainly to race and postmodernity. His is a complex body of work. I have sought to locate its organizing principles and motive forces in its overriding and persistent concerns with Africa and the effort to do research and scholarship from an African perspective.

Notes

1. It is clear that Du Bois follows themes in *The Phenomenology of Mind*. For example, in *The Souls of Black Folk* one finds many parallels to *The Phenomenology of Mind*—especially chap. 3, "Force and Understanding: Appearance and the Supersensible World," and its sections "Independence and Dependence of Self-Consciousness: Leadership and Bondage" and "Freedom of Self-Consciousness: Stoicism, Skepticism and the Unhappy Consciousness"; chap. 4; and the opening section of chap. 6. Lewis points out that Du Bois had a genuine affinity for Hegel's *Phenomenology of Mind*, "and for all James' supposed pragmatic and empirical influence upon him, Du Bois found in the Hegelian World-Spirit, dialectically actualizing itself through history, a profoundly appealing concept" (Lewis 1993, 139).

2. James's and Dewey's psychological theories followed their pragmatic philosophy. In this sense, streams of consciousness that were in a continual state of flux, whose alterations reflected physiological changes within the individual, determined psychological states. Their stance, as with pragmatism generally, was a form of extreme methodological individualism and ahistoricism (James [1890] 1950; Dewey [1916] 1997).

References

Bourdieu, Pierre. 1977. *Outline of a Theory of Practice*. New York: Cambridge University Press.

Dewey, John. [1916] 1997. Theories of Knowledge. In *Pragmatism: A Reader*, ed. Louis Menand. New York: Vintage Books.

Du Bois, W.E.B. [1896] 1986. *The Suppression of the African Slave Trade to the United States of America 1638-1870*. New York: Library of America.

———. [1897] 1986. The Conservation of Races. In *W.E.B Du Bois: Writings*, ed. Nathan Huggins. New York: Library of America.

———. [1898] 1973. The Study of the Negro Problems. In *W.E.B. Du Bois on Sociology and the Black Community*, ed. Dan S. Green and Edwin D. Driver. Chicago: University of Chicago Press.

———. [1899] 1996. *The Philadelphia Negro: A Social Study*. Philadelphia: University of Pennsylvania Press.

———. [1903] 1986. *The Souls of Black Folk*. New York: Knopf.

———. [1904] 1996. On the Souls of Black Folk. In *W.E.B. Du Bois: A Reader*, ed. Eric J. Sundquist. New York: Oxford University Press.

———. [1924] 1992. *The Gift of Black Folk: The Negroes in the Making of America*. Millwood, NY: Kraus-Thomson Organization.

———. [1935] 1992. *Black Reconstruction in America 1860-1880*. New York: Atheneum.

———. 1939. *Black Folk Then and Now*. Millwood, NY: Kraus-Thomson Organization.

———. [1940] 1995. *Dusk of Dawn: An Essay Toward an Autobiography of a Race Concept*. New Brunswick, NJ: Transaction.

———. [1947] 1995. *The World and Africa*. New York: International.

———. [1961] 1996. Toussaint L'Ouverture. In *W.E.B. Du Bois: A Reader*, ed. Eric J. Sundquist. New York: Oxford University Press.

———. 1968. *The Autobiography of W.E.B. Du Bois*. New York: International.

———. 1995. The African Roots of the War. In *W.E.B. Du Bois: A Reader*, ed. David Levering Lewis. New York: Henry Holt. First published in *Atlantic Monthly* 115(May 1915):707-14.

Galton, Francis. 1869. *Hereditary Genius: An Inquiry into Its Laws and Consequences*. New York: D. Appleton.

Gooding-Williams, Robert. 1991-92. Evading Narrative Myth, Evading Prophetic Pragmatism: Cornel West's *The American Evasion of Philosophy*. *Massachusetts Review* Winter: 517-42.

Hegel, G.W.F. 1966. *The Phenomenology of Mind*. London: Allen & Unwin.

James, William. [1890] 1950. *Principles of Psychology*. Vol. 1. New York: Dover.

Lewis, David Levering. 1993. *W.E.B Du Bois: Biography of a Race 1868-1919*. New York: Henry Holt.

Marx, Karl. [1845] 1969. Theses on Feverback. In *Karl Marx and Frederick Engles: Selected Works in Three Volumes*. Vol. 1. Moscow: Progress.

Moses, Wilson. 1978. The *Golden Age of Black Nationalism, 1850-1925*. New York: Oxford University Press.

Rampersad, Arnold. 1976. *The Art and Imagination of W.E.B. Du Bois*. Cambridge, MA: Harvard University Press.

Smedley, Audrey. 1993. *Race in North America*. Boulder, CO: Westview Press.

Spencer, Herbert. 1889. *An Epitome of the Synthetic Philosophy*. London: Williams & Norgate.

West, Cornel. 1989. *The American Evasion of Philosophy: A Genealogy of Pragmatism*. Madison: University of Wisconsin Press.

Zamir, Shamoon. 1995. *Dark Voice: W.E.B. Du Bois and American Thought, 1888-1903*. Chicago: University of Chicago Press.

ANNALS, *AAPSS*, **568**, March 2000

W.E.B. Du Bois and "The Negro Church"

By BARBARA DIANNE SAVAGE

ABSTRACT: This article surveys W.E.B. Du Bois's political thought on the appropriate role of African American religion and religious institutions in the struggle for African American empowerment. More broadly, the discussion illuminates a vigorous debate in the early decades of the twentieth century among a wide variety of African American intellectuals and activists on this very question. The article concludes with a call for renewed research on the place of the church in political struggles, as this remains an area about which much is assumed but little is actually written.

Barbara Dianne Savage is assistant professor of history at the University of Pennsylvania. She is the author of Broadcasting Freedom: Radio, War, and the Politics of Race, 1938-1948 *(1999) and is currently working on an intellectual history of black religion and black politics.*

A MONG his many other achieve-ments, W.E.B. Du Bois is one of the scholars often credited with pioneering the field of black church history. Yet there has been little consideration of his ideas on the question of where "the Negro church" or African American religious beliefs ought to fit, if at all, in strategies for the political and economic advancement of black people. An impassioned but overlooked debate on that very question marked the early decades of twentieth-century African American history. This article analyzes Du Bois's place in that discussion and concludes by renewing his 1899 call for more historical research on black religion and religious institutions, expanded by my own appeal for special attention to the relationship between African American religion and political empowerment.

Assessments of Du Bois's personal religious sentiments have come to mixed conclusions, with Herbert Aptheker defending him as an agnostic and not an atheist but also as someone sympathetic to social Christianity (Aptheker 1982). Manning Marable has written a brief but nuanced account of what he calls Du Bois's "revulsion" and "curious attentiveness" to the black church. Marable concludes that Du Bois ultimately endorsed the notion that black Christianity had met the challenge of its radical potential, not only in the United States but in the larger world (Marable 1985).

However, Du Bois's overall stance toward black Christianity and the black church remained far from celebratory. Even when he acknowl-edged the centrality of the church to black life, including black political life, his greatest ideological consistency was seeing that fact not as a strength but as an impediment to be overcome or managed. I also argue that in this respect Du Bois was not singular but one among a chorus of African American intellectuals and activists spanning a variety of political viewpoints and religious orientations. This brief exploration of African American political thought on black religion and racial advancement also illuminates how variegated those ideas are, including those of Du Bois, whose multiplicity eludes the dichotomous paradigms often imposed upon him. In this way, I align myself with those who warn against tendencies to reduce Du Bois and the rich diversity of African American political ideas to oversimplified monolithic slogans (Reed 1997; Moses 1992, 1998).

DU BOIS ON BLACK RELIGION

What is most striking about Du Bois's 1898 *Annals* article, "The Study of the Negro Problems," is how little attention he devotes to black religion and the black church as he lays out his brief research agenda. He did include among his defining social characteristics of black people the fact that they were "members of Christian churches"; he also suggested that historical studies of enslaved Americans include attention to their "conversion to Christianity," which he saw as a part of the "social evolution" which separated them from their "savage ancestors." It was in his call for historical study that he placed "the rise of such peculiar expressions of Negro social history, as the Negro church." So again, his interest in the church was historical in this piece, and not statistical or anthropological or sociological, the other three broad areas of study he outlined (Du Bois 1898, 4, 5, 14, 18).

It is somewhat ironic that, as Du Bois envisioned his research project then, the church of his own day did not figure in it, even as it would become somewhat more prominent in the actual study published a year later. In that study, The Philadelphia Negro, Du Bois characterized the organized church as a "curious phenomenon" that represented "all that was left of African tribal life" and that blended both family and ritual functions in an all-encompassing way. "So far-reaching are these functions of the church," he concluded, "that its organization is almost political" (Du Bois [1899] 1996, 197, 201).

Elsewhere in this same study, Du Bois cast the church first as a social institution, then as a religious institution. Because of their unique position as black institutions, Du Bois concluded that "all movements for social betterment are apt to centre in the churches" where the "race problem in all its phases is continually being discussed." Yet his praise of the church rang faintly, as he ended by chiding churches for what he saw as the distractions of extravagance and internal dissension which spoiled their greater potential (Du Bois [1899] 1996, 205, 207, 234).

In an essay written a year later and subsequently published as a chapter in The Souls of Black Folk, Du Bois reaffirmed the prominence of the church in black life but was more openly critical of the passivity implicit in Christian doctrine. He judged that its principles were well suited to the slave but unsuitable for contemporary political and social needs which in his view were being ignored by the black Methodist and Baptist churches with their emphasis on "religious feeling and fervor" (Du Bois 1900). When Du Bois published his Atlanta University study The Negro Church in 1903, his frustration was more apparent in a statement in which he, joined by Mary Church Terrell and sociologist Kelly Miller, called for a religious rebirth for black people—one that would move the church away from "emotional fervor" toward becoming a "mighty social power" and the "most powerful agency in the moral development and social reform of 9,000,000 Americans of Negro blood" (Du Bois 1903a, 207-8).

Despite Du Bois's poignant embrace of the power of black spirituals in The Souls of Black Folk (Du Bois [1903b] 1997), he also reasserted there his sense of failed potential in black church leadership, even as he continued to accept the significance of the church in black communities. In editorials written for The Crisis in the decade to follow, Du Bois continued this pattern of praising the black church but harshly criticizing its leadership for being "pretentious," "dishonest and immoral"; for failing to address the real economic needs of its members; and for driving away educated and energetic black men and women who do not subscribe to "unimportant dogmas and ancient and outworn creeds" (Du Bois 1912, 1916).

AFRICAN AMERICAN THOUGHT ON BLACK RELIGION AND CHURCHES

Although this critique may seem all too familiar, it is valuable to be reminded that the church was viewed at the beginning of the twentieth century not as a powerfully engaged political actor but rather an aged, sleeping giant squandering its potential. And Du Bois was by no means alone in this assessment. When Carter G. Woodson first published *The History of the Negro Church* in 1921, a book which to date has no rival as a claimed history of the black church, he echoed many of these same criticisms in his narrative historical account (Woodson 1921; Raboteau 1990). Woodson diagnosed the church as suffering not only from a generational divide, a class divide, and a regional one but ultimately from a division over differences in ideas about the "importance of the church in the life of the community" (Woodson 1921, 130, 141, 145).

Indeed for Woodson, rather than being a unifying force for black people, the church had become its primary divisive force, splitting the black community into conservatives who embraced the old-time religion in style and doctrine, and progressives who wanted both religion and education and a more modern style of worship and theology—divisions which themselves mirrored larger political differences. At the same time, he did credit the church with doing some good and deflected some of the criticism of the black church onto white Christianity, which he characterized as "not interested in the real mission of Christ," adding as an aside that Jesus would be lynched if he were on the scene (Woodson 1921, 224, 226-27, 230, 282-83, 295, 301).

Still, like Du Bois, Woodson did not, or perhaps could not, advocate for an absolute dismissal of church life but rather argued for its reform from within. In this way, he too conceded the enduring staying power of black churches and preachers but urged that they embrace the "things of this world—promoting education, health, recreation, social welfare." But on the specific question of black preachers' involvement in political activity, Woodson cautioned that "preachers have done their best political work by protest from outside the machine" (Woodson 1921, 257, 288, 295, 299).

The criticisms of the black church Du Bois and Woodson outlined in these early works were voiced by others as well. For example, Kelly Miller, in a 1914 article on "The Ministry," argued boldly that Du Bois's so-called talented tenth of the race ought to simply take over the leadership of black churches, pleading that otherwise, "if the blind lead the blind, will not both fall into the ditch?" More explicitly, he suggested that the talented ought to simply flood into the ministry itself and assume the leadership of black religious institutions and life (Miller [1914] 1969, 203-4, 214, 217).

Black women writers and activists in this period attributed some of their disappointment about the black church specifically to ministerial domination of church policy. Ida B. Wells and Fannie Williams, for example, were among many black woman activists who described black preachers as "corrupt" and "ignorant," with Williams arguing that black advancement was "more hindered" by the ministerial leadership "than by any other single cause" (White 1999, 73-74).

Indeed, Wells had left a church in disgust when a bishop failed to remove a minister who had been implicated in a morals scandal. Wells's more pointed general criticism, however, was that some black preachers were too timid politically, based on her experience trying to organize protest meetings about lynchings. For example, in the aftermath of a 1908 lynching in Springfield, Illinois, Wells could not convince her own church or any other in Chicago to allow her to hold a public meeting about it. That action led her to use her own home instead as a site for a series of meetings on that and other political issues (Duster 1970, 297-304; Townes 1993, 162).

Even as Wells aimed her criticism directly at the political timidity of ministerial leadership, some other black women observers shared, along with their male counterparts, an abhorrence for traditional black religious practices that were, in their

eyes, unrefined and too emotionally charged. Anna Julia Cooper called that style of worship "ludicrous" and "semi-civilized." For Mary Church Terrell and Alice Dunbar-Nelson, expressions of religious fervor by black women were especially distasteful and frightful to some extent, with Terrell calling it "discouraging and shocking to see how some of the women shout, holler and dance during services." Dunbar-Nelson chided those who participated for reinforcing negative images of black women in particular as primitive and, though unstated, as highly eroticized as well (White 1999, 72).

Here, and in the writings of men like Du Bois, Woodson, and others in this period, one sees quite clearly the intraracial class bias implicit in these critiques of black worship practices. Black religiosity itself had become a central class marker, intertwined with notions about workingclass, rural southerners or their recently migrated northern urban kin.

Nevertheless, Evelyn Higginbotham cautions that many black Baptist women who objected to the emotionalism of black worship practices were not rejecting the practices themselves, as some of them also engaged in similar expressions during worship services. Rather, Higginbotham concluded, they were objecting to an excessive reliance on emotionalism in the absence of any meaningful social program. Nannie Burroughs, the activist founder of the Women's Convention of the National Baptist Convention, argued that "the church should not substitute shouting for service," as she chastised the black clergy for preaching "too much Heaven and too little practical Christian living" (Higginbotham 1993, 175-76).

Black women's criticisms of ministers were often twofold then, aimed both at what they saw as their lack of moral or intellectual leadership and their political conservatism. Burroughs and other black Baptist women had in their minds a model of the black church's public responsibilities that shared some philosophical similarity to the settlement house, social gospel, and other progressive movements of the late nineteenth and early twentieth centuries. They emphasized a service-oriented church, actively engaged in helping to meet the day-to-day needs of its community, such as literacy training, medical care, clothing and feeding the poor, and recreational services. Indeed, Burroughs argued in 1914 that "no church should be allowed to stay in a community that does not positively improve community life" (Higginbotham 1993, 172-74, 176).

Burroughs's vision of an engaged black church was not limited, however, to the notion of spiritual and social service provider. Along with other black Baptist women leaders like Willie Layten, she also actively encouraged black women to enter the world of electoral politics, initially as church-based organizers and political educators but then, more emphatically, as newly franchised voters after the passage of women's suffrage. Layten specifically urged that black churches become centers for voter education in an attempt to take political advantage of the growing numbers of northern black urban dwellers during the great migration (Higginbotham 1996, 149, 151-53; Higginbotham 1990, 199-220; Terborg-Penn 1983, 1998).

PUBLIC DEBATES
ON BLACK RELIGION
AND BLACK POLITICS

Concerns among certain black intellectuals and activists about the social and political responsibility of the black church became much more public in the 1920s and early 1930s when a passionate debate about these issues played itself out on the pages of popular newspapers and magazines, both black and white. The proliferation of attention to the black church in this period stems from several demographic, cultural, and political factors. This interwar period of economic depression had brought with it a steady stream of black migration, a rise in black church memberships, and a growing variety of black religious sects, developments apparent to many observers. Garveyism, a movement that has been characterized as a religious movement itself, also rose to popularity during this time (Burkett 1978; Wilmore [1973] 1983; Marable 1989).

This was an era also marked by the growth of the secular black press, a fact usually overlooked in discussions of this period. As a consequence of that development, the domination of reporting about religious issues by black denominational publishing houses also came under challenge. Black newspapers in the late 1920s and 1930s reported widely on religion and on the activities of various churches and denominations.

These papers also devoted prominent attention to the unscrupulous practices, financial and sexual, of black preachers and denominational leaders, including several notorious and scintillating cases of alleged abuses. There also was a fair amount of sensationalized reporting on the emergence of alternative black religious groups, which were characterized as cults, including, for example, close attention to black Jews and followers of Father Divine, Elder Micheaux, Mother Catherine, and others.

In all these ways, the black press itself emerged as a new forum for considering the issue of the black church's political responsibility. And yet this was also a forum where the voices of black women in particular remained largely unheard, so that the public debates about the church's public duties and potential largely excluded the people most likely to be church members and church workers.

The editorial pages and opinion columns in black newspapers in the 1920s and 1930s reflected several sides of the continuing debate about the political role of the black church, including the points of view of men who staunchly defended the church against liberal critics whether black or white. One example illustrates the complexity of these exchanges. In 1925, Kelly Miller, who as noted earlier held his own critical views of the church, nonetheless used his column in the *Amsterdam News* to counter a speech to the NAACP by Clarence Darrow in which he reportedly had urged blacks to turn away from religion, to stop depending on God, and to learn to depend on themselves for their own advancement. Darrow, who had successfully defended a black Detroit doctor against charges of murder in protecting his home from attack by a white mob, was considered an ally in the cause for black justice, but Miller sharply chastised him for straying from the field of legal to that of religious advice (Miller 1925).

Miller argued that "religious reliance" had been the mainstay of black existence and survival and that it also gave the race "great moral advantage" in its appeals to the conscience of white Americans, conceding that because they lacked the "compulsion of power," blacks were forced to rely on moral appeals (Miller 1925). In effect, Miller carried forward an argument based on the view of the black church as the institutional home for political and moral claims for racial advancement; abandoning it without an alternative was unthinkable for him—even as he continued to criticize aspects of black church life.

This incident with Clarence Darrow also drew Du Bois's attention, as he used the incident both to defend Darrow's right to criticize black churches and to praise the implicit arguments in those criticisms. In Du Bois's view, Darrow was only saying what African American church members were already saying, that the church was "spending too much money for church edifices, and not enough for the social uplift which Christianity stands for." Du Bois also used the incident to caution black churches away from excluding dissident views, a malady he associated specifically with white Christianity. Arguing against the practice of letting theological differences divide political allies, Du Bois concluded by asking, "What difference does it make whether the whale swallowed Jonah or Jonah swallowed the whale, so long as Justice, Mercy and Peace prevail?" (Du Bois 1983b, 516).

Even as Du Bois agreed with some of Darrow's criticisms, he did not argue for the outright rejection of black Christianity or the church itself as Darrow had suggested. In this way, Du Bois's stance was consistent with that of other African Americans who questioned but did not dismiss the links between black religion and black political empowerment. Perhaps the most notable aspect of this controversy is the paucity of arguments for the church's or religion's political irrelevancy.

In fact, even A. Philip Randolph, the well-known Socialist and labor leader, took a cautious stance on the question of the place of black religion in the struggles of black workers. At a 1929 conference on labor and religion, Randolph instead prodded the black church to champion a proletarian philosophy and align itself with the struggle of black workers who formed the mass of church members. But his arguments were couched in deferential terms and offered with a homage to the importance of the church to past political gains made by the race (Randolph 1969).

This mixed approach owed itself to Randolph's own experience organizing Pullman porters, where, although he observed that it was rare to find a black preacher who was committed to the cause of unionism per se, he also admitted that church meeting spaces and financial support from individual preachers and churches had been crucial to his movement's strength. He included a list of those who had supported the Pullman porters, calling them "outstanding, independent, progressive, intellectual Negro preachers" (Randolph 1969, 634).

So Randolph's was not a dismissive critique but a rather respectful one asking for the church's continued support as "a constructive social, educational and spiritual service to the Negro workers"—a plea the Socialist Randolph grounded in biblical imperative. "If the Church, white or black, is to express the true philosophy of Jesus Christ, Himself a worker," he concluded, "it will not lend itself to the creed of oppressive capitalism which would deny to the servant his just hire" (Randolph 1969, 636).

As Randolph's remarks remind us, leaders of black political and civic organizations often depended on black churches for meeting space and for support of their programs. Some black religious leaders were especially irked when these same organizations would denounce black churches, and the fact of their reliance on church resources was sometimes raised to counter those criticisms. For example, when the NAACP's *Crisis* magazine published an especially critical article on the black southern church and the "preachocracy" in 1935, an editorial writer defending the church in the *Washington Tribune* made just that point: "Abuse of the church is a favorite theme for many Negro intellectuals—but when any of them desire to stage a 'drive' or 'put over a program,' straight way he seeks the preacher to furnish the audience and the opportunity" ("Southern Negro" 1935).

WHITE CRITICS, BLACK DEFENDERS

Some of the harshest criticisms of black churches in this period came from white intellectuals, some of whom were critical of religion generally and of black religion in particular. In these cases, as with the Darrow incident, African American intellectuals and religious leaders who were themselves critical of some aspects of black religion nonetheless vigorously defended the church against these attacks. In 1927, Kelly Miller, who had countered Darrow, also debated the question of whether Christianity handicapped black progress with V. F. Calverton, editor of the *Modern Quarterly*. Calverton attacked black Christians as naive, with Miller once again defending black religious faith itself—and not just the church as an institution—as politically necessary especially in the absence of an alternative or substitute. "Like Ghandi, of India," Miller argued, "the Negro must employ passive, moral resistance until he is able to match power with power" ("Christian Religion" 1927).

Other white intellectuals also aimed pointed criticism at African American religion and churches. H. L. Mencken, who opposed religion generally, wrote an essay in 1931 for *Opportunity* magazine in which he characterized black Christianity as "extraordinarily stupid, ignorant, barbaric and preposterous," arguing that it rested on the teachings of "moron Negro theologians" who were "bold and insatiable parasites." In this case, the Reverend Adam Clayton Powell responded by reminding Mencken that the black church was the "only church that has persistently opposed lynching" and that "the Negro pulpit is the only pulpit that has unceasingly preached the brotherhood of man." But Powell also agreed with Mencken's assessment that there were too many black churches and that too many of its leaders were in fact "parasites" (Mencken 1931; Powell 1931; "Dr. A. Clayton Powell" 1931).

Du Bois used the liberal Protestant magazine *The Christian Century* as a forum to reenter these discussions about religion and political responsibility. He shifted critical focus away from the black church onto white Christianity in an essay entitled "Will the Church Remove the Color Line?" In answering the specific question he had posed, Du Bois concluded that the Christian church would ignore the race problem as long as possible and then claim credit for any subsequent progress that did occur. For Du Bois, the Christian church was "consistently on the wrong side" of political issues, rejecting the despised, the lowly, and the unfortunate, standing on "the side of wealth and power" (Du Bois 1931, 1554, 1556).

Du Bois's broad critique of white Christianity was not a new theme but an enduring one for him. Indeed, one of his most developed analyses of white Christianity had come in 1907, in an address delivered before the Philadelphia Divinity School. There, Du Bois asserted that as a matter of history African Americans looked "upon the white churches not as examples but with a sort of silent contempt and a real inner questioning of the genuineness of their Christianity." For him, white Christianity suffered from an ethical paradox because of its practices of racial and class-based exclusions (Washington and Du Bois 1907, 176, 181).

Although he criticized white Christianity in general, Du Bois also specifically pointed to southern Christians as being in a particular ethical dilemma. He had concluded that there was "no more pitiable paradox than that of the young white Christian in the South today who really believes in the ethics of Jesus Christ. . . . Who can doubt that if Christ came to Georgia to-day one of His first deeds would be to sit down and take supper with black men, and who can doubt the outcome if He did?" (Washington and Du Bois 1907, 176, 177, 181).

Similarly, nearly two decades later in 1923, Du Bois had concluded that one of the defining characteristics and strengths of the black church was its refusal to engage in exclusionary practices, which kept it from becoming the closed and hypocritical institution he believed the white church and white Christianity to be.

And for him, the racially and economically exclusionary nature of white churches rendered them ill-suited to claim the banner of Christianity at all. Indeed, he argued ultimately that black Americans occupied a singular place as a true American exemplar of Christian ethics and that their brand of Christianity was part of what made black people a national asset (Du Bois 1982). This idea of the redemptive or messianic potential of black Christianity was an enduring theme among a variety of African American thinkers, extending back at least as far as David Walker (Moses 1992).

MODELS FOR CHANGE

Even as he reserved his harshest criticism for white churches and white Christianity, Du Bois did not cease in his reproach of black churches, but he did shift once again in his characterization of their institutional responsibility. In 1937, as he had in his earliest writings about the church, he cautioned against judging the black church as a religious institution at all, as it was in his view primarily a social and an economic institution rather than a religious one. For him, the tantalizing potential of the black church rested in its enormous economic potential. Citing the scale of property owned by black churches, built "literally from the pennies of the poor," Du Bois argued that "we get some idea of . . . how easily it could be for the Negro, properly led, to do in a more purely economic field the same sort of thing" (Du Bois 1983a, 212).

By the late 1930s, then, Du Bois had returned to his earlier notion that the black church was not so much a religious institution as a potential unit of economic cooperation and unity. This change was very much in keeping with broader shifts in his own thinking in this period on the importance of building a new economic base for black people. He conceived then of "the new Negro Church" that would inspire its members with "high ideals of good deeds, and not simply entertain them or scare them or merely yell at them." But "above all, the business activities of the new Negro Church must be more systematic"; it should "buy and pay for homes of the church members" and get them jobs and organize "buying clubs and co-operative effort" (Du Bois [1917] 1985, 85). That would be its greatest strategic, empowering role—its greatest political offering in strategies for black advancement.

Du Bois had concluded that both the black church and the white church were essentially economic institutions, with the black church offering to its members its potential as a cooperative communal enterprise. The white church had always in his view been an economic organization where "any action or program that threatens income has little chance for recognition and none for adoption" (Du Bois [1939] 1997, 195).

While Du Bois was conceiving of the church as an economic unit, others in this period also had ideas about the potential power implicit in consolidating black religious organizations. There had been proposals in the late nineteenth century to combine the various black Methodist denominations under a single unit, and that idea received renewed attention in the 1930s as well (Walker 1982).

Carter Woodson proposed something more provocative, calling for the creation of a single United Negro Church, encompassing all black churches, erasing all other denominational affiliations. Unlike Du Bois, with his emphasis on the black church's economic potential, Woodson was interested in the political power that could come from creating a single national black mass organization of such magnitude. Others in this period, like Bishops Reverdy Ransom and R. R. Wright, Jr., of the African Methodist Episcopal Church, advocated linking black churches across denominations around a single program of social service delivery and public policy engagement (Woodson 1931; Wills 1978; Wright 1965; Sawyer 1994).

These quite different ideas all reflect attempts in the 1930s to convert congregations of black people across regional and denominational lines into a mass organizing base for greater political, social, and economic power. Although unrealized at the time, this notion had such appeal precisely because of the tantalizing potential of creating a nation of black people united by religion but organized for political purposes.

CONCLUSION

Revealed here are a variety of ideas among African American intellectuals and activists in the early decades of this century about the place of black religion and black religious institutions in the struggle for black advancement. Implicit in the chorus of complaints against the church is a call for the church to be all things to all people, to be the savior institution at a time when the institutional infrastructure—economic, political, and social—of the African American community was seen as so very limited.

The litany of criticisms also points to a gap between reality and perception, between history and myth perhaps, but more important toward the need for historical attention to this entire subject. Some have dismissed criticisms of the church as being limited to antireligious secular intellectuals, but that is not the case. Many of those men and women who questioned and defended the church's political position were themselves believers or church members, like Miller, Woodson, and Burroughs, or even church leaders like Powell, Ransom, and Wright. The debate about what the church ought to be doing or how religion ought to be employed involved a wide range of African Americans, spanning generations, ideologies, and regions.

Often it also is our impression that objections to the black church focus narrowly on class-bound notions of parasitic preachers, religious primitivism, and ignorant parishioners. But, clearly, it was a broader critique even as the use of those images may have masked that complexity. The criticisms often had shifting targets— sometimes the religious leadership, sometimes it was church members, sometimes the hypocrisy and racism of American Christianity, sometimes the conservatism and passivity of black Christianity.

One part of that debate over what the church's political role ought to be is a tug-of-war for political leadership between African Americans who favored a religiously based leadership and those who did not, between those who saw the enormous political potential of church-based organizing and those who feared the unchecked political influence of religious leaders. But it also appears to be a debate that did not rest particularly upon a critique of religion as dampening or anesthetizing the political will of the masses. Rather, these specific ideas reflected broader varieties of political thought among African Americans on the quite different question of how the church could best advance the race or how it could make itself more politically relevant, and perhaps even more central to the lives of people than it already was for many.

More subtle and nuanced layers of this debate are yet to be uncovered, some of which will be revealed through an examination of core definitional questions concerning, for example, the evolution of the concept of "the Negro church" itself, a phrase which most use quite confidently and loosely without ever defining it—a pattern which extends to the term "black church." Neither term captures the variety of black religious practices, organizations, and activities within that broad configuration.

In addition, more attention to the concept of the "political" itself is essential, especially here where the notions of spiritual and political empowerment overlap but where the spiritual is often ignored or under-emphasized in analyses which rely on scholarly tools unsuited to the task of examining the spiritual. By adopting a wide rather than narrow definition of the political, one is better able to include also the ideas and work of those usually excluded from the public sphere of traditional definitions of politics—in this case, the women who constituted the mass of black church memberships. For what is absent from both this article and most historical accounts about the black church are the voices of the people who filled the pews, the choirs, the usher boards, the auxiliaries, in effect, the lay members and leaders of these religious organizations—predominantly voices of women.

For those black men and women who were both devout and devoted, the church offered some vital appeal as a source of spiritual nurturance and power. How those people who in turn empowered the church answered the question of the church's political role remains largely a mystery at this point, but it is also a line of inquiry which I am most eager to see pursued. Without the voices of those who constituted, supported, and maintained the wide variety of black religious activity captured under the rubric of "the black church," we cannot answer the broader questions at hand. After all, religious organizations are among the most voluntary and independent of associations, and for those who tried to move black churches, individually and collectively, toward greater political agency, the

questions that also beg are whose church is it and who defines its meaning and its missions, whether political or otherwise.

A century after Du Bois sketched out his research plan, his call for scholarly attention to black religion and religious institutions still requires our response. As for Du Bois, blessed as he was with a long life, his views on African American religion and the place of the church in political struggles would continue to shift over time, in periods beyond the 30 years examined in this article. But today, with the renewal of calls for faith-based initiatives, black religion and religious institutions are once again expected to deliver black communities out of the wilderness created by centuries of economic, political, and social isolation. In some ways, as history teaches us, the more things change, the more they remain the same.

References

Aptheker, Herbert. 1982. W.E.B. Du Bois and Religion: A Brief Reassessment. *Journal of Religious Thought* 39(Spring/Summer):5-11.

Burkett, Randall K. 1978. *Garveyism as a Religious Movement: The Institutionalization of a Black Civil Religion.* Metuchen, NJ: Scarecrow Press.

Christian Religion Called Handicap to Negro in Debate. 1927. *Amsterdam News*, 17 Apr.

Dr. A. Clayton Powell Makes Bitter Attack on Henry L. Mencken's View on Negro Ministers and Christianity. 1931. *New York Age*, 28 Feb.

Du Bois, W.E.B. 1898. The Study of the Negro Problems. *The Annals* of the

American Academy of Political and Social Science, Jan.:1-23.

————. [1899] 1996. *The Philadelphia Negro*. Philadelphia: University of Pennsylvania Press.

————. 1900. Of the Faith of the Fathers. *The New World: A Quarterly Review of Religion, Ethics and Theology* 9(Dec.):614-25.

————. 1903a. *The Negro Church: Report of a Social Study Made Under the Direction of Atlanta University*. Atlanta, GA: Atlanta University Press.

————. [1903b] 1997. *The Souls of Black Folk*. Boston: Bedford Books.

————. 1912. *The Crisis* 1(May):4.

————. 1916. *The Crisis* 6(Apr.):11.

————. [1917] 1985. The New Negro Church. In *Against Racism: Unpublished Essays, Papers, Addresses, 1887-1961*, ed. Herbert Aptheker. Amherst: University of Massachusetts.

————. 1931. Will the Church Remove the Color Line? *Christian Century* 9 Dec.:1554-56.

————. [1939] 1997. Letter to Reverend William Crowe, Jr., 9 August. In *Correspondence of W.E.B. Du Bois*. Vol. 2, *Selections, 1934-1944*, ed. Herbert Aptheker. Millwood, NY: Kraus-Thomson Organization.

————. 1982. The Negro as a National Asset. In *Writings by W.E.B. Du Bois in Periodicals Edited by Others*, vol. 2, *1910-1934*, ed. Herbert Aptheker. Millwood, NY: Kraus-Thomson Organization. Reprinted from *Homiletic Review* 86 (July 1982):52-58.

————. 1983a. The Co-Operative Negro Church. In *Newspaper Columns of W.E.B. Du Bois*, vol. 1, *1883-1944*, ed. Herbert Aptheker. White Plains, NY: Kraus-Thomson Organization. Reprinted from *Pittsburgh Courier*, 19 June 1937.

————. 1983b. Darrow. In *Writings in Periodicals Edited by W.E.B. Du Bois: Selections from* The Crisis, vol. 2, *1926-1934*, ed. Herbert Aptheker. Millwood, NY: Kraus-Thomson Organization. Reprinted from *The Crisis* 35(June 1928):203.

Duster, Alfreda, ed. 1970. *Crusade for Justice: The Autobiography of Ida B. Wells*. Chicago: University of Chicago Press.

Higginbotham, Evelyn Brooks. 1990. In Politics to Stay: Black Women Leaders and Party Politics in the 1920s. In *Women, Politics, and Change*, ed. Louise A. Tilly and Patricia Gurin. New York: Russell Sage Foundation.

————. 1993. *Righteous Discontent: The Women's Movement in the Black Baptist Church, 1880-1920*. Cambridge, MA: Harvard University Press.

————. 1996. Religion, Politics, and Gender: The Leadership of Nannie Helen Burroughs. In *This Far by Faith: Readings in African-American Women's Religious Biography*, ed. Judith Weisenfeld and Richard Newman. New York: Routledge.

Marable, Manning. 1985. The Black Faith of W.E.B. Du Bois: Sociocultural and Political Dimensions of Black Religion. *Southern Quarterly: A Journal of the Arts in the South* 23(3):15-33.

————. 1989. Religion and Black Protest Thought in American History. In *African American Religious Studies*, ed. Gayraud S. Wilmore. Durham, NC: Duke University Press.

Mencken, H. L. 1931. The Burden of Credulity. *Opportunity* Feb.:40-41.

Miller, Kelly. [1914] 1969. *Out of the House of Bondage*. New York: Arno Press.

————. 1925. Darrow's Advice to the Negro. *Amsterdam News*, 26 Dec.

Moses, Wilson Jeremiah. 1992. *Black Messiahs and Uncle Toms: Social and Literary Manipulations of a Religious Myth*. University Park: Pennsylvania State University Press.

———. 1998. *Afrotopia: The Roots of African American Popular History*. New York: Cambridge University Press.

Powell, A. Clayton. 1931. H. L. Mencken Finds Flowers in a "Dunghill." *Opportunity* Mar.:72-73.

Raboteau, Albert J. et al. 1990. Retelling Carter Woodson's Story: Archival Sources for Afro-American Church History. *Journal of American History* 77(1):183.

Randolph, A. Philip. 1969. Negro Labor and the Church. In *A Documentary History of the Negro People of the United States, 1910-1932*, ed. Herbert Aptheker. Secaucus, NJ: Citadel Press. Reprinted from *Labor Speaks for Itself on Religion: A Symposium of Labor Leaders Throughout the World* (New York: Macmillan, 1929).

Reed, Adolph. 1997. W.E.B. *Du Bois and American Political Thought: Fabianism and the Color Line*. New York: Oxford University Press.

Sawyer, Mary R. 1994. *Black Ecumenism: Implementing the Demands of Justice*. Valley Forge, PA: Trinity Press.

Southern Negro and the Church, The. 1935. *Washington Tribune*, 4 Apr.

Terborg-Penn, Rosalyn. 1983. Discontented Black Feminists: Prelude and Postscript to the Passage of the Nineteenth Amendment. In *Decades of Discontent: The Women's Movement, 1920-1940*, ed. Lois Scharf and Joan M. Jensen. Westport, CT: Greenwood Press.

———. 1998. *African American Women in the Struggle for the Vote, 1850-1920*. Bloomington: Indiana University Press.

Townes, Emilie M. 1993. Because God Gave Her Vision: The Religious Impulse of Ida B. Wells-Barnett. In *Spirituality and Social Responsibility: Vocational Vision of Women in the United Methodist Tradition*, ed. Rosemary Skinner Keller. Nashville, TN: Abingdon Press.

Walker, Clarence E. 1982. *A Rock in a Weary Land: The African Methodist Episcopal Church During the Civil War and Reconstruction*. Baton Rouge: Louisiana State University Press.

Washington, Booker T. and W.E.B. Du Bois. 1907. *The Negro in the South: His Economic Progress in Relation to His Moral and Religious Development*. Philadelphia: G. W. Jacobs.

White, Deborah Gray. 1999. *Too Heavy a Load: Black Women in Defense of Themselves, 1894-1994*. New York: Norton.

Wills, David. 1978. Reverdy C. Ransom: The Making of an A.M.E. Bishop. In *Black Apostles: Afro-American Clergy Confront the Twentieth Century*, ed. Randall K. Burkett and Richard Newman. Boston: G.K. Hall.

Wilmore, Gayraud. [1973] 1983. *Black Religion and Black Radicalism: An Interpretation of the Religious History of Afro-American People*. Maryknoll, NY: Orbis Books.

Woodson, Carter G. 1921. *The History of the Negro Church*. Washington, DC: Associated.

———. 1931. A United Negro Church. *New York Age*, 15 Aug.

Wright, Richard. R., Jr. 1965. *87 Years Behind the Black Curtain*. Philadelphia: A.M.E. Book Concern.

ANNALS, *AAPSS*, **568**, March 2000

Romancing the Body Politic:
Du Bois's Propaganda of the Dark World

By HERMAN BEAVERS

ABSTRACT: Although best known for his work as a sociologist, historian, and editor, W.E.B. Du Bois also authored numerous works of fiction and poetry. Despite their dismissal by critics as not much more than failed experiments that test the boundary separating poetry and prose, this article suggests that Du Bois's acts of creative composition are driven by his desire to exert critical force as part of his contribution to the effort of studying "Negro problems." Du Bois's creative writing can be understood as recapitulations of his enterprise as a social scientist and as an attempt to dramatize the workings of the American body politic. As social scientist, Du Bois manifests a vision of what his training allowed him to assert through organized, scientific study. However, as creative writer, Du Bois mediates this project by positing the need for heroic action in issues of gender and sexuality and presents a way to think about African American representations of masculinity in the twentieth century.

Herman Beavers is associate professor of English and director of the Afro-American Studies Program at the University of Pennsylvania. He is the author of two books: A Neighborhood of Feeling *(1986), a chapbook of poems, and* Wrestling Angels into Song: The Fictions of Ernest J. Gaines and James Alan McPherson *(1994). He is currently at work on* Prodigal Allegories, *a study on representations of African masculinity in the twentieth century and a collection of poems entitled* Still Life with Guitar.

I T is perhaps more than a coincidence that Esau, the disinherited brother of Jacob, figures into a number of texts produced by African American male writers at the beginning of the twentieth century. As we can observe in works by Paul Laurence Dunbar, James Weldon Johnson, and W.E.B. Du Bois, Esau's decision to trade his birthright figures into discussions that are meant to evoke the tenuousness, if not the futility, of black political life in America. Johnson's invocation of Esau comes at the end of *The Autobiography of an Ex-Colored Man*, where the nameless protagonist, having denounced his claim to membership in the black race, declares, "I cannot repress the thought that, after all, I have chosen the lesser part, that I have sold my birthright for a mess of pottage" (Johnson [1927] 1965, 511).

Dunbar's collection of stories, *The Strength of Gideon*, published in 1900, some 12 years prior to Johnson's novel, finds him turning to prose fiction in order to protest racial injustice of the sort to be found in the United States at the turn of the century. That injustice, Dunbar suggests, is most evident in the realm of electoral politics, particularly as it relates to the black community's relationship to the Republican Party. Dunbar's decision to depict the exigencies of political participation has ironic overtones in light of the disenfranchisement of Southern blacks. But as a Northerner writing about the world with which he is most familiar, Dunbar undertakes to depict in "A Mess of Pottage" (which could be where Johnson got the idea for how to end his novel), "Mr.

Cornelius Johnson, Office Seeker," and "A Council of State" the ways that even in the North, blacks play at best a marginal role in electoral politics. In these stories, Dunbar does not hesitate to provide images of black folk undone by their self-importance and political naïveté.

Du Bois takes up the image of Esau early on in *Darkwater: Voices from the Veil*, where in The Credo he asserts,

I believe in the Training of Children, black even as white; the leading out of little souls into the green pastures and beside the still waters, not for pelf or peace, but for life lit by some large vision of beauty and goodness and truth; lest we forget, and the sons of the fathers, like Esau, for mere meat barter their birthright in a mighty nation. (Du Bois [1920] 1969, 4)

It is easy to note the lyricism of the passage, but consider as well the way Du Bois links education to communal memory, as if to suggest that the role of the educator is (as his reference to the Twenty-Third Psalm would indicate) that of both shepherd and repository of collective memory. As Du Bois insists, lack of education creates a community ripe for exploitation, prone to squander its political resources (their "birthright in a mighty nation") in exchange for spoils that have little value in the public sphere.

Looking more closely at Dunbar, one notes that the figure of Esau has much to do with his realization that the black community is often driven, like Esau, by a sense of immediacy, an investment in short-term strategies that are characterized by negotiation and barter for goods which threaten black political capital. In the biblical narrative, Esau "sells" his birthright to Jacob when his bodily needs outweigh his investment in the future. For Dunbar and Du Bois to invoke him intimates the ways that each was aware of the need for a unified and coherent political agenda for the black community, one which avoided becoming bogged down in the quagmire of electoral politics, opting instead for a more messianic vision.

This is much more manifest in Du Bois's work than in Dunbar's. Dunbar opts to rely instead on ironic portrayals of black political ineffectualness. In "A Mess of Pottage," he depicts a black community, referred to as "Little Africa," as the object of a political struggle between the Democratic and Republican Party candidates during a gubernatorial election. As the story opens, Dunbar characterizes the Democratic Party as a group resigned to its lack of influence in the black community. Besides distributing money in Little Africa to gain influence, an act Democrats believe will not work to their advantage, the black community is seen as being so solidly Republican that the latter party takes them for granted, noting, "We've got 'em just like that" (Dunbar, 1900, 212).

As it turns out, however, the Democratic candidate for governor decides that winning the election means going to the black community in person, "carrying the war into the enemy's country" (241). As a man with "a convincing way of making others see as he [sees]," Mr. Lane concludes that black votes go to the Republican Party because "those people go one way because they are never invited to go another" (242), at which point he resolves to meet with the leading Republican power broker in Little Africa, Deacon Isham Swift.

When Lane discovers that all the claims about Swift are true—that the old man is staunchly Republican and indignant at the suggestion of voting otherwise (which means that others will be persuaded to think likewise)—he turns to the Reverend Ebenezer Clay of Mount Moriah, who proves to be much more acquiescent to his entreaties. As he introduces Mr. Lane to give a speech before his congregation, Dunbar's Reverend Clay proudly declares, "Of co'se Brothah Lane knows we colo'ed folks're goin' to think our own way anyhow" (244). Dunbar is clearly relying on irony to make his point; the black community does not exercise independence of thought; rather, they are a community whose political activity is a matter of rote behavior, not negotiation. And, as Dunbar's decision to give Swift's adversary the surname Clay suggests, too often the black community is a malleable substance to be shaped according to the majority's political desires.

After Lane's speech and after the congregation files out and heads home, there is an obvious split in sentiment that Dunbar reveals to be generational in nature:

Twenty years ago such a thing could not have happened, but the ties which had bound the older generation irrevocably to one party were being loosed on the younger men. The old men said, "We know;" the young ones said, "We have heard," and so there was hardly anything of the blind allegiance which had made even free thought seem treason to their fathers. (245)

Note the manner in which Dunbar makes the distinction between knowledge and hearsay, the effect of which is that solidarity is by no means a given. Deacon Swift's response to this rift is to denounce the Reverend Clay's decision to lead Little Africa down such a "treacherous course." As he gives an emotional speech, in which he insists, once more, that the party of Lincoln has demonstrated its devotion to Little Africa, the Deacon's son, Tom, sits unmoved by his father's rhetoric. When election day arrives, he sells his vote to the Democrats for five dollars, a transaction which becomes known to the entire community.

What motivates his betrayal, Dunbar suggests, is that, without ties to slavery, he "is not made of the same stuff" as his father. Dunbar prompts us to believe that his father, because of his sixth-grade education, lacks tough-minded integrity and feeling. Believing that he knows more than his father about political matters, Tom represents the sort of failed memory produced by an adherence to a materialism which negotiates on the basis that material prosperity is not a means, but an end in itself. Further, Tom's political involvement, because it represents a kind of ethical bankruptcy, is not the product of political subjectivity; rather, his decision to accept money from the Democrats is also a substantive break from the past. But as the passage above proposes, there is a marked difference between a political consciousness born of experience and that produced by indirect contact with historical events, and so we need to understand Tom's actions as those of an ahistorical subject.

Deacon Swift, in a fit of fatherly rage, makes Tom return the five-dollar note to the Democrats. Interestingly, Dunbar's investment in irony is such that he neglects to inform the reader which candidate wins the election. The reason for this is not only that we should assume the Republicans maintain their hold on Little Africa but also that who wins is beside the point. What is more important, as evidenced by the story's final scene, is the need for Little Africa to increase its distance from electoral politics. During a Wednesday night prayer meeting, Deacon Swift gets up and, in an interesting twist, announces, "Des' a minute, brothahs . . . I want to mek a 'fession. I was too ha'd an too brash in my talk de othah night, an de Lawd visited my sins upon my haid. He struck me in de bosom o' my own fambly. My own son went wrong. Pray fu' me!" (253). The call for prayer that closes Dunbar's short story surely points to the need for a closing of ranks and a reassessment of the past. But I also want to press a bit harder here and insist that it also speaks to the ways that to be political is likewise to risk patriarchal crisis.

Although it is no revelation to see Dunbar's story working out a vision of politics as a bastion of male participation and agency, I want to suggest here that Dunbar's story reveals the ways that even as democracy was conceived as a break from monarchy, American politics retains the notion that power, as an instrument of patriarchy, can be handed from one generation to the next. This explains the way that Isham Swift views Tom's transgressions as a subset of his own actions. The dynastic anxieties we see worked out in this story intimate Dunbar's skepticism regarding black participation in American politics, electoral or otherwise. Because it is difficult to amass the kind of resources necessary to resist the temptation of corrupt behavior, Dunbar's story ends with the spiritual rumination of prayer, which means that the story actually depicts a regression of political agency rather than an advance. In lieu of power in the secular world, Dunbar suggests, there must be integrity which can, at the very least, lead the son to adopt the worldview of the father.

Irony notwithstanding, Dunbar's story bears relation to Du Bois's novel, *Dark Princess* ([1928] 1995), largely because he argues in "A Mess of Pottage" for how little there is to be gained by black participation in the electoral politics. As he demonstrates in "Mr. Cornelius Johnson, Office Seeker" and "A Council of State," the patronage that blacks seek is meant as a way to configure their marginality in political matters, not their influence. Dunbar's decision to depict this situation ironically may be more a product of his ambivalence about the role of the black artist in society, but this nonetheless leaves him with no way to propose an alternative.

Moreover, we might even consider the ways that Dunbar's growing disillusionment as an artist influences his depiction of black political possibility. Evidence of this arises when we look at the deacon's name, Isham Swift; buried within the name is an anagram which forms the question, "Is Ham (or perhaps more rightly the 'sons of Ham') swift?" Dunbar's in-joke leads us to conclude that whites certainly do not believe this to be so, especially if "swift" is intended to mean political savvy. But, as Darwin Turner has asserted about Dunbar, part of the difficulty here is one, given Dunbar's growing marginality and isolation as an artist, that suggests the possibility that it is Dunbar himself who poses the question (Turner 1969). If this be the case, then what "A Mess of Pottage" and the other political critiques of Republican abuse in the collection argue is either that blacks lack the adequate civilization to participate in the politics of modernity or that, like Esau, blacks lack the ability to defer immediate gratification, which suggests that only a short time out of slavery, they have become the epitome of the modern subject: enslaved to public forms of material consumption, with these becoming the "pottage" traded for not once, but time and again.

If Jacob, as biblical trickster, bears any relation to African American narrative, it is because he represents stealth, but a form of stealth, cunning, and forethought that works well in the political arena. Further, he represents the act of linking futurity with nationhood, for as "the Supplanter" of his brother's status, his actions determine not only his own prosperity but that of his ancestral line as well, which is synonymous with nationhood (in the form of

Israel). But this points to what is lacking in Dunbar's critique, namely, that the question of black patronage in northern electoral politics is a product of the anxieties that are easily located in the white majority.[1] Dunbar, so disillusioned about African Americans' lack of political power, mirrors his own artistic confinement and thus fails to consider that there is, in fact, power to be exercised in the black community. If there is a messianic impulse in Dunbar's fiction, it is up to his readership to discern it. There is little possibility of this, however, because recognition of the ironic in political matters becomes an end in itself.

Dunbar's decision to depict black political impotence ironically has much to do with a pragmatism that ultimately works against the interests of the collective. His political commentaries in *The Strength of Gideon* all end with solitary black men, struck dumb by the speed of their falls from political grace. Because they are men who glory in hubris, they are doomed to suffer their sin with the sense that comfort from the black community is an inadequate replacement for political influence. It is here that we need to turn to W.E.B. Du Bois, first, because he dares to imagine Africa as a site of both cultural and political density rather than as the site of either backwardness or generational collapse.

But we can also note in Du Bois's fiction that he chooses optimism over despair, and so we find him working in *Dark Princess* to transform Esau into the Prodigal Son. This is no easy maneuver, for in addition to the difficulty of bringing New Testament

symbolic machinery into play, Du Bois must also eschew the irony that Dunbar uses to enjoin political critique in favor of allegory and romance, which requires a different approach to language and thematic framing. Further, it also means that if we are to decipher Du Bois's novel as a commentary on the state of African American political activity of the 1920s, then his decision to incorporate the parable of the Prodigal Son into his novel has a great deal to do with a desire to complicate matters surrounding the political subject, to problematize perhaps the propensity of the black community to fall into neatly arranged camps whose interests diminish the community's collective power.[2]

DU BOIS THE ARTIST

Much has been said about Du Bois's forays into creative writing, which can be seen as early as "On the Coming of John" and "On the Passing of the First-Born" in *The Souls of Black Folk* (1965) where he utilizes the fictive and the autobiographical, respectively, to good effect. And irrespective of one's critical assessment of it, his creative output is an impressive corpus of poems, autobiography, novels, and sketches. In thinking about this article, however, I have tried to imagine Du Bois holistically, as the romantic who authors *Dark Princess*, the social scientist who calls for a systematic (statistical) approach to the study of black life in "The Study of the Negro Problems" (1898) (and later, of course, *The Philadelphia Negro* [1995]), and the historian who produces *The*

Suppression of the African Slave Trade (1899) and *Black Reconstruction* (1969). Such an endeavor is difficult; Du Bois's creative writing is not quite good enough for us to consider him in a class with Langston Hughes, Jean Toomer, Nella Larsen, or Zora Neale Hurston. But it is not so poorly conceived or realized that we can dismiss it either.

What is at issue here is how to reconcile Du Bois's notion that "the Negro is primarily an artist," an assertion he makes in 1913 in "The Negro in Literature and Art," which he published in *The Annals* of the American Academy (alongside a piece by Booker T. Washington on industrial education) with his assertion in "The Study of the Negro Problems," published some 15 years earlier, where he declares, "Consequently, though we ordinarily speak of the Negro problem as though it were one unchanged question, students must recognize the obvious facts that this problem, like others, has had a long historical development, has changed with the growth and evolution of the nation; moreover, that it is not one problem, but rather a plexus of social problems, some new, some old, some simple, some complex" (Du Bois 1898, 3). The question of reconciliation is perhaps best approached by noting Keith Byerman's observation that Du Bois was "a theorist and historian of black writing," and as such

Du Bois tended to see himself as a man of letters, one who demonstrated significant literary skills regardless of the subject matter. He was also specifically a writer of literature, with a number of published poems, stories, parables, reviews, novels, as well as many more writings that were never published. (Byerman 1994, 100)

For Du Bois, "art helps to name the ideal ends for which the political struggle is carried on" (Byerman 101). Thus, art was always a matter of propaganda. He begins "Criteria of Negro Art," which appeared in *The Crisis* in 1926 (Du Bois 1994), by juxtaposing two viewpoints, one which symbolizes a skepticism toward the value of artistic expression and the other which delights in the relationship between aestheticism and pleasure. He goes on to dismiss both viewpoints summarily. "Let me tell you," he writes, "that neither of these groups is right. The thing we are talking about . . . is part of the great fight we are carrying on and it represents a forward and an upward look—a pushing onward" (Du Bois 1994, 61).

In looking at his novel *Dark Princess*, I want to suggest that Du Bois's approach exemplifies his assertions in "Criteria of Negro Art," for the novel represents the act of bringing together what would appear on the face of things to be disparate enterprises. But as Byerman notes, Du Bois's investment in art making is of a piece with the writing of history. "The novelist, not less than the historian or social scientist, does not render a pure creation of fancy; quite the contrary, he stays as close to the facts as possible. The novelist, in other words, is a historian who feels the necessity to speak even if he cannot prove everything he says" (Byerman 1994, 139).[3] Byerman helps us to understand that Du Bois's approach to novel writing is less grounded in generic practice than it is messianic discourse.

To write novels, Du Bois suggests, is to write a version of the truth. As such, the novel creates a world that has an analogue in the real world. Looking at *Dark Princess*, we cannot say that Du Bois partakes, however, of the social realism that will be the vogue of the 1930s with the advent of Richard Wright, but he does see the novel as performing cultural work of the sort represented by prophecy, in this instance providing the reader with a strategy of interpretation through which one can construct a vision of the future. As prophet, Du Bois frees himself of the social scientist's and historian's dilemma of looking at what is or what was in order to imagine what can be.

POLITICS AND ALLEGORY:
DARK PRINCESS

Commentators on *Dark Princess* have all located the novel in the realm of political allegory, and I see nothing in the novel to dissuade me from such a conclusion. But what interests me, and what occupies the remainder of this article, is Du Bois's attempt to transform Esau, the disinherited, into the Prodigal Son. What this means, at least in political terms, is that Du Bois imagines a world where change does not issue from controlling societal conditions from the top downward in order to produce positive outcomes for the whole, but from letting the positive aspects of a life lived "below" flow upward.

In ways more reminiscent of Johnson's handling of the figure of Esau, Du Bois actually links an image of prosperity and upward mobility to his characterization. Indeed, this goes a long way toward asserting that political consciousness is not the product of material comfort. Rather, the truly committed freedom fighter will eschew comfort. This revisionary posture toward the biblical narrative has much to do with the ways in which even as we find Du Bois utilizing scripture, the narrative arc of his fictional treatment is a product of secular energies, marking the distance Du Bois sees between spirituality and political agency.

As Arnold Rampersad has observed, *Dark Princess* did not "find favor with the general public." Matthew Towns, the novel's hero, moves "between poles of passion and self-denial" (Rampersad 1976, 202). While I agree with this assessment, I would amplify Rampersad's remarks and insist that Matthew Towns's problem in the novel is largely a matter of embodiment. As Wilson Moses has observed, Du Bois, though no lover of Christianity, was enamored of the notion of heroic redemption through suffering (Moses [1982] 1993, 142). The novel's messianic configuration, the way the novel ends with the birth of Matthew's son, "the Messenger and Messiah of the Darker Worlds" (Du Bois [1928] 1995, 311), as the sign of Matthew's ultimate redemption, intimates that not only is the political future of blacks in America at issue, but masculine subjectivity as well. Moving through *Dark Princess*, we find Towns struggling with the exigencies of language; his is a life fraught with the need to make himself understood, for his story to be viewed in light of its representativeness. The difficulty Du Bois sets for himself in creating a romantic figure like Towns is creating a figure who is the embodiment of a redemptive consciousness but who eschews the impulse to channel this into religiosity, opting instead to locate redemption as a secular phenomenon.

What makes this important is Du Bois's vision of the body politic. For if Matthew Towns seeks redemption, he must do so because the body politic requires it, not for personal ends. Thus, we need to pay close attention to the references the novel makes to the body and physical exertion because, located in an allegorical framework, these carry symbolic weight. For example, late in the novel, after Matthew has fallen out of favor in the world of electoral politics, he consummates his relationship with Princess Kautilya, his political and romantic counterpart, and gets a job digging the new subway. Though one of the men working for political boss Sammy Scott offers him a job as a foreman or a timekeeper, Matthew says, "I told him I wanted to dig." In what represents an instance where Du Bois's ideological fervor overwhelms his artistic restraint, Kautilya observes, "We start to dig, remaking the world," leading Matthew to launch into the following speech:

We must dig it out with my shovel and your quick wit. Here in America black folk must help overthrow the rule of the rich by distributing wealth more evenly first among themselves and then in alliance with white labor, to establish democratic control of industry. During the process they must keep step and hold tight hands with the other struggling darker peoples. (Du Bois [1928] 1995, 256)

In a realist novel, perhaps, we might expect a very different response, one that draws more heavily on the vernacular in order to manifest Matthew's desire to be a "man of the people" in a more believable fashion. But in Du Bois's version of political allegory, this is not a necessity. He can work in proximity to his own sense of appropriate speech, even as he articulates the beginnings of what will become much stronger socialist leanings in the decades to follow.

The problem, of course, is that Du Bois sees the emergence of a critical consciousness that can "establish control of democratic industry" as a by-product of physical labor. But more important, as an instance where wage labor assumes a transformative posture, labor must become part of something larger, more grand in scope. It must unloose itself from a machine of accumulation (capitalism) and harness itself to a different, newer machine, whose emphasis is sharing and redistribution in a form of democratic socialism.[4] Having chosen to produce a novel so steeped in allegory, Du Bois overcomes his own Victorian impulses in order to bridge the gap between mind and body.

What this means for Du Bois is that allegory is nothing short of a tactical maneuver. But as such, it plays for much higher stakes than irony because allegory, as Angus Fletcher argues, appears to express conflict between rival authorities, as in times of political oppression we may get "Aesop-language" to avoid censorship of dissident thought. At the heart of any allegory will be found this conflict of authorities. One ideal will be pitted against another, its opposite: thus the familiar propagandistic function of the mode, thus the conservative satiric function, thus the didactic function. (Fletcher 1964, 22)

Dark Princess delights, then, in a plethora of oppositions: country versus city, electoral politics versus ritual politics, materialism versus aestheticism, to name a few. But we need to remember that Du Bois conceives *Dark Princess* as an allegorical project that utilizes the social realist elements of its plot to counterpoint its romantic impulses. Thus, Du Bois wishes to depict the triumph of good over evil, but ultimately, he casts this within the context of a global industrial democracy and the "joining of black America with the rest of the nonwhite world" (Du Bois [1928] 1995, 132).

But it is here that I find *Dark Princess* to be a troublesome work of fiction. To accomplish this, Du Bois must perform a maneuver that aligns the erotic with political agency. This is a necessity foreshadowed when Matthew decides to marry Sara Andrews, a decision which Du Bois describes thus:

He had not noticed Sara much hitherto. He had not noticed any woman, since— since—But he knew Sara was intelligent and a hard worker. She looked simple, clean and capable. She seemed to him noticeably lonely and needing someone to lean on. She could make a home. He never had had just the sort of home he wanted. He wanted a home—something like his own den, but transfigured by capable hands—and devotion. Perhaps a wife would stop this longing—this inarticulate Thing in his soul. (136)

Although Sara has a moment in the novel when she looks at Matthew with something akin to erotic desire, their union privileges the material over the erotic. After the wedding, Matthew tries to place his arm about Sara's shoulders, but she warns him, "Be careful of the veil" (144). As a woman fair-skinned enough to pass for white, Sara is remarkable as a character in African American fiction in that she possesses a high level of political savvy and drive, traits Du Bois finds redeeming. But her impulse to protect the placement of the veil not only recalls the controlling metaphor found in *The Souls of Black Folk* but demonstrates the manner in which it becomes a signifier of erotic impoverishment.

Caught in this dilemma, Matthew's task is to find a way to link body and action, to free himself from purgatory—symbolized by his participation in electoral politics and his marriage—and find redemption. When Princess Kautilya returns to the novel, having disappeared for over 100 pages (during which time she has become a union organizer and laborer and thus shuns temporarily the advantages of high birth), Matthew runs away with her, spurning the opportunity to have a seat in Congress. Their brief union leads at novel's end to the birth of their son, the "Maharajah of Bwodpur."

The messianic ethos of *Dark Princess* needs to be considered in light of Du Bois's attempt to recuperate Matthew from a state of disinheritance, to make him a prodigal. He accomplishes this move by deferring Matthew's marriage to the princess, organizing the fourth section of the novel as a series of letters between them, where they discuss the relation of work to revolution. This needs to be understood in the context of Du Bois's vision of art as propaganda. But here we need to understand that the word "propaganda" is derived from the Latin word *propagare*, which means "propagate." The romance that ensues between Matthew Towns and Princess Kautilya is a clear example of having one's cake and eating it too. I say this because we find Matthew one minute extolling the virtues of work, quitting all ties to politics and taking up the aforementioned job as a ditchdigger, but by novel's end, he is wealthy, powerful, and the father of a male heir, which means that his sexual potency is, in the way of all wealthy patriarchs perhaps, political capital as well.

In thinking about the idea of a body politic, I am reminded of Moira Gatens's observation that "the modern body politic is based on an image of the masculine body" (Gatens 1991, 84). Trying to envision a body politic redeemed by the rise of the "darker worlds," Du Bois produces what is, in my view, an allegory that collapses into masculine narcissism. Which is to say that, even as Sara Andrews and Princess Kautilya represent women who are remarkable for their intellect and political consciousness,

ultimately Du Bois cannot find a way to value them equally, to allow them to be the agents of political change, no matter how catalytic their presence may be. The princess, the mother of Matthew Towns's son, is caught in a political dilemma: her kingdom, the Indian province of Bwodphur, requires that she either enter an arranged marriage or produce a male heir; she is enjoined by her sex from ruling the kingdom alone. Thus, at novel's end she announces, "Bwodphur needs not a princess, but a King" (Du Bois [1928] 1995, 308).

This suggests that Du Bois's investment in allegory and romance is mediated by notions of propaganda to be sure, but propaganda of the sort whose success rises and falls (pun intended) on the male member. Indeed, the notion of the "darker worlds" assuming membership in the hall of nations, has much to do, as Wilson Moses has suggested, with a Wagnerian design, reminding us of opera's propensity to excess. *Dark Princess* is at once a hearkening back to the operatic tradition and a call for a heroic art (Moses [1982] 1993, 144). Thus, we might place the novel, as Moses does, as the harbinger of "new tradition in black writing," but it is also important, I think, to site the novel, not only in terms of its racial politics, but also its gender politics.[5]

However, Du Bois's adherence to romance and allegory represents his decision to privilege a rhetoric of the body and suggests that the discursive intersection of race and masculinity requires nothing less than the tactical maneuver allegory assumes in *Dark Princess*: to make masculinity's perpetual crisis into a sacrificial cross. Indeed, *Dark Princess* gives us repeated instances where Matthew Towns (and to a lesser degree, his consort, Princess Kautilya) moves from one sacrifice to the next, each one progressively smaller in scale, moving from his life in the public world inward, toward his private life. Thus, the novel begins with Towns being forced to give up medical school and later the opportunity to serve in Congress, and finally, in order to prepare himself for a struggle as yet undefined, he gives up his relationship to Kautilya altogether (only to be reunited with her at novel's end).

This is also played out when Matthew's part in the foiled attempt to destroy a train carrying a group of Klan members (and, coincidentally, the princess as well) is revealed. When he is sentenced to prison, Matthew protects the princess from being implicated in the conspiracy, taking the punishment upon himself. Although we are meant to see this sacrifice as a noble gesture, what interests me here is the way this scene serves a revisionary function, providing Du Bois with the opportunity to return to the rhetorical territory of his 1890 Harvard graduation address, entitled "Jefferson Davis as a Representative of Civilization." In Du Bois's rendering, Davis is a romantic figure, worthy of emulation and admiration when one considers his individual traits apart from civilization. "A soldier and a lover, a statesman and a ruler; passionate, ambitious, and indomitable; bold reckless guardian of a people's All—judged by the whole standard of Teutonic civilization, there is something noble in the figure of Jefferson Davis" (Du Bois [1890] 1995, 17). But as a symbol of the ways that white supremacy plays a destructive role in the world, Davis is a figure to be regarded with some measure of skepticism. The civilization Davis and men like him augur in is one whose "foundation is the idea of the Strong Man—Individualism coupled with the rule of might" (17).

As a man of heroic temper, Matthew Towns could most certainly function in such a way in Du Bois's novel, but the plot of *Dark Princess* turns on the relationship between sacrifice and redemption. In that sense, we see Du Bois reconstituting the romantic hero. The civilization in which Davis functions, as Teutonic hero, is one where Du Bois observes "the overweening sense of the I and the consequent forgetting of the Thou" (Du Bois [1890] 1995, 18). In many ways, the Harvard graduation address lays out, in ways that are mirrored in *Dark Princess*, "the change made in the conception of civilization," namely, the act of "adding to the idea of the Strong Man, that of the Submissive Man." As the address insists, no one is better suited for this role than the Negro, who represents "the peculiar embodiment of the idea of Personal Submission" (Du Bois 1890 [1995], 19).

This brings us back to where we began: Esau as a figure of indulgence being transformed into the Prodigal Son, who returns to find himself restored to power and status. In the former story, what justifies Jacob's triumph is that it represents an instance of the weak outmaneuvering the strong. In the latter narrative, what we see is the magnanimity of patriarchal power on one hand, but also the spoils that are the lot of the submissive man on the other. The ultimate challenge for Matthew Towns is one of mastering, of bringing into conceptual proximity political consciousness and an awareness of the body that arises from physical exertion. That Kautilya has their child unbeknown to him suggests that he is unaware of the fate that awaits him; he must submit, without knowing it, to political destiny. The birth of his child accomplishes this, not only because it is the result of an erotic endeavor but also because Matthew's relationship to the princess ensures, ostensibly, that the child will be the "text" upon which a new social contract is inscribed. And so, Matthew and Kautiliya's act of consummating their relationship needs to be understood for the revisionary rhetoric that it is, for what it suggests, as an allegorical gesture, is that the redemption of civilization results, not from a cultural hybridity resulting from contact with whites, but from the "darker peoples" discovering their mutual interests and acting upon them.

But Matthew's return to his mother's cabin in Virginia is also Du Bois's rhetorical nod back to "Of the Meaning of Progress," a chapter in *The Souls of Black Folk*. While that experience marked an epiphany for the younger Du Bois, it was characterized by transience. To be sure, Du Bois wishes to suggest that it was a formative experience, necessary for the man who would do social science research in Philadelphia's Seventh Ward, but it also marks a transition which he cannot recover: "My log schoolhouse was gone. In its place stood Progress; and Progress, I understand, is necessarily ugly." The chapter ends with Du Bois musing on the irrecoverable past while riding to Nashville in the Jim Crow car. The end of *Dark Princess*, with its beautiful consort and male heir and the reconciliation with the mother, a former slave, is Du Bois's opportunity to link the African American past to a world of "darker races" beyond, whose common language is that of patriarchal discourse.

As Claudia Tate observes in the introduction to the latest edition of *Dark Princess*, Du Bois "aligns his political agenda with the pleasure principle" (Tate 1995, xix). In its pages, we find the articulate hero who, contrary to the mores of the 1920s, represents the effort to link erotic desire to the search for an all-encompassing form of political subjectivity. Unfortunately, the form it takes, optimistic as it may be, is a relationship animated by patriarchal conventions. While it is clear that Esau is redeemed, the transformation into the Prodigal Son does not speak to the issue of gender oppression. Redemption, such as it is, means that Matthew is saved from the exigencies of racial prejudice.

But I want to suggest that our work in the future, as Professors Griffin and Collins have insisted in their articles, must seek to problematize some of Du Bois's formulations—and nonformulations—about gender. Although Du Bois's intellectual prowess with respect to the discourses of race and class was ahead of its time in the 1920s, his attitude regarding gender, while tending toward progressivism, was highly reflective of the historical moment. As we ponder the new millennium (and Du Bois's place in it), we hope new ways to calculate performances of masculinity will emerge; thus we might view black feminist discourse and its call for gender equality not as threat but as legacy, indeed, as birthright, an invitation to see power as a shared and treasured thing.

Notes

1. It is there we find a community whose interests, should they become linked to those of their immigrant counterparts (who do not immediately fit comfortably in the category of whiteness), mean a shift in the political tide.

2. This may be giving Du Bois credit for an intentionality that he does not possess. For in some ways it would mean that his novels would be less formulaic, more prone to either parody, satire, or outright realist critique. The fact that Du Bois's novel lacks this quality speaks nonetheless to an investment in his novel that needs to be taken every bit as seriously as his scholarly writing.

3. Byerman continues, noting Du Bois's novels are instances where the writer is not telling a tale at all but recounting real events. The novel form, in other words, is a measure of the historian's humility and deserves attention for its truth content, if not its art. But there is a conflicting, if not contradictory, reason for the choice of genre. He recognizes the necessity of storytelling, with its referential character, but also of the "pure imagination": "By allowing for the imagination, he can express his moral indignation and his version of the apocalypse without being accused of emotional excess or subjectivity. He puts words in the mouths of madmen and conspirators, so that he can say what he feels must be said but what would be scandalous and perhaps even irresponsible to say in his own voice. To the roles of historian and novelist he adds that of prophet" (Byerman 1994, 139-40).

4. Although it is doubtful that Du Bois himself would have referred to his model of resistance in this fashion (at least in the 1920s), what is clear is that his notion of the "talented tenth" was slowly being revised.

5. *Dark Princess* occurs at a time during the twentieth century when antiheroic representations of masculinity came to the fore. This is not to suggest that writers like Hemingway, Eliot, Fitzgerald, Faulkner, and the other male proponents of literary modernism were any less invested in male supremacy but rather that they had abandoned the notion that male superiority was rooted in a spiritual context.

References

Byerman, Keith. 1994. *Seizing the Word: History, Art, and Self in the Works of W.E.B. Du Bois*. Athens: University of Georgia Press.

Du Bois, W.E.B. [1890] 1995. Jefferson Davis as a Representative of Civilization. In *W.E.B. Du Bois: A Reader*, ed. David Levering Lewis. New York: Henry Holt.

———. 1898. The Study of the Negro Problems. *The Annals* of the American Academy of Political and Social Science Jan.:1-23.

———. 1899. *Suppression of the African Slave Trade*. Boston: Longman, Green.

———. 1913. The Negro in Literature and Art. *The Annals* of the American Academy of Political and Social Science Sept.: 233-37.

———. [1920] 1969. *Darkwater: Voices from the Veil*. New York: AMS Press.

———. [1928] 1995. *Dark Princess*. Jackson: University of Mississippi Press.

———. 1965. *The Souls of Black Folk*. New York: Avon Books

———. 1969. *Black Reconstruction*. New York: Atheneum.

———. 1994. Criteria of Negro Art. In *Within the Circle*, ed. Angelyn Mitchell. Durham, NC: Duke University Press. First printed in *The Crisis*, Oct. 1926.

———. 1995. *The Philadelphia Negro*. Philadelphia: University of Pennsylvania Press.

Dunbar, Paul Laurence. 1900. *The Strength of Gideon and Other Stories*. New York: Arno Press and New York Times.

Fletcher, Angus. 1964. *Allegory: The Theory of a Symbolic Mode*. Ithaca, NY: Cornell University Press.

Gatens, Moira. 1991. Corporeal Representation in/and the Body Politic. In *Cartographies*, ed. Rosalyn Disprose and Robyn Ferrel. North Sydney, Australia: Allen & Unwin.

Johnson, James Weldon. [1927] 1965. *Autobiography of an Ex-Colored Man*. New York: Alfred A. Knopf.

Madsen, Deborah L. 1996. *Allegory in America: From Puritanism to Postmodernism*. New York: St. Martin's Press

Moses, Wilson Jeremiah. [1982] 1993. *Black Messiahs and Uncle Toms: Social and Literary Manipulations of a Religious Myth*. University Park: Pennsylvania State University Press.

Rampersad, Arnold. 1976. *The Art and Imagination of W.E.B. Du Bois*. Cambridge, MA: Harvard University Press.

Tate, Claudia. 1995. Introduction. *Dark Princess*, by W.E.B. Du Bois. Jackson: University of Mississippi Press.

Turner, Darwin. 1969. Introduction. *The Strength of Gideon and Other Stories*, by Paul Lawrence Danbar. New York: Arno Press and *New York Times*.

ANNALS, *AAPSS*, **568**, March 2000

Du Bois's Humanistic Philosophy of Human Sciences

By LEWIS R. GORDON

ABSTRACT: One of the many challenges W.E.B. Du Bois faced in the study of African Americans was the pervasive racism that affected how social scientists acquired data on people of African descent. Moreover, the historical reality in which such data were gathered was one in which there were indications of genocidal aims on the part of the dominant population. Du Bois needed to show that African Americans should receive rigorous study and that rigorous study was a part of the struggle for African American upliftment. In his effort to address both challenges, Du Bois, in effect, developed several bases for rigorous human study that included the importance of recognizing the humanity of the subjects under study. He touched upon several central concerns in the philosophy of the human sciences including the viability of studying metastable subjects; the relationship between epistemological and ontological categories in the cultural sphere; and the lived reality of action in the face of behavioral imposition.

Lewis R. Gordon is chairperson of Afro-American studies at Brown University, where he also is professor of Afro-American studies, contemporary religious thought, and modern culture and media, and a faculty member of the Center for the Study of Race and Ethnicity in America. He edits Radical Philosophy Review *and co-edits a book series,* Studies in Africana Thought. *His books include* Bad Faith and Antiblack Racism; Fanon and the Crisis of European Man; Her Majesty's Other Children; *and* Existentia Africana.

I N his 1903 classic *The Souls of Black Folk*, W.E.B. Du Bois made a prognosis that has haunted the twentieth century: "Herein lie buried many things which if read in patience may show the strange meaning of being black here at the dawning of the Twentieth Century. This meaning is not without interest to you, Gentle Reader; for the problem of the Twentieth Century is the problem of the color line" (1903, 41). When Du Bois wrote "Gentle Reader," he was being more than rhetorical, for this "Reader," for whom there was once presumed a lack of interest and, therefore, (falsely) a lack of relevance, is here alerted that his or her condition, being other than black, was inscribed in the core of the problems in question.

The black, whose "strange meaning" and "being" were also called into question as "the Negro problem," represented also a tension in the presumed order. Du Bois did not here write about being black but about its meaning. He announced a hermeneutical turn that would delight even his most zealous philosophical successors. This hermeneutical turn signaled a moment in a complex struggle, a moment marked by its admission of incompleteness and probably impossible closure. The black, subject to interpretation, became a designation that could be held by different groups at different times and as such was both concrete and metaphorical. If the color line is at the mercy of interpretive blackness, then its boundaries carry risks, always, of changing and overlapping. The Gentle Reader's possibilities are announced, then, as paradoxically

less fixed in their fixedness than he or she may be willing to admit. Such a Reader may intensify, then, his or her effort to take "precautions."

Du Bois's announcement has played itself out, prophetically, in this regard: race/color has marked a course through the twentieth century like a rift through the planet, while its heaps of ideological rubbish have piled themselves up, in their characteristic divides, like casualties on the Western front. Deny it as we may, as a consequence or cause of a multitude of evils, the problem of the color line is a persisting problem, a problem that, in the eyes of some, is here to stay (for example, Bell 1992). Born from the divide of black and white, it serves as a blueprint of the ongoing division of humankind. The color line is also a metaphor that exceeds its own concrete formulation. It is the race line as well as the gender line, the class line, the sexual-orientation line, the religious line—in short, the line between "normal" and "abnormal" identity.

The twentieth century was also marked by another pronouncement of grave import: the struggle for liberation and, hence, revolution. There were revolutionary struggles in Asia, decolonization struggles in Africa and the Caribbean, civil rights struggles in the United States, and indigenous struggles worldwide. Like the fate of Du Bois's announcement on color, many of the revolutionary efforts at the century's morn have fallen into ill repute at its twilight. But the forces that gave them validity haunt our present. Global economic inequality intensifies in the face of First World dismissal of the relevance of revolution and, hence, revolutionary consciousness. We are in a sorry moment, as the question of an active consciousness, of taking a stand of resistance, has shifted its foci from systems to intrasystemic "critique." There is no longer the radical, Leninist revolutionary call of what is to be done. Instead, there is the pathetic retreat: What can one do?

Two announcements heralded the dawn of the twentieth century: identity and liberation. Despite addressing "color lines," Du Bois's explorations have charted a genealogical thematic of "fundamental" thoughts on the twentieth-century subject, of the twentieth-century self: his anguished voice was, after all, addressing problems of identity, the resolution of which later culminated to a voice of revolution. His final autobiography, *A Soliloquy on Viewing My Life from the Last Decade of Its First Century*, charts a course from New England liberalism in Barrington, Massachusetts, and Cambridge, Massachusetts, to Communist internationalism in Harlem, New York, and Accra, Ghana, although the closing remarks reveal a beautiful fusion of Marxism with African American existentialism:

I just live. I plan my work, but plan less for shorter periods. I live from year to year and day to day. I expect snatches of pain and discomfort to come and go. And then reaching back to my archives, I whisper to the great majority: To the Almighty dead, into whose pale approaching faces, I stand and stare. . . . Teach living man to jeer at this last civilization which seeks to build heaven on Want and Ill of most men and vainly builds on color

and hair rather than on decency of hand and heart. Let your memories teach those wilful fools all which you have forgotten and ruined and done to death. . . . Our dreams seek Heaven, our deeds plumb Hell. Hell lies about us in our Age: blithely we push into its stench and flame. Suffer us not, Eternal Dead to stew in this Evil—the Evil of South Africa, the Evil of Mississippi; the Evil of Evils which is what we hope to hold in Asia and Africa, in the southern Americas and islands of the Seven Seas. Reveal, Ancient of Days, the Present in the Past and prophesy the End in the Beginning. . . . Let then the Dreams of the dead rebuke the Blind who think that what is will be forever and teach them that what was worth living for must live again and that which merited death must stay dead. Teach us, Forever Dead, there is no Dream but Deed, there is no Deed but Memory. (Du Bois 1968, 422-23)

Identity and liberation are two themes that lay beneath the waves of twentieth-century thought. Identity calls for the question of a being's relation to itself. Thus, we find identity questions in ontological questions, questions of being, essence, and meaning—in short, of the existential force of the question, in the end, What am I?

In the liberatory question, we head, too, through a series of philosophical turns. Although the two meet on the question of who is to be liberated, the liberating animus charts a course of value that at times transcends being, although not always essence. Liberation is a teleological concern, a concern about purpose, a concern about ought and whys: Whatever we may be, the point is to focus energy on what we ought to become.

A powerful dimension of Du Bois's work is the extent to which he straddled both the identity and liberatory divides, divides of research and divides of policy. In his writings, the search reveals the normative and the normative reveals the search. His classic essay, "The Study of the Negro Problems," which this issue of *The Annals* of the American Academy of Political and Social Science commemorates, offers several challenges on how researchers in the human sciences should go about studying racialized people. I say "racialized people" because, as we will see, the normativity achieved by some members of a racist society enables them to live as though freed of racial designation. The research challenges present a unique feature of African American thought; such thought raises the metatheoretical level of investigation even at the level of methodological involvement. This article explores some of the philosophical richness of Du Bois's argument and presents a case for its continued relevance as we face our humanity in the aftermath of a trenchant, postmodern, misanthropic era.

THE CONTEXT

In 1896, the year in which the Supreme Court of the United States affirmed segregation of the races in the landmark case of *Plessey* v. *Ferguson*, Du Bois, then 28 years of age, was called upon by the University of Pennsylvania to conduct a study of the black populations of the Seventh Ward, a ghetto, in the city of Phila-

delphia. Nearly seven decades later, he recounts the invitation and the situation with the sensibility of an elder attuned to both the wisdom and naïveté of his youth:

It all happened this way: Philadelphia, then and still one of the worst governed cities, was having one of its periodic spasms of reform. A thorough study of causes was called for. Not but what the underlying cause was evident to most white Philadelphians: the corrupt, semicriminal vote of the Negro Seventh Ward. Everyone agreed that here lay the cancer; but would it not be well to give scientific sanction to the known causes by an investigation, with imprimatur of the University? It certainly would, answered Samuel McCune Lindsay of the Department of Sociology. And he put his finger on me for the task. (Du Bois 1968, 194)

He continues:

If Lindsay had been a smaller man and had been induced to follow the usual American pattern of treating Negroes, he would have asked me to assist him as his clerk in this study. Probably I would have accepted having nothing better in sight for work in sociology. But Lindsay regarded me as a scholar in my own right and probably proposed to make me an instructor. Evidently the faculty demurred at having a colored instructor. But since I had a Harvard Ph.D., and had published a recognized work in history [*Suppression of the African Slave-Trade to the United States of America*], the University could hardly offer me a fellowship. A compromise was hit on and I was nominated to the unusual status of "assistant" instructor. Even at that there must have been some opposition, for the invitation was not particularly cordial. I was offered a salary of $900 for a period limited to one year. I was given no real academic standing, no official recognition of any kind; my name was eventually omitted from the catalogue; I had no contact with students, and very little with members of the faculty, even in my own department.

Nevertheless, Du Bois took the challenge:

I did not hesitate an instant but reported for duty with a complete plan of work and outline of methods and aims and even proposed schedules to be filled out. My general plan was promptly accepted and I started to work, consulting Lindsay regularly but never meeting the faculty. With my bride of three months, I settled in one room in the city over a cafeteria run by a College Settlement, in the worst part of the Seventh Ward. We lived there a year, in the midst of an atmosphere of dirt, drunkenness, poverty, and crime. Murder sat on our doorsteps, police were our government, and philanthropy dropped in with periodic advice. (194-95)

And here is his mature reflection on how he understood the so-called Negro problem in his youth:

The Negro problem was in my mind a matter of systematic investigation and intelligent understanding. The world was thinking wrong about race, because it did not know. The ultimate evil was stupidity. The cure for it was knowledge based on scientific investigation. At the University of Pennsylvania I ignored the pitiful stipend. It made no difference to me that I was put down as an "assistant instructor," and even at that, that my name never actually got into the catalogue; it goes without saying that I did no instructing save once to pilot a pack of idiots through the Negro slums. (197)

Du Bois faced a formidable task. That he was given only a year, with-

out assistance, to present a systematic study of the black population in the Seventh Ward of Philadelphia betrayed the bad faith of the institutions that commissioned that study. In effect, Du Bois was set up to fail but with the provision that his failure count as the best possible effort to study that community and, thus, serve as affirmation of the pathologies of the community under study. In other words, Du Bois's study was to serve as a form of theodicean legitimation of Philadelphian society (and by implication, U.S. society). Theodicy is the effort to reconcile the goodness of an all-powerful deity with the existence of evil. In modern times, theodicy has been secularized through making political systems or systems of rationalization stand for the fallen god and by making social evils or contradictions stand for the annoying evils or imperfections of the system. Du Bois's labors were expected to demonstrate that Philadelphia's evils were extrasystemic, were features of the black populations, rather than intrasystemic, things endemic to the system and, hence, things done to the black populations.

We see here an ironic relation to research, for if Du Bois were successful at what he was commissioned to do, he would have been a failure at what he had set out to do, which was to find out the "truth," as it were, of the Philadelphia black population's situation. The glitch in the institution's expectations was Du Bois himself. He was, after all, W.E.B. Du Bois, the future dean of African American scholarship. That title eventually came to him from the pioneering work he produced from *The*

Philadelphia Negro (1899) through to *Black Reconstruction in America* ([1935] 1992) and other subsequent work in history, sociology, political economy, and philosophy. The 28-year-old Du Bois knew that he was hired as a lackey to legitimize policies premised upon black pathology, but, being a "race man," he knew, as well, that opportunities for black folk to succeed instead of to fail were few and far between. He knew that any effort on his part to study and demonstrate the ordinary required extraordinary efforts, efforts that were no less than Promethean. Reflecting on the opposition he faced, he later wrote:

Of the theory back of the plan of this study of Negroes I neither knew nor cared. I saw only here a chance to study an historical group of black folks and to show exactly what their place was in the community. . . . Whites said: Why study the obvious? Blacks said: Are we animals to be dissected and by an unknown Negro at that? Yet, I made a study of the Philadelphia Negro so thorough that it has withstood the criticism of 60 years. (1968, 197)

Indeed, he had. Du Bois's work withstood 60 years of criticism because he not only studied the black populations in Philadelphia but also questioned the study of black folk in the United States and, by implication, other anti-black societies. The paper he presented to the American Academy of Political and Social Science, "The Study of the Negro Problems" (1898b), inaugurated a profound turn in the study of human beings in the modern era. The title brought the turn into focus succinctly by its focus on study. Du Bois, in effect, announced the metatheoretical question of how theory is formulated. There is something peculiar, he suggests at the outset, about how blacks are studied—key to consider is whether they are studied at all—which requires reflection on one's method more than one would with populations who are normative. Practices of systematic inquiry and critical self-assessments are often put to the wayside by commentators in favor of opinionated statements of what, supposedly, must be so with regard to blacks. In effect, the Negro problems were thrown out of the sphere of human problems into the sphere of necessity premised upon pathologies. Consequently, the Negro problems often collapsed into the Negro Problem—the problem, in other words, of having Negroes around. In this regard, it was, as commentators (for example, Fanon 1967) subsequently noted, a predominantly white problem.

FROM PROBLEMATIC
PEOPLE TO PEOPLE'S PROBLEMS

The problem of problematized people is well known among existential and phenomenological theorists (see Freire 1990; Gordon 1995a, 1995b, 1997a, 1997b). It can be understood in terms of the spirit of seriousness. The spirit of seriousness emerges when there is a collapse in the divide between values and the material world (compare with Gordon 1995a, chap. 6). In such instances, the material world becomes a cause of values and vice versa. In other words, there is such an isomorphic relation between values and objects of value that they become one. Thus, the object fails any longer to signify or suggest a particular value or meaning. It becomes that value or meaning. In cases of a problematic people, the result is straightforward: they cease to be people who might face, signify, or be associated with a set of problems. They become those problems. Thus, a problematic people do not signify crime, licentiousness, and other social pathologies; they, under such a view, are crime, licentiousness, and other social pathologies (see, for example, Fanon 1967, chap. 6).

How does one study problems faced by a people without collapsing them into the problems themselves? Du Bois begins by offering a definition of social problems: "A social problem is the failure of an organized social group to realize its group ideals, through the inability to adapt a certain desired line of action to given conditions of life" (1898b, 2). That Du Bois focuses on the social is already a theoretical advance. For in his time, the tendency was to approach the study of a people in terms of either phylogenic or ontogenic considerations. The phylogenic focuses on species' differences where, especially with regard to the "racial" status of blacks, debate took the form of whether they were members of the human species. The ontogenic consideration had limitations in its focus on the individual organism. With such a focus, one would address simply an individual organism that works and another that fails—as are easily found in any study of a set of human subjects—but the meaning of working and failing transcends the organism itself. The problems, matters relating to success or failure, require a third mediating consideration: the social world (compare with Fanon 1967, intro.). The social world mediates the phylogenic and the ontogenic and presents, through the complexity of social life—life premised upon intentions, actions, and the ongoing achievement of intersubjective relations—a world of agency, deliberation, and contingency. It is a world without accident yet without, as well, necessity. It is a world that brings things into being that need not have been brought forth. By focusing on the social, then, Du Bois has, in one sweep, taken the U.S. discourse on blackness onto unfamiliar ground.

The unfamiliar ground of social analysis requires a different way of reading problems:

Thus a social problem is ever a relation between conditions and action, and as conditions and actions vary and change from group to group from time to time and from place to place, so social problems change, develop and grow. Consequently, though we ordinarily speak of the Negro problem as though it were one unchanged question, students must recognize the obvious fact that this problem, like others, has had a long historical development, has changed with the growth and evolution of the nation; moreover, that it is not *one* problem, but rather a plexus of social problems, some new, some old, some simple, some complex; and these problems have their one bond of unity in the act that they group themselves about those Africans whom two centuries of slave-trading brought into the land. (1898b, 3)

That social problems are not static raises the question whether it is possible to conduct systematic study of a constantly changing or metastable subject. The metastability of the subject here is a function of human reality. The human being is a subject that constantly challenges the permanent relevance of data. In effect, the tendency to stratify the Negro problem betrays a tendency to address black populations as though they were not human populations. As human populations, they are metastable. Such a reminder brings into focus an important dimension of the problem of studying black folk. For if an error in studying black folk emerges from a failure to recognize their humanity, one might think that such an error could easily be alleviated by simply studying them as human beings. The question brings into focus the problem with racial analysis. Can a racial formation be rigorously studied as a human formation?

Du Bois addresses this problem by raising another dimension of the human being that is not addressed simply by recognizing its capacity for change. After raising the social, he explores the historical specificity of blacks in the United States. The historical reality of blacks in America is one of struggling against conquest, kidnapping, enslavement, and a constant reconstruction of racial hierarchies at each moment of seeming triumph over racial oppression. The Civil War, he points out, eradicated legalized chattel slavery without eliminating the conditions that racialized slavery in the first place. The result was, then, a reassertion of forces against the freedom of black folk. This dialectic between freedom and unfreedom is such that it raises, as well, the question of a dialectic between the past and the future. In taking heed of historical impositions and the possibilities sought in present inquiry, Du Bois brings another problem into focus—the problem of the political: "They do not share the full national life because there has always existed in America a conviction . . . that people of Negro blood should not be admitted into the group life of the nation no matter what their conditions might be" (1898b, 7).

The political problem, although not explicitly stated as such, has the consequence of political nihilism—the view that one's political institutions are incapable of responding to one's social needs. Such nihilism is an understandable consequence of the nation's anxieties over black inclusion. In Du Bois's words:

They rest . . . on the widespread conviction among Americans that no persons of Negro descent should become constituent members of the social body. This feeling gives rise to economic problems, to educational problems, and nice questions of social morality; it makes it more difficult for black men to earn a living or spend their earnings as they will; it gives them poorer school facilities and restricted contact with cultured classes; and it becomes, throughout the land, a cause and excuse for discontent, lawlessness, laziness and injustice. (1898b, 8)

A consequence of this social problem is the widespread credo, Why bother?

The equating of blacks with failure has played itself out over the course of the twentieth century. It is what troubled Frantz Fanon in the 1950s, when he reflected on the sociogenic conditions of failure in anti-black societies (Fanon 1967), and it was a recurring theme of the 1980s and 1990s. Cornel West (1993) has, for instance, rearticulated this problem as one of nihilism in the black community, and I have examined this problem as a larger problem of political nihilism in a postmodern world (Gordon 1997b, chap. 5). Du Bois is, however, linking the problem of nihilism to a peculiar dimension of social reality in the formation of a concept not mentioned in his seminal article but serves as its subtext—namely, oppression.

ON OPPRESSION

Oppression is a function of the number of options a society offers its members. Where there are many options, choices can be made without imploding upon those who make them. If a set of options are considered necessary for social well-being in a society, then trouble begins when and where such options are not available to all members of the society. In effect, such options have an impact on membership itself. In a world where I have only two options but everyone else has three, it is highly likely that my choices will exceed my options more quickly than would the others. Where there are only two options, I may use up two choices before I begin to make inward, abstract choices, like "neither," or "I will choose X or Y affirmatively or reluctantly," and so on. Eventually, it becomes clear that to make more than two choices without collapsing onto myself and the way I make choices, I will need to expand my options. But to do so would put me in conflict with a world that has only given me two options. In effect, then, to live like everyone else places me in a situation of conflict. Here, we see the problem brought into philosophical focus. For, to live like everyone else, to live as "ordinary," as "normal," would require of me an "extraordinary" act—to change the system, which may require powers beyond my capacity, or to change myself, which, although a localized exercise of power, would require something of me that is not demanded of others. In either formulation, I would have to work harder than others.

That is what Du Bois means to point out in his list of hardships faced by social limitation (see, for example, Du Bois 1898b, 8). The problem is particularly stark if we consider Jim Crow. In limiting the options available for blacks in the everyday negotiation of social life, Jim Crow increased the probability of black social life being in conflict with American social life; it increased the probability of blacks breaking the law on an everyday basis. Such limited options forced every black to face choices about the self that placed selfhood in conflict with humanhood.

In the post–Jim Crow era, problems continue as the collapse of blacks into pathologies is such that it limits the options available for blacks in civil society. Many blacks, for instance, in going about their everyday life, incur a constant risk of incarceration. Under such circumstances, blacks take extraordinary measures to live an ordinary life; an ordinary life, after all, should not involve expected encounters with the criminal justice system.

The study of the Negro problem then calls for a provocative form of human study—the study of a human population whose humanity is a structurally denied feature of the society in which they are studied. Implicit in Du Bois's call for such a study, then, is an indictment of the society itself: "The sole aim of any society is to settle its problems in accordance with its highest ideals, and the only rational method of accomplishing this is to study those problems in the light of the best scientific research" (Du Bois 1898b, 10).

And what is the best scientific research? The best scientific research has criteria that will, at best, put into relief some (if not all) of the prejudices of the researchers. Du Bois adds to his appeal the claim that "the American Negro deserves study for the great end of advancing the cause of science in general. . . . [And those who fail to do so] hurt the cause of scientific truth the world over, they voluntarily decrease human knowledge of a universe of which we are ignorant enough" (Du Bois 1898b, 10-11). The best research is guided by a search for the universal. Data that purport to cover the human species without inclusion of blacks and other peoples of color are at best true over a subset of the human species. The humanity of black folks, then, is a necessary addition for the rigorous practice of the human sciences.

Du Bois's insight has been repeated by many scholars and writers throughout the twentieth century. Each of them, from Alain Locke (1989) to Ralph Ellison (1987) through to the genealogical poststructural work of V. Y. Mudimbe (1988) and the black feminist arguments of bell hooks (1981, 1984, 1990) and Joy James (1996, 1997) echo this point—that the structural collapse of universality into whiteness (and masculineness) has exemplified a false universal. One may find a more complete picture of a society in those places its members often seek to avoid. In African American philosophy, for instance, one will find studies of both what (white) American philosophy is willing to face and what it is unwilling to face. In effect, it requires a reenvisioning of both what America is and what it means to do philosophy in America. The same applies to social science and the human sciences in general.

Du Bois then returns to the question of study with an addendum of humanistic study, which calls for recognizing the limitations of essentialistic claims across a social group: "What is true of the Negro in Massachusetts is not necessarily true of the Negro in Louisiana; . . . what is true of the Negro in 1850 was not necessarily true in 1750" (Du Bois 1898b, 17). He then advances two categories of study—the social group and the social environment. The four suggestions for the study of the social group—historical, statistical, anthropological measurement, and sociological interpretation—have been hinted at in our discussion thus far. Given the impact of Hegel's introduction to his *Philosophy of History* (1956), it was a long-standing view that blacks were not historical. Du Bois's advancement of the historical here was, in this area of thought, Copernican. The quantitative suggestions were less problematic because of the dominant ideology that placed blacks in close proximity to nature. It seems odd, then, that Du Bois had to reiterate their importance. His advancement of quantitative analysis makes sense, however, if we consider another feature of the dehumanization of blacks, a feature that hits the heart of inquiry itself—namely, the impact racism has on epistemological openness and epistemological closure.

Epistemological openness pertains to the anonymity that undergirds the social dimension of each social group. A social group is such that each member can occupy the role that exemplifies it. When the theorist encounters a member of that group and identifies, usually by virtue of the role the member performs, the social group to which he or she belongs, it is good practice to restrict judgments to the context and to the social role but not over the full biography of the individual who plays that role. Those aspects remain anonymous, nameless. Thus, to pass by a student and to recognize him or her as a student need not entail the role "student" to cover the entire scope of that student's life and being. Such is the case with many other social roles and groups. There is always more that one could learn about the individual who occupies that social role.

In the case of epistemic closure, however, the identification of the social role is all one needs for a plethora of other judgments. In effect, to know that role is to know all there is to know about the individual. In effect, there is no distinction between him or her and the social role, which makes the individual an essential representative of the entire group. The group, then, becomes pure exterior being. Its members are without "insides" or hidden spaces for interrogation. One thus counts for all. The guiding principle of avoiding the fallacy of hasty generalizations is violated here as a matter of course. Du Bois's counsel, then, is toward opening this space of inquiry.

Our turn to anonymity brings us to sociological interpretation. To break out of epistemic closure, one needs to recognize that blacks have points of view on the world. Such an approach "should aim to study those finer manifestations of social life which history can but mention and which statistics can not count, such as the expression of Negro life as found in their hundred newspapers, their considerable literature, their music and folklore and their germ of esthetic life—in fine, in all the movements and customs among them that manifest the existence of a distinct social mind" (Du Bois 1898b, 20).

The second category, the peculiar social environment, addresses the problem of options raised before. Du Bois ends the essay by issuing a call that has lost its power today in light of recent efforts to discard the study of race: "True lovers of humanity can only hold higher the pure ideals of science, and continue to insist that if we would solve a problem we must study it" (Du Bois 1898b, 23). The transition from Negro to Black to Afro-American to African American has been marked, as well, by the transition from race to contemporary claims of its scientific invalidity and its so-called social and political irrelevance (for example, Appiah 1992). In response, critics have issued the same objection as Du Bois did a century ago: deny as we might the continued relevance of race and racism in the lives of large segments of the American population, how will those who continue to bear the brunt of discrimination present their case without data that identify them as targets of the discrimination?

EPISTEMIC LIMITATIONS OF RACE REPRESENTATION

The problem with data is that they must be rigorously gathered. Rigor here means that the process of gathering and interpreting data must be guided by an understanding of the challenges raised by human studies and an understanding of the logic of social action and claims of universality. Moreover, the challenge addresses the integrity of the theorist as well, especially the theorist who might be a member of the community under discussion. As Du Bois observed later in his *Soliloquy*:

I became painfully aware that merely being born in a group, does not necessarily make one possessed of complete knowledge concerning it. I had learned far more from Philadelphia Negroes than I had

taught them concerning the Negro Problem. (Du Bois 1968, 198)

A member of a group does not live his or her everyday experience in a way that constitutes the reflection of study. To study one's lived reality requires a displacement and a new set of questions about that reality that render one's experiences, at best, data to be added to the stream of data to be interpreted. But more, the theoretical questions raised may be such that there is no precedent for them, which means that by raising them, one has placed oneself outside of a privileged sphere of knowledge. How one lives in a community is not identical with the sort of knowledge involved in how one studies a community.

A striking feature of Du Bois's recommendations for rigorous study, however, is that in the midst of all his almost positivistic conceptions of objectivity in the study of black folk, there are also the hermeneutical considerations and the experiential considerations of looking at blacks from the inside. These are concerns that Du Bois himself deploys in another essay from the period, "On the Conservation of the Races" (1898a), a paper that he presented to the Negro Academy the same year in which he presented "The Study of the Negro Problems" to the American Academy of Political and Social Science. The two academies represented a historical reality that took existential and phenomenological forms in Du Bois's two essays. For it is "inside," so to speak, to a community of black intellectuals, that Du Bois brought forth the existential phenomenological reading of the nihilistic threat of denied membership as a struggle of twoness, of two souls, of double consciousness (Du Bois [1898a] 1998, [1903] 1995; Allen 1997).

Double consciousness raises not only the experience of seeing the world from an American point of view and a black point of view, from the point of view of the black diaspora but also from the contradictions encumbered by such experience. Must "black" be anathema to "American"? What black folks experience are the contradictions of American society; it is an experience of what is denied, an experience of the contradictions between the claims of equality and the lived reality of inequality, between the claims of justice and the lived reality of systematic and systemic injustice, between the claims of a universal normativity and the lived reality of white normativity, between the claims of blacks not having any genuine points of view and the lived reality of blacks' point of view on such claims (compare with Gordon 1998).

By raising the question of black problems from blacks' point of view, Du Bois raised the question of an "inside" that required an approach to social phenomena that puts the theorist in a position to break down the gap between himself or herself and the subjects of study. For in principle if the theorist can imagine the black point of view as a point of view that can be communicated, then already a gap between the theorist and the black subject of study has been bridged. The theorist, whether white or of color, must work with the view

of communicability and, simultaneously, a process of interrogation that will bring forth what black subjects are willing to divulge. In short, the method presupposes agency, freedom, and responsibility, which transforms the epistemological expectations of inquiry. From the "outside," one could receive limited data. From the "inside," one could, as well, receive limited data. Combined, one receives "good" data, "solid" data, "rigorously acquired" data, but never "complete" data. It is by staying attuned to the incompleteness of all data with regard to human beings that one makes the approach humanistic. It is a method that reveals that, when it comes to the human being, there will always be more to learn and, hence, more to research.

SOME CONCLUSIONS

Our times are marked by a profound divide in approaches to human study. The sentiments, as we have seen, gear toward total abandonment of liberatory questions in favor of identity questions. Without the liberatory calling, identity questions become struggles over definition or the rejection of definitions, ironically, on supposedly purely theoretical grounds. The result has been, on one hand, the continued, often reactionary influence of neopositivistic approaches, where the effort is to imitate the natural sciences through quantitative conceptions of objectivity. At the other extreme is the postmodern rejection of all "totalizations" and concepts like "progress" and "rigor" and even the adjective "human" in human study. There, hermeneutics or interpretation has taken a path to the seemingly trivial (Rickman 1998). For African Americans, the situation is particularly moribund, for how could a denial of humanity benefit a people who have spent more than 300 years struggling for it? How can African Americans take seriously the constructivity of their situation when social reality continues to smack them in the face as a reality that is hardly fictitious? And as for neopositivism, with its demand of value neutrality, a similar criticism applies: it is only the powerful who can afford a world devoid of value since they are already situated in a position to be its beneficiary.

Neopositivism and postmodernism are not, however, the only alternatives. Interpretations can be socially situated by the complex network of questions that pertain to the study of the human being as a metastable subject that is coextensive with a set of values, including the values of freedom and expectations for the sort of life appropriate to mature members of a society. I say mature because without a coherent conception of maturity, all members of a social group, regardless of age, would be infantilized and, hence, problematic. Such an approach requires both taking seriously the conditions of objectivity raised by the intersubjective dynamics of the social world and the existential problematic of how human beings live. I have argued elsewhere that such a call is for an existential sociology (Gordon 1997b, chap. 4).

Now, a century after Du Bois's encomia, we face a population called African Americans. This population has been studied to the point of serving, throughout the twentieth century, as the bedrock of much sociological and anthropological work. That African Americans have been reinscribed into the grammar of race signification is such that the forces that precipitated the Negro problems are clearly problems that have made their way to the dawn of another century.

In his later years, Du Bois came to the conclusion that the study of a problem was a necessary but insufficient means of eliminating it. He did, as is well known, defy the adage of radicalism in youth and conservatism in old age by reversing its order. Du Bois became a revolutionary because, in the end, he saw that knowledge by itself does not compel action. For knowledge to become effective, it needs to achieve a degree of historical force. Part of the Du Boisian legacy is the rich body of texts on which to build our contemporary understanding of people of African descent. In effect, he contributed to the epistemic project of transforming a population of people through transforming the conditions of historic recognition. While the struggle for new social relations continues, the project of humanistic study is such that the possibilities offered by a richer understanding of human diversity may help set afoot, as well, the world for which Du Bois so faithfully struggled. It is with such thoughts in mind that I come to a close with a repetition of his words:

Let then the Dreams of the dead rebuke the Blind who think that what is will be forever and teach them that what was worth living for must live again and that which merited death must stay dead.

Teach us, Forever Dead, there is no Dream but Deed, there is no Deed but Memory. (Du Bois 1968, 422-23)

References

Allen, Earnest. 1997. On the Reading of Riddles: Rethinking Du Boisian "Double Consciousness." In *Existence in Black*, ed. Lewis R. Gordon. New York: Routledge.

Appiah, K. Anthony. 1992. *In My Father's House: Africa in the Philosophy of Culture*. New York: Oxford University Press.

Bell, Derrick. 1992. *Faces from the Bottom of the Well: The Permanence of Racism*. New York: Basic Books.

Du Bois, W.E.B. [1896] 1969. *The Suppression of the African Slave-Trade to the United States of America, 1683-1870*. New York: Schocken Books.

———. [1898a] 1998. On the Conservation of the Races. In *African Philosophy: An Anthology*, ed. Emmanuel Chukwudi Eze. Cambridge, MA: Blackwell.

———. 1898b. The Study of the Negro Problems. *The Annals* of the American Academy of Political and Social Science 11(Jan.):1-23.

———. 1899. *The Philadelphia Negro: A Social Study*. Philadelphia: University of Pennsylvania Press.

———. [1903] 1995. *The Souls of Black Folk*. New York: Signet/Penguin.

———. [1935] 1992. *Black Reconstruction in America, 1860-1880*. New York: Atheneum.

———. 1968. *The Autobiography of W.E.B. Du Bois: A Soliloquy on Viewing My Life from the Last Decade of Its First Century*. Ed. Herbert Aptheker. New York: International.

Ellison, Ralph. 1987. *Going into the Territory*. New York: Vintage.

———. 1992. *Shadow and Act*. New York: Vintage.

Fanon, Frantz. 1967. *Black Skin, White Masks*. Trans. Charles Lam Markmann. New York: Grove Press.

Freire, Paulo. 1990. *Pedagogy of the Oppressed*. Trans. M. B. Ramos. New York: Continuum.

Gordon, Lewis R. 1995a. *Bad Faith and Antiblack Racism*. Atlantic Highlands, NJ: Humanities Press.

———. 1995b. *Fanon and the Crisis of European Man: An Essay on Philosophy and the Human Sciences*. New York: Routledge.

———. 1997a. *Existence in Black: An Anthology of Black Existential Philosophy*. New York: Routledge.

———. 1997b. *Her Majesty's Other Children: Sketches of Racism from a Neocolonial Age*. Lanham, MD: Rowman & Littlefield.

———. 1998. The Problem of Autobiography in Theoretical Engagements with Black Intellectual Production, *Small Axe: A Journal of Criticism* 4(Sept.): 47-64.

Hegel, G.W.F. 1956. *The Philosophy of History*. Trans. J. Sebree. New York: Dover.

hooks, bell. 1981. *Ain't I a Woman? Black Women and Feminism*. Boston: South End Press.

———. 1984. *Feminist Theory from Margins to Center*. Boston: South End Press.

———. 1990. *Yearning: Race, Gender, and Cultural Politics*. Boston: South End Press.

James, Joy Ann. 1996. *Resisting State Violence*. Minneapolis: University of Minnesota Press.

———. 1997. *Transcending the Talented Tenth: Black Leaders and American Intellectualism*. New York: Routledge.

Locke, Alain. 1989. *The Philosophy of Alain Locke: Harlem Renaissance and Beyond*. Ed. Leonard Harris. Philadelphia: Temple University Press.

Mudimbe, V. Y. 1988. *The Invention of Africa*. Bloomington: Indiana University Press.

Outlaw, Lucius T. 1996. *On Race and Philosophy*. New York: Routledge.

Rickman, H. P. 1998. Deconstruction: The Unacceptable Face of Hermeneutics. *Journal of the British Society for Phenomenology* 29(3):299-313.

West, Cornel. 1993. *Race Matters*. Boston: Beacon Press.

ANNALS, *AAPSS*, **568**, March 2000

W.E.B. Du Bois on the Study of Social Problems

By LUCIUS T. OUTLAW, JR.

ABSTRACT: This close reading and interpretation of Du Bois's "The Study of the Negro Problems" (Du Bois 1898b) focuses on several matters: the historical and biographical contexts within which Du Bois produced and presented the essay; what the author takes to be Du Bois's convictions regarding the nature and production of scientific, truthful knowledge, and the importance of such knowledge for resolving social problems and thereby contributing to progressive social evolution. These convictions presupposed and were conditioned by a particular conception of social reality in terms of which Du Bois formulated a conception of "social problems," particularly those having to do with "the Negro" in the United States. Finally, the author reviews Du Bois's critique of then-prevailing social science and his proposed "Program for Future Study" of "Negro problems" and concludes with a brief assessment.

Lucius T. Outlaw, Jr., teacher and essayist, is T. Wistar Brown Professor of Philosophy at Haverford College (Pennsylvania), where he has been a member of the faculty since 1980. He has held visiting professorships at Spelman College, Howard University, Hamilton College, and Boston College. He has authored a collection of essays entitled On Race and Philosophy *(1996).*

DU BOIS prepared "The Study of the Negro Problems" for presentation at the 44th meeting of the American Academy of Political and Social Science in Philadelphia in November of 1897.[1] He had come to Philadelphia from Wilberforce, Ohio, after gladly accepting an offer from the University of Pennsylvania to conduct sociological studies of Philadelphia's Seventh Ward that would eventuate in *The Philadelphia Negro* (Du Bois 1899). He and his new wife, Nina, arrived during the summer of 1896 and remained in Philadelphia into December of 1897, when they moved to Atlanta, where Du Bois took a position at Atlanta University.

It is important to note that "The Study of the Negro Problems" was but one among several seminal research, creative thinking and writing, and persuasional presentational efforts undertaken by Du Bois during the years in Philadelphia while he was preoccupied, first and foremost, with the Seventh Ward work of door-to-door surveying, tabulating and analyzing, and writing:

— 5 March 1897: Presentation of "The Conservation of Races" as the second in the series of Occasional Papers of the American Negro Academy during a founding meeting at Lincoln Memorial Church in Washington, D.C.;
— July and August 1897: Survey work conducted in Virginia published as "The Negroes of Farmville, Virginia: A Social Study" in the U.S. Department of Labor Bulletin of January 1898 (Du Bois 1898a);

— August 1897: "Strivings of the Negro People" published in Atlantic Monthly (Du Bois 1897b), republished in 1903, with minor revisions, as "Of Our Spiritual Strivings," the first chapter in *The Souls of Black Folk*; and
— 19 November 1897: "The Study of the Negro Problems" read at a meeting of the American Academy of Political and Social Science and published in *The Annals* in January 1898.

Of particular interest to me are the differences with regard to agenda, subject matter, audience, and mode of articulation of these endeavors and writings in light of what might be taken to be Du Bois's intentions and for whom intended. "The Conservation of Races" was meant to serve as an articulate agenda for and to motivate a very particular audience of Negroes and was thus different from those persons to be served and motivated by "Strivings of the Negro People," a work which was directed, to a significant degree I believe, at whites as well as Negroes. "The Negroes of Farmville, Virginia: A Social Study" and "The Study of the Negro Problems" are directed at different audiences while serving importantly different, though related, agendas: to provide scientific accounts of Negro life in service to efforts of social reform.

These writings provide early examples of Du Bois engaging in what David Levering Lewis (1993) characterizes as "a seductive Apache dance" amidst "several clashing premises" in the later *The Philadel-*

phia Negro. However, Lewis does not convince me that what he takes to be the premises which Du Bois committed to in rationalizing his efforts in *The Philadelphia Negro* did, in fact, clash. I am convinced, however, that Du Bois was endeavoring to fashion a program and strategies for resolving problems of Negro life and thereby enhance the progressive development of a Negro racial group plagued by the complexly interrelated effects on them of racial prejudices and economic exploitation by white folks, and of problematic orientations and practices that had become characteristic of Negro social and cultural life in the United States that Du Bois (among a number of Negroes) was convinced were inimical to the resolution of social problems affecting their lives and impairing their progressive social evolution. As I understand Du Bois, he was convinced that the complexities of the problems, among these the vested interests of various white and Negro folks and organizations of different socioeconomic groupings and orientations, required a program for problem resolution and strategies of implementation attentive to these complexities and persuasive for important persons in the various groups.

For Du Bois, such a program had to be science-certified as truthful and ethically appropriate in helping to bring about freedom and justice for Negroes, who were for him a distinct race with a message of value for the United States and the world (Du Bois [1897a] 1992). Furthermore, as a young, highly educated, Negro man with an attitude unhampered by self-doubt and on a mission to lead

efforts to redeem and uplift his race but not blinded by his own self-assurance or his idealism, Du Bois knew that his efforts would require astute dexterity in a rapidly developing, world-historic young nation that, though supposedly "founded in Liberty and dedicated to the proposition that all men are created equal" (in the words of Abraham Lincoln), was thoroughly structured by programs serving white racial supremacy and by the enslavement and suppression otherwise of Africans becoming American Negroes. He would know that he must do a dance, if you will.

But, characteristic of the man, it was a decidedly pragmatic dance of the intellect choreographed largely by himself and performed in and through novel empirical and historical research, critical interpretations, and scholarly and creative writings all with a breadth of learnedness, arresting nuance, penetrating insights, and frequent prescience that, of those I have read and reread, I continue to find especially impressive. As a Harvard-trained, very promising, ambitious young Negro scholar and social scientist, Du Bois had been recruited by white folks, Lewis reasons (Lewis 1993, 188), to conduct a sociological study of Philadelphia's troubled and troubling Seventh Ward, with its high concentration of Negroes, in order to legitimate, by his being the Negro social scientist in charge of the study, the credibility of an expected report of deplorable conditions that would confirm white folks' judgments of the Negro's inherent backwardness and inferiority. By providing such a report, Du Bois would aid Philadelphia's notable and influential whites in determining what type of quarantine they should impose, and for how long, to contain the "black plague" threatening the city's "healthy native stock" of white folks (188).

Du Bois, however, had ideas regarding races different from those of the white notables, about the then present and future of race relations in the United States especially, and about the importance of right thinking, truthfulness, social reform, and social evolution relative to the Negro. Many of the notables, Du Bois was convinced, social scientists and reformers among them, were not thinking correctly about such matters. Moreover, he thought most people, including blacks, quite ignorant of these matters. He was determined, then, to conceive and make operational a conception of scientific study of the social world that would produce truthful, scientific accounts of the problems affecting Negroes that would be sufficient to compel right thinking and corrective social action.

For Du Bois to be successful, astute dexterity in several related lines of endeavor would be required involving and directed at different audiences—Negro and white—of different social and economic status and drawing on different sources and types of resources. David Levering Lewis offers the following assessment of Du Bois's dance as he finds it played out in *The Philadelphia Negro*:

Seeing himself as the custodian of privileged insights capable of transforming American race relations, Du Bois was determined to gain the widest and most respectful hearing possible. But to do this, he obviously must have calculated that it would be necessary to write what amounted almost to two books in one—one that would not be immediately denounced or ridiculed by the arbiters of mainstream knowledge, influence, and order for its transparent heterodoxy; and a second one that would, over time, deeply penetrate the social sciences and gradually improve race-relations policy through its non-immediately apparent interpretive radicalism. He set about, then, to write a study affirming and modifying yet also significantly subverting, the received sociological wisdom of the day. . . . Behind the moralizing, and the stern admonitions to black people to behave like lending-library patrons, the book would speak calmly yet devastatingly of the history and logic of poverty and racism. (Lewis 1993, 189-90)

Lewis is on to something important. Consequently, in examining "The Study of the Negro Problems," produced during the period when Du Bois was engaged in studying Negroes in Philadelphia's Seventh Ward and in Farmville, Virginia, I have found it helpful to keep in mind the constrained and highly charged intellectual—as well as the social, political, and economic—maneuver spaces in which he was compelled to work while devising and pursuing his mission of scientific study of social problems. I have also found it helpful to remind myself of his concerns and efforts in "The Conservation of Races," written for and presented to a Negro audience six months before he presented "The Study of the Negro Problems" to the mostly white producers and custodians of social scientific knowledge organized for such as the American Academy of Political and Social Science. With these reminders, I am better able to appreciate "The Study of the Negro Problems" as one among several of Du Bois's determined efforts during 1897 to correct thinking about race and race relations in the United States while pursuing his mission to lead efforts to uplift the Negro.

DU BOIS ON SCIENTIFIC TRUTH, PROBLEM RESOLUTION, AND SOCIAL EVOLUTION

One might characterize "The Study of the Negro Problems" as audacious (though the African American vernacular expression "bodacious" strikes me as more apt). Of course, there is its deftness and clarity of purpose and articulation. By the end of the essay's fourth paragraph, Du Bois has done the following: set forth a poignant assessment of "the present period in the development of sociological study" in terms of observations of the growth and evolution of U.S. society; pronounced the enterprise of sociology and its results lacking; announced his discovery of an unrecognized field of opportunities for scientific inquiry arising from the presence in the United States of eight million black people; and enumerated "certain considerations concerning the study of the social problems affecting American Negroes" to which he will devote his attention in the presentation (Du Bois 1898b, 1, 3). But there is more: the confidence with which he appropriates and positions himself as an appropriate—even authoritative—

pursuer and acquirer of scientific truth gained through rigorous, objective, empirical study.

For Du Bois, such truthful and thereby ethically appropriate knowledge of the races in the United States especially was to be the normative knowledge by which to guide policy formation and implementation, social practices, and the social evolution of the Negro race and of the nation as a complex whole. Epistemological concerns (that is, concerns regarding the production, validation, and legitimation of truthful, scientific knowledge of social realities) and pragmatic concerns for social evolution (that is, for civilizational development: the humane, progressive development of social life conditioned by freedom and justice, for the Negro especially) were thus intimately related matters for him. Already there had been attempts, he acknowledged, to "put the nation in possession of a body of truth in accordance with which it might act intelligently" (Du Bois 1898b, 11). However, many of the most powerful and influential nation-building white folks, among them many of the white arbiters and custodians of the scientific production of knowledge of social realities, were bent upon having these sciences underwrite white racial supremacy. Du Bois took the opportunity provided him to speak at the meeting of the American Academy of Political and Social Science to present a case for systematic and comprehensive studies not just of Negro problems but of the results of social scientific studies in the United States completed up to that time. He dared to go even further: he gave his audience instruction as to "the scope and method which future scientific inquiry should take . . . and . . . the agencies by which the work can best be carried out" (2).

Why such audacity? In my judgment, because primarily Du Bois was an especially self-assured and determined young man with firmly held convictions, reasoned faith, and science-inspired optimism. He was convinced that, ultimately, human history was a matter of thoroughly human social (in the widest sense) activities and processes that conform to a particular kind of natural social lawfulness, processes and activities involving human interactions in and through social structures (institutions, organizations, family arrangements, patterns of activity) that were a function of willful human agency (formulating and acting to realize particular ideals, engaging in various practices). He was convinced that the acquisition and application of truthful scientific knowledge of social realities was necessary for realizing and enjoying flourishing life in freedom and justice and thus was fundamental to the full development and proper exercise of human agency (at the time often characterized as "mature manliness"). The truth, Du Bois believed, could set all free; thus, in his presentation he spoke with conviction of the need to safeguard the sanctity of truthful scientific knowledge. He was convinced, as well, of the ability and responsibility of the most talented among every people to acquire truthful knowledge and to use it to lead others in its proper application so as to guide the progressive evolution of life socially, politically, economically, and culturally.

Du Bois, then, was the living embodiment, the living exercise, of a decisive combination of convictions that drew on empiricist epistemology, a progressive philosophy of history, and evolutionary accounts of social realities. This combination was further enhanced (and complicated) by a racialist philosophical anthropology (that is, regarding the human species as made up of several distinct races—the defining raciality of which was determined by historical and sociological factors, hardly at all by heritable biological factors—each of them with distinct cultural "messages" to contribute to the storehouse of human civilization [Du Bois (1897a) 1992]) and influenced significantly by both Christian and secular humanist ethical convictions. I dare to say the latter were among the more important constitutive features and driving forces of Du Bois's character and personality, of his worldview, of his life in the world, and thus of his mission on behalf of the Negro race and the development of the United States of America as indeed a nation-state of freedom and justice for all. These convictions and faith had been cultivated and enhanced through Du Bois's formal studies and extracurricular learning experiences while at Fisk, Harvard, and the University of Berlin. They informed his empirical investigations of urban life in the Seventh Ward of Philadelphia and of rural life in Farmville, Virginia. These were the motivating and orienting convictions at the heart of Du Bois's conception of and agenda for scientific study of problematic social realities, of Negro life in particular, as set forth in "The Study of the Negro Problems."

DU BOIS'S CONCEPTIONS
OF SOCIAL REALITY
AND "SOCIAL PROBLEMS"

Du Bois, I have noted, understood human history as constituted by the transgenerational efforts of psychologically, culturally bonded and sociologically bounded self-reproducing social collectivities to maintain group and individual life conditioned by, and in response to, circumstances of time and place while guided by accounts of the past and present, and by anticipated or hoped-for futures. Such a social collectivity, what he called "an organized social group" (Du Bois 1898b, 2), was for him the principal agent of human history-making and was thus a major element in his inventory of social realities (though a few years later he would argue that "exceptional" individuals comprising a "talented tenth" of each collectivity must play leading roles in the making of the group's history [Du Bois (1903) 1992], and many years later, he would reexamine and restate this theory of group leadership as the "guiding hundredth" [Du Bois (1948) 1996]). Furthermore, Du Bois thought of these social groups as organized in and through shared ideals, which also provide the defining and orienting meanings and values that motivate and guide social activities—individual and group, mundane and extraordinary—and provide for shared sociocultural life.

However, when a group is situated such that it "cannot realize its group ideals, through the inability to adapt a certain desired line of action to given conditions of life," then the group's life situation has become problematic: they are living—and may thus become for themselves and for other social groups with whom they are in contact—a "social problem" (Du Bois 1898b, 2).

When analyzing social realities, two complex factors are crucial for Du Bois in determining whether an organized social group's life is problematic. One factor is the circumstances in which members of the collectivity fashion and live their group-conditioned lives, circumstances that can be evaluated in terms of whether they are conducive to the collectivity's members realizing their individual and shared ideals. The other factor is the character of a group's collection of action-guiding ideals and beliefs and of the activities its members engage in as they seek to make a life in particular circumstances: that is, whether these ideals, beliefs, and actions are appropriate to the challenges and opportunities of circumstances such that they promote adaptive success in meeting and resolving challenges and exploiting opportunities in ways that result in the group's survival and progressive evolution.

Furthermore, Du Bois noted, the circumstances of social life vary historically and globally and in each setting change continuously, in large part due to human activity. Successful living, he reasoned, requires that organized social groups adapt, particularly those whose members move—or are moved—from one set of circumstances to others substantially, even drastically, different: that is, through experience and learning, members of the group must adjust their repertoires of action-guiding beliefs and ideals and their actions to changed and changing circumstances so as to survive, reproduce, develop, and flourish. Doing so would constitute, for Du Bois, progressive social evolution. But achieving such evolution requires adaptation: that is, more or less substantial changes to prevailing circumstances or to a group's ideals, beliefs, and practices—or to both. It is the challenging responsibility of scientists of the social world, Du Bois argued, to determine objectively and truthfully (that is, scientifically) the nature and extent of problematic social life that impedes progressive evolution. The living realities of Negro life in the United States of America, when measured against the nation's founding ideals, were, for Du Bois, a truly historic opportunity to provide scientific explanation of profoundly problematic social existence in order to guide efforts of reformation.

However, there were substantial complications to be attended to in providing such explanatory guidance. The world, Du Bois noted, was not constituted by a single organized social group of the kind of concern to him, but by several: namely, by the world's great races as he had referred to them in his "On the Conservation of Races" ([1897a] 1992). Developments definitive of the new historical configuration of developments constituting Western modernity had resulted in unprecedented circumstances of subgroupings of several of the great races coming into contact, increasingly so in particular nation-states. One of the most novel and complex of these circumstances, in Du Bois's estimation, had been formed in the United States when subgroups of two of what were widely regarded as the most dissimilar of races—white and Negro—were brought together through the massive enslaving continental relocations of Negroes by white folks who were intent on fashioning a nation-state in which their race's interests and ideals, including their invidious prejudices against the Negro, would reign supreme.

By Du Bois's reckoning, Negroes' success in surviving—to say nothing of thriving—in these novel and extremely challenging circumstances was thus conditioned by a great deal more than their own ideals and practices. Racialized enslavement, prompted and sustained by the economic motives and racial prejudices of white folks, had become a decisive factor in the Negro's history of distorted and impeded development in the Americas and a key impediment to realizing group ideals conducive to their flourishing. A future life of growing in freedom and justice required, then, novel adaptive strategies appropriate to the circumstances and effective in changing the circumstances. Neither success-producing adaptive strategies nor changes to circumstances to allow for greater successful adaptation were to be had without the most adequate and appropriate understanding of conditioning circumstances and possibilities for living differently and better.

With regard to the problematic life of the Negro, that understanding, Du Bois was convinced, could only be had in the form of rigorously historical, thorough and systematic, objective, scientific knowledge, based on empirical observation and comparison, of the nature, causes, and development of problematic Negro life, especially during slavery. No such knowledge had been produced, Du Bois claimed, in part because the Negro's situation in the Americas and that of the young United States of America were entirely novel historically.

Here, then, was both great need and great opportunity. Du Bois was motivated by especially heightened senses of human history-making in general, and of the United States in particular, as a result of studies and travels that prompted his developing critical perspectives on the historical development of various peoples in the world to which to compare the development of Negroes in the United States. He was ready to seize the moment and bring science of the social world to bear in careful, systematic, and critical studies of problematic Negro life in order to resolve the race's problems and allow for its progressive evolution and that of the nation-state. But by bringing social science to bear on novel circumstances challenging the nation, the mission of science—the production of a systematic body of true knowledge "worth the knowing"—would thereby be legitimated and advanced (Du Bois 1898b, 1). Du Bois was convinced that here was a moment of historic possibility: need could be met and opportunity realized through the proper study of "the Negro problems."

Why did Du Bois believe the achievement of both these ends—one epistemological (the production of truthful scientific knowledge of problematic social realities), the other a matter of social pragmatics (using that knowledge to resolve the problems and enhance social evolution)—could be assisted by successful study of the problems facing Negro Americans? Answering this question requires a closer look at Du Bois's related conceptions of social reality and of historically informed, scientifically produced explanatory knowledge of social reality. The "Negro problems" are the prism that factors out the two conceptions and their intimate relations.

A DIALECTICAL CONCEPTION OF SOCIAL DEVELOPMENT

Again, for Du Bois a social problem is constituted by the inability of an organized social group to adapt particular preferred strategies of action for realizing certain group ideals to particular life conditions. Ideals and action strategies are always in mutually conditioning relation to the circumstances of life: the actions following from—or in violation of—ideals are either appropriate and lead to success—that is, survival and progressive development as a consequence of the resolution of problems— or they are inappropriate because unsuccessful—that is, they impair living that might otherwise promote progressive development. Conditions, however, change, and so action strategies and ideals must change and adapt accordingly. The problematic situation of the American Negro is thus not "one unchanged question" but one with a "long historical development" that changes with the nation's "growth and evolution" (Du Bois 1898b, 3). Furthermore, the Negro social problematic, he had determined, was not one problem but a "plexus" (3) of new and old, simple and complex social problems. And what makes a particular plexus of social problems distinctively Negro problems? Only that they "group themselves about those Africans whom two centuries of slave-trading brought into the land" (3). This, he argued, is the "one bond of unity" among the various problems that, taken together, constitute the plexus of social problems, which it is appropriate to call "the Negro problems."[2]

Du Bois makes several especially deft moves of great significance at this early point in the essay. In accounting for the "bond of unity" in what he referred to as the "plexus" of Negro problems by reasoning that the problems "group themselves about" Africans and African-descended persons present in the country as a result of two centuries of enslavement, Du Bois offered a substantially different account of the problematic realities of Negro life, a substantially different philosophical and social anthropology of the Negro, than the prevailing accounts of that era. He contradicted those who reasoned that the Negroes' problems were functions of their inherent racial character, of their essential

nature as a race of Negroes. Du Bois sought to redirect the focus of explanatory causality away from the raciality of the Negro to the action strategies and ideals of the Negro, on one hand, and to historical and socioeconomic circumstances, on the other. But the circumstances of Negro life, to a great extent, were directly and indirectly conditioned by white folks and their prejudices against and economic exploitation of black folk.

The full force of Du Bois's conception of the problematics of Negro social life conveyed by the phrase "they group themselves about" was not—is not—immediately obvious, I suspect, which makes for the deftness—and the danger—of his articulation: that is, the possibility that its full meaning and force as intended by Du Bois might well be missed and prevailing notions of the inherent deformity and inferiority of the Negro not only not be disputed and disrupted, but be reinforced by self-serving (mis)interpretations by white listeners and readers that Du Bois was confirming their prejudicial judgments. That he was not, I believe, is evidenced by his arguments on behalf of sustaining the Negro race advanced in "On the Conservation of Races," which he presented to the American Negro Academy eight months before his presentation of "The Study of the Negro Problems" during the November meeting of the American Academy of Political and Social Science.

Even closer note should be taken, then, of Du Bois's efforts in "The Study of the Negro Problems" for the novel contributions he makes to knowledge of the complex inter-workings of the social world and to the production of such knowledge by his understanding of the "interplay of race and economics" (Lewis 1993, 203) that inform his essay. The empirical work he was conducting in Philadelphia's Seventh Ward had prompted questions about possible influences of circumstances of origin on the lives of Negroes who had migrated to Philadelphia from the South. Du Bois went to rural Farm-ville, Virginia, to investigate the historical development of Negroes under conditions of slavery to better understand the lives of those who migrated to urban settings such as Philadelphia. Consequently, Du Bois had come to a rather poignant understanding of what Lewis terms "the novel triad of race-class-economics" (208) that would form the basis of analysis and interpretation of *The Philadelphia Negro* (Du Bois 1899).

However, Du Bois's account of the interworkings of race, class, and economics in "The Study of the Negro Problems" is not without difficulties. He made a valiant effort to identify economic motives, rather than invidious racial prejudice, as the initial generative cause of Negro problems, beginning with their enslavement. According to Du Bois (1898b, 3-4), initially, during the late seventeenth and early eighteenth centuries, there was an "all-absorbing economic need" in the Americas for "the creation of a proper labor supply to develop American wealth." In the West Indies, he argued, this need was met by enslaving Negroes and Indians; in mainland colonies the need was met by importing "Negroes and

indented servants." "Immediately then," Du Bois continued, "there arose the question of the legal status of these slaves and servants; and dozens of enactments . . . were made 'for the proper regulation of slaves and servants' . . . to solve problems of labor and not of race or color." Subsequently, he concluded, "the economic superiority of the slave system" and "the fact that the slaves were neither of the same race, language nor religion as the servants and their masters" were the two circumstances that gave rise to problematic differentiations in the labor supply. "In laboring classes thus widely separated there naturally arose a difference in legal and social standing. Colonial statutes soon ceased to embrace the regulations applying to slaves and servants in one chapter, and laws were passed for servants on the one hand and for Negro slaves on the other."

What is both striking and problematic about Du Bois's explanatory developmental account is that, after asserting that creating a proper labor supply was the driving economic need and thus the generative source of the development of problems that will "group themselves about the Negro," Du Bois reasoned that in the colonies of the mainland this need was met by the importation of slaves and servants, the latter group, apparently, being persons who were not Negroes. Yet, in the very next sentence he wrote "of the legal status of these slaves and servants" (Du Bois 1898b, 3). Negroes were enslaved; non-Negro indented servants were not. Thus, the historically sequential explanatory account

Du Bois offered—that the Negro become slave and the non-Negro become servant were the subsequent development of a racially segmented labor market—seems to have been undercut by the very terms of his account: Du Bois himself used racial distinctions to explain the initial development of the labor supply. That is, from the outset it seems, the labor supply was racially segmented and, by Du Bois's own reckoning, had economic significance only (Negro slaves versus [non-Negro] indented servants) before these "laboring classes" were transformed into racialized distinctions of "legal and social standing" (3).

According to Du Bois's own descriptive/explanatory account, the differences of "legal and social standing" seemed to have been operative from the start, namely, with the categorization of laborers at importation. The question of "a proper labor supply" for the colonies of the mainland was "answered by the importation of Negroes and indented servants" (Du Bois 1898b, 3). If correct, then the earliest efforts to create "a proper labor supply to develop American wealth" (3), defined the classes of labor by function and status (enslaved, indented) and distinguished the labor classes on racial terms: those imported as indented servants (not Negroes), those enslaved in the West Indies (Negroes and Indians), and those imported as slaves (Negroes). This racialized segmentation was not a subsequent development, as Du Bois proposed, though shortly after the importation of the first African laborers there would indeed be subsequent

substantial changes, anchored in racial distinctions, in the legal, social, economic, and political—in the very ontological—meanings of the categories used to distinguish among groups of laborers.

Nonetheless, of lasting significance was Du Bois's conception of the centrality of particularities of historical development involving the interrelations of race, class, and economics to the problematic nature of Negro life. (Equally significant, we can see with hindsight, aided substantially by the work of Joy James [1997], among others, was the absence of what we now regard as appropriate considerations of gender as an important element at play in conditioning the problematic nature of Negro life.) This was not, however, a matter of the development of Negro life in and of itself, but of the interrelated development of the Negro as part and parcel of the development of Euro-American, racialized, capitalist modernity, particularly the Negro slave-based economy of the South that became "not only an economic monstrosity, but a political menace" (Du Bois 1898b, 6) which led to a social crisis that resulted in civil war.

The ending of that war, however, did not resolve the originating problems: "The Civil War simply left us face to face with the same sort of problems of social condition and caste which were beginning to face the nation a century ago" (Du Bois 1898b, 6). Thus, the compelling need for systematic scientific investigation of post–Civil War Negro problems, though their origins preceded the war: the problems are "living, growing social questions whose progeny will survive to curse the nation, unless we grapple with them manfully and intelligently" (6). For Du Bois, social growth is but "a succession of problems"; the Negro problems a result of "275 years of evolution" distinguished by failure to incorporate the Negro into the group life of the nation consistent with the nation's ideals of freedom and justice due to invidious white prejudice against and economic exploitation of the Negro on one hand, and thereby the backwardness (ignorance, crime, and social degradation) and impaired group life and ideals of the Negro on the other.[3] What, then, was to be done?

DU BOIS'S CRITIQUE OF PREVAILING SOCIAL SCIENCE AND "PROGRAM FOR FUTURE STUDY"

Du Bois envisioned "a broad and systematic study of the history and condition of the American Negroes" (Du Bois 1898b, 15) so thorough that the scope and duration would require massive resources—human, fiscal, and intellectual—and years of coordinated effort. No such venture had even been attempted. And what work had been done, he judged, "bears but small proportion to the work still to be done" though he took pains not to "disparage in any way the work already done by students of these questions" (11). That work he judged unsystematic, not based on thorough knowledge of the details of Negro life, uncritical, and, an especially serious failure, as having treated Negro slaves "as one inert changeless mass [with] no conception of a social

evolution and development among them" (14).

The Negro problems as social problems were consequences of the impaired social evolution of the nation and of the Negro and, Du Bois warned, were a curse threatening the nation. The source and nature of that threat—as Du Bois recounted first in "The Study of the Negro Problems," then again, according to David Levering Lewis, in *The Philadelphia Negro*—were other than supposed and feared by the custodians of social science meeting as the American Academy of Political and Social Science. Both they and white folks generally were partly responsible: the former because, as scientists of the social world, they had not yet appreciated the novel field of study the Negro problems offered as an unprecedented instance of problematic social evolution awaiting scientifically informed corrective intervention; white folks generally because of their invidious prejudices against the Negro that barred the race from full and proper integration into the life of the nation. With calm and articulate confidence, Du Bois set forth his proposal for the rehabilitation and advancement of social science through the proper study of the Negro problems.

That rehabilitation was no small matter for Du Bois. At issue was the validation and legitimation of the sanctity of science as the means to the discovery of truths regarding social problems which must be available to all peoples to be used to guide progressive social evolution. However, audacious still, Du Bois took care to stake out an objectivity-preserving, nonpartisan position on the matter: namely, that social reform must be a mediate—not an immediate—aim of the quest for truth. Confusing the two aims, he warned, would result in the defeat of both. Moreover, he urged, the truth, when discovered by those who study the social world, must not be dallied with "to humor the whims of the day," for by doing so such persons would "degrade the high end of truth-seeking in a day when they need more and more to dwell upon its sanctity" (Du Bois 1898b, 11). Du Bois laid out in his presentation a philosophy of the social sciences that was already guiding and structuring his own empirical studies in Philadelphia; had structured his fieldwork in Farmville, Virginia; and would produce in the form of *The Philadelphia Negro*, by Lewis's assessment, a singularly "breakthrough achievement" in his breaking with the social theorizing characteristic of the times that attributed social life and practices to determination by heritable factors and in his bold efforts to develop a truly objective science of the social world (Lewis 1993, 201-2). Du Bois would later characterize his philosophy as an effort to "put science into sociology through a study of the conditions and problems of my own group" (Du Bois 1984, 15).

Proper, truth-seeking scientific study of the Negro problems would require additional structuring postulates. First needed was a recognition that the field of study is quite large; varied historically and by concrete settings; and made distinct by the ways, extent to which, and reasons why the problems "group themselves about" the Negro. Further, the uncompromising Du Bois requires of his white audience the explicit admission that "the Negro is a member of the human race ... is capable to a degree of improvement and culture, is entitled to have his interests considered according to his numbers in all conclusions as to the common weal" (Du Bois 1898b, 17).

The determined and audacious young Negro social scientist went further to divide the study of the Negro into two categories. The first category was that of "an organized social group," the study of which, Du Bois proposed, could be conducted most practicably if organized into four divisions:

1. Historical study. "Historical research must be subdivided in space and limited in time by the nature of the subject, the history of the different colonies and groups being followed and compared, the different periods of development receiving special study, and the whole subject being reviewed from different aspects."

2. Statistical investigation. "The concrete social status of the Negro can only be ascertained by intensive studies carried on in definitely limited localities, by competent investigators, in accordance with one general plan."

3. Anthropological measurement. "The most obvious peculiarity of the Negro—a peculiarity which is a large element in many of the problems affecting him—is his physical unlikeness to the people with whom he has been brought into contact. This difference is so striking that it

has become the basis of a mass of theory, assumption and suggestion which is deep-rooted and yet rests on the flimsiest basis of scientific fact. That there are differences between the white and black races is certain, but just what those differences are is known to none with an approach to accuracy."

4. Sociological interpretation. "It should include the arrangement and interpretation of historical and statistical matter in the light of the experience of other nations and other ages; it should aim to study those finer manifestations of social life which history can but mention and which statistics can not count, such as the expression of Negro life . . . in all the movements and customs among them that manifest the existence of a distinct social mind" (Du Bois 1898b, 18-20).

The second category of study Du Bois proposed was that of the "peculiar environment" of the Negro. Here the task was to isolate and study all cases of the "tangible phenomena" of prejudice against the Negro; the effect of prejudice on the physical development, mental acquisitiveness, and moral and social condition of the Negro as manifested in economic life, legal sanctions, crime, and lawlessness; and the influence of prejudice on American life and character generally (Du Bois 1898b, 20).

How to conduct, thoroughly and properly, such studies? It was clear to Du Bois that detailed, comprehensive, and properly coordinated studies of the Negro as he conceived of them and proposed to his audience of political and social scientists would

be long, difficult, and costly, requiring years of effort and mobilization of talent and resources that, in his estimation, only two agencies were capable of accomplishing: the government and the university. The former, however, should "confine itself mainly to the ascertainment of simple facts covering a broad field" (Du Bois 1898b, 21-22). The university, in Du Bois's estimation, was the only competent agency "for the study of these social problems in their more complicated aspects, where the desideratum is intensive study, by trained minds, according to the best methods" (22). And mindful, no doubt, of the politics of knowledge production in a racialized United States of America, Du Bois thought a southern Negro college (such as Atlanta University, Tuskegee, or Hampton, where research conferences had already been organized and hosted) a most appropriate institutional context for conducting the studies, though in collaboration with the likes of the University of Pennsylvania, Harvard, Columbia, or Johns Hopkins universities (21).

Du Bois would devote substantial energies in the years following his presentation of "The Study of the Negro Problems" engaging in carefully choreographed gentleman-scholar prospecting for the resources to undertake his visionary studies on the scale and with the comprehensive sweep and authoritative scientific integrity that he proposed. But he would not be successful. The white custodians of philanthropic resources and of social scientific investigation of racial matters, and of the preservation and evolution of the U.S. racial order, having found their Negro leader and broker in Booker T. Washington after his address at the Atlanta Exposition of 1895, were deliberate in their determination not to fund such efforts by the "radical" Du Bois. Instead, nearly half a century later some among their successors would recruit Swedish social scientist Gunnar Myrdal to organize and direct such studies as Du Bois proposed and to produce a final report in the form of *An American Dilemma: The Negro Problem and Modern Democracy* (Myrdal 1944).

DU BOIS'S CLOSING REMINDER AND EXHORTATION

Du Bois ended his essay and presentation with a critical assessment of what he took to be a prevailing attitude toward the work of scientists, describing the period as one in which there was "much flippant criticism of scientific work," mistaken regard for the truth seeker, and sneering at "the heroism of the laboratory" (Du Bois 1898b, 23). He moved to appropriate to his double mission—to study the Negro problems scientifically and, in the process, to rehabilitate, advance, and sanctify science while pointing to "the quickest path toward the solution of the present difficulties" (21)—all of the legitimating moral significance and responsibilities that come with committing oneself to being, and being recognized as, a "lover of humanity": "At such a time true lovers of humanity can only hold higher the pure ideals of science, and continue to insist that if we would solve a problem we must study it, and that there is but one coward on earth, and that is the coward that dare not know" (23).

Audacious to the very end of his presentation, Du Bois admonished his white colleagues in the political and social sciences: if they were truly lovers of humanity and committed to the pure ideals of science and if Negro life is problematic, then they must study it properly and thoroughly in order to understand why and in order to resolve the problems. Were they to continue to conduct themselves otherwise, he signified, were they to continue to dally with truth and the sanctity of scientific knowledge production, they would be cowards who dare not know the truth, without which neither the problems gathered about the Negro could be resolved successfully and appropriately, nor the U.S. civilizational project realize fully its highest ideals. As perhaps very few persons at the time had the courage or perspicacity to see, Du Bois understood exceedingly well the intimate, pragmatic relationships of truthful and adequate scientific knowledge of social reality, social problematics, and progressive social evolution, and how utterly crucial such knowledge was for resolving America's great racial curse. "The Study of the Negro Problems" remains one of the most astute articulations of such understanding, an exemplary case of a philosophy of social science appropriate to a U.S. context—then and now.

Notes

1. My understanding of the relevant historical and biographical contexts is much as-

sisted by the magisterial first volume of David Levering Lewis's biography of Du Bois (Lewis 1993, 179-210).

2. It would be worthwhile to explore Du Bois's aid to thought of the notion of a "fixed center" around which problems "group themselves" as they develop, and explore at some length his idea of investigating such a grouping through the "development of successive questions about one centre" because "given any fixed condition or fact . . . and problems of society will at every stage of advance group themselves about it" (Du Bois 1898b, 6).

3. "The points at which they [Negroes] fail to be incorporated into this group life constitute the particular Negro problems, which can be divided into two distinct but correlated parts, depending on two facts: First—Negroes do not share the full national life because as a mass they have not reached a sufficiently high grade of culture. Secondly—They do not share the full national life because there has always existed in America a conviction—varying in intensity, but always widespread—that people of Negro blood should not be admitted into the group life of the nation no matter what their condition might be" (Du Bois 1898b, 7).

References

Du Bois, W. E. Burghardt. [1897a] 1992. On the Conservation of Races. In *African-American Social and Political Thought 1850-1920*, ed. Howard Brotz. New Brunswick, NJ: Transaction.

———. 1897b. Strivings of the Negro People. *Atlantic Monthly* 80:194-98.

———. 1898a. The Negroes of Farmville, Virginia: A Social Study. U.S. Department of Labor *Bulletin* 14(Jan.).

———. 1898b. The Study of the Negro Problems. *The Annals* of the American Academy of Political and Social Science (Jan.):1-23.

———. 1899. *The Philadelphia Negro*. Philadelphia: University of Pennsylvania Press.

———. [1903] 1992. The Talented Tenth. In *African-American Social and Political Thought 1850-1920*, ed. Howard Brotz. New Brunswick, NJ: Transaction.

———. [1948] 1996. The Talented Tenth Memorial Address. *The Boulé Journal* 15(Oct.):3-13. In *The Future of the Race*, ed. Henry Louis Gates, Jr. and Cornel West. New York: Knopf.

———. 1984. *Dusk of Dawn: An Essay Toward an Autobiography of a Race Concept*. New York: Harcourt, Brace & World, 1940. Reprint, New Brunswick, NJ: Transaction.

James, Joy. 1997. *Transcending the Talented Tenth: Black Leaders and American Intellectuals*. New York: Routledge.

Lewis, David Levering. 1993. *W.E.B. Du Bois: Biography of a Race*. New York: Henry Holt.

Myrdal, Gunnar. 1944. *An American Dilemma: The Negro Problem and Modern Democracy*. New York: Harper.

ANNALS, *AAPSS*, **568**, March 2000

The Washington and Du Bois
Leadership Paradigms Reconsidered

By MARTIN KILSON

ABSTRACT: From the end of Reconstruction in the 1880s to the 1940s, the African American population confronted the complex issue of how to lead African Americans in an emergent industrial American nation-state system that applied rigid white supremacist practices in its interface with African Americans. One can hypothesize two generic types of modern ethnic group leadership: (1) the social organization type which focuses on the nuts and bolts of outfitting a group with agencies, mechanisms, networks, and institutions related to modern social development; and (2) the guidance type or mobilization type which focuses on the character of an ethnic group's status, citizenship rights, human rights, and honor in a modern nation-state society. This article revisits the classic leadership contest from the 1890s to the 1940s between the leadership paradigms of Booker T. Washington and W.E.B. Du Bois in terms of the two generic types of modern ethnic group leadership. It concludes with a critique of efforts by neoconservatives today to revive the Washington leadership paradigm, which historically has been a distorted variant of the generic social organization type leadership.

Martin Kilson is Frank G. Thompson Research Professor at Harvard University, where he has taught since 1962. He is author or coauthor of several books, including Political Change in a West African State *(1966);* The African Diaspora: Interpretive Essays *(1976); and* The Making of Black Intellectuals: Studies on the African American Intelligentsia *(three volumes) (forthcoming).*

WITHIN less than two decades of the defeat of the secessionist southern states in the Civil War, the affirmative action policy of broad federal government support for the full-fledged social and political incorporation of African Americans into the American social system—the policy known as Reconstruction—was threatened by right-wing restorationist southern forces. By the mid-1880s, these restorationist forces were well on the way toward smashing Reconstruction completely, replacing it with what can only be called the imposition of an authoritarian system of political control between the white social system and the black social system in the South.

Although democratic political patterns prevailed within the white social system, the federal government's inability to sustain voting rights and broader citizenship rights for African Americans in the South inevitably translated into a parallel authoritarian subplot alongside the democratic mainstream southern system. Outside the South, where by 1910 around 10 percent of the African American population had settled, the authoritarian interface between the white and black social systems that dominated in the South was not reconstituted.

Nonetheless, a broad range of non-democratic maneuvers prevailed typically outside the South as ways of restricting full access to democratic participation by African American communities, which resulted in a three-generation delay in the production of a full-fledged black elected political class for African American communities outside the South. So, in general, for the African American population—both in the South and outside the South—it was not until the passage of the major civil rights legislation of the middle 1960s and later that the typical black citizen could claim full citizenship and human rights on one hand and full electoral participation rights on the other. Only then, therefore—virtually 100 years following the defeat of the South in the Civil War—was it possible for a mature black elected political class to evolve. For example, when the Voting Rights Act of 1965 was enacted, only about 350 black elected officials existed nationwide, at which time the African American population numbered about 20 million.

Thus, with the collapse of Reconstruction by the 1880s, African Americans became a unique American ethnic community in regard to its leadership and political processes. Apart from American Indians, African Americans in general could not interlock the development of their ethnic group or ethnic community leadership patterns (their internal group authority processes) with the systemic political processes within the evolving American industrial social system. Irish Americans, Italian Americans, Jewish Americans, white Anglo-Saxon Protestant Americans (WASPs) and other white groups could claim from the 1880s onward that special ethnic group political status associated with being able to interlock their ethnic group leadership patterns with the system-wide political processes in the

American system as a whole (at town, city, county, state, and federal levels).

It was because of this generic difference between the citizenship status of African Americans and white American groups that the phenomenon of a Booker T. Washington–W.E.B. Du Bois leadership paradigm conflict emerged in the first place. No white ethnic group experienced this kind of generic leadership conflict as they faced the task of transforming themselves into viable ethnic communities, as their members commenced to make themselves effective participants in the evolving industrial American society of the late nineteenth century. In short, only African Americans had to go back to square one, so to speak, in order to tackle the question of how do you lead black folks as they enter a raucously industrializing American society, a capitalist system that was buffeting human beings about like leaves in the wind. And, of course, owing to the white supremacist marginalization and pariahization of blacks' status in America from the late nineteenth century to the 1960s—usually reinforced by vicious vigilante and/or official violence— the issue of black leadership was all the more difficult to resolve.

Let me first address this generic query with a brief reference to my ancestral origins among that special leadership stratum among African Americans before the Emancipation Proclamation, known by its U.S. Census Bureau label "Free Negro Head of Household." My father was an African Methodist clergyman (the Reverend Martin Luther Kilson) as

was my father's brother (the Reverend Delbert Kilson). Their great-grandfather, born in the early 1800s to a free Negro family, was a landowning farmer and an educated African Methodist Episcopal clergyman. My great-great-grandfather, the Reverend Isaac Lee, mortgaged his farmland to build the first African Methodist Episcopal Church in Kent County, Maryland, between the 1840s and 1853. He also supported the abolitionist movement, and members of his clan picked up guns to join the battle for freedom of all Negroes.

On my maternal side, my great-grandfather Jacob Laws helped to build and sustain modern communities among free Negroes before the Civil War in Maryland, Delaware, and Pennsylvania. And like my father's forebears, Jacob Laws also supported the abolitionist movement, and he too picked up guns, paid for his own uniform, joined the U.S. 24th Colored Infantry in Philadelphia, and went to battle for the freedom of Negro slaves. Happily, he came back to Pennsylvania alive, moved with a small cadre of black Civil War veterans to small towns around Philadelphia, settling in Ambler, Pennsylvania, in the late 1870s, where he helped build the social organization of that town's African American community. He helped build the black community's houses as a carpenter, and he was one of three organizers in 1885 of the first African Union Methodist Protestant Church (AUMP) in Eastern Montgomery County, Pennsylvania. He and other organizers of Ambler's AUMP Church mortgaged their own homes to gain the financing necessary to build their church. It was the Ambler black community's first church.

What does this tale of my ancestors tell us about the interaction between Booker T. Washington, W.E.B. Du Bois, and the generic black leadership issue of how to lead black folks? I think this ancestral tale provides a historical framework for identifying core features and dynamics that faced African Americans in their formative developmental phase from the 1880s and 1890s into the early twentieth century. From this ancestral tale, I suggest that we can posit at least two essential functions of leadership.

One function can be characterized by the term that anthropologists often use—social organization. That is, leadership is concerned with fashioning the nuts and bolts of a social system, the infrastructure of agencies and networks that allow individuals and a people as a whole to realize the purposes required for a viable human existence. Thus, one core type of leadership we can call social organization type leadership.

A second function of leadership is to offer guidance and goals for a community, to direct a community to certain ends and purposes. This leadership function is concerned with a group's status, rights, and honor. This second core type of leadership we can call guidance type or mobilization type leadership. It is from this second type of leadership in a modern nation-state society that political leadership evolves, whether activist or social movement leadership or elected politician leadership.

In general, for African Americans the end of Reconstruction and the imposition of racial caste marginalization of black citizens in American society placed a barrier to the natural growth of guidance or mobilization type leadership. Within the South, where the vast majority of African Americans resided between the 1890s and the 1950s, mobilization type leadership was extremely limited, aggressively restricted by the authoritarian white racist patterns. For example, by 1940 only 5 percent of the adult black population in the South had been allowed to become registered voters. White violence and white bureaucratic coercion were employed to impose this lowest level participation ceiling on African American citizens.

As a result, a massive federal government intervention was required to alter this situation (which finally came with the Voting Rights Act of 1965), and meanwhile the majority community of African Americans in the South had to resort to that more primary (or embryonic) form of leadership that I call social organization leadership. Indeed, a variant of social organization leadership was articulated along systemic lines by the most prominent African American political figure in the South from the late 1880s to his death in 1915. That figure was Booker T. Washington.

THE WASHINGTON LEADERSHIP PARADIGM

If we could magically transport ourselves back 100 years or so to Atlanta, Georgia, in 1895, we would have experienced an extraordinary event. That event would shape the metamorphosis of African American leadership processes—and thus the processes of black political incorporation in American life—for the first four generations of the twentieth century.

The extraordinary event I refer to was the presence of Booker T. Washington at a capitalist industrial exposition. As a keynote speaker at the 1895 Atlanta Exposition, Washington told an audience of white entrepreneurs—the leading figures of an exploding American industrial capitalism—that all they had to worry about in regard to a troublesome American working class was the white working class. As Washington was well aware, the white working class had or could bid for full citizenship status (they were within the American social contract) and thus could participate in helping to define the emergent industrial nation-state's public purposes.

But what about the black working class? Above all, the black working class was outside the American social contract—and brutally outside it at that. Most (over 90 percent) of the African American working class was an oppressed agrarian proletariat whom historians, cognizant of its dilapidated attributes, labeled a peonage agrarian class. In other words, the African American working class was not just overwhelmed by massive social oppression but overwhelmed as well by judicial, police, and political oppression. The cruelest kind of systemic oppression under capitalism was endured by the southern branch of the black working class—perhaps one-third of whom faced the horrible experience of prison labor under vicious white superintendence from the 1890s to the 1950s, or, nearly as bad, they experienced the terrible threat of imprisonment for the purpose of becoming prison labor (Oshinsky 1995).

Booker T. Washington's message to the assembled industrial capitalists was at the other end of the political spectrum from what that young African American who was just finishing his doctorate at Harvard University in 1895—W.E.B. Du Bois—would have told the Atlanta Exposition participants had he been invited to it. In direct reference to that core query—how do you lead black people?—Booker T. Washington's Atlanta Exposition speech belittled the possibility of using politics to advance African American needs, concerns, and status in a raucously evolving industrial capitalism. He said, "Start . . . a dairy farm or truck garden" instead. Raising his two hands, Washington proclaimed that, in matters of political rights and status, whites and blacks would be as "separate as the fingers on my hands." In short, Washington's address rejected the guidance type or mobilization type leadership model, favoring instead the social organization type leadership model.

From these groundwork propositions, then, Washington sought to strike a bargain with America's captains of industry and, through them, with America's operational authoritarian white supremacist overrule of some 10 million black people. Washington opined that if the white elites and leadership would funnel financial and institutional resources to what I call his social organization type black leadership, this Washington brand of black leadership would, on one hand, advance the African American social system while, on the other hand, neglect the quest for full-fledged citizenship status and human rights—rights that were by 1895 some 30 years old, enshrined in the Constitution on pain of a bloody Civil War and elaborated by federal legislation known as the Civil Rights Codes of 1865, 1866, and 1867. In *The Future of the American Negro*, Booker T. Washington presents his accommodationist formulations:

I believe the past and present teach but one lesson—to the Negro's [white] friends and to the Negro himself—that there is but one hope of solution; and that is for the Negro in every part of America to resolve from henceforth that he will throw aside every non-essential [citizenship and human rights] and cling only to essential—that his pillar of fire by night and pillar of cloud by day shall be property, economy, education, and Christian character. To us just now these are the wheat, all else the chaff. (Washington 1899, 132)

There was in Washington's accommodationist schema no timetable for the establishment of African American citizenship and human rights parity. Gunnar Myrdal's classic appraisal of African American citizenship status as of the middle 1940s states that, "Through thrift, skill, and industry the Negroes were gradually to improve so much that, at a later stage, the discussion again could be taken up concerning his

rights. This was Washington's philosophy" (Myrdal 1944, 739).

Booker T. Washington was not, of course, a simpleton. He knew that if he could get the American elites in 1895 to generate financial and material resources to advance blacks in education, job opportunities, and neighborhood development, this very process of social system development would inevitably converge with the American political system. He also knew that, given his autocratic leadership style, he would be the top client type or errand boy black leadership figure.

Alas, even though the American elites of the nineteenth and early twentieth centuries with whom Washington interacted never even approximated generating the material resources for African American modernization that Washington's compromise formula implied, Washington nevertheless evolved to that unique and curious role as top client type black leader. So whatever the inadequate supply of financial and material resources from white elites for African American modernization was, Booker T. Washington exercised an inordinate sway over its allocation among blacks. Washington's top client type black leader role also saw him functioning as the main advisor among African American leadership to President Theodore Roosevelt and President William Taft on those torturous issues related to blacks' authoritarian-delineated interface with the American social contract.

What were the salient political issues requiring Washington's advice? (1) voting rights or rather the steady and cynical disenfranchisement of African Americans well into the twentieth century; (2) pervasive institutional discrimination and/or segregation toward blacks throughout American life; and (3) massive, pernicious violence against blacks generally and against any particular black citizen the perpetrators of white supremacist violence wished to target. Such violence was often taken to the point of taking a black life, by mob lynching or police brutality, the wretched tale of which is related more effectively in Gunnar Myrdal's *An American Dilemma* (1944) than in many other sources.

Thus, what historians have labeled the accommodationist leadership method of Booker T. Washington produced at best sparse and problematic social system advancement—social organization metamorphosis—for the typical African American citizen by, say, World War I. At the time of Washington's death in 1915, over 90 percent of the 11 million blacks in the United States were still massively poor. The so-called bargain that Washington struck with white elites in regard to opening up industrial job markets for the black working class was an utter failure because the white capitalist class made no serious effort to incorporate African American workers at parity with white workers. Neither was the other half of Washington's so-called bargain with white elites any more successful—the goal of educating the illiterate offspring of slaves through the special financial and resource assistance of white elites. The bulk of the southern black population

remained wretchedly educated by the 1930s (Bond 1938).

Finally, while full credit belongs to Booker T. Washington for his important contributions to the development of the African American professional class or intelligentsia—with Washington himself founding a key black institution of higher education, Tuskegee Institute—this important class within the African American social system was minuscule at the time of Washington's death in 1915. Nor was the black professional stratum any more fulsome by the start of World War II, mainly because the white elites in general and the white capitalist class in particular failed to keep its pathetic Faustian bargain with Booker T. Washington that commenced with his Atlanta Exposition address in 1895.

In opting for the social organization type black leadership, Washington painted himself and African Americans generally into a leadership cul-de-sac. And had Washington lived perhaps one more generation, the devastating impact of his leadership cul-de-sac in regard to constraining the growth of the guidance type or mobilization type black leadership would have been unbearable (see Kilson forthcoming).

THE DU BOIS LEADERSHIP PARADIGM

The mainstream black leadership as we know it today (what I call the pragmatic activist strand among the African American professional class as represented in the leadership of black professional organizations and especially black civil rights organizations) owes a lot—maybe everything—to W.E.B. Du Bois. What Du Bois did between the early 1900s and the 1940s in the leadership realm of African American life was to put substance into the guidance type or mobilization type black leadership paradigm. Du Bois thereby helped to correct the devastating flaws in Washington's social organization type black leadership paradigm. Du Bois, in challenging the accommodationist leadership paradigm, revolutionized what became the mainline African American leadership methodology in three special respects:

— he articulated the core attributes of a mobilization type leadership process for African Americans;
— he fashioned an intellectual discourse that propelled arguments and thinking along mobilization type leadership lines, and thus encouraged thinking that critiqued the sell-out attributes of Washington's accommodationist leadership—its surrender of blacks' citizenship and human rights; and
— he fashioned an intellectual discourse that upheld and defended black honor, which fervently challenged the presumption of most white Americans that defaming African Americans' cultural presence in American society was their natural privilege as whites—a defamation mania that often resulted in loss of African American lives.

Indeed, from today's vantage point, it seems almost incredible that proponents of the Booker T. Washington leadership paradigm could entertain a leadership methodology that either ignored or warred against a guidance type or mobilization type black leadership position. In the final analysis, all that the Washington leadership paradigm could generate was a clientage form of leadership mainstreaming of African American society. On balance, the clientage type black leadership methodology served only a small, cynical inner circle of the black elite.

Du Bois was convinced early in his intellectual career that the pseudo-leadership mainstreaming mode that Booker T. Washington fostered was simply unworkable for guiding the interests of a massively outcast African American community in an industrializing nation-state society like America (Lewis 1993). Worse still, this Washington paradigm was dishonorable—an insult to already horrendous injury visited upon blacks by the American branch of Christian civilization. That special interplay of his strong black personhood, his brilliant mind, his nimble and bold intellect, and his deep disdain for the authoritarian arrogance of white America's racial caste patterns virtually ensured Du Bois's rejection of the Washington paradigm. It was virtually preordained that Du Bois would play a major role in fashioning an alternative leadership mainstreaming paradigm—a politically viable mainstreaming paradigm (Lewis 1993).

Thus, the Du Bois paradigm fashioned a protracted but viable antidote to the Booker T. Washington clientage leadership mainstreaming methodology, focusing on the guidance type leadership modalities, which is to say protecting a group's rights, status, and honor. Du Bois pursued essentially a three-pronged strategy. First, he forged a citizenship rights leadership cadre— a group of individuals committed to translating American social contract rights into rights for black people; committed to challenging status-denying racist values, ideas, and cultural practices; and committed to mobilizing popular support against group defamation. The founding of the NAACP was the key prong in this strategy, especially its multilayered evolution as a political mobilizing agency and a legal rights or human rights enhancing agency (Tushnet 1987).

With the NAACP in place, Du Bois and his African American colleagues (Monroe Trotter, J. Milton Waldron, Clement Morgan, and others) cultivated a network of loyal white allies among the white middle class and upper class—mainly from that small but strategic segment of elite WASPs that sociologists have aptly labeled the cosmopolitan segment. Allies also hailed from members of the emerging Jewish American bourgeoisie who were early supporters of that cosmopolitan segment of America's elites from the 1920s onward. The cosmopolitan segment of America's middle class and upper class, whatever their particular ethnic group patterns might be, are committed to a leadership or political ethos that cherishes equality of citizenship and equality of opportunity as core

American values—values to which such cosmopolitan elites are willing to lend their personal influence, social leverage, and wealth to advance (Baltzell 1964). In these respects, the cosmopolitan white bourgeois elements differ markedly from those bourgeois whites at the other end of the leadership attitudinal spectrum—the parochials who employ their strategic and social capacities to restrict these values.

A third strand among America's bourgeoisie inhabits the center, tilting under circumstances sometimes to the cosmopolitans and sometimes to the parochials. Some analysts have labeled this segment of America's bourgeoisie establishmentarians— and, as Du Bois and his black colleagues searched for a broad range of white elite allies, they occasionally landed some allies among the establishmentarians.

At any rate, it was typically just a small cadre of either cosmopolitans or establishmentarians among mainly the WASP, Jewish, and Irish American bourgeoisie who grasped the moral imperative required to challenge America's white supremacist patterns in alliance with Du Bois and the NAACP. That we still lack serious study of whites as antiracist allies in college curriculums generally (even within Afro-American or black studies departments) is a lacuna that must be corrected, for the fulsome understanding of what Du Bois and the NAACP achieved (and later other elements of the antiracist and civil rights movement) is impossible without this knowledge.

The third prong of the Du Bois paradigm involved the need to mobilize the federal government into a major role in fostering the development of citizenship rights equality for African Americans. During Du Bois's period of leadership and influence in the NAACP and within black leadership processes generally (from World War I to the early 1930s), he and his NAACP colleagues experimented with political mobilization or political movement tactics that, a generation later, were broadcast across the country during the years of the civil rights revolution—1955 to 1975. For example, Du Bois pioneered the first march on Washington movement during World War I in order to let the white supremacist-minded federal government know that, under his citizenship rights-oriented leadership, blacks were deadly serious about gaining full-fledged citizenship status—so serious that they would demand the right to fight America's wars and thus the right to die for America.

Seeking legislation in the U.S. Congress and/or testing the authority of the federal courts on behalf of the protection of black life against white terrorist violence were other politicization tactics developed under the Du Bois paradigm. These approaches failed, though out of them came an even greater influence on the federal courts to advance the status and quality of African American citizenship. Though Du Bois himself was no longer in a formal leadership role in the NAACP, the brilliant civil rights lawyer and dean of Howard University Law School, Professor Charles Houston, would maneuver the NAACP into organizing the NAACP Legal Defense Fund

in the late 1930s. Under the directorship of Houston's brilliant protégé Thurgood Marshall—who later became U.S. Supreme Court Justice Marshall—the Legal Defense Fund directed a long and arduous legal battle to dismantle the total juridical infrastructure of racial segregation and discrimination. This juridical dismantling of American racism would not have seen the light of day under Washington's paradigm.

Thus, as the 1930s closed and America entered World War II, it was apparent that the clientage type leadership mainstreaming mode of the Washington paradigm had been displaced by the citizenship rights leadership of the Du Bois paradigm. Rooted in a generic guidance type leadership process, Du Bois's citizenship rights political mobilization achieved a general consensus among both black Americans and their small community of white allies. In short, the Du Bois leadership paradigm had achieved a mainstream presence. The Du Bois paradigm strove to bring the poorest, weakest, and least educated black individuals into mainstream citizenship rights—that is, into the same body of citizenship rights enjoyed by white Americans. In addition, Du Bois's paradigm had become mainstream by World War II among the majority of African Americans, as the multilayered network of agencies in black civil society identified the Du Bois paradigm as their own. This was the case whether one was speaking about the black clergy leadership, black lawyers leadership, black doctors leadership, black businesspersons leadership, black working-class leadership, black women's organizations, and also that small but advancing cadre of elected black officials who existed by World War II (there were two congressmen and perhaps 50 other elected black officials nationwide by 1945).

Of course, the establishmentarian or conservative sector of African American middle-class and professional families and associations during the years between the two world wars preferred the accommodationist view of what I call the social-organization leadership approach that Booker T. Washington represented. However, during this same period, there was a significant section of African American middle-class associations—a crucial element of black civil society—that sympathized with the activist political outlook of W.E.B. Du Bois and the NAACP. But, at the same time, this activist sector of the African American middle class also understood the need to simultaneously advance the social-organization processes in African American society (for example, black colleges, black secondary schools, black businesses, black professional groups, black churches, black trade unions, and so on). And the top intellectuals who were allied to the activist sector of the African American middle class simultaneously supported the advancement of the social-organization infrastructure of black American life—intellectuals like Charles Johnson, William Hastie, Horace Mann Bond, St. Clair Drake, John Aubrey Davis, L. D. Reddick, James Nabrit, and others. In short, though they supported the activist leadership outlook of W.E.B.

Du Bois, this activist sector of the black middle class never allowed the Booker T. Washington leadership sector to have a monopoly over the social-organization approach to African American development during the first 40 years of the twentieth century. There is no doubt whatsoever—the historical record supports it—that Du Bois and his followers among the African American bourgeoisie lent their talents and resources to advance schools for black children (whether private or public), advance black colleges, assist the growth of black business, professional associations, trade unions, women's organizations, and sundry other black civil society agencies. No monopoly in this sphere was surrendered to the Booker T. Washington leadership paradigm, although many conservative analysts today would have us believe that this happened. It did not.

Moreover, unfortunately for Washington and his leadership paradigm, the conservative segment of the white elites who were Washington's patrons failed miserably in their patron obligation, in their purported transfer to the Washington paradigm camp of that degree of financial and material resources and support capable of forging a viable African American civil society and, through this, viable social mobility. By the 1940 census, some 90 percent of African Americans remained in the ranks of the poor and working class, barely 5 percent were middle class and above, and barely 5 percent were stable working class.

In short, the white elite side of the Washingtonian compromise—of the accommodationist trade-off—defaulted. Put more bluntly, the Washington paradigm was double-crossed by white American conservatism. There is no evidence that American conservatism ever had the slightest intention of allowing or enabling the Washington paradigm—or its various offshoots in our contemporary era that revolve around the so-called black conservatives—to forge viable paths to citizenship and social mobility equality for African Americans.

WASHINGTON'S PARADIGM AND NEOCONSERVATISM

As American society settled into the postwar era of the late 1940s and 1950s, the Du Bois paradigm's sway in the ranks of mainstream black leadership was unmistakable—a reality that Du Bois himself lived to witness. Throughout the 1950s, 1960s, and 1970s, the black leadership heirs of Du Bois stayed the course, as it were, pressing and challenging America's white supremacist patterns on behalf of African American citizenship rights and equal opportunity for social mobility. Relative success was achieved through a battery of federal civil rights legislation and other policies like the war on poverty program and the overall affirmative action practices that the Kennedy and Johnson administrations established and the Nixon, Ford, and Carter administrations more or less sustained.

Numbering some 8000-plus black officials and perhaps 80,000 administrators and political technicians, the black political class—a key element of the overall mainstream black leadership—epitomizes the attainments of the Du Bois paradigm, as do the overall social mobility advancements among African Americans through the 1970s and 1980s—assisted importantly by affirmative action practices. By the 1990s, what I call the mobile stratum among blacks included 40 percent black middle-class households and 25 percent black stable working-class households, placing 65 percent of black families in this mobile stratum. But some 30 percent of black households failed to succeed to the mobile stratum as did 5 percent of black poor working-class households; these two segments comprise a static stratum of 35 percent of black households. What is worse, of course, are the great numbers of broken families (mainly headed by women) and the concomitant high rates of unwed mothers (mostly teenagers) who have produced a generation of urban poor children. Riddled by a massive drug trade, these urban poor children are now viewed as responsible for inefficient welfare programs and high crime rates, two crises that have denigrated the black poor in the eyes of most white Americans over the past 25 years.

One might have thought that the success of the black American mobile stratum through federal civil rights policies and mobility pump-priming policies that the Du Bois paradigm helped put on the national agenda would be welcomed by most white Americans. This has not been the case. In the era of neoconservatism that began with Reagan's 1980 presidential victory and continued under a long Republican reign, conservatives generally and Republicans in particular have ideologically and politically manipulated the crises of that 30 percent of poor black households so as to diminish the aura associated with the Du Bois paradigm's success among the 65 percent mobile stratum black households. This neoconservative ideological manipulation of black crises has involved neoracist backlashing and race-baiting, much of it amounting to pandering to long-standing white supremacist assumptions among most white Americans regarding their phobias toward African Americans as possible neighbors, professional peers, school mates, and political allies.

The neoconservative backlash against civil rights advances and the crisis of black poverty gained support among electorally critical communities of white voters who were nursing many-sided mobility and status anxieties, galvanized mainly by civil rights legislation advances and the beginnings of viable incorporation of blacks into the American social contract (Rieder 1985).

As Rieder's study reveals, Alabama Governor George Wallace's presidential campaigns were the first electoral beneficiaries of the preference of many white Americans to cling to long-standing pariah (racist) characterizations of black people. Nationally, Wallace logged 14 percent of the presidential vote in 1964 and 1968, and but for his injury by a would-be assassin, he might have bettered 14 percent in 1972. Nixon, however, picked up where Wallace left off, fashioning his own version of Wallace's race-baiting strategy that

some commentators dubbed Nixon's southern strategy.

The Reagan and Bush Republican administrations added their own contribution to the savvy conservative electoral strategy of backlashing liberal public policies that have fundamentally advanced the social and political status of black Americans in the post–civil rights era. Above all, the success of conservative Republican forces—within both the electoral realm and the intellectual sphere—in backlashing public policies favorable to black Americans ultimately depends upon strong latent racist or Negro-phobic norms and patterns in American life and among white American citizens. Given this underlying quantum of Negro-phobic norms and patterns that persist in American life, both neoliberal and conservative white politicians and intellectuals now advise the mainline African American leadership to surrender its long-standing commitment to the Du Boisian leadership paradigm in exchange for the Washingtonian accommodationist paradigm.

A CONCLUDING NOTE

As already noted, it is the existence in our post–civil rights era of an African American social system which contains a sizable weak working-class and poor constituency—one that participates disproportionately in the national crime rate especially and one that relies disproportionately on welfare public policies—which ultimately fuels Negro-phobic backlashing conservative politics. The Republican party during the past 30 years has very shrewdly used this Achilles' heel of black American life as a political scapegoat among middle-class and working-class white voters. This cynical manipulation by conservatives of the weaknesses of black American life also has been embarrassing to the mainline African American leadership and intelligentsia because it is so patently unfair. Conservatives do not go about posturing in the face of, say, the Irish American bourgeoisie about the crisis of that other drug addition, alcoholism, among the Irish working class, about which Andrew Greeley (1972) so sensitively writes. They do not go about posturing in the face of the Italian American bourgeoisie about the massive criminality of working-class and poor Italians connected with the Mafia, which plays a prominent role in the drug trade that is devastating American life and communities—black and white. And they do not go about posturing in the face of the WASP bourgeoisie about the multilayered social disarray among white rural poor working-class sectors in Appalachian states and elsewhere—WASP sectors with high rates of broken families, drug use, and sundry criminality that is one of our country's best kept secrets.

Propagation of a revival of the Washington paradigm as a kind of magic-wand solution to the crises surrounding the poverty-stricken 30 percent of African American households is now common fare among conservatives, with special contributions from black conservatives like Glenn Loury, Shelby Steele, and Robert Woodson. A few conservative organizations even have distributed funds to community development and neighborhood uplift projects in a few inner-city black communities, mainly through Robert Woodson's neighborhood development organization, which appears to be a kind of pilot project on the efficacy of the Washington paradigm. But these funds—from Heritage Foundation and the Olin Foundation and others—have been minuscule, no more serious relative to the task of ameliorating the economic crises facing the black poor today than were the funds made available to Booker T. Washington a century ago by parochial conservative elites. Just compare the stingy funds and resources conservative elites currently extend to the crises facing the African American poor to the funds and resources liberal elites running the Ford Foundation, Rockefeller Foundation, Carnegie Corporation, Mellon Foundation, Annenberg Foundation, MacArthur Foundation, and others currently extend to ameliorating these problems.

Those conservatives who are reviving the Washington leadership paradigm as a kind of magic-wand solution to the crises of the black poor are just not credible. Indeed, the major part of the financial resources delivered by conservative networks and foundations to African American issues have gone into propagandistic or ideological projects focused on black audiences. For example, there are now nearly a dozen black conservative talk radio stations that target black communities in major metropolitan areas, including Baltimore, Denver, Atlanta, and Detroit.

Conservative money has also targeted black intellectuals, the most recent manifestation of which was the launching in 1994 of a bimonthly militant black conservative magazine titled *Destiny*. Leading black conservative intellectuals such as Thomas Sowell (of the Hoover Institution) and Walter Williams (of George Mason University) are members of *Destiny*'s governing board.

In general, then, this throwing by conservatives of a back-to-Washington paradigm discourse into the faces of African American leadership (the genuine heirs of the Du Bois paradigm) is mainly ideological and political maneuvering. It has been clever, too, in its purpose of deflating the aura of the Du Bois paradigm among white Americans and thereby limiting the political alliance capability of black leadership. This Washington paradigm revivalism by conservatives is part of a 20-year process of critiquing and trashing the policies that liberals, moderates, and progressives fashioned under the Kennedy and Johnson administrations and, with bipartisan support among some Republicans, sustained through the 1970s. These policies went farther than any previous national policies ever did toward closing the black/white political power gap and social mobility gap that white supremacist patterns have long sustained in American life.

So far, the current Washington paradigm revivalism propagated by conservatives is behaving true to form. There is no credible evidence that today's conservatives are any more willing to generate the resources required to advance the social system of poor African Americans today than the conservative patrons of Booker T. Washington were willing to do a century ago. Today's white conservatives are just as likely to double-cross the Washington paradigm today as their counterparts did earlier in the twentieth century. But should today's white conservatives discover the moral fiber necessary to end white America's long-standing state of denial of its horrendous injury to black Americans through its white supremacist practices, I have no doubt that inventive members of conservative groups can evolve from their current reactive conservatism to a proactive conservatism—that is, from a cynically manipulative plutocratic conservatism to problem-solving conservatism, a helping-hand conservatism. When the wealthy conservative foundations like Olin Foundation, Bradley Foundation, Richardson Sciafe Foundation, among sundry others, design and fund viable programs of scholarships for high-achieving working-class and poor black children or viable programs for serious economic regeneration of inner-city black communities (and rural ones too), then I and other heirs of the Du Bois paradigm among the African American intelligentsia will roundly applaud American conservatism. To expect anything less would be to dishonor William Edward Burghardt Du Bois.

References

Baltzell, Digby. 1964. *The Protestant Establishment*. New York: Oxford University Press.

Bond, Horace Mann. 1938. *Negro Education in Alabama: A Study in Cotton and Steel*. Washington, DC: Associated.

Greeley, Andrew. 1972. *That Most Distressful Nation: The Taming of the American Irish*. Chicago: Quadrangle Books.

Kilson, Martin. Forthcoming. *The Making of Black Intellectuals: Studies on the African American Intelligentsia*. N.p.

Lewis, David Levering. 1993. *W.E.B. Du Bois: Biography of a Race 1869-1919*. New York: Henry Holt.

Myrdal, Gunnar. 1944. *An American Dilemma*. Vol. 2. New York: Harper & Bros.

Oshinsky, David. 1995. *Worse Than Slavery*. New York: Oxford University Press.

Rieder, Jonathan. 1985. *Canarsie: The Jews and Italians of Brooklyn Against Liberalism*. Cambridge, MA: Harvard University Press.

Tushnet, Mark. 1987. *The NAACP's Legal Strategy Against Segregated Education 1925-1950*. Chapel Hill: University of North Carolina Press.

Washington, Booker T. 1899. *The Future of the American Negro*. New York: Negro Universities Press.

INDEX

314

Portable

Life in the fast lane. It usually involves a few sacrifices. Your insurance coverage doesn't have to be one of them. Whether you're moving on or even out on your own, insurance offered through your AAPSS membership won't end just because you've changed jobs. It travels right in your back pocket.

Take advantage of one of your best membership benefits. Affordable coverage. Reliable providers. Portable benefits. **Call 800 424-9883** to speak to a customer service representative. Because an established benefits package fits your changing lifestyle.

4 ways to order and share the best scholarship in your field

■ Back Issues

Make sure you didn't miss any important articles that you need for your own practice, research or classroom. Back issues are available at 20% discount. To order, call Sage Customer Service at (805) 499-9774 or email: order@sagepub.com.

■ Reprints

Customize your instructional materials to fit your classroom and symposia needs with powerful, new ideas from leading scholars in the field. Reprints make cost-effective additions to your course materials and conference packets. They are convenient and easy to obtain. To order multiple copies of a recent article, call Sage Reprint Services at (805) 499-0721, Ext 7535 or email: reprint@sagepub.com.

■ Special Issues

Occasionally an entire issue is devoted to a single relevant topic, viewing it at length and in depth. The pertinent information in these Special Issues is something you will refer to again and again. Sage offers discounts of up to 60% on multiple copies for classroom adoption. For more information on multiple-copy prices call (805) 499-0721, ext. 7528 or email: adopt_jnl@sagepub.com.

■ Sample Copies

Sample copies (up to two) may be obtained on request directly from Sage Publications, by calling Sage Customer Service at (805) 499-9774 or e-mail:jsamples@sagepub.com.

SAGE PUBLICATIONS, INC.
2455 Teller Road, Thousand Oaks, CA 91320
Tel: (805) 499-0721 ■ Fax: (805) 499-0871
Visit us at http://www.sagepub.com